Perspectives on Countering Extremism

Perspectives on Countering Extremism

Diversion and Disengagement

Edited by
Shashi Jayakumar

BLOOMSBURY ACADEMIC
LONDON • NEW YORK • OXFORD • NEW DELHI • SYDNEY

BLOOMSBURY ACADEMIC
Bloomsbury Publishing Plc
50 Bedford Square, London, WC1B 3DP, UK
1385 Broadway, New York, NY 10018, USA
29 Earlsfort Terrace, Dublin 2, Ireland

BLOOMSBURY, BLOOMSBURY ACADEMIC and the Diana logo
are trademarks of Bloomsbury Publishing Plc

First published in Great Britain 2023
Paperback edition published in 2024

Series design by Adriana Brioso

Library of Congress Cataloging-in-Publication Data
Names: Jayakumar, Shashi, editor.
Title: Perspectives on countering extremism : diversion and
disengagement / edited by Shashi Jayakumar.
Description: New York, NY : Bloomsbury Academic, 2023. |
Includes bibliographical references and index.
Identifiers: LCCN 2022038920 (print) | LCCN 2022038921 (ebook) |
ISBN 9781350253841 (hardback) | ISBN 9781350253858 (epub) |
ISBN 9781350253865 (pdf) | ISBN 9781350253872
Subjects: LCSH: Violence–Prevention.
Classification: LCC HM1116 .P43 2023 (print) | LCC HM1116 (ebook) |
DDC 303.6–dc23/eng/20221018
LC record available at https://lccn.loc.gov/2022038920
LC ebook record available at https://lccn.loc.gov/2022038921

ISBN: PB: 978-1-3502-5388-9
          ePDF: 978-1-3502-5386-5
          eBook: 978-1-3502-5385-8

Typeset by Integra Software Services Pvt. Ltd.

To find out more about our authors and books visit www.bloomsbury.com
and sign up for our newsletters.

For Miranda –
Far More than a Diversion

Contents

Contents

List of figures

List of tables

Contributors

Dr Amarnath Amarasingam is an Assistant Professor in the School of Religion and cross-appointed to the Department of Political Studies at Queen's University in Ontario, Canada. He is also a Senior Fellow with the International Centre for the Study of Radicalisation. His research interests are terrorism, radicalization and extremism, online communities, diaspora politics, post-war reconstruction, and the sociology of religion. He is the author of *Pain, Pride, and Politics: Sri Lankan Tamil Activism in Canada* (2015) and the co-editor of *Stress Tested: The COVID-19 Pandemic and Canadian National Security* (2021) and *Sri Lanka: The Struggle for Peace in the Aftermath of War* (2016). He has published various peer-reviewed articles and book chapters, presented papers at over 100 national and international conferences, and has written for *The New York Times*, *The Monkey Case*, *The Washington Post*, CNN, *Politico*, *The Atlantic* and *Foreign Affairs*.

Sean Arbuthnot has been a CVE Practitioner in the UK since 2013 and is currently the Prevent Coordinator for the city of Birmingham. He is also a Fellow at the Centre for Analysis of the Radical Right (CARR) and a Visiting Fellow of Cranfield University. Prior to this, he enjoyed a varied twelve-year policing career and has a Masters in Conflict Resolution from Lancaster University.

Kamalle Daboussy has more than thirty-three years of experience working in the fields of migrant and refugee settlement support with culturally and linguistically diverse youth and in international humanitarian aid. For the last eighteen years, he has been CEO of Western Sydney Migrant Resource Centre, having worked actively and strategically across civil and political spheres to further the participation and successful settlement of diverse communities, including with Sydney's Muslim communities, the Department of Foreign Affairs and Trade, AusAID, and with Parliamentary Ministers and MPs. Kamalle has also been involved in numerous other organizations, such as Settlement Services International and the Southwest Legal Sydney Centre, and civil society organizations that work on social disadvantage. Over the last three years, Kamalle has been an advocate for the repatriate of Australian women and children who are trapped in Northeast Syria. Kamalle's daughter and grandchildren were coerced into Syria, where they found themselves amongst the sixty-plus individuals in al-Hawl and al-Roj Camps, following the fall of the Islamic State.

Muhammad Abdullah Darraz is a Senior Researcher in the Central Board of Muhammadiyah. He was formerly executive director of the MAARIF Institute for Culture and Humanity, where he focused on countering violent extremism and community peacebuilding through interfaith dialogue and collaboration. Darraz has conducted programmes on mainstreaming human rights values in high schools and strengthening moderate views among students. In 2011, he started the National Youth Camp for senior high school students to prevent violent extremism. In partnership with Google Indonesia, he hosted social media trainings on enhancing students' capacity to counter violent extremism. Darraz has a master in Islamic Philosophy (Paramadina University) and a bachelor in Islamic Studies (Islamic State University). In 2019, he studied management and leadership at the Korean Development Institute (KDI) School of Public Policy and Management. He also participated in an advanced summer programme on 'Preventing, Detecting, and Responding to the Violent Extremist Threat' at Leiden University. He has received several awards for his achievements in promoting Indonesian Islamic Moderation among the younger generation, including the Discovery Indonesian Islam (2016, British Embassy), Short Term Award in Understanding Contemporary Terrorism (2017–18, the Australia Awards and Deakin University) and the Professional Development Programme Fellowship from the Asia Foundation (2019–20).

Brad Galloway became the Coordinator at the Centre on Hate, Bias and Extremism in September of 2020. Brad brings a wealth of experience from his work in the countering and preventing violent extremism and terrorism space, and his more recent work in intervention and case management with NGO's such as Life After Hate. He conducts consultancy work centred around the Evolve program at the Organization for the Prevention of Violence (OPV). He also worked as a Research Assistant on a number of projects that are currently funded by Public Safety Canada and the Canadian Network for Research on Terrorism, Security and Society (TSAS). Moreover, Brad has served as a consultant for Google, Moonshot CVE, and the Institute for Strategic Dialogue (ISD), among others. His primary research interests include right-wing extremism and terrorism, preventing and countering violent extremism, and the roles of former extremists in combating violent extremism.

Dr Antje Gansewig holds a Magister Artium in sociology and German philology from the Martin Luther University Halle-Wittenberg (Germany). She obtained a PhD from the Carl von Ossietzky University of Oldenburg (Germany) for her thesis on the involvement of former right-wing extremists in German schools. Since 2013 she has worked in the fields of political extremism, crime prevention and civic education for several institutions (e.g., State Prevention Council Schleswig-Holstein, National Center for Crime Prevention, Federal Agency for Civic Education).

Dr. Fernán Osorno Hernández is currently an honorary research affiliate at the University of Bristol's School of Sociology, Politics and International Studies (SPAIS) and the Centre for the Study of Ethnicity and Citizenship. His research is focused on grassroots efforts to prevent and counter violent extremism (P/CVE) in the UK. More specifically, it is concerned with the complex relationship between policy design and grassroots implementation, with a particular focus on how youth workers interpret, challenge, enact and adapt P/CVE policies to meet their pre-existing safeguarding practices. He has recently relocated to the United States where he is the Education Manager at Hello Neighbor, a non-profit resettlement organisation.

Dr Shashi Jayakumar was educated at Oxford University where he studied History (BA 1997, DPhil, 2001). He was a member of the Singapore government's Administrative Service from 2002 to 2017. He has published widely on various topics within the field of radicalization and political violence. He is the editor of *Terrorism, Radicalisation & Countering Violent Extremism: Practical Considerations & Concerns* (Palgrave Pivot, 2019).

Dr Clarke Jones is a Senior Research Fellow (Criminology) based at the Research School of Psychology at the Australian National University. He also works as a consultant for the United Nations Office of Drugs and Crime in the Philippines. His expertise includes youth interventions, community engagement, prison radicalization, correctional reform, violent extremist offenders and prison gangs. He has applied his research in two key areas: prison reform (Philippines) and community-based work with Muslim communities in Australia. He has published extensively, including *Inmate Radicalisation and Recruitment in Prisons*. Before entering academia in 2010, he worked for over fifteen years in several areas of Australian national security, including in the police, military and intelligence service. In 2002, he was awarded the Chief of the Australian Defence Force Fellowship to complete a PhD at the University of New South Wales.

David Jones is the Manager of Applied Research at the Organization for the Prevention of Violence (OPV), based in Alberta, Canada and a Junior Research Affiliate at the Canadian Network for Research on Terrorism, Security and Society. The OPV is a non-government organization that operates a direct intervention programme intended to help individuals disengage from violent extremism. He holds a graduate degree from the University of Alberta.

Dr Farhad Khosrokhavar is a Retired Professor at Ecole des Hautes Etudes en Sciences Sociales in Paris, France. His latest books include *Muslims in Prison: A Comparative Perspective between Great Britain and France* (with James Beckford and Danièle Joly, 2005), *Suicide Bombers, The New Martyrs of Allah* (translated from French into seven languages, 2005), *Inside Jihadism: Understanding Jihadi Movements Worldwide* (2009), *Jihadist Ideology, The Anthropological Perspective* (2011), *The New Arab Revolutions That Shook the World* (2012), *Radicalization, Why Some People Choose the Path of Violence* (2016), *Jihadism in Europe, European Youth and the New Caliphate* (2021) and a co-edited volume with Jérôme Ferret, *Family and Jihadism, A Socio-anthropological Approach to the French Experience* (2022).

Christian Damgaard Kristoffersen holds a master of Political Science from Aarhus University and has been a consultant for several years at the Department of Children and Youth in the City of Aarhus. He has worked with the city's PVE efforts aimed at children and youth, covering a wide variety of perspectives such as radicalization, extremism, discrimination, digital literacy, internet culture, critical thinking, dialogue and pedagogical methodology. He has been a coordinator for several workshops for children and youth in Aarhus with the aim of creating dialogue on the above topics. He has also co-developed several of the current PVE initiatives by the Department of Children and youth. He is currently a consultant at the Department of Culture and Arts in the City of Odense.

Anne Sofie Skare Rasmussen holds a master in anthropology and experience economy. She works as a consultant in the Department of Children and Youth in the City of Aarhus and has been working for the Aarhus model since 2014. She works with the city's PVE efforts aimed at children and youth, covering a wide variety of perspectives such as radicalization, extremism, discrimination, digital literacy, internet culture, critical thinking, dialogue and pedagogical methodology. She is also working with preventing negative social control and children and youth's risk behaviours online.

Justin Richmond is founder and executive director of Impl. Project, a US-based humanitarian organization that conducts projects throughout the Philippines and around the world. Justin began his international career on the island of Sulu in 2009 and has continued to work among the Bangsamoro people to deliver livelihoods projects and relief aid. Impl. Project Philippines is based in Marawi City and delivers data-driven programming among the Philippines' most vulnerable populations.

Alasdair Roy is one of Australia's leading child rights specialists, with over thirty years of experience promoting and protecting the rights of children and young people. Alasdair currently provides consultancy services to domestic and international government, private and not-for-profit organizations. He is also a Visiting Lecturer at the Singapore University of Social Sciences. From 2008 to 2016, Alasdair was the Children and Young People Commissioner in Canberra, Australia, and from 1997 to 2008, the Deputy Community Advocate for Children and Young People in Canberra. He holds full registration with the Psychology Board of Australia, the British Psychological Society, the Singapore Psychological Society and the Middle East Psychological Association. In 2016, Alasdair was awarded a Medal of the Order of Australia (OAM) for services to children and young people, and in 2015, a Churchill Fellowship to examine service delivery for children in Iceland, Norway and Sweden.

Dr Stijn Sieckelinck has since March 2021 been Professor at the Hogeschool van Amsterdam University, the Netherlands, where he coordinates research on youth work. He holds a PhD in Social Educational Theory. He publishes on social pedagogy, citizenship education, polarization, radicalization and idealism. Previously, he worked at VU University Amsterdam, McGill University and Utrecht University. Dr Sieckelinck is concerned with issues regarding social education. His work aims to contribute to better insights and approaches in science, practice, and policy, especially where relationships with young people are concerned. In his book 'Reradicaliseren' (2017), he presents a pedagogical vision on the radicalization of young people.

Cameron Sumpter is a Research Fellow at the Centre of Excellence for National Security (CENS) at the S. Rajaratnam School of International Studies (RSIS) in Singapore, where he focuses on the policy and practice of preventing and countering violent extremism (P/CVE), particularly in Indonesia. Cameron's primary interest is the reintegration of former prisoners and those who have returned from extremist activity abroad. He also analyses prison-based disengagement programmes, risk assessment instruments and the development of P/CVE policy in different nations. Cameron is widely published on these issues. He presents his findings at international forums and consults with outside organizations, such as the United Nations Office on Drugs and Crime (UNODC).

Alexander Van Leuven collects youth voices on CPVE-related grievances, threats and protective factors. He is a PhD candidate at KU Leuven University in Media Anthropology, with a BA in Social Work (AP University College of Antwerp) and an MA in Social and Cultural Anthropology (KU Leuven). After a decade as a CPVE officer in the City of Mechelen, bridging policy and practice, Alexander became a researcher at the Hannah Arendt Institute, bridging research and policy. He is recording youth voices on and through the practice of safe spaces in Mechelen (Belgium), Dordrecht (Netherlands), Portsmouth (UK) and Calais (France) within an EU project called ORPHEUS, which aims to divert grievances away from violent extremism through the creation of safe spaces.

Dr Maria Walsh holds a Magister Artium and a PhD in educational sciences and criminology from the Ludwig Maximilian University Munich (Germany). She has worked as a researcher at the Max Planck Institute for Foreign and International Criminal Law and as a senior researcher and deputy head at the National Center for Crime Prevention. Her research focuses on crime prevention, juvenile delinquency, desistance and former extremists in PVE.

Acknowledgements

The ideas underpinning this volume have different wellsprings. The initial spark was a 2017 presentation on youth diversion given under the Chatham House rule at the Online Radicalisation Research Community of Practice (ORRCOP), hosted by the National Security Coordination Secretariat, Singapore. My thoughts were considerably enriched through other fora, including the annual workshops on radicalization and countering violent extremism held by the Centre of Excellence for National Security (CENS) at the S. Rajaratnam School of International Studies (RSIS), Singapore. This long-running series, together with the CENS Distinguished Visitor Programme as well as a separate programme, the Asia-Pacific Programme for Senior National Security Officers (APPSNO), has seen a constellation of academics, researchers and experts come to Singapore and generously share their time with an audience of policymakers, researchers and practitioners. I am grateful to all who have come over the years. These include Scott Atran, Shiraz Maher, Richard Barrett, Bartolomeo Conti, Mikkel Hjelt, Daniel Köhler, Alex Schmid, Andrew Silke, Ali Soufan and Lorenzo Vidino; I should also mention, in particular, alumni of our events who have contributed to the present volume (Amarnath Amarasingam, Sean Arbuthnot, Clarke Jones, Alex Van Leuven and Christian Damgaard Kristoffersen). These are many others (too many to name) who have not just shared their expertise in workshops but have generously made time when, say, interested parties informally bumped into them over the buffet table (a CENS speciality).

Planning for this volume was well advanced when the Covid-19 pandemic hit in 2020. The subsequent period was a trying time for all of us, including the present writer and several contributors. Some, faced with personal and professional pressures, elected quite understandably to withdraw. Others (equally understandably) needed considerably more time than originally envisaged to complete their contributions. To all, and especially to those who stayed the course, I am profoundly grateful. My thanks finally go to Julia Lau and Daryl Ong for their invaluable contributions in preparing this volume for publication as well as for saving me from many errors. Needless to say, all errors that remain are mine alone.

Shashi Jayakumar
Senior Fellow
Head, Centre of Excellence for National Security
Executive Coordinator, Future Issues and Technology
S. Rajaratnam School of International Studies (RSIS), Singapore

Introduction

Perspectives on countering extremism: Diversion and disengagement

Shashi Jayakumar

This volume seeks to contribute to the study of early upstream interventions in the field of radicalization and preventing/countering violent extremism (P/CVE). The contributors are in the main experts familiar with diversion and disengagement, practitioners who have designed interventions or scholars who have studied the effects of various interventions.

There are of course numerous works within the burgeoning field of CVE which deal with deradicalization, disengagement and other modes of stemming (or reversing) radicalization at either the individual or the community level. Some explanation is therefore necessary to set this volume against the backdrop of work done in the field and to take stock of the original contributions.

Definitions and distinctions

Any work dealing with the radicalization/CVE space almost inevitably needs to begin by making the commonplace – but necessary – observation that despite decades of scholarship on the issue, there is in fact no academic consensus on what the key terms – extremism and radicalization, to name two – actually mean.[1] The lack of consensus becomes even more apparent in the arguments concerning what makes an individual 'radicalized', or, for that matter, what is involved in the actual process of transition from 'radical' to terrorism or violence.[2] Many works would at this stage insert an enormous number of footnotes citing the key articles and books in the field, but, given that this volume is aimed as much at the practitioner and policymaker (or the general interested lay reader) as it is the academic expert and given that the core focus of this volume is not primarily radicalized individuals, I have chosen to limit such references.

One of the definitions put forward that I have found the most useful and relevant is by Anja Dalgaard-Nielsen, who describes a radicalized individual as

> ... *a person harbouring a deep-felt desire for fundamental socio-political changes, [and radicalization] is understood as a growing readiness to pursue and support far-reaching changes in society that conflict with, or pose a direct threat to, the existing order.*[3]

The Dutch security service, the AIVD, has defined radicalization as

> *the (active) pursuit of and/or support to far-reaching changes in society which may constitute a danger to (the continued existence of) the democratic legal order (aim), which may involve the use of undemocratic methods (means) that may harm the functioning of the democratic legal order (effect).*[4]

This is especially useful to understand radicalization in Western contexts. But while radicalization in the West is what many readers will be more familiar with, this volume goes beyond this and includes contributions from practitioners and experts with experience in other locations. Given this and given also that several of the contributions in this volume are from individuals knowledgeable about the 'street level' conditions that can give rise to radicalization, it is relevant here to reflect on a pared-down definition, one which comes from a youth worker who regularly comes into contact with individuals at risk of radicalization:

> 'Radicalisation happens when a person or group deviates from what is desirable in society. It is about deviating thoughts and in the worst case, turning words into deeds.'[5]

The occasionally heated debates concerning radicalization and violent extremism are matched by the fervour with which experts discuss the processes that attempt to reverse them: deradicalization and disengagement.

Again, there is a vast literature on this.[6] 'Deradicalization' seeks to change thoughts, views or convictions – efforts to change an extremist's worldview so the individual no longer agrees with radical ideas or ideology formerly held. These ideas, which may have brought him or her close to committing violence, may have been held at a personal level, or by movement the individual belonged to – in which case, the process of deradicalization means that the individual no longer agrees with the movement's tactics or ultimate goals. Some deradicalization efforts are under the auspices of state-run programmes, which typically (but not always) attempt to change the views of offenders who have been incarcerated. 'Disengagement', on the other hand, can be taken to mean the process by which individuals holding radical ideas (sometimes ideas that bring them close to the category of potential violent extremists) disassociate themselves from an extremist movement he/she may have belonged to (but not necessarily renouncing its ultimate goals). Where a movement or organization is not involved, disengagement at the individual level may also mean distancing oneself from the idea of committing a violent act (being persuading for example that violence is not the best way of achieving one's goals), while still holding ideas deemed radical by mainstream society. A disengaged individual may therefore still be a radical one.

The public health model

Experts and national authorities focused on prevention of radicalization and violent extremism have increasingly in recent years started to discuss interventions with reference to the public health model. As Cameron Sumpter observes in his contribution to this volume, the use of the public health lens when discussing violence has had a long history, with agencies such as the World Health Organization (WHO) in its seminal 2002 report on violence and health dividing and interventions into three levels – primary (broadly focused prevention), secondary (more targeted prevention) and tertiary (post-crime intervention).[7]

This conceptual approach has been adapted within the realm of CVE, with several of the contributors making some form of reference to it. Broadly understood, primary prevention in CVE programmes is designed to address the *potential* for radicalization in a community or population. Initiatives falling within this category often take the form of awareness campaigns and general education programmes. They can also refer to initiatives (efforts aimed at fostering critical thinking and resilience for example) that aim to reduce the social vulnerabilities thought to foster radicalism – to individuals or communities who are not radicalized or have not yet begun proceeding down a certain pathway.

Secondary prevention ('pre-clinical' using the public health lens) refers to interventions aimed at individuals identified as being in the process (usually at the beginnings of the process) of radicalization, or individuals or communities that have begun to exhibit risk factors or behaviours that might, if left unchecked, lead to a radicalized trajectory. The aim of secondary prevention initiatives is to halt the progress of the process underway, and, where possible, to bring the individual back into mainstream thinking, or into mainstream society.

Finally, tertiary interventions (treatment at the 'acute' stage) are aimed at individuals (or, occasionally, communities) who have clearly manifested signs of radicalization. Often, the interventions concern individuals facing the criminal justice system. The interventions can also extend to rehabilitation or building resilience (to prevent recidivism for example) of individuals who have been deemed radicalized and/or faced the criminal justice system.[8]

Diversion and disengagement: Going (further) upstream

Deradicalization programmes exist around the world, with some of the well-known programmes being state-led ones (for example, in Saudi Arabia and Singapore).[9] There are also models which are mistakenly called 'deradicalization' programmes, but which in reality encompass programmatic interventions which, taken together, represent efforts to get an individual to disengage from a certain worldview.[10] Broadly speaking, these often fall within the secondary and tertiary phases of intervention.

Rehabilitation and deradicalization programmes will continue to play a key role, even as they continue to evolve. But there has been increasing agreement amongst policymakers, practitioners and experts (and even from former radicals and extremists) in recent years that work in countering violent extremism (CVE) needs to shift away from 'deradicalization' to upstream work and prevention efforts.[11] Why the focus? The idea (again using the public health lens) is that symptoms should be spotted and treated before they become manifest and also that there is uncertainty about the effectiveness of some deradicalization programmes.

Partly as a result of this thinking, there has been a noticeable shift in some locations to work at the local and community level, not necessarily working to de-programme ideologies (whatever they may be) out of individuals, but to ameliorate or mitigate behaviour associated with violent extremism.[12] There has been in recent years a concomitant interest on the part of practitioners and policymakers in going further upstream to tackle the wellsprings of radicalization.[13]

Some of the contributions in this volume are concerned with circumstances that could drive individuals into a radicalized trajectory, as well as the early interventions that could have an effect in driving individuals away from this path. Some of the interventions approach the issue from a disengagement lens while others deal with early interventions to a more specific population where the people in question might not be radicalized themselves but exist in a milieu or geographic area which might make for recruitment into extremist groups. There are also contributions dealing the even earlier stages – awareness initiatives which target groups such as students which could not be said as a whole to be 'at risk', although there might be individuals within the targets groups themselves who might be more vulnerable than others.[14]

Here, a further term needs to be introduced and defined, given that several contributions deal with it either in part or whole: diversion.

This is a term which like so many in the field has several possible meanings. Diversion can be a similar strategy to disengagement but conducted *before* an individual is devoted to the movement or ideology. Some disengagement efforts might for example aim to tackle issues deep in the psyche responsible for radical thought (and may indeed elide into deradicalization), but diversion initiatives can ignore these entirely and try to provide off-ramps without grappling with the issue of commitment to a radical ideology at all. In this meaning, diversion would be further 'upstream' than disengagement – for example, initiatives seeking to nudge at-risk individuals into positive outcomes. It is possible to go even further upstream: diversionary programming at the primary stage may be aimed at a target group of individuals which may not yet have manifested signs of proceeding down a radicalized trajectory, *or who may not even be at risk*. This is the approach taken for example by Christian Kristoffersen and Anne Sofie Skare Rasmussen in this volume to describe sessions involving critical thinking and reflections in schools in Aarhus, Denmark (with the two authors explicitly using the term diversion) and arguably by Antje Gansewig and Maria Walsh (who do not) whose contribution deals with the use of 'formers' to engage students in schools to prompt reflection and, presumably, an avoidance of that trajectory.

The definition, however, is not that simple a matter. Diversion can mean different things to different people and there is in fact no agreement amongst experts (or amongst the contributors). Amarnath Amarasingham, Bradley Galloway and David Jones for example in their contribution situate diversion within the secondary and tertiary levels of programming – a useful counterpoint to the idea that diversionary programming takes place at the earliest stages (indeed, before one has even 'staged'). Notwithstanding what has been said above about broad-based diversion initiatives, it could be argued that the more common interpretation of diversionary programmes is that of interventions seeking to identify individuals at risk of committing acts of violent extremism (in other words, at risk of radicalization or having proceeded partway down that trajectory) and seeking to offramp them. The chapters that follow give examples from a wide spread of locations.

For those who take the position that both diversion and disengagement are individually focused and targeted at identified risk factors, it would follow naturally that these would be secondary or tertiary interventions. This position entails a rejection of the notion that public messaging campaigns aimed at loosely defined vulnerable populations or even broad-based interventions at the population level (social resilience measures, critical thinking, promoting tolerance, etc.) can constitute diversionary programming.

These might seem to be irreconcilable disagreements, but even as one accepts some definitional tension, it is possible to glimpse overlaps which are useful and indeed perhaps constructive. Although the type of diversion concerning individuals who are considered 'radicalized' and/or facing the criminal justice system might have specific interventions (for example, schemes for ex-offenders to reintegrate back into society in a manner aimed at minimizing the risk of recidivism), there are in fact various other interventions – resocialization, teaching life skills, mentoring, to name some – which can be common to both upstream and downstream diversion.

Some of this can be seen when we attempt the comparison with diversion in another field which has many learning lessons for CVE experts – criminal justice and the pre-criminal space. In this field (covered in the following paragraphs) diversion can mean attempts to head the individual off from *further* contact with the criminal justice system, but it is also employed in for juveniles (who might have offended at the juvenile justice level) who are at the risk of more serious offending.

The pre-criminality comparison: A (relevant) digression

Diversion in the criminal and juvenile offending space has for some considerable time been used to good effect in various parts of the world.[15] The programmes themselves can take many forms. Some programmes are skills-based and aimed at improving education levels, offering better employment prospects. There are also school-based programmes (or programmes aimed at retaining students in school and minimizing delinquency). Some schemes (both in and out of school) that seem to hold promise focus on behavioural and life skills. Given that offending has been linked in some cases to poor decision-making ability, cognitive-behavioural training social competence has also been shown to have some positive effect in terms of reducing criminal activity. Diverting young offenders from the criminal justice system (or from further contact with either the youth or criminal justice systems which can have its own knock-on criminogenic effects) benefits the individual, the criminal justice system and society as a whole.

In the CVE sphere, the Diversion Operations Team of the Australian Federal Police (AFP) for example has led interventions the purpose of which 'is to provide services so that at-risk individuals can disengage from violence and reconnect with their family and community before they harm themselves or others'.[16] The diversion work relies on a triage of supporting agencies, civil society and community partners to devise and implement early intervention and violence disengagement strategies for individuals. This includes connecting at-risk individuals with services such as mentoring, counselling, education and employment support. There are diversion initiatives at the state and local level as well, which see community organizations given support to tailor plans for people for whom diversion interventions are indicated.[17]

There are various youth diversion schemes for youth delinquency and minor offending in Singapore, a country which like several others has a system of 'pre-court diversion'.[18] Interventions for youth at risk are holistic: the National Committee on Prevention, Rehabilitation and Recidivism (NCPR) oversees national efforts to prevent offending in triage with police, relevant government agencies, social workers, as well as voluntary welfare organizations in the social support sector. A key aim is to detect social issues at an early stage and, where appropriate, to make referrals to social support services, rather than sending the individual for reformative training or to face the courts. These are measures and tailored programmes help to divert youths (especially out-of-school youth, or youths involved with gangs or drugs) who had committed minor offences from the court system by engaging them via suitable rehabilitation programmes to develop pro-social mindsets and life skills. The programmes emphasize remaining in the educational system and can include group work and individual sessions that promote pro-social mindsets and inculcate life skills such as decision-making, or being meaningfully engaged through vocational training and or employment.[19] Where appropriate, case management and outreach involving individual, group or family sessions are used to help youths develop their identity and resilience to a level where they can dissociate from gangs or other undesirable activities.[20]

The efforts do not stop there. A related, but further upstream set of programmes in Singapore is aimed at students assessed to be at risk, *but who have not yet offended*. Facets of the various programmes include providing a safe after-school environment, mentoring by credible adults and peers, and providing opportunities for the youth-at-risk to be meaningfully engaged through studies (given that some display emerging absenteeism issues), work or opportunities relating to interest groups. Some of the programmes target primary and secondary students from disadvantaged backgrounds. Identified students and their families receive coordinated multi-agency upstream support, in partnership with schools and other community partners, with referrals to relevant social services made as appropriate.[21] At the individual level, the aim is to develop resilience and problem-solving ability.

The extant literature concerning interventions around the world throws up several salient learning points. First, more informal interventions may increase engagement and are more likely to have a positive impact.[22] Second, programmes that work across multiple social settings, such as the family, school, peers and the community, also seem to have more of an impact compared to interventions seeking to simply address one risk factor. Third, the overall, emerging consensus seems to be that those designing community interventions should focus on developing programmes that strengthen social bonds of the individual (or offender) to the community (key components include family, pro-social peers, school and work). These are considered more effective in reducing offending, and can help the offender reintegrate into the community.[23] The community itself stands to benefit: well-adjusted, productive youths make for a safer society.[24]

All this has a bearing on some of what follows.

Youth diversion in Europe

Before considering chapters which discuss actual initiatives, it is useful to first consider the chapter by Farhad Khosrokhavar, which describes the lived experiences of many French Muslims. The overall feeling is one of rejection by society and prejudice against their faith (reinforced by the policy of *Laïcité*). Daily life is punctuated with 'small humiliations' against the overall backdrop of stigmatization – the feeling of being held responsible for the crimes (extremist actions) of other Muslims. As a result, many within the French Muslim community feel culturally rejected or undervalued. The marginalization is particularly acute for those who live in the socio-economically disadvantaged *banlieues*.[25] Inhabitants of the *banlieue* face everyday discrimination, economic marginalization and lack of access to the job market. Many of them have so deeply imbibed this sense of exclusion and stigmatization that it has in fact become part of their identity.

The sense of being rejected by society and a loss of faith in it leads some – a minority – to 'a high level of aggressiveness, a distrust towards the others, and a lack of self-esteem that leads to the hatred of the Self and the others'. Being radicalized and choosing violence is from their perspective a reaction to social injustice and humiliation experienced daily.

Some of these feelings – particularly of exclusion, stigmatization, alienation and the lack of opportunities – are of course felt not just by Muslims in France but by others elsewhere in Europe. The two chapters that follow describe programmatic interventions designed to tackle these and other risk factors.

Using the case study of the Belgian city of Mechelen (which from 2014 onwards saw a number of youths travelling to Syria to fight for ISIS), Alexander Van Leuven describes an intervention which emphasizes Positive identity and Societal Resilience (PiM). As Van Leuven observes, he receives different types of referrals – some related to drugs and others related to extremism. Some of the interventions consist of tackling early-stage social alienation. Some youths are given meaningful constructive activity under the Jongeren BuurtZorg (Youth Neighbourhood Care). Youngsters employed under this initiative for brief stints realize their own capabilities and gain esteem.

For Van Leuven, the key element of diversion is a form of life coaching. But what seems to be critical is getting credible individuals to give alienated youths a 'nudge', which helps in the process of unlocking the individual's potential, or sense of esteem. These credible figures (volunteers and professionals) are empathetic and trustworthy, have the requisite skills to not just deal with the underlying issues in within the minds of individuals referred, but also form a *connection*. These coaches also construct alternative pathways for individuals, many of whom express sympathy with ISIS as a 'cry for help', but who are also targeted by the manipulative nudges of recruiters from extremist groups – recruiters who appeal to the individual's sense of worth.

Van Leuven's points and assessments find close parallels in Stijn Sieckelinck's piece on Arnhem in the Netherlands. The intervention Sieckelinck observes, Buro Zend-Uit (BZU), was co-created by youth workers and social researchers with support from the municipality. Like parts of Mechelen, the area in question, Presikhaaf, is socio-economically deprived and has been a recruiting ground for ISIS (in addition to facing issues with criminality). Those tempted by the call of ISIS but who did not make the journey face other issues such as social alienation, lack of opportunities and discrimination in the labour market. They have very few positive experiences, even at school: 'For every single individual participating in this programme, the two key areas of socialisation and identity development, home and school, are sources of stress rather than resilience.' This leads to combativeness and/or to further social alienation, increasing the attractivity of the criminal/extremist milieu.

In the pilot programme, selected youths are intensively supported and assisted in the identification and upgrading of life goals, and assisted also to spot their vulnerabilities (as well as their hidden talents). This is facilitated by a mentoring programme not unlike what we have encountered with Mechelen.[26] In time, with successful cases, the individuals become more aware of their inner capacities and opportunities for personal growth.

A common strand running through both contributions is that youth who are made aware of their capacities (especially through a guided process of self-examination which may also see them set self-directed goals) and who feel valued are better able to withstand the seemingly attractive lure of destructive or antisocial solutions. The latter possibility is always present. Sieckelinck observes that ISIS presents itself as an agency where no discrimination exists, calling to mind Van Leuven's observation in his contribution that hidden talents can be spotted and nurtured by mentors, but also by extremist groups.

The attractions of the radical path seem clear. Joining a group fulfils various needs – it can provide status and identity, fulfil the need for belonging and give meaning to young people in particular.

Van Leuven's central argument is that these processes can be the extension of a very *normal* process that we all have to deal with, especially as emerging adults. Strong ideals can occur naturally in the course of identity development (especially when difficulties in life are encountered; in addition, there are also interactions taking place during upbringing, at school and through the internet).[27] The development of strong beliefs constitutes a stage in cognitive, psychosocial and identity formation. Joining an extremist group can be the answer to a young person's existential doubts, as these groups also provide an opportunity to match words with deeds.[28]

This chimes with a body of work that has emerged in recent years concerning the quest on the part of the individual for meaning and significance – 'the fundamental desire to matter, to be someone, to have respect'.[29] It has increasingly been recognized that young people do engage in ideological exploration or with radical perspectives when wrestling with issues of identity.[30] A related approach, the 'uncertainty-identity theory', suggests that self-uncertainty (brought on by personal circumstances or other factors) can lead individuals to identify with types of groups that provide a clear identity together with prescriptions on behaviour and belief. The uncertainty in and of itself can lead in the direction of extremism while validation is provided by group identification.[31] A key proponent of this approach, Michael Hogg, has persuasively argued that the way to protect individuals from this type of validation is to ensure that there are alternative (and less destructive) identities available that go some way to ameliorating feelings of uncertainty.[32]

The Mechelen Model and BZU approaches target youths at uncertain times of their lives, while they are preoccupied by issues of identity, and in some cases suffering from alienation or stigmatization.[33] These programmes offer alternatives and opportunities for youths to express themselves, without necessarily having to completely de-programme themselves of all ideals.[34] As Stijn Sieckelinck has elsewhere argued, there is nothing objectionable at all in being 'reasonably passionate' – and indeed this is something that should be encouraged.[35]

Schools, society and beyond

The case studies given above concern interventions introduced partly to counter the effects of an insalubrious milieu. But as discussed earlier, interventions can take place further upstream, even before issues develop, and it is also useful within the broad prevention umbrella to contemplate initiatives that take place in safe environments, where the groups targeted by interventions might not be classified as high risk.

An example of this is described in the contribution on the Danish city Aarhus by Christian Damgaard Kristoffersen and Anne Sofie Skare Rasmussen. Aarhus has of course given its name to a famed approach to prevention known (wrongly) in some quarters at the 'Aarhus deradicalisation model'. There is a large extant literature on the model itself, which rests on strong historical cooperation between the police, schools and social services.[36] Some of the better-known aspects of the model are the parts dealing with individuals planning to join ISIS (or returnees from Syria). The contribution by Kristoffersen and Rasmussen concerns a different and somewhat unheralded aspect: voluntary workshops offered to every public school in Aarhus for children aged ten to eighteen years. This is the most upstream part of the overall Aarhus prevention effort.

The core pedagogical aspect of these workshops is inclusive dialogue on specific themes (between the workshop instructors and the students, as well as among the students themselves) in an equal setting, where all are encouraged to speak out. While radicalization (and, in recent years, online radicalization) features, this is only one plank. Others include critical thinking and digital literacy.

What these workshops amount to is the provision of a set of cognitive tools for young and sometimes impressionable individuals. As the contributors note, the workshops 'are intended to strengthen and work with community, understanding, empathy, a broader perspective on the world among several other things among the students. In a nutshell, we try to give the students the tools to understand themselves, their classmates, and the world they live in as well as tools to interpret their experiences.'[37]

There seems to be a particular use case for older students who are starting to orientate themselves towards the wider society, with the programming for this age group tailored to encourage and inspire democratic participation in society. This is very much in keeping with moves in Denmark in recent years, with increasing emphasis on inculcating resilience from a young age, strengthening critical thinking skills, and making students understand the value of citizenship and the role they play as citizens.[38]

The object is not prevention in terms of off-ramping students from negative outcomes. No specific racial or religious groups or neighbourhoods are targeted. The objective is not to measure outcomes either. That said, and as the contributors note, positive feedback has been received, especially concerning how the workshops are an ideal setting for creating and nurturing common understanding and empathy and fostering community in the classroom.

The Aarhus workshops facilitate, in effect, the creation of safe spaces that enable open and frank discussion. This bears comparison with points made in another contribution in the volume by Fernan Osorno Hernandez, who examines grassroots prevention work in the UK. Practitioners organize workshops where individuals can engage in discussion and disagree without feeling there is a right or wrong answer (this aspect is also strongly present in the Aarhus workshops). The key difference is that the interventions Osorno Hernandez describes facilitate safe spaces in more downstream (and troubled) settings, with specific groups and individuals either being selected or invited to participate. The practitioners are using these methods to challenge belief systems and facilitate the development of critical thinking skills within groups or individuals which have already been imbued with strongly held points of view or pre-dispositions.

The initiatives in schools in Denmark or Germany (in the contribution by Maria Walsh and Antje Gansewig) concern upstream interventions where the targeted students are not considered at risk. The interventions described by Mohammad Abdullah Darraz in Indonesian schools on the other hand are very different in terms of circumstance and context. In Indonesia, broad-based interventions are needed because whole swathes of the community might be at risk of falling into a radicalized mindset. Indonesia has for decades prided itself on its pluralism, diversity and cultural acceptance of various groups within society. This is on the wane at many levels, as Darraz points out in his contribution. He shows through alarming survey data rising intolerance and the othering of minorities (both minorities within the Islamic fold and other religious groups) that has taken place within the mindsets of many within of the mainstream (Sunni) majority towards other minorities. Increasing intolerance can be a precursor to extremism: a number of the younger generation share these views, with some feeling that it is acceptable to take up violence against these other groups.

Darraz paints a fascinating picture of interventions by the Maarif Institute in 'red zones' or areas known prone to extremist rhetoric. One issue is that of the existence of school extracurricular activities created in the name of strengthening religious education. This has on some occasions allowed ingress of radical groups and thinking, as has the trend of student councils which are networked with Islamist boarding schools (*pesantren*) of a Salafi-Wahabi hue, which has made for the hardening of religious attitudes.

What can be done? There is of course no antidote. There are, however, approaches which have promised as bulwarks against creeping extremism. The first is exposure and awareness. The organization that Darraz leads, the Maarif Institute, actively facilitates activities for educators at all levels to raise awareness of attempts by radical groups to infiltrate the school environment. The second approach to erode radical and intolerant mindsets is the mainstreaming of diversity within internal school practices – this might include reinforcing principles of togetherness and equality, involving minority students in school activities, and celebrating all religious holidays, including those of the minority.

The approaches sketched out by Darraz are set into context by and should be read together with Cameron Sumpter's survey of the diverse landscape of primary and tertiary prevention in Indonesia.[39] Some of the interventions Sumpter describes are government-led (or government-supported), but the overall picture is an extremely complex one (while many intervention providers do genuinely worthwhile work, some providers are lured into the scene primarily by donor money). From time to time, there may well be worthy initiatives such as those discussed by Darraz, but whether at the group or individual level, they will (as Sumpter observes) be more likely to emerge organically in particular settings where strong communities, charismatic personalities and other favourable conditions create genuine opportunities for diversion or more broad-based attempts to instil resilience and tolerance.

Diversion/disengagement as official strategy

Some of the initiatives described by Osorno Hernandez, briefly mentioned above, stand outside of the UK's official Prevent programme, which operates in the space of supporting people who are vulnerable to radicalization or extremism. At the heart of Prevent is Channel, the multi-agency programme that identifies individuals at risk of radicalization and devises support plans. Channel and Prevent have suffered from negative press in the past (especially when it comes to the stigmatizing of the Muslim community, and the perception of an over-securitization of the overall approach).[40] In his contribution, Prevent coordinator Sean Arbuthnot does not ignore these criticisms but points to the successes that can be achieved when interventions are driven by a local, multi-agency approach that can assess a referral's vulnerability and take decisions on the appropriate support package.

Arbuthnot observes that PREVENT is not about deradicalization. It aims instead 'to engage people as far upstream as possible, whilst they are on a path to radicalization, *before* they are actually radicalized or criminalized. Its aim is to turn people away from violence'. Specific successful interventions he describes (which are for both Islamist and right wing) can be creative and tailored to individual needs. In addition (echoing some of what is at work in the BZU and the Mechelen Model), the diversionary activities work to foster a positive mindset, tap into a referral's interests or provide them with skills and qualifications that enhance their career prospects or life skills.

Again, discourse and discussion are important within this journey. Arbuthnot points to the effectiveness of mentoring and, with this, the development of critical thinking skills. The mentors used depend on the circumstances of the specific case: they may include religious scholars, psychologists, counsellors, youth workers and mental health practitioners. Some are former extremists themselves. What they hold in common is experience, credibility and the ability to establish an environment of trust and empathy.

Like Arbuthnot, Fernan Osorno Hernandez has a deep familiarity with PREVENT, but from a different perspective: extensive interactions and fieldwork with PVE practitioners and Youth workers engaged in upstream interventions. Their insights are thought-provoking and echo themes we have already encountered. One set of observations concerns problems with an overly securitized approach to P/CVE. This can lead to blinkered mindsets which ignore the overall milieu – one full of contributive and often intersecting factors such as gang violence, racism, Islamophobia, social stigmatization, domestic violence, knife crime, education disengagement and other local issues. Youth workers can be caught between doing multi-modal work, tackling the variegated root causes in a holistic way, and on the other hand solely doing PREVENT counter-radicalization referral work.[41] The two approaches need not necessarily be exclusive, but some of the most useful youth work that Osorno Hernandez describes takes place when youth workers incorporate P/CVE work into their pre-existing practices which *do* take into account and tackle these other root causes. It is this approach – one that seeks to identify and tackle the different factors that may make someone fall into criminality or violence (or terrorism) that is preferred by the most insightful of the practitioners interviewed by Osorno Hernandez.

Interventions in and out of official strategy: The community

A theme running through several of the contributions is the perception of the community as well as its own role and agency. Sometimes the entire community can be stigmatized (as we shall see in Farhad Khosrokhavar's contribution) but there are instances where the community also comes together to mobilize resources or makes a change within itself as the result of facilitation by an external actor. This mobilization within the community is the centrepiece of Justin Richmond and Reed Mikkelsen's contribution.

The intervention in question, carried out by the NGO Impl project, is styled as a diversionary development programme conducted over the 2015–20 period in Butig,

Mindanao, the Philippines. This is the staging ground of various militant groups, including the Maute Group, which was behind the 2017 siege of nearby Marawi. The root issues in the Butig area which make young men vulnerable to recruitment by groups like the Maute are not principally (and not in the first instance) religious. What was instead at play was an interconnected mesh which included vendettas, discrimination, poverty, the lack of education and opportunities, and the attendant resentment. Besides leading to a tendency towards criminal activity, all this also made for fertile ground for Salafi-jihadi ideology that could be exploited by groups like the Maute, which offered youth a path to wealth and respect that they otherwise would not have had.

The premise behind Impl project's interventions was simple. Young men from the area were taught construction tradecraft (which could lead at least some of them to be gainfully employed) and an economic cooperative was also set up, which (as the contributors explain) led to a decreased rate in farmers pulling their sons out of school. These became bulwarks against the short-term allure of recruitment efforts by extremist organizations. The initiatives in question did not attempt to 'diagnose' or still less treat Islamist extremism, nor did they make all core conditions leading to recruitment go away. But there was a diminution of these conditions as a result of the initiatives introduced, along with a more socially positive mindset and an improvement in the level of community resilience, which meant that there was no longer broad-based sympathy for the extremist groups.

ISIS has attracted tens of thousands of adherents. Many have been killed, but large numbers – both combatants and their families – are held at the time of writing in various camps, principally in Northeast Syria. Clarke Jones, Alasdair Roy and Kamalle Dabboussy (whose daughter and her three children are being held at one of these camps) have devised a programme, Changing Tides, which can be put into use for returnees should the conditions allow (given developments in late 2022 with some being brought back, there seems to be a pressing need for such an intervention).

The programme, developed in consultation with groups within the Australian Muslim community, is a diversionary framework that consists of a range of preventative and support mechanisms. The framework uses elements that have been found to be effective in other interventions, such as those promoting desistance from street and prison gangs, drug and alcohol-related offending, and youths involved in antisocial and violent behaviours. Given that the target group would have been exposed to significant trauma, individuals will be provided psychological and mental health assistance (in addition to other services such as legal support where needed).

What Jones, Dabboussy and Roy are pointing to is not an exercise in 'deradicalization' but more accurately, resocialization and reintegration. They accept that some of the individuals should they return might be at risk of engaging in potentially harmful behaviour (and might in any case be of interest to law enforcement agencies). They argue however that these risks can be mitigated through the proposed community-led programme developed specifically for them. Many of the details of Changing Tides will no doubt need to be fleshed out – or even perhaps rethought – should the target group ever return to Australia and their individual case needs are assessed. Suffice to say at this point, however, that Jones, Dabboussy and Roy provide a provocative (others might suggest persuasive) alternative to state-led CVE programmes, which they argue can be stigmatizing and which has led to a lack of trust on the part of the community when it comes to government-led programmes.[42]

Cautionary contributions

We have already encountered in some of the chapters the issue of varied root causes leading individuals to radicalization and joining extremist groups. Some practitioners and organizations attempt the complicated task of devising multi-modal interventions targeting violence, gang activity, other criminal behaviour and uncertain identities. But as Amarnath Amarasingam, Brad Galloway and David Jones observe, while all these myriad factors are suggestive and quite often present in various combinations in the trajectories of extremists, the factors themselves are present in the stories of a great many people who *never* take a turn to extremism. The corollary is that it is not easy to discern within all this any clear, common factors that *specifically* make individuals likely to join a violent extremist group.

Reflecting on their involvement and looking back, many former extremists alluded to the seemingly random process of becoming involved. The former extremists interviewed by Amarasingam, Galloway and Jones could articulate programming that would have prevented their slide to extremism – even, tellingly, formers who subsequent became involved in P/CVE.

The takeaway is not that it is futile to design programmes. What the contributors suggest, however, is that a great deal of care and thought should go into programme design and implementation, precisely on account of the varied factors that may drive the turn to extremism and violence. If interventions are to be effective, they need to be designed to be adaptive and should not make presuppositions on needs that can be very specific, nor should practitioners be too quick to discount driving forces that can be individual in nature (for example when it comes to ideological and political grievances).

Amarasingam, Galloway and Jones point out the difficulties that formers have in discerning what would have worked for them. Uncertainty concerning formers also features in a different way in the chapter by Antje Gansewig and Maria Walsh – here, doubt is expressed as to whether ad hoc interventions in schools feature formers work. The chapter deals primarily with talks and presentations given by former left and right-wing extremists in German schools. While these can be generally well-received, the impact study (in one case) conducted by the authors showed no sign of any meaningful impact on the attitudes of the audience members when it came to extremist attitudes, violence and delinquency. Gansewig and Walsh point out that there has been no definitive study of the PVE programming using former extremists in schools showing that there have been lasting effects on students for the prevention of extremism or crime. Indeed, as they point out, this type of programming could in some cases lead to a fascination with extremist lifestyles – precisely the opposite of what was intended.

Uncertainty does not mean (as we see in the chapter by Amarasingam, Galloway and Jones) that the intervention in question has no value. Gansewig and Walsh observe that rigour is needed when designing these types of school-based interventions and clarity is needed in identifying the target group and the aim (whether the intention is a broad awareness or diversion at a secondary level).[43] In addition, even when these are met, it may be more useful to embed this programming within an overall school-based prevention and awareness curriculum, not as a one-off occurrence.[44]

Conclusion

This volume represents an attempt to contribute to a body of knowledge in terms of what has been tried in early interventions in the P/CVE space. It has *not* set out to answer the vexed question of what definitively works and what does not in the field, nor has the primary purpose been to set out what 'success' might look like. Still, some observations can be made from the insights shared by contributors.

In early-stage engagements when the target group is not strictly speaking at risk, an intervention which takes the form of talks or workshops can be about almost any topic. But here, the key question is what one is trying to achieve. The answer is likely not diversion or disengagement, but a general pro-social awareness.

In many locations, it might be reasonable to posit that interventions in schools (the loci of so much social capital) are useful. The programmes look different depending on location and circumstance: in the West, value of democratic participation and citizenship, and developing critical thinking skills (or at least developing the ability to have reasoned discussion across a range of topics) are important. In other contexts or circumstances, what may be needed are tailored programmes at a community level, especially where tolerance or basic building blocks of society are being eroded (as we have seen with the chapters dealing with Indonesia).

On diversion and disengagement further downstream: the existence of risk factors (including rootlessness, identity issues, the lack of opportunities) either singly or in combination does not mean a natural progression to radicalization and violence, but it can be conducive for potential progression down this pathway. We see this in the Philippines (chapter 10), where the lack of opportunities is a critical factor when it comes to joining an extremist organization and where gainful work or training (or opportunities to be in school) improves resilience among individuals and in the community.

In the case studies we have seen in the West, at the level of the street, alienation and anger stemming from various causes can meld into a mix where the various component factors become harder to distinguish and are subsumed by the authorities under the label 'radical'. The interventions which seem to hold some promise may be those which seek to engage holistically all these factors, even though many of the so-called 'risk factors' being observed have, seemingly, a weak direct association with radicalization to violent extremism.[45]

Some of the interventions are not a quick fix and do not 'solve' all the risk factors, or still less promote comprehensive desistance from negative behaviours or actions. In some cases, the approach is more about reducing vulnerability. What should be looked for as results of interventions are indicators of more positive pro-social behaviours and for the individual more preparedness to take positive steps (such as acknowledging issues or improving his or her prospects). Factors that facilitate this include school support, civic engagement, involvement with the community, training (including vocational training), projects where one can gain esteem, and mentoring.

A final conclusion is that, where possible, unsecuritized approaches to diversion and disengagement at the community level are those which should be tried. It will also be apparent that while some of the core work has been done by NGOs, youth workers, and intervention providers in the community, these organizations and individuals do not necessarily loom over-large in the stories we have seen. Successful approaches involve being non-judgemental, getting to know the community (or the youth), understanding needs and spending time with the target group or individuals, without being over-focused on the radicalization aspect. The backdrop should (in the ideal) be one of trust between those at the forefront of any programme and those receiving intervention.[46]

This is lengthy and intense, resource-intensive work. Rather than attempt to 'measure effectiveness' in each and every case, it might be preferable for there to be an in-built recognition that for some of the interventions, it takes time for the community's resilience to improve or (at the individual level) for attitudes to change, for alienation to dissipate, and for motivations and behaviour to be shaped in more pro-social ways. Time enough such that for at least some who are on their own individual journeys, alternative, more positive pathways will become clearer.[47]

Notes

1   For discussion, see A. P. Schmidt, 'Radicalisation, De-radicalisation, Counter-radicalisation: A Conceptual Discussion and Literature Review', *The International Centre for Counter-Terrorism – The Hague* 4, no. 2 (2013). https://icct.nl/publication/radicalisation-de-radicalisation-counter-radicalisation-a-conceptual-discussion-and-literature-review/ (accessed 28 January 2022).

2   See for example Randy Borum, 'Radicalization into Violent Extremism I: A Review of Social Science Theories', *Journal of Strategic Security* 4, no. 4 (2011): 7–36; Clark McCauley and Sophia Moskalenko, 'Mechanisms of Political Radicalization: Pathways Toward Terrorism', *Terrorism and Political Violence* 20, no. 3 (2008): 415–33, and F. M. Moghaddam, 'The Staircase to Terrorism. A Psychological Exploration', *American Psychological Association* 60, no. 2 (2005): 161–9. My own thoughts on these issues (part of a collaborative project with other experts) can be found in Bartolomeo Conti, Ekaterina Sokirianskaia, Fredrick Ogenga, Phil Gurski, Rahma Dualeh and Shashi Jayakumar, 'Deradicalisation', *International Panel on Exiting Violence: Final Report* (International Panel on Exiting Violence/*La Fondation Maison des sciences de l'homme*, 2019), available at: https://www.ipev-fmsh.org/wp-content/uploads/2021/06/Final-Report-IPEV-EN.pdf pp. 33–7 (accessed 28 January 2022).

3   Anja Dalgaard-Nielsen, 'Violent Radicalization in Europe: What We Know and What We Do Not Know', *Studies in Conflict & Terrorism* 33, no. 9 (2010): 798.

4   *From Dawa to Jihad: The Various Threats from Radical Islam to the Democratic Legal Order*, General Intelligence and Security Service (AIVD), 2005, 13. https://english.aivd.nl/publications/publications/2005/03/30/from-dawa-to-jihad (accessed 28 January 2022).

5 Annemarie van de Weert and Quirine A. M. Eijkman, 'Subjectivity in Detection of Radicalisation and Violent Extremism: A Youth Worker's Perspective', *Behavioral Sciences of Terrorism and Political Aggression* 11, no. 3 (2019): 200.

6 As explained above, I do not propose (given the nature of this volume and intended audience) to overwhelm the reader with references on deradicalization and disengagement. Works that I have found useful for understanding both concepts and cases include: *Understanding Deradicalisation: Methods, Tools and Programs for Countering Violent Extremism* (London and New York: Routledge, 2017), at 1–28, Mary Beth Altier, Christian N. Thoroughgood and John G. Horgan, 'Turning away from Terrorism: Lessons from Psychology, Sociology, and Criminology', *Journal of Peace Research* 51, no. 5 (September 2014): 647–61; Anja Dalgaard-Nielsen, 'Promoting Exit from Violent Extremism: Themes and Approaches', *Studies in Conflict & Terrorism* 36, no. 2 (2013): 99–115; John Horgan, Mary Beth Altier, Neil Shortland and Max Taylor, 'Walking Away: The Disengagement and De-radicalization of a Violent Right-wing Extremist', *Behavioral Sciences of Terrorism and Political Aggression* 9, no. 2 (2017): 63–77; and Mary Beth Altier, Emma Leonard Boyle, Neil D. Shortland and John G. Horgan, 'Why They Leave: An Analysis of Terrorist Disengagement Events from Eighty-seven Autobiographical Accounts', *Security Studies* 26, no. 2 (2017): 305–32.

7 The goal of primary preventions is to stop the initial emergence of violent extremism before it takes root. Secondary and tertiary preventions (going by the original definitions) are respectively focused on avoiding violence, immediately responding when it does occur, and ensuring long-term care in its wake. Etienne G. Krug, Linda L. Dahlberg, James A. Mercy, Anthony B. Zwi and Rafael Lozano (eds.), *World Report on Violence and Health* (World Health Organization, 2002), 15, available at: http://whqlibdoc.who.int/publications/2002/9241545615_eng.pdf (accessed 25 January 2022). See also K. Bhui and E. Jones, 'The Challenge of Radicalisation: A Public Health Approach to Understanding and Intervention', *Psychoanalytic Psychotherapy* 31, no. 4 (2017): 401–10, and *Countering Violent Extremism through Public Health Practice: Proceedings of a Workshop* (Washington, DC: National Academies of Sciences, Engineering, and Medicine. The National Academies Press, 2017): 63–8, available at: https://cphd.ph.ucla.edu/sites/default/files/downloads/Countering%20 Violent%20Extremism%20Through%20Public%20Health%20Practice1_0.pdf (accessed 14 February 2022).

8 For explanations of the primary/secondary/tertiary approach as it pertains to CVE, see for example Shandon Harris-Hogan, Kate Barrelle and Andrew Zammit, 'What Is Countering Violent Extremism? Exploring CVE Policy and Practice in Australia', *Behavioral Sciences of Terrorism and Political Aggression* 8, no. 1 (2016): 8–13; M. J. Williams, J. G. Horgan and W. P. Evans, *Evaluation of a Multi-faceted, U.S. Community-based, Muslim-led CVE Program* (US Department of Justice, 2016), 10–11, available at https://www.ojp.gov/pdffiles1/nij/grants/249936.pdf), 10–11, and *Levels of prevention at the CPRLV* (Center for the Prevention of Radicalisation Leading to Violence, 2017; available at: https://info-radical.org/wp-content/uploads/2017/03/cprlv-intervention-at-every-level.pdf (accessed 14 February 2022). These explanations come with variations and nuances; in my own treatment above, I have chosen to offer a view taking into account the main interpretations without necessarily attempting to reconcile all of them.

9 Both programmes have an extensive literature. See Andreas Capstack, 'Deradicalization Programs in Saudi Arabia: A Case Study', *Middle East Institute*,

10 June 2015, http://www.mei.edu/content/deradicalization-programs-saudi-arabia-case-study#_ftn3., and Shashi Jayakumar, *Deradicalisation in Singapore: Past, Present and Future, The International Centre for the Study of Radicalisation (ICSR) Report*, King's College London, United Kingdom, 20 August 2020. https://icsr.info/wp-content/uploads/2020/08/ICSR-Report-Deradicalisation-in-Singapore-Past-Present-and-Future.pdf (accessed 13 February 2022).

10 See the discussion and references given to the 'Aarhus Model' further below, n.36.

11 'These folks are also the early *prevention* network we so desperately need to invest in right now, although many don't yet realize their potential to help counter extremism before it ever takes hold. No amount of "deradicalization" will make enough of a necessary impact if we can't proactively prevent people from becoming "radicalized." Prevention and accountability are key.' Christian Picciolini, 'I'm Closing Free Radicals Project – Here Are My Reasons, and Why a Shift in Focus Is Needed', *Medium*, 10 November 2021. https://medium.com/@cpicciolini/free-radicals-project-forced-to-close-its-doors-a88e29661d21 (accessed 11 November 2021).

12 See the remarks of van de Weert and Eijkman, 'Subjectivity in Detection of Radicalisation and Violent Extremism', 191–2.

13 As Eric Rosand observes, 'awareness needs to be raised among criminal justice officials and practitioners, as well as the wider public, to make clear that "off-ramp" programs for those who have come to the attention of law enforcement, or have been arrested and even charged with a terrorism offense, is not being "soft" on security but rather a successful outcome of the criminal process – and one that, if implemented properly, will lead to a reduction of the threat. Lessons can be learned from work with gangs that have led to lowering recidivism rates.' 'Taking the Off-ramp: A Path to Preventing Terrorism', *War on the Rocks*, 1 July 2016. https://warontherocks.com/2016/07/taking-the-off-ramp-a-path-to-preventing-terrorism/ (accessed 14 February 2022).

14 Two contributions (those by Cameron Sumpter and Farhad Khosrokhavar) do not deal with specific interventions but give general useful overviews of Indonesian CVE policy (Sumpter) and of the conditions in France that make French Muslims vulnerable to radicalization (Khosrokhavar).

15 It is well understood that criminological research can provide comparative insights for terrorism researchers (for example, how desistance from criminal activity might hold lessons for the study of leaving of extremist groups). Nonetheless, this remains an under-explored topic. See the remarks of Daniel Koehler in his book *Understanding Deradicalisation*, at 30–4. There has been still less work done on the body of work on criminal and pre-criminal diversion might be relevant for CVE practitioners. For the general concepts and approaches, see *Practical Lessons, Fair Consequences: Improving Diversion for Young People in Victoria* (Department of Justice, 2012), 18. https://library.bsl.org.au/jspui/bitstream/1/4056/1/Practical_lessons%20fair_consequences_improving_diversion_for_young%20people%20victoria.pdf, and *What Works in Reducing Young People's Involvement in Crime?* (Australian Institute of Criminology, 2002). https://www.aic.gov.au/sites/default/files/2020-05/what-works-in-reducing-young-peoples-involvement-in-crime.pdf (accessed 14 February 2022). The paragraphs in this section derive from the material on criminal (and pre-crime) diversion in Australia and Singapore, which have comparatively mature approaches in this area; the point however is that approaches detailed in the literature are also used in other locations and in some cases can translate to the CVE context.

16 'National Efforts' (Australian Federal Police, n.d.). https://www.afp.gov.au/what-we-do/crime-types/fighting-terrorism/national-efforts. For diversion in Australia, see Jenny Cartwright, 'Diversion in Australia: Not Your Traditional Counter-terrorism Response', *AFP Platypus Magazine*, April 2016: 30–2. http://www5.austlii.edu.au/au/journals/AUFPPlatypus/2016/10.pdf (accessed 31 January 2022) and 'Countering Violent Extremism (CVE) Intervention Programs', Australian Government Department of Home Affairs. https://www.homeaffairs.gov.au/about-us/our-portfolios/national-security/countering-extremism-and-terrorism/cve-intervention-programs (accessed 31 January 2022). See also Adrian Cherney, 'Working with Radicalised Individuals: Insights from a Secondary and Tertiary Prevention Program', *Behavioral Sciences of Terrorism and Political Aggression* (2022; ahead of print), 1–21. As Cherney observes concerning the intervention in one Australian state (15), 'The main strategy to address the vulnerabilities and needs evident amongst our client sample was to provide alternative pathways and to promote pro-social activities.'

17 Kate Campbell, 'Anti-radicalisation Alliance Set Up in WA', *PerthNow*, 20 June 2017. https://www.perthnow.com.au/news/wa/anti-radicalisation-alliance-set-up-in-wa-ng-68b33e2b0bb4ff17a3fa724b6665308f (accessed 31 January 2022). In neighbouring New Zealand, there is no official diversion strategy, but have been examples of 'off-ramps'. For example, in 2018, a judge in Christchurch decided on a course of rehabilitative measures instead of punishment when sentencing a young convert who planned an attack. The youth was then mentored by people in the Muslim community and given other activities. David Clarkson, 'Kiwi Teenager Radicalised Online Planned Mass Killing in Christchurch "for Allah"', *Stuff.co.nz*, 16 February 2018. https://www.stuff.co.nz/national/crime/101480988/kiwi-teenager-radicalised-online-planned-mass-killing-in-christchurch-for-allah (accessed 14 February 2022).

18 For Singapore, see Kumaralingam Amirthalingam, 'Criminal Justice and Diversionary Programmes in Singapore', *Criminal Law Forum* 24 (2013): 527–59 at 552–3, *Report on Youth Delinquency. Key Trends and Upstream Measures* (Singapore: Central Youth Guidance Office, Ministry of Social and Family Development, 2019 at 40–53; https://www.msf.gov.sg/NCPR/Our-Initiatives/Documents/FA_MSF_Report%20on%20Youth%20Delinquency%202019%20%28Medium%20Res%29.pdf), and *Report on Youth Delinquency 2021* (Singapore: National Committee on Prevention, Rehabilitation and Recidivism), esp.20–30. See https://www.msf.gov.sg/NCPR/Our-Initiatives/Documents/FA_MSF_Report_on_Youth_Delinquency_2021.pdf (links accessed 28 January 2022).

19 *Report on Youth Delinquency 2021*, 32.

20 *Report on Youth Delinquency 2021*, 33. The information provided in these paragraphs at p.6 is not meant to suggest that the level of organization in tackling these matters in Singapore is in any way unique; the intention is to give some sense of what broadly takes place in the pre-court diversion space. Many of the specific interventions in Singapore have close parallels elsewhere.

21 *Report on Youth Delinquency 2021*. Information on the Singapore interventions had also benefitted from information and materials concerning diversion, probation and community rehabilitation shared by senior staff from the Probation and Community Rehabilitation Service and Central Youth Guidance Office at a 2019 event under the Chatham House Rule.

22 *Practical Lessons, Fair Consequences*, 18.

23 C. Gill, 'Community Interventions', in *What Works in Crime Prevention and Rehabilitation: Lessons from Systematic Reviews*, D. Weisburd, D. P. Farrington,

and C. Gill, eds. (New York: Springer, 2016), 104; and *What Works in Reducing Young People's Involvement in Crime? Review of Current Literature on Youth Crime Prevention*, 8. Some experts in early interventions for crime prevention have used the term 'developmental prevention' – interventions targeted at children and adolescents aimed at having a positive effect on risk factors at the individual, family and school levels. See David P. Farrington, Maria M. Ttofi and Friedrich A. Lösel, 'Developmental and Social Prevention', in *What Works in Crime Prevention and Rehabilitation*, D. Weisburd, D. P. Farrington and C. Gill, eds., 15–16. As the authors observe (16), 'Many programs focus on individual children or youth by providing training in social competencies, interpersonal problem solving, and other behavioural or cognitive skills. Other programs concentrate on the family by providing training in parenting skills, counselling on child rearing, or coping with family stress.' For developmental prevention, see also *E4J University Module Series: Crime Prevention and Criminal Justice: Module 2: Crime Prevention. Topic Two Continued – Detailed Explanation of Tonry and Farrington's Typology*, at https://www.unodc.org/e4j/en/crime-prevention-criminal-justice/module-2/key-issues/2a–detailed-explanation-of-tonry-and-farringtons-typology.html (accessed 27 January 2022). Some of the developmental intervention approaches described have parallels in some of the work described by contributors to this volume. Also useful is T. I. Herrenkohl, J. D. Hawkins, I. J. Chung, K. G. Hill and S. Battin-Pearson, 'School and Community Risk Factors and Interventions', in *Child Delinquents: Development, Intervention and Service Needs*, R. Loeber and D. P. Farrington, eds. (Thousand Oaks, CA: Sage, 2001), 211–46; see especially Table 10.1 at 217).

24   *Practical Lessons, Fair Consequences*, 18.

25   As Khosrokhavar observes, some French middle-class Muslims (a minority) feel strongly rooted in their French identity and have a harmonious relationship with society, even though to reach this status, they had to (and continue to have to) struggle against daily social prejudices against them.

26   This is not the place for a full discussion of mentoring (which is also employed in the pre-crime space) and its effectiveness, but it is worth observing that this features in some of the interventions described in this volume. Common strands include making a connection and giving the individual a sense of competence and control over their lives, while at the same time reducing vulnerability. Mentoring can be used both for at-risk individuals and for individuals already deemed to be part way into the radicalisation process. See B. Spalek and L. Davies, 'Mentoring in Relation to Violent Extremism: A Study of Role, Purpose, and Outcomes', *Studies in Conflict & Terrorism* 35, no. 5 (2012): 354–68, B. Spalek and L. Davies, *Key Evaluation Findings of the West Midlands (WM) 1-2-1 Mentoring Scheme* (University of Birmingham, 2010). (http://www.birmingham.ac.uk/Documents/collegesocial-sciences/social-policy/IASS/news-events/west-midlands-1-2-1-evaluation-findings.pdf), and (for the experiences of a mentor within the renowned 'Aarhus Model'), [Anonymous], 'Mentoring and Deradicalisation', in *Terrorism, Radicalisation & Countering Violent Extremism*, Shashi Jayakumar, ed. (Singapore: Palgrave Pivot), 19–28.

27   Marion van San, Stijn Sieckelinck and Micha de Winter, 'Ideals Adrift: An Educational Approach to Radicalization', *Ethics and Education* 8, no. 3 (2013): 277.

28   'Ideals Adrift: An Educational Approach to Radicalization', 279.

29   Arie W. Kruglanski, Michele J. Gelfand, Jocelyn J. Bélanger, Anna Sheveland, Malkanthi Hetiarachchi and Rohan Gunaratna, 'The Psychology of Radicalization and Deradicalization: How Significance Quest Impacts Violent Extremism', *Political Psychology* (35, Supplement 1 – *Advances in Political Psychology*, February 2014): 73.

30 Stijn Sieckelinck, Femke Kaulingfreks and Micha De Winter, 'Neither Villains nor Victims: Towards an Educational Perspective on Radicalisation', *British Journal of Educational Studies* 63, no. 3 (2015): 331.

31 Michael A. Hogg, 'From Uncertainty to Extremism: Social Categorization and Identity Processes', *Current Directions in Psychological Science* 23, no. 5 (2014): 338–42.

32 Hogg, 'From Uncertainty to Extremism: Social Categorization and Identity Processes', 341.

33 Readers with the interest in other European city and national-level interventions that involve (*inter alia*) working with youth, offering alternative points of view, developing critical thinking and psycho-social support activities should consult *Prevention of Juvenile Radicalisation: Manual for Professionals.* International Juvenile Justice Observatory, 2018, 60ff. https://www.oijj.org/sites/default/files/archivospaginas/ pralt_manual_en.pdf (especially relevant are the various national reports). See also Tore Bjørgo and Yngve Carlsson, 'Early Intervention with Violent and Racist Youth Groups', Norwegian Institute of International Affairs (Norsk Utenrikspolitisk Institutt), no. 677, 2005. https://www.files.ethz.ch/isn/27305/677.pdf (links accessed 14 February 2022).

34 As Preben Bertelsen (an academic whose work underpins the theoretical approach behind the 'Aarhus Model' for 'deradicalization') notes bluntly: 'The message (…) has to be: it's great that you have religious, political convictions, that you're critical of society. Just, please, find some way to deal with them that does not involve violence'. Jon Henley, 'How Do You Deradicalise Returning Isis Fighters?' *The Guardian*, 12 November 2014, at https://www.theguardian.com/world/2014/nov/12/deradicalise- isis-fighters-jihadists-denmark-syria (accessed 4 February 2022).

35 Stijn M. A. Sieckelinck and Doret J. de Ruyter, 'Mad about Ideals? Educating Children to Become Reasonably Passionate', *Education Theory* 59, no. 2 (2009): at 183 and 186. '(…) becoming a person depends on developing an identity and for this one needs to discover which ideals or ultimate values of one's community and society are ideals for oneself' (186).

36 For an introduction, Preben Bertelsen, 'Danish Preventive Measures and De- radicalization Strategies: The Aarhus Model', *Panorama*, no. 1 (2015): 243–51, at https://psy.au.dk/fileadmin/Psykologi/Forskning/Preben_Bertelsen/Avisartikler_ radikalisering/Panorama.pdf, and Toke Agerschou, 'Preventing Radicalization and Discrimination in Aarhus', *Journal for Deradicalization*, no. 1 (2014): 5–22.

37 The authors emphasize the need to bring the students closer to mastering life skills and also acknowledge the debt that is owed in this aspect to the *Life Psychology* model formulated by Prof Preben Bertelsen. For this, and for how this sits with other approaches such as Significance Quest Theory, see Arie W. Kruglanski and Preben Bertelsen, 'Life Psychology and Significance Quest: A Complementary Approach to Violent Extremism and Counter-Radicalisation', *Journal of Policing, Intelligence and Counter Terrorism* 15, no. 1 (2020): 1–22.

38 The role of citizenship and having a meaningful place in society is a key aspect within overall Danish P/CVE efforts. See for example *An Introduction to the Danish Approach to Countering and Preventing Extremism and Radicalisation* (Danish Institute of International Studies Report [15], 2015), 24–5. https://www.ft.dk/ samling/20151/almdel/reu/bilag/248/1617692.pdf (accessed 14 February 2022), and 'Efforts to Prevent Extremism in the Nordic Countries: Mapping' (Rambøll Management Consulting, December 2017), http://uim.dk/publikationer/efforts-to- prevent-extremism-in-the-nordic-countries/ (link no longer accessible).

39   As Sumpter explains in his chapter, while Indonesian 3P/CVE landscape is fertile
     ground for initiatives both by government and the NGO sector, the 'secondary'
     prevention scene (as defined by the public health model) sees comparatively fewer
     interventions.

40   For an introduction to the issues, see Talene Bilazarian, *Countering Violent
     Extremism: Lessons on Early Intervention from the United Kingdom's Channel Program*
     (GW Program on Extremism, October 2016). https://extremism.gwu.edu/sites/g/files/
     zaxdzs2191/f/downloads/Channel%20CVE%20UK.pdf, and Frank Gardner, 'Prevent
     Scheme: Why the Government's Programme Is So Difficult', *BBC*, 20 October 2021.
     https://www.bbc.com/news/uk-58975385 (links accessed 14 February 2022).

41   The need to take into account these other factors (violence, crime, gang activity,
     hostile relations with the police) and address them holistically within the context
     of PREVENT has been recognized for some considerable length of time. See Laura
     Zahra McDonald, 'Engaging Young People within a Counter-Terrorism Context',
     in *Counter-Terrorism Community-Based Approaches to Preventing Terror Crime*,
     B. Spalek, ed. (Palgrave Macmillan, 2012), 126 and 128. In the earlier years of
     PREVENT, some Channel work was outsourced to collaborators who worked with
     communities where these issues were endemic. Interventions included creating
     safe spaces for discussion, giving individuals skills and confidence to resist negative
     influences, and unlocking social capital of individuals through provision of
     education and vocational training. See Jack Barclay, *Strategy to Reach, Empower,
     and Educate Teenagers (STREET): A Case Study in Government- Community
     Partnership and Direct Intervention to Counter Violent Extremism* (Center on Global
     Counterterrorism Cooperation, December 2011). https://www.globalcenter.org/wp-
     content/uploads/2012/07/barclay_policybrief_1114.pdf (accessed 15 February 2022).

42   For a comparison (concerning the proposed pathways for European returnees,
     but reflecting several of the concerns and considerations laid out by Jones and
     Dabboussy, including the need for community involvement and multiagency
     support), see M. Meines, M. Molenkamp, O. Ramadan and M. Ranstorp, *Responses
     to Returnees: Foreign Terrorist Fighters and Their Families* (The Netherlands:
     Radicalisation Awareness Network Centre of Excellence, 2017), 50. https://ec.europa.
     eu/home-affairs/system/files_en?file=2020-09/ran_br_a4_m10_en.pdf (accessed
     9 February 2022).

43   Some of these observations bring to mind the points made in the chapter by Osorno
     Hernandez. The youth workers Osorno Hernandez interacts with also conduct talks
     in schools and in the community with the aim of raising awareness of vulnerability,
     and of how easily one can proceed down the pathway to radicalization. But the
     approach by these practitioners and the range of ground covered appears much more
     multifaceted than what is seen in the talks by formers in Germany: 'Revealing these
     pathways to young people often requires reviewing case studies of radicalisation/
     grooming and engaging with the stories of "former" extremists. It also involves
     talking about religion, racism, violent and non-violent extremism and socio-
     economic contextual factors such as access to education, employment and housing.'

44   For useful remarks on mainstreaming this type of programme within educational
     curricula (and which aspects should be prioritized, going simply beyond warning
     youths of the dangers of extremism), see Stijn Sieckelinck and Micha de Winter
     (eds.), *Formers & Families: Transitional Journeys In and Out of Extremisms in the
     United Kingdom, Denmark and The Netherlands* (The Hague: National Coordinator
     for Security and Counterterrorism, 2015), 95–6.

45 As experts studying radicalization in an immigrant/diasporic community that has often been problematized using the lens of violent extremism (the Somali-American community in the United States) have remarked, '[Risks] need to be understood not only from the perspectives of criminal justice, politics, history or theology but also from a psychosocial perspective – one that considers community and family processes.' Stevan Weine, John Horgan, Cheryl Robertson, Sana Loue, Amin Mohamed and Sahra Noor, 'Community and Family Approaches to Combating the Radicalization and Recruitment of Somali-American Youth and Young Adults: A Psychosocial Perspective', *Dynamics of Asymmetric Conflict* 2, no. 3 (November 2009): 181–200 at 182.

46 See the remarks of Håvard Haugstvedt, 'Trusting the Mistrusted: Norwegian Social Workers' Strategies in Preventing Radicalization and Violent Extremism', *Journal for Deradicalisation* 19 (2019): 152–3: 'A key observation in one study of universal and selective prevention workers was the need for a trusting relationship between participants in an intervention and the local community where the intervention is located.'

47 My sincere thanks to the anonymous reviewers of this manuscript whose suggestions strengthened the volume considerably. I am also grateful to Cameron Sumpter for reading this introduction and making helpful suggestions. All errors that remain are my own.

Bibliography

Agerschou, T. 'Preventing Radicalization and Discrimination in Aarhus'. *Journal for Deradicalization*, no. 1 (2014): 5–22.

Altier, M. B., Thoroughgood, C. N. and Horgan, J. G. 'Turning Away from Terrorism: Lessons from Psychology, Sociology, and Criminology'. *Journal of Peace Research* 51, no. 5 (September 2014): 647–61.

Altier, M. B., Leonard Boyle, E., Shortland, N. D. and Horgan, J. G. 'Why They Leave: An Analysis of Terrorist Disengagement Events from Eighty-seven Autobiographical Accounts'. *Security Studies* 26, no. 2 (2017): 305–32.

Amirthalingam, K. 'Criminal Justice and Diversionary Programmes in Singapore'. *Criminal Law Forum* 24 (2013): 527–59.

Australian Federal Police. (n.d.). 'National Efforts'. https://www.afp.gov.au/what-we-do/crime-types/fighting-terrorism/national-efforts

Australian Government Department of Home Affairs. 'Countering Violent Extremism (CVE) Intervention Programs'. https://www.homeaffairs.gov.au/about-us/our-portfolios/national-security/countering-extremism-and-terrorism/cve-intervention-programs (accessed 31 January 2022).

Australian Institute of Criminology. *What Works in Reducing Young People's Involvement in Crime?* (2002) https://www.aic.gov.au/sites/default/files/2020-05/what-works-in-reducing-young-peoples-involvement-in-crime.pdf (accessed 14 February 2022).

Barclay, J. *Strategy to Reach, Empower, and Educate Teenagers (STREET): A Case Study in Government-Community Partnership and Direct Intervention to Counter Violent Extremism* (Center on Global Counterterrorism Cooperation, December 2011). https://www.globalcenter.org/wp-content/uploads/2012/07/barclay_policybrief_1114.pdf (accessed 15 February 2022).

Bertelsen, P. 'Danish Preventive Measures and De-radicalization Strategies: The Aarhus Model'. *Panorama*, no. 1 (2015): 243–51, available at https://psy.au.dk/fileadmin/Psykologi/Forskning/Preben_Bertelsen/Avisartikler_radikalisering/Panorama.pdf

Bhui, K. and Jones, E. 'The Challenge of Radicalisation: A Public Health Approach to Understanding and Intervention'. *Psychoanalytic Psychotherapy* 31, no. 4 (2017): 401–10.

Bilazarian, T. *Countering Violent Extremism: Lessons on Early Intervention from the United Kingdom's Channel Program* (GW Program on Extremism, October 2016) https://extremism.gwu.edu/sites/g/files/zaxdzs2191/f/downloads/Channel%20CVE%20UK.pdf (accessed 14 February 2022).

Bjørgo, T. and Carlsson, Y. 'Early Intervention with Violent and Racist Youth Groups'. Norwegian Institute of International Affairs (Norsk Utenrikspolitisk Institutt), No. 677 (2005). https://www.files.ethz.ch/isn/27305/677.pdf (accessed 14 February 2022).

Borum, R. 'Radicalization into Violent Extremism I: A Review of Social Science Theories'. *Journal of Strategic Security* 4, no. 4 (2011): 7–36.

Campbell, K. 'Anti-radicalisation Alliance Set Up in WA'. *PerthNow*, 20 June 2017. https://www.perthnow.com.au/news/wa/anti-radicalisation-alliance-set-up-in-wa-ng-68b33e2b0bb4ff17a3fa724b6665308f (accessed 31 January 2022).

Capstack, A. 'Deradicalization Programs in Saudi Arabia: A Case Study'. *Middle East Institute*, 10 June 2015, http://www.mei.edu/content/deradicalization-programs-saudi-arabia-case-study#_ftn3

Cartwright, J. 'Diversion in Australia: Not Your Traditional Counter-terrorism Response'. *AFP Platypus Magazine*, April 2016, pp. 30–2. http://www5.austlii.edu.au/au/journals/AUFPPlatypus/2016/10.pdf (accessed 31 January 2022).

Center for the Prevention of Radicalisation Leading to Violence. *Levels of Prevention at the CPRLV*, 2017; available at: https://info-radical.org/wp-content/uploads/2017/03/cprlv-intervention-at-every-level.pdf (accessed 14 February 2022).

Cherney, A. 'Working with Radicalised Individuals: Insights from a Secondary and Tertiary Prevention Program'. *Behavioral Sciences of Terrorism and Political Aggression* (2022; ahead of print): 1–21.

Clarkson, D. 'Kiwi Teenager Radicalised Online Planned Mass Killing in Christchurch "for Allah"'. *Stuff.co.nz*, 16 February 2018. https://www.stuff.co.nz/national/crime/101480988/kiwi-teenager-radicalised-online-planned-mass-killing-in-christchurch-for-allah (accessed 14 February 2022).

Conti, B., Sokirianskaia, E., Ogenga, F., Gurski, P., Dualeh, R. and Jayakumar, S. 'Deradicalisation', *International Panel on Exiting Violence: Final Report* (International Panel on Exiting Violence/La Fondation Maison des sciences de l'homme, 2019). Available at: https://www.ipev-fmsh.org/wp-content/uploads/2021/06/Final-Report-IPEV-EN.pdf, pp. 33–7 (accessed 28 January 2022).

Dalgaard-Nielsen, A. 'Violent Radicalization in Europe: What We Know and What We Do Not Know'. *Studies in Conflict & Terrorism* 33, no. 9 (2010): 797–814.

Dalgaard-Nielsen, A. 'Promoting Exit from Violent Extremism: Themes and Approaches'. *Studies in Conflict & Terrorism* 36, no. 2 (2013): 99–115.

E4J University Module Series: Crime Prevention and Criminal Justice: Module 2: Crime Prevention. Topic Two Continued – Detailed Explanation of Tonry and Farrington's Typology. https://www.unodc.org/e4j/en/crime-prevention-criminal-justice/module-2/key-issues/2a--detailed-explanation-of-tonry-and-farringtons-typology.html (accessed 27 January 2022).

Farrington, D. P., Ttofi, M. M. and Lösel, F. A. 'Developmental and Social Prevention'. In *What Works in Crime Prevention and Rehabilitation: Lessons from Systematic Reviews*, D. Weisburd, D. P. Farrington, and C. Gill, eds., 15–76. New York: Springer, 2016.

Gardner, F. 'Prevent Scheme: Why the Government's Programme Is So Difficult'. *BBC*, 20 October 2021. https://www.bbc.com/news/uk-58975385 (accessed 14 February 2022).

General Intelligence and Security Service (AIVD), *From Dawa to Jihad: The Various Threats from Radical Islam to the Democratic Legal Order*, 2005. Available at: https://english.aivd.nl/publications/publications/2005/03/30/from-dawa-to-jihad (accessed 28 January 2022).

Gill, C. 'Community Interventions'. In *What Works in Crime Prevention and Rehabilitation: Lessons from Systematic Reviews*, D. Weisburd, D. P. Farrington and C. Gill, eds., 77–110. New York: Springer, 2016.

Harris-Hogan, S., Barrelle, K. and Zammit, A. 'What Is Countering Violent Extremism? Exploring CVE Policy and Practice in Australia'. *Behavioral Sciences of Terrorism and Political Aggression* 8, no. 1 (2016): 6–24.

Haugstvedt, H. 'Trusting the Mistrusted: Norwegian Social Workers' Strategies in Preventing Radicalization and Violent Extremism'. *Journal for Deradicalisation* 19 (2019): 149–83.

Henley, J. 'How Do You Deradicalise Returning Isis Fighters?' *The Guardian*, 12 November 2014. Available at: https://www.theguardian.com/world/2014/nov/12/deradicalise-isis-fighters-jihadists-denmark-syria (accessed 4 February 2022).

Herrenkohl, T. I., Hawkins, J. D., Chung, I. J., Hill, K. G. and Battin-Pearson, S. 'School and Community Risk Factors and Interventions'. In *Child Delinquents: Development, Intervention and Service Needs*, R. Loeber and D. P. Farrington, eds., 211–46. Thousand Oaks, CA: Sage, 2001.

[Hjelt, Mikkel]. 'Mentoring and Deradicalisation'. In *Terrorism, Radicalisation & Countering Violent Extremism*, Shashi Jayakumar, ed., 19–28. Singapore: Palgrave Pivot.

Hogg, M. A. 'From Uncertainty to Extremism: Social Categorization and Identity Processes'. *Current Directions in Psychological Science* 23, no. 5 (2014): 338–42.

Horgan, J. G., Altier, M. B., Shortland, N., and Taylor, M. 'Walking Away: The Disengagement and De-radicalization of a Violent Right-wing Extremist'. *Behavioral Sciences of Terrorism and Political Aggression* 9, no. 2 (2017): 63–77.

An Introduction to the Danish Approach to Countering and Preventing Extremism and Radicalisation (Danish Institute of International Studies Report (15), 2015). https://www.ft.dk/samling/20151/almdel/reu/bilag/248/1617692.pdf (accessed 14 February 2022).

Jayakumar, S. *Deradicalisation in Singapore: Past, Present and Future, The International Centre for the Study of Radicalisation (ICSR) Report*, King's College London, United Kingdom, 20 August 2020. https://icsr.info/wp-content/uploads/2020/08/ICSR-Report-Deradicalisation-in-Singapore-Past-Present-and-Future.pdf (accessed 13 February 2022).

Koehler, D. *Understanding Deradicalisation: Methods, Tools and Programs for Countering Violent Extremism*. London and New York: Routledge, 2017.

Krug, E. G., Dahlberg, L. L., Mercy, J. A., Zwi, A. B., and Lozano, R. (eds.). *World Report on Violence and Health*. World Health Organization, 2002, 15. Available at: http://whqlibdoc.who.int/publications/2002/9241545615_eng.pdf (accessed 25 January 2022).

Kruglanski, A. W., and Bertelsen, P. 'Life Psychology and Significance Quest: A Complementary Approach to Violent Extremism and Counter-Radicalisation'. *Journal of Policing, Intelligence and Counter Terrorism* 15, no. 1 (2020): 1–22.

Kruglanski, A. W., Gelfand, M. J., Bélanger, J. J., Sheveland, A., Hetiarachchi, M. and Gunaratna, R. 'The Psychology of Radicalization and Deradicalization: How Significance Quest Impacts Violent Extremism'. *Political Psychology* (Vol. 35, Supplement 1 – *Advances in Political Psychology*, February 2014): 69–93.

McCauley, C. and Moskalenko, S. 'Mechanisms of Political Radicalization: Pathways toward Terrorism'. *Terrorism and Political Violence* 20, no. 3 (2008): 415–33.

McDonald, L. Z. 'Engaging Young People within a Counter-Terrorism Context'. In *Counter-terrorism Community-based Approaches to Preventing Terror Crime*, B. Spalek, ed., 119–36. Palgrave Macmillan, 2012.

Meines, M., Molenkamp, M., Ramadan, O. and Ranstorp, M. *Responses to Returnees: Foreign Terrorist Fighters and Their Families*. The Netherlands: Radicalisation Awareness Network Centre of Excellence, 2017. https://ec.europa.eu/home-affairs/ system/files_en?file=2020-09/ran_br_a4_m10_en.pdf (accessed 9 February 2022).

Ministry of Social and Family Development, Singapore. *Report on Youth Delinquency. Key Trends and Upstream Measures*. Singapore: Central Youth Guidance Office, 2019, https://www.msf.gov.sg/NCPR/Our-Initiatives/Documents/FA_MSF_Report%20 on%20Youth%20Delinquency%202019%20%28Medium%20Res%29.pdf (accessed 28 January 2022).

Moghaddam, F. M. 'The Staircase to Terrorism. A Psychological Exploration'. *American Psychological Association* 60, no. 2 (2005): 161–9.

National Academies of Sciences, Engineering, and Medicine. *Countering Violent Extremism Through Public Health Practice: Proceedings of a Workshop*. Washington, DC: National Academies of Sciences, Engineering, and Medicine. The National Academies Press, 2017. Available at: https://cphd.ph.ucla.edu/sites/default/files/ downloads/Countering%20Violent%20Extremism%20Through%20Public%20 Health%20Practice1_0.pdf (accessed 14 February 2022).

National Committee on Prevention, Rehabilitation and Recidivism, Singapore. *Report on Youth Delinquency 2021* (Singapore: National Committee on Prevention, Rehabilitation and Recidivism), esp.20–30. https://www.msf.gov.sg/NCPR/Our-Initiatives/Documents/FA_MSF_Report_on_Youth_Delinquency_2021.pdf. (accessed 28 January 2022).

Picciolini, C. 'I'm Closing Free Radicals Project — Here Are My Reasons, and Why a Shift in Focus Is Needed'. *Medium*, 10 November 2021. https://medium.com/@cpicciolini/ free-radicals-project-forced-to-close-its-doors-a88e29661d21 (accessed 11 November 2021).

Practical Lessons, Fair Consequences: Improving Diversion for Young People in Victoria (Department of Justice, 2012), 18. https://library.bsl.org.au/jspui/bitstream/1/4056/1/ Practical_lessons%20fair_consequences_improving_diversion_for_young%20 people%20victoria.pdf (accessed 14 February 2022).

Prevention of Juvenile Radicalisation: Manual for Professionals. International Juvenile Justice Observatory, 2018. https://www.oijj.org/sites/default/files/archivospaginas/ pralt_manual_en.pdf (accessed 14 February 2022).

Rambøll Management Consulting. 'Efforts to Prevent Extremism in the Nordic Countries: Mapping' (Rambøll Management Consulting, December 2017), http://uim.dk/ publikationer/efforts-to-prevent-extremism-in-the-nordic-countries/ (link no longer accessible).

Rosand, E. 'Taking the Off-ramp: A Path to Preventing Terrorism'. *War on the Rocks*, 1 July 2016. https://warontherocks.com/2016/07/taking-the-off-ramp-a-path-to-preventing-terrorism/ (accessed 14 February 2022).

Schmidt, A. P. 'Radicalisation, De-radicalisation, Counter-radicalisation: A Conceptual Discussion and Literature Review'. *The International Centre for Counter-terrorism – The Hague* 4, no. 2 (2013). https://icct.nl/publication/radicalisation-de-radicalisation-counter-radicalisation-a-conceptual-discussion-and-literature-review/ (accessed 28 January 2022).

Sieckelinck, S. and de Ruyter, D. J. 'Mad about Ideals? Educating Children to Become Reasonably Passionate'. *Education Theory* 59, no. 2 (2009): 181–96.

Sieckelinck, S. and de Winter, M. (eds.). *Formers & Families: Transitional Journeys In and Out of Extremisms in the United Kingdom, Denmark and The Netherlands*. The Hague: National Coordinator for Security and Counterterrorism, 2015.

Sieckelinck, S., Kaulingfreks, F., and De Winter, M. 'Neither Villains nor Victims: Towards an Educational Perspective on Radicalisation'. *British Journal of Educational Studies* 63, no. 3 (2015): 329–43.

Spalek, B. and Davies, L. *Key Evaluation Findings of the West Midlands (WM) 1-2-1 Mentoring Scheme*. University of Birmingham, 2010. http://www.birmingham.ac.uk/Documents/collegesocial-sciences/social-policy/IASS/news-events/west-midlands-1-2-1-evaluation-findings.pdf

Spalek, B. and Davies, L. 'Mentoring in Relation to Violent Extremism: A Study of Role, Purpose, and Outcomes'. *Studies in Conflict & Terrorism* 35, no. 5 (2012): 354–68.

van de Weert, A. and Eijkman, Q. A. M. 'Subjectivity in Detection of Radicalisation and Violent Extremism: A Youth Worker's Perspective'. *Behavioral Sciences of Terrorism and Political Aggression* 11, no. 3 (2019): 191–214.

van San, M., Sieckelinck, S. and de Winter, M. 'Ideals Adrift: An Educational Approach to Radicalization'. *Ethics and Education* 8, no. 3 (2013): 276–89.

Weine, S., Horgan, J., Robertson, C., Loue, S., Mohamed, A. and Noor, S. 'Community and Family Approaches to Combating the Radicalization and Recruitment of Somali-American Youth and Young Adults: A Psychosocial Perspective'. *Dynamics of Asymmetric Conflict* 2, no. 3 (November 2009): 181–200.

Williams, M. J., Horgan, J. G. and Evans, W. P. *Evaluation of a Multi-faceted, U.S. Community-based, Muslim-led CVE Program*, US Department of Justice (2016). Available at: https://www.ojp.gov/pdffiles1/nij/grants/249936.pdf

Part One

Youth diversion in Europe

2

France's Muslims: Secularism and radicalization

Farhad Khosrokhavar

In recent years, France has been the Western European country with the largest number of jihadist deadly attacks and the highest death toll.[1] Between 2001 and 2017, there were twenty-three jihadist attacks in France, compared to ten in the UK, five in Germany, two in Spain and seven in Belgium which led to losses of life.[2] The uniqueness of France lies in its brand of strict secularism – *radical laïcité* – and the perception on the part of French Muslims that they are being treated in an increasingly 'colonial' manner on account of their religion, Islam. Some of this feeling is shared by other Muslims in Europe, but it is far stronger in France. Other European countries have developed their own brand of radical Islam due to characteristics that they share with France (for example, in terms of Islamophobia and the seclusion or segregation of large groups of lower-class Muslims in stigmatized neighbourhoods). But strict secularism – secularism in its radicalized version – serves to delegitimize Islam and is one of the specific causes of heightened radicalization in French youths.

Institutional mechanisms favouring fundamentalism and radicalization

France stands out from other European countries through its adoption of secularism (*laïcité*). The history of secularism is complex, with at least seven different versions of *laïcité* having existed.[3] *Laïcité* exists on a spectrum, ranging from a moderate version to one we shall call fundamentalist or radical secularism. The moderate version of secularism which prevailed in 1905 led to the famous law of 1905 on the separation of church and state. According to this law, the state was to remain strictly neutral towards all religions and state officials were to wear no religious insignia (this restriction did not however apply to civil society).

Laïcité in its actual implementation brought about problems with the Catholic Church. In the 1960s, however, the general impression was that French society had managed to solve its issues with the church and that a consensus had been reached between Catholic France and Republican France, in particular after Vatican II and the opening of the Catholic church to reform and to the acknowledgement of an increasingly secular European world.

From the 1980s onwards, there were further *laïcité*-related problems. This time, the issue was tinged with colonial suspicion and linked to the settling of immigrant Muslim (and at the beginning, predominantly North African) individuals. These were mostly migrant workers who, rather than returning home, chose to stay and settle with their families in France. The question of the Islamic headscarf arose in 1989 with the so-called incident of the 'Creil headscarfs' in a northern Parisian suburb. A few middle school girls of Moroccan descent wore headscarves to school. This incident set in motion the first institutional mobilization to ban headscarves in public (state-run) schools. Ultimately, the outcome was the 2004 law banning religious insignia (such as headscarves) in public schools (teachers had been banned from wearing religious insignia since 1905).[4] Other incidents included the so-called Baby Loup nursery school affair between 2010 and 2014, which saw an employee who wore a headscarf being fired. The nursery school was a private association which did not directly depend on the state, but it also banned its teachers from wearing religious insignia.

There have been many related issues and debates, including one on the banning of headscarves in universities for students[5] and on some beaches, in restaurants,[6] medical offices and hospitals,[7] for jury duty in court[8] and separately, the issue of the *niqab* (resulting in a 2010 law banning anyone from hiding their face in public). These issues and official action against the *niqab* or the headscarf also exist to some extent in other parts of Europe, but what sets France apart are the cultural mechanisms that oppose each other: on the one hand *laïcité* and on the other hand Islam, which mobilizes intellectuals and part of public opinion.

Every ten to fifteen years in France, voices arise proclaiming that France is becoming more Islamized and that it is losing its secular soul to a dominating and anti-republican Islam. In the early 1990s, the book *The Lost Territories of the Republic*[9] was published. In 2020, another collective volume *The Conquered Territories of Islamism* was published.[10] These two publications created a huge media sensation and contributed to an increasing suspicion of Muslims. The consequence was the establishment of increasingly restrictive laws as noted above pertaining to the outward forms of Islamic expression in schools, associations and more generally, in public.[11] The actual social and economic roots of this apparent 'Islamization' in some poor and excluded neighbourhoods were put aside; what began to take hold in people's minds was a vision of Islam as an exclusivist way of thinking and acting, perceived as an enemy to French secularism.

The French paradox is that these laws and such thinking reinforce religious fundamentalism, with a minority of Muslims becoming convinced that French society is anti-Islamic and that the only possible way is to retreat into a closed and sealed fundamentalist identity in order to protect Muslims. These circumstances also favour the growth of radical Islam, which finds in the extremist version of secularism an opportunity to claim that French modernity is against Islam and that the only way to fight it is by using violence.[12]

Secularism and the unease of the French Muslim Faith Community (FMFC)

The feeling of being misunderstood or even despised and rejected by global society is something we encountered often in the interviews with a significant group of practising and non-practising Muslims from the lower and middle classes. Marginalization is multiple and the reasons brought up for it are varied and often contradictory, depending on the interviewees. The FMFC is not monolithic. A significant part of it is deeply secularized and for these individuals, their unease is rooted in the realization that in France, their secularism is not taken seriously and the desire is to label them 'Muslims' at any cost. Another part of the community finds it very challenging that the dual identity of 'French *and* Muslim' is not accepted in France. French citizenship imposes a monolithic framework which excludes French-Muslim dual identity (unlike in other countries such as the United States, where dual or multiple identities, for example, of African-Americans or Latinos, are accepted).

This raises tremendous problems. Secularism defines 'French monoculturalism' but is in opposition to the multiculturalism that is seen in many European countries; the French model does not accept the constitution of specific identities such as defining oneself as French-Moroccan, French-Algerian or French-Muslim and the public space is considered exclusively as one for secular citizenship. A third minority group defines itself as entirely Muslim and is challenged by secularism in its quest for a religious identity which is characterized by religious fundamentalism. Another small minority, recruited mainly from the poor suburbs but which since 2013 has also drawn from middle-class youths, intends to cross swords with society in the name of Islam's 'Holy War' (*jihad*).

The French/Muslim/Arab identity is a very diversified concept: it reflects how some individuals define themselves not only as French citizens but also as members of specific sub-groups in society. They see themselves through multiple layers of an identity which cannot be reduced to a simple linear relationship between individuals and society, as French Republicanism demands. The multiple groups that define French Muslims have divergent attitudes towards society and Islam, but mainstream society tends to reduce this heterogeneity to a homogeneous attitude that is contrary to *laïcité* and Republicanism.

The French who define themselves as being of Muslim faith are not united and do not form a strong cohesive group. A large part of the FMFC is stratified and is part of the working class; a great majority of them live in the *banlieues* (or 'poor suburbs'). Their incarceration rate is much higher than their proportion of the population in French society. This phenomenon is not unique to France and is reflected elsewhere in Western Europe, where the general pattern is of an incarceration rate several times greater than their proportional representation in European societies.[13]

It is commonly accepted that in France and in a large part of Europe, the unease of the younger generation of Muslim immigrants in poor neighbourhoods (known as banlieues in France) has an economic dimension. But besides this, there are also dimensions of urban segregation and cultural stigmatization. Once the immigrant integrates into the middle class, it is assumed that the problem is largely resolved. The surveys carried out in the context of our numerous studies reveal the overly simplistic nature of this assumption.[14] It is true that those of the FMFC who integrate into the middle class focus on protecting their status and avoiding proletarianization, as do many in the middle classes. However, a large majority of them are far from 'happy' or feel that they are treated equally, or even feel like full citizens. Their perception is that French society is making them pay for their colonial heritage, for the deplorable image of fundamentalist and radical Islam, and for the image of poor suburban youths, by making them guilty of the latter's unsocialized attitudes. These multiple viewpoints burden their daily life with an array of customary accusations thrown at them: they are not secular enough, they are not French enough, they are not openly condemning radical Islam enough, and they are not genuinely Republican citizens (that is, they are not authentic, secular, democratically minded people).

Immigrant middle classes are integrated economically, unlike the youths of the *banlieues* who suffer from economical marginalization and lack of access to jobs. The latter are not simply excluded from society: a large number of them have internalized this socio-economic exclusion, making it an integral part of their identity even though at the same time they *oppose* this negative perception along with its inevitable stigmas held by themselves and by others. The result is a high level of aggressiveness, a distrust towards others and a lack of self-esteem that leads to the hatred of the Self and the Other.

I use the expression 'cultural alienation' for middle-class people of the Muslim faith who are economically integrated but who often experience cultural unease, which can easily turn into existential unease. The main issue this group faces is secularism in its increasingly uncompromising and very often contradictory form. In the middle-class Muslims' view, if they act as secular people, they are treated as suspicious and untrustworthy Muslims by other Muslims but if they act as Muslims, they are criticized for not being secular enough and, therefore, fake citizens by mainstream French society.

One observation stands out: once secularization has settled in, in the sense of French Muslims taking individual steps out of the ethnic-religious relationship which hitherto defined part of their mentality, they acquire an understanding which serves to reduce their differences with mainstream society. A significant observation from interviews is the phenomenon of 'deep secularization' in a large number of French Muslims who have lost specific reference to their country of origin and Muslim faith, and whose consequent point of view is one from which religious, ethnic or geographic origin has entirely faded, with their sense of belonging to the Nation being much stronger. Even then, public opinion constantly reminds them of their 'non-Frenchness' or their 'incomplete Frenchness', with the attendant suspicion of a lack of adherence to secularism or *laïcité*.

Cultural alienation of French Muslims

Cultural alienation is based on the notion of a 'target community'. The FMFC does not constitute a true community, but society attributes a false unity and cohesion to it based on history and imagination linked to facts which are deeply anchored in the collective identity of mainstream society. For example, middle-class Arabs are categorized into a uniform group based on Islam or their North African origins or even the Arabic language, even though this uniformity does not exist: most individuals within the FMFC do not even speak Arabic or use elementary forms of colloquial Arabic.

The second trait which characterizes target communities including middle-class French Muslims is the predicament they face – a form of symbolic aggression – where they are seen to bear responsibility for matters over which they have no influence. They are associated with and even accused of wrongdoing allegedly carried out by the *banlieue* youths (such as drug dealing, theft, aggression) and, more generally, for radical Islamism and Islamic fundamentalism. Society attributes responsibility to the members of the target community – they may be charged in public by the media and mainstream society without being able to contest this social bias and prejudice, and with no possibility of reply.

The third trait attributed to members of the target community is that of not being 'transparent'. They are suspected of being different from who they pretend to be, of being not genuine in their attitudes or sincere in their public statements. For example, if an 'Arab' denounces the jihadist attacks carried out by Mohamed Merah or Amedy Coulibaly, it is considered either a formality, insincerity or a delayed apology. The target community is always in the spotlight: nobody believes its alleged members and they are considered to be fundamentally untrustworthy. There is always a halo of uncertainty surrounding them.

This is why many individuals within the FMFC feel culturally rejected or undervalued. Daily life is punctuated with 'small humiliations': 'Arab' or 'Muslim' individuals pay for their integration into society with constant reminders of their non-French past. This phenomenon of micro-aggressions is also present in the United States, where the Black middle class is constantly reminded of its non-white origins in attitudes which range from condescending kindness to explicit rejection.[15]

Cultural alienation is thus caused by an exhausting situation of 'in-between-ness': Muslims who are economically integrated even if not treated equally but who are harassed in particular because of the identification which reduces them to being no more than an 'Arab', that is, sharing the traits of the Arab immigrants from the poor suburbs who live in delinquency, Islamic radicalization and other socially stigmatized situations. Joining the middle classes should have freed these individuals from this negative 'Arabness' which attaches to poor suburban youths of the *banlieues*. Yet they surrender themselves to the fact that the negativity of the 'Arab' label is insurmountable and this is even more so if, as is often the case, they are more religious and less secularized.

Even when they reach middle-class status, French Muslims and more generally European Muslims[16] feel the pinch of stigmatization. With similar qualifications, 'Arabs' (citizens of North African origin) viscerally feel the inequality and the lack of access to jobs compared to French people of non-Muslim or non-Arab origin. The probability of a French Muslim being hired is two to three times lower than that of a non-Muslim.[17] This incites French Muslims to search for jobs with anonymous entry tests or those that are less sought after, such as positions in the army,[18] police forces or prison administration.

Despite the inequality of job access, some French Muslims still manage to reach middle-class status. However, this does not mean the end of their disadvantages in a society where merely being Muslim arouses suspicions. The best solution for such individuals is to start a small company, if possible. The status of being self-employed (in French, *auto-entrepreneur*) makes things easier as long as the individual can find clients. An alternative is working for companies like Uber, where customer relations are managed remotely by the internet.

Middle-class individuals of immigrant origin[19] feel a deep unease of cultural alienation: they feel unrecognized and rejected in their 'Arab', 'Turkish' or 'Non-French' origin. A large majority of the Muslim middle class feels unease due to the mainstream society's lack of understanding of, or at best condescending attitude towards, Islam and Arabness. Islam becomes the emblem of the unease of this cultural alienation. A significant number of French Muslims have become secularized. They do not practise their religion and would like to be treated fully as citizens according to the French model of ignoring one's origins in the public sphere, but even they feel the lack of consideration with regard to Islam. They feel contempt towards their identity, are constantly reminded of their origins on various occasions where people encourage them to behave as 'good Muslims' and are frustrated by the lack of respect for the religion of Allah. Whether they are secularized or practising Muslims, they feel 'Arab' in a derogatory sense and more generally, feel others treating them with arrogance. This lack of respect is experienced as the continuation of colonial contempt in a neo-colonial form. The minority that has embraced orthodoxy and even ultra-orthodoxy (fundamentalism) feels even more rejected and culturally alienated, as they directly oppose *laïcité*.[20]

A minority of French middle-class Muslims feel strongly rooted in their French identity and have a harmonious relationship with society, even though they have had to and continue to have to struggle against daily social prejudices against them. This social group is diverse. There are those who secured their social positions through associations,[21] in particular in the poor suburbs, thanks to public funds for cultural activities. Some became entrepreneurs and succeeded; others managed to climb socially thanks to sporting prowess, in particular in football, following Zinedine Zidane, but also in boxing,[22] judo or other cultural activities, in particular *raï* singing, hip-hop and French rap, which show many signs of French Muslim influence. Many young people from *banlieue* backgrounds attain middle-class status through music careers.

The suspicion and denial of recognition by mainstream society towards the French Muslim middle class create an 'unhappy consciousness' among many of the latter. Although the economic integration of this group is a significant step towards their adoption of a civic identity,[23] this is not sufficient since in most cases it is not partnered with cultural integration into society.[24] Being economically integrated does not provide the feeling of social or cultural belonging, nor does it mean people are happy to be part of society even if the individual does not feel underprivileged economically. There is a major difference between cultural integration and cultural alienation. Many middle-class individuals of Muslim origin do not feel socially or culturally recognized and feel they are being stigmatized in their deepest identity, which should bring together Frenchness but also Islam, and as the case may be, Arab or Turkish identity.

This feeling of being rejected by society leads a minority of Muslims to lose faith in their integration into society and to choose radicalization and violence at the service of an extremist version of Islam – *jihad*. This is of course not particular to France and is a shared feeling among some Muslims all over Europe but is of heightened intensity as mentioned above on account of the French brand of secularism.

Muslims in poor and marginalized districts and the 2015 attacks

The 2015 terrorist attacks in France (on 7 and 9 January against *Charlie Hebdo* magazine and the Hypercacher kosher supermarket near Paris which killed seventeen and injured twenty, and the 13 November attacks near the Stade de France and at cafes and restaurants at the Bataclan theatre, killing 131 and injuring 413) were among the most deadly in Europe. In order to measure the impact of the 2015 attacks on French society, it is important to ask how they were understood by immigrant youths in the *banlieues*, who have much higher unemployment and incarceration rates, and a lower standard of living than the national average.

Interviews were carried out in 2019 in Le Champ de la Ville, a deprived neighbourhood in Gien in the Loiret region of France. In this neighbourhood, several hundred families live in social housing. The neighbourhood has two mosques, a Turkish one and a North African one. The relationship between the Turkish and North African Muslim communities appears at first glance to be neutral, but the North Africans do not usually attend the Turkish mosque and vice versa. One member of the Turkish mosque, aged around thirty, was quite clear about the relationship:

Question: What do you think of the January and November 2015 attacks when around 150 people were killed in Paris?

Answer: You know, the January 2015 attacks or those of November 2015, they were not committed by the Turkish. They were mostly carried out by North Africans and, sometimes, Black people. They attacked Charlie Hebdo and the Jewish supermarket in January and in November it was the massive attack in Paris. The problem is that public opinion holds all Muslims responsible. They are accused of being the perpetrators of the attacks, but we, the Turkish people, played no role in it. In fact, even crime rates in Turkish (-origin) youths are marginal compared to North African (origin) youths. However, we suffer from being Muslims and public opinion places all Muslims in the same basket.

What's the use of being law-abiding citizens if a handful of North Africans tarnish your reputation even though we have nothing to do with the situation? That's the problem! We try to monitor our youths and we succeed more or less, but young North

Africans should be monitored by their parents and their community and they don't
succeed, apparently. They think they represent Islam, when in reality they represent
the problems in their community and they tarnish Muslims in public opinion.

In our discussion with the Turkish *imam*, one of his friends who was present declared that we were moving towards groups and even cities which were increasingly 'communitarized' (close-knit communities, rejected by French Republicanism as being antagonistic to the French definition of citizenship), with Turkish and North African people constituting more or less impermeable blocs. The implication was that large families with migrant backgrounds grow up together and share mutual convictions and a form of culture which integrates social and economic exclusion as one of their major features, along with segregation and self-confinement. Furthermore, each group of older migrants considers the new migrants as groups with whom they should not mix. New waves thus oppose old waves. They are moving towards segmentation of these groups, which create more or less impermeable 'layers', with diversity developing extremely slowly.

The *imam* of the Turkish mosque lived in the neighbourhood from 1999 to 2002. According to him, this is a poor neighbourhood where a dozen or so 'young villains' hold sway. This has had a negative effect on the neighbourhood. Youths respect no rules, blocking the road to police cars when they are in the middle of illegal activities, mostly selling drugs and vandalism. In one area, light bulbs were systematically broken. The Turkish *imam*'s mother still lived in the neighbourhood and was afraid to go out at night. According to the *imam*, the youths in question were of North African origin and were not Turkish. Many Turkish people worked hard and left the neighbourhood as soon as they could, to settle down in another town and to keep their children from mingling with the deviant youths of the neighbourhood.

According to our Turkish interlocutor, there were tense relations between Algerian-origin youths and French society. 'France crushed us and it is our turn to crush them now!' say the Algerian-origin youths, he claimed. Other Turkish members of this community said that their members rarely deviated and were not attracted to radical Islamism. Turkish people did not, by the *imam*'s account, let their children hang out on the streets, unlike North Africans. They were 'nationalists' in the Turkish sense of the word (their affiliations and links were with political groups in Turkey). The Turkish mosque was affiliated with *Diyanet* in its Parisian branch, the State institution in Turkey which supervises *imams* and obstructs radicalization. *Imams* usually come to France for four years and often preach in Turkish. The youths understand the language, according to the Turkish *imam*, although this is not necessarily true for the second- or third-generation youths of Turkish origin, as they do not master Turkish, unlike their parents.

In the 1990s, there was a partnership between the police and the community groups in the neighbourhood. Nowadays this type of relationship no longer exists, meaning that there is an absence of possible mediation between state institutions and the local population in the neighbourhood. This also poses the question of radicalization. Individuals of North African origin are commonly accused of being violent and radicalized while individuals of Turkish origin seem less exposed to such accusations.[25]

The feeling of being held responsible for other people's crimes

In La Reynerie, a poor suburb of Toulouse, a major southwestern city in France, a young Arab of this neighbourhood in his second year of studying for a master's degree was interviewed:

Question: What do you think of the Charlie Hebdo and Bataclan attacks in Paris?
Answer: I feel uneasy. When I talk to teachers or other students who are not from the poor suburbs, they talk to me as if I were already guilty, almost as if I had committed the attacks or was an accomplice. It's always the same story. How am I concerned? Why do I always need to justify myself (in front of the others)? I did not commit these attacks and I shouldn't have to take a stance on this.

Question: I wasn't asking the question to accuse you, but to have your opinion, just as I ask other citizens.

Answer: In my neighbourhood, they said the journalists who were killed by the Kouachi brothers [in the Charlie Hebdo attack] deserved it. Why did they insult the Prophet of Islam? According to the people in the neighbourhood, if the journalists insulted him, it means they wanted to insult us, the second- or third-generation Arabs. The banlieue youths feel that the caricatures of the Prophet of Islam were aimed at them in particular. For once, we saw parents and children united in their outrage: the parents because the figure of the Prophet is untouchable, the children because they are tired of the insults and they cannot accept more humiliation.

Question: But there is more to it than that. The neighbourhood has become religious and I am told that compared to ten years ago or so, religious fundamentalism prevails of a much stricter type than before.

Answer: As you can see, the neighbourhood is becoming more and more religious. It is not by chance. I, myself, am not that religious, but I understand these youths. For them it is like a sort of refuge, they find an identity as you say in social sciences, a refuge identity which protects them from a society which does not like them, which despises them. Becoming a Muslim is also rejecting laïcité, rejecting a society which refuses people from different origins and colonies they wish would disappear as distinct, assimilate them as they say. Well! Arabs cannot be assimilated. They want to live like everyone but they don't want to be humiliated because of their different past, or change religions and names to please everyone. It's my conclusion in a little study I carried out for my Master's dissertation: there is a colonial continuity for these youths, they are humiliated just like in the past. They believe that insulting Islam is a way of humiliating them and their parents with different means. Before they would humiliate 'Bougnoules' (a derogatory word for 'Arabs'), now it's Muslims. It's the same contempt.

Question: But what about the attack on 13 November 2015? Arabs and Muslims were also killed in the attack.

Answer: I will tell you something that I don't like either. For the youths of the neighbourhood, when they saw the Parisian Arabs, those who were in the cafés with the 'French', well! Those were no longer people they respected. They had become like the French, they lived like them, they weren't from the neighbourhood and belonged to the society of integrated people. There was a difference: the youths of the neighbourhood didn't approve of the massacres, but it wasn't their problem, and the Arabs who were killed with French people, that didn't move them.

Question: Apparently, in the demonstrations on 10 and 11 January 2015, according to some like Philippe Corcuff there were many Muslims who spoke out against the death of the journalists.[26]

Answer: But these are Muslims who are on the other side, they live like the French, they don't live in the poor suburbs. They are, as you could say, economically integrated into society, unlike the youths, who are socially and mentally excluded. For the youths, those Muslims are not any of theirs, they are like service Arabs, 'sold', paid by the 'Whites'.

Question: For you, the border line is the Cité [poor neighbourhood], *not the fact of being Muslim!*

Answer: Of course, it's obvious for these youths. They are locked up in the Cité and all those who leave it are traitors in their eyes. That's tragic.

Question: What do you think of the radicalisation of the youths in the poor suburbs?

Answer: It's also a way of accusing us more. This radicalisation is rooted in the living conditions of these youths who feel excluded, despised and rejected by society. They react to the violence of society by opposing their own counter-violence in the name of Islam. To them, what's important is the injustice and humiliation they feel every day and to which they react by becoming radicalised.

This interview, chosen among from about thirty carried out with youths and social workers, reflects the mental boundary between the poor *banlieues* populated by ethnic minorities and mainstream society. For many young French Muslims, society has rejected them, relegating them to the poor neighbourhoods where they become part of the group 'abandoned by France'.[27]

In this context, 'radicalization' is in reality experienced by many youths as an unfair and unfounded accusation of global society against them. Being radicalized and even violent, in their perspective, is a way of reacting to the social injustice, disdain and humiliation that Muslims are suffering throughout Europe, but particularly in France, due to the radical secularism that distinguishes it from the rest of Europe.

What makes radicalization less significant in much of Europe now compared to recent years and particularly in France is the disappearance of the Islamic State in Iraq and Syria in October 2017. This has robbed many European Muslim youths of an alternative utopia. But still, in France, radical secularism in France continues to worsen misunderstandings between Muslim minorities and mainstream society. In fact, the sentiment all over Europe, as evidenced through the coercive policies towards the perceived threat of radicalization, is the rejection of Islamic identity rather than more tolerance towards it.

Positing solutions is not an easy matter and it is more difficult in France than in other European countries on account of the official ideology of *laïcité* and also the positions taken by certain quarters in the Muslim community. On the issue of the veil, for example, there is a perception within these groups that France's restrictive laws are being promulgated to control their religious practices. One suggestion would be a serious dialogue between the state and representatives of different strands of thinking within the French Muslim community. The difficulty with this is that the French Muslim community lacks intellectuals capable of articulating and defending the thinking within their community in the public sphere unlike, say, French Jews who have eminent intellectuals who know how to lend legitimacy to the claim of their Jewishness vis-à-vis the state.

In addition, as observed earlier, the jihadist attacks of the last decade have had the effect of distorting perceptions in the public space, further disadvantaging the French Muslim community – they are ever more suspected of having sympathy for fundamentalist and extremist versions of Islam. A large part of French society is therefore in favour of coercive laws regarding Islam in the public space. The Muslim community is unable to argue in a rational and effective way against this. It would take a new generation of Muslims to articulate their views effectively – this would involve finding ways to carve out an acceptable religious space within French society while being cognizant of and perhaps accommodating concerns and viewpoints from mainstream society. If this happens, it will necessarily be a gradual process.

Notes

1   Farhad Khosrokhavar, *Le nouveau Jihad en Occident* [The New Jihad in the Western World] (Paris: Robert Laffont, 2018).

2   As many as 247 deaths in France, 93 in England, 15 in Germany, 36 in Belgium and 208 in Spain.

3   See Jean Beaubérot, *Les sept laïcités françaises. Le modèle français de laïcité n'existe pas* [The Seven French Secularities. There Is No Such Thing as the French Model of Secularism] (Paris: Maison des Sciences de l'Homme) 2015.

4   Private schools, the majority of which were managed by Catholics, were not subject to this restriction.

5   Caroline Beyer, « Un rapport officiel préconise l'interdiction du voile à l'université » [*An Official Report Recommends Banning Headscarves in Universities*], in *Le Figaro*, 6 August 2013.

6   Claire Digiacomi, « *Les deux femmes voilées exclues du restaurant 'Le Cénacle' à Tremblay-en-France ont porté plainte* » [*The Two Women Wearing Headscarves Who Were Rejected from Entering the 'Le Cenacle' Restaurant File a Lawsuit*], *Le Huffington Post*, 29 August 2016.

7   Fatima Achouri, Pas de voile à l'hôpital: la CEDH valide une décision juridique française [No Headscarves in Hospitals: the CEDH Confirms French Judicial

Decision by Fatima Achouri, 27 November 2015, at http://fatimaachouri.com/paroles-de-femmes-musulmanes/

8   Caroline Piquet, « *Une jurée exclue du tribunal pour avoir refusé d'enlever son voile pour prêter serment* » [*A Member of the Jury Excluded From Court after Refusing to Remove her Headscarf to Take Oath*], *Le Figaro*, 9 May 2015.

9   Georges Bensoussan (dir.), *Les Territoires perdus de la République–antisémitisme, racisme et sexisme en milieu scolaire*, [*The Lost Territories of the Republic - Antisemitism, Racism and Sexism in Schools*] (Paris: Mille et Une Nuits Editions, 2002).

10   Bernard Rougier (dir.), *Les territoires conquis de l'islamisme* [*The Conquered Territories of Islamism*] (Paris: Presses universitaires de France, 2020).

11   Anne-Sophie Lamine, Les foulards et la République, Revue des Sciences Sociales, [*The Headscarves and the Republic, Social Science Review*] 2006, No. 35; Le Monde avec Reuters, « *Le Parlement vote l'interdiction du voile intégral* », [*Le Monde with Reuters, 'Parliament Votes to Ban the Niqab', Le Monde*], 14 September 2010.

12   See Farhad Khosrokhavar, *Jihadism in Europe* (Oxford University Press, 2021).

13   Citing only the English case, where statistics are available, in December 2014 there were 12,225 Muslim prisoners out of a prison population of 85,509 individuals compared to just 4.8 per cent of Muslims in English society: almost 15 per cent of Muslims are in prison. See Danny Shaw, 'Why the Surge in Muslim Prisoners?', *BBC News*, 11 March 2015.

14   This work is based on several empirical studies, including the one on middle classes of immigrant origin financed by the Victims of Terrorism Support Portal (FAVT) in 2014, research on prisons financed by the Ministry of Justice (2011–13), and research on the *banlieue* suburbs of Greater Paris financed by the Paris Bureau of HLM government housing between 2010 and 2018, as well as studies on Islam between 2010 and 2018.

15   See Elijah Anderson, *Code of the Street* (New York and London: W.W. Norton & Company, 1999).

16   See an extensive discussion on this issue in Khosrokhavar, *Jihadism in Europe*.

17   See Claire Adida, David Laitin and Marie-Anne Valfort, Mesurer la discrimination, Apports de l'économie expérimentale [*Measuring Discrimination, Experimental Economics*], 2013; Marie-Anne Valfort, Musulmans: la réalité des discriminations au travail [*Muslims: The Reality of Discrimination at Work*], 9 April 2015, http://www.latribune.fr/opinions/tribunes/musulmans-la-realite-des-discriminations-au-travail-467384.html In 1997, the phenomenon had already been analysed. See Philippe Bataille, *Le racisme au travail*, [*Racism at Work*] (Paris: La Découverte, 1997).

18   In the French army in 2005, 10–20 per cent of the staff were supposedly of majority North African origin. See Christophe Bertossi and Catherine Wihtol de Wenden, *Les couleurs du drapeau: l'Armée française face aux discriminations [The Colours of the Flag: the French Army in the Face of Discrimination]* (Paris: Robert Laffont, 2007).

19   In her work *Musulmans au Quotidien* [The Daily Lives of Muslims] (Paris: La découverte, 2015), Nilüfer Göle focuses on the middle-class 'ordinary Muslims' who would like to experience their faith quietly in French society (and more widely, European society) who raise real and symbolical obstacles against them.

20   The unease of cultural alienation is also based on the sometimes warped interpretation of reality of an 'international conspiracy'. Individual members of the FMFC sometimes layer on top of their alienation a mythical, generalized conspiracy (such as the Jewish conspiracy or a Freemason conspiracy) or of illegitimate

domination (Western interventions in the Arab revolutions which made them fail), according to some French Muslims in our interviews.

21 Rémy Leveau and Catherine Wihtol de Wenden, *La beurgeoisie: Les trois âges de la vie associative issue de l'immigration* [Beurgeoisie: The Three Ages of Assiocative Life from Immigrant Backgrounds] (CNRS Editions, 2001).

22 See Jérôme Beauchez, *L'empreinte du poing, La boxe, le gymnase et leurs hommes*, [The Mark of The Fist, Boxing, Gyms, and their Men] (EHESS Editions, 2014).

23 Jonathan Laurence and Justin Vaisse, *Intégrer l'Islam [Integrating Islam]* (Odile Jacob, 2007).

24 See Bernard Godard, *La question musulmane en France [The Muslim Question in France]* (Fayard, 2014), which shows the failure of the state but also of Muslim institutions in promoting the integration of the followers of the religion of Allah in France.

25 See Khosrokhavar, *Jihadism in Europe*.

26 See the report by Jane Weston Vauclair and David Vauclair, *De Charlie Hebdo à #Charlie*, [From Charlie Hebdo to #Charlie] (Eyrolles, 2016).

27 See Eric Marlière, *La France nous a lâchés! Le sentiment d'injustice chez les jeunes des cités* [France Has Abandoned Us! The Feeling of Injustice of the Youths in the Suburbs] (Fayard, 2008).

Bibliography

Achouri, Fatima. Pas de voile à l'hôpital: la CEDH valide une décision juridique française, 27 November 2015. Available at: http://fatimaachouri.com/paroles-de-femmes-musulmanes/

Adida, Claire, Laitin, David and Valfort, Marie-Anne. *Mesurer la discrimination, Apports de l'économie expérimentale*. 2013.

Anderson, Elijah. *Code of the Street*. New York and London: W.W. Norton & Company, 1999.

Beaubérot, Jean. *Les sept laïcités françaises. Le modèle français de laïcité n'existe pas*. Paris: Maison des Sciences de l'Homme, 2015.

Beauchez, Jérôme. *L'empreinte du poing, La boxe, le gymnase et leurs hommes*. Editions EHESS, 2014.

Bensoussan, Georges (ed.). *Les Territoires perdus de la République – antisémitisme, racisme et sexisme en milieu scolaire*. Paris: Editions Mille et Une Nuits, 2002.

Bertossi, Christophe and de Wenden, Catherine Wihtol. *Les couleurs du drapeau : l'Armée française face aux discriminations*. Paris: Robert Laffont, 2007.

Beyer, Caroline. « Un rapport officiel préconise l'interdiction du voile à l'université », in Le Figaro, 6 August 2013.

Digiacomi, Claire. « *Les deux femmes voilées exclues du restaurant "Le Cénacle" à Tremblay-en-France ont porté plainte* », The Huffington Post, 29 August 2016.

Godard, Bernard. *La question musulmane en France* (Fayard), 2014.

Göle, Nilüfer. *Musulmans au Quotidien*. Paris: La découverte, 2015.

Khosrokhavar, Farhad. *Le nouveau Jihad en Occident*. Paris: Robert Laffont, 2018.

Khosrokhavar, Farhad. *Jihadism in Europe*. Oxford: Oxford University Press, 2021.

Lamine, Anne-Sophie. « Les foulards et la République », *Revue des Sciences Sociales*, no. 35 (2006): 14–25.

Lapeyronnie, Didier. *Ghetto Urbain. Ségrégation, violence, pauvreté en France aujourd'hui.* Paris: Robert Laffont, 2008.

Laurence, Jonathan and Vaisse, Justin. *Intégrer l'Islam.* Odile Jacob, 2007.

Le Monde and Reuters. «*Le Parlement vote l'interdiction du voile intégral*», *Le Monde*, 14 September 2010.

Leveau, Rémy and de Wenden, Catherine Wihtol. *La beurgeoisie: Les trois âges de la vie associative issue de l'immigration.* CNRS Editions, 2001.

Marlière, Eric. *La France nous a lâchés! Le sentiment d'injustice chez les jeunes des cités.* Fayard, 2008.

Piquet, Caroline. « *Une jurée exclue du tribunal pour avoir refusé d'enlever son voile pour prêter serment* », Le Figaro, 9 May 2015.

Rougier, Bernard (ed.). *Les territoires conquis de l'islamisme.* Paris: Presses universitaires de France, 2020.

Shaw, Danny. 'Why the Surge in Muslim Prisoners?'. *BBC News*, 11 March 2015.

Valfort, Marie-Anne. 'Musulmans: La réalité des discriminations au travail', 9 April 2015, http://www.latribune.fr/opinions/tribunes/musulmans-la-realite-des-discriminations-au-travail-467384.html

Vauclair, Jane Weston and Vauclair, David. *De Charlie Hebdo à #Charlie.* Eyrolles, 2016.

Part Two

Diversion as part and parcel of genuine prevention

3

Evidence-inspired prevention of violent extremism in the Belgian city of Mechelen: Evaluation and recommendations

Alexander Van Leuven

This chapter studies diversion as a practice within the Prevention of Violent Extremism (PVE). The focus of this chapter is the Belgian city of Mechelen. The Mechelen Model for PVE has social alienation as a central perspective and organizes interventions for the re-socialization of individuals alienated from societal institutions. To have a genuinely preventive effect, these interventions must be carried out before recruitment into extremist networks, paramilitaries, informal activities or any illegal entity for that matter. Moreover, these interventions are generally aimed at those who have lost faith in institutionalized interventions. That is where diversion comes into play. This chapter ultimately offers practical conclusions and recommendations for effective PVE.

Situating the Mechelen Model

Prevention of Violent Extremism (PVE) refers to that grey zone where no laws are broken, but where there is a rising concern for a fellow citizen who might or might not be on the path to breaking the law. Belgium has much in common with other nations in facing these issues but also has its particular challenges. The country is a federal state composed of multiple partly overlapping regions with specific capacities. Such dispersion has a negative effect on its ability to make consistent policies tackling violent extremism. Northern regions, identifying with the historic feudal principality of Flanders, are especially slow to recognize the antecedents of violent extremism, with welfare services ill-equipped to take on associated challenges.

A systematic overview of Belgian PVE policies has been given by others.[1] Maarten De Waele has recounted the history of Islamist violent extremism in Belgium, also explaining the federal safety structures and how they link to prevention actors (e.g., youth workers) in a municipal body joining all relevant actors.

Building on that contribution, this chapter recounts the Belgian approach to violent extremism and social insecurity from a perspective that is more relevant to municipalities, especially the City of Mechelen. A key facet of the Belgian approach has been a focus on local perspectives as a method of overcoming the intra-federal complexity. Safety policies are a federal capacity, but prevention policies are strictly speaking a regional capacity. Ultimately, municipalities have the largest preventative ability because they are in continuous contact with reality.

Historically, Mechelen is not part of the Flemish feudal region, but nowadays it is incorporated in the Northern regions, which increasingly identify with an exclusivist Flemish identity. This results in prevention policies that are disproportionally informed by a different interest, namely the safeguarding of Flemish culture.[2]

Flemish regions have a troubled history with their Muslim communities. In times of globalized risks,[3] confidence in and support for social policies is waning.[4] Nadia Fadil and Martijn de Koning specifically identify *integration policies and anti-poverty policies as* corrupted by securitization – suggesting that they have been practically replaced by PVE policy.[5] This is also mirrored at the federal level: the incomplete *Plan M* policy, which was to somehow protect (white) Belgians from Islam, particularly was seen as the influence of immoderate foreign Islamic entities in the form of Saudi-funded Wahhabi mosques. *Plan M* was itself the precursor to the *Plan R* policy, on *Radicalization/violent extremism*.[6] *Plan R* does not limit itself to regulating security affairs, but outlines the goals for federally funded *de-radicalization officers* embedded in local prevention services.[7] An integrated approach to security also informs prevention policies. However, heavily securitized prevention of radicalization treats people in danger of being recruited as dangerous people. This has acted in some cases as a form of self-fulfilling prophecy, pushing them towards recruitment and endangering the success of preventative interventions.

When a large number of Belgian youth started travelling to war-struck Syria to fight the Assad regime,[8] Belgian policymakers reacted exactly as ISIS terrorists wanted them to: with vigorous measures targeted at Muslims in general.[9] In this complicated context, it takes a creative twist to make progress. This happened on the local level, when in spring 2013, the Mayors of Antwerp, Maaseik, Mechelen and Vilvoorde confronted with the departure of youth [...] to fight in Syria, started to pilot locally tailored prevention responses, also obtaining federal subsidies to that end.[10]

Where is the urban space called Mechelen (on PVE)?

In autumn 2013, I was appointed Local Coordinator for the Prevention of Violent Extremism (PVE) in the City of Mechelen. I was to develop what would become known as the Mechelen Model.[11] For reasons that will become apparent, I immediately changed the title of PVE coordinator to PiM coordinator. PiM is a Dutch anagram referring to 'Positive Identities and Societal Resilience' and is at the core of the Mechelen Model.

In this section, I will explain the unique traits of that Model. I first discuss the context of the Mechelen community and then I discuss how PVE practice is the most functional for the locality. Finally, some elaboration is given on how diversion works within the overall PVE model.

The Mechelen community

In the 1990s, the Belgian City of Mechelen was characterized as 'Chicago on the Dijle river'. People felt highly insecure in public spaces, caused by bouncer violence and youth nuisance, ranging from informal gatherings in public spaces to vandalism, intimidation and drug dealing.[12]

In 2012, Mayor Bart Somers enacted a plan starting with a new narrative for the community.[13] The plan invested in the infrastructure of the city with its medieval heart and modern urban and industrial appearance. The city council created recreational spaces for tourists and residential spaces for middle-class families, increasing revenue for the city treasury, without raising taxes. All 86,000 inhabitants became inheritors of an enviable history that restored the grandeur of Mechelen as the capital of the Low Countries and the seat of the Supreme Court of the Burgundian Netherlands – Mechelen was widely known as the place where you go to for justice.

The local police force was strengthened in numbers too and massive camera surveillance was installed. This new approach consisted of more than merely hard security measures. Somers was equally receptive to the insights of the now deplored KU Leuven criminologist Dr. Stef Christiaensen to develop a large prevention service alongside the safety policy.[14] To date, that prevention service builds on the notion of responsive community cohesion.[15] This cohesion generally characterizes the Mechelen community; simultaneously, this characterization is very outspoken within the Belgo-Moroccan sub-community, which is relatively speaking the largest Belgo-Moroccan community (15 per cent of the municipal population) and definitely the most targeted Belgian subgroup for recruitment in the Syrian civil war. Furthermore, this cohesion is responsive for the simple reason that when a person disconnects from societal institutions, someone else will immediately sacrifice time and energy to re-socialize those for whom they have concern.

Social alienation

The Mechelen Model is mostly a code of conduct that ensures that the engagement for said responsiveness will be applied hands-on, in any case and for anyone.[16] It actively promotes referral of any concern with regard to social alienation, preferably (but not exclusively) before any kind of violent extremist recruiter steps in. This code of conduct is known in Dutch as *Positieve identiteit en Maatschappijvorming* or translated into English, 'Positive identity and Societal Resilience (PiM)' (a full elaboration follows below). To understand it, one must acknowledge that it is a prevention model rather than a safety model. One must also appreciate the dynamics of the Mechelen community and understand the theoretical underpinnings of the model.

Some believe that a turn to violent extremism comes swiftly. This belief is most strikingly depicted in a testimonial I once heard, about two Brusseleirs going from wearing mini-skirts to jihad in three weeks. That might be the gist of what safety officers observed, but for prevention this view is problematic. This 'skirts to jihad' moment is just a fraction of what really happens and does not offer any meaningful guidance for intervention. Aside from some cases with a certified mental condition at play, where recruits were used to spread propaganda, the Mechelen PVE casework does not support the claim that a turn to violent extremism happens swiftly.

My experience is that the processes leading to violent extremism are the extension of a very normal process that we all have to deal with, especially as emerging adults. In our identity development, everyone incidentally encounters difficulties, which can grow into frustrations that require the support of others to overcome.[17] Luckily, we can rely on an entire web of social institutions to help us do this.[18] These institutions (see Figure 3.1) are mainly in the categories of family, school or work and leisure associations. However, in some instances, the intervention of care, police and justice services are sometimes required. A very special institution is (social) media, which is both a social institution and an entity that influences other social institutions.[19]

PVE is concerned with the occasional instances of what Loïc Wacquant describes as institutional failure that breaks the social contract, which permits our fellow citizens to slip through the meshes of the safety net that comprises society, welfare state and rule of law.[20] This phenomenon can be conceptualized as social alienation.[21] Therefore the city council of Mechelen provides civilians and professionals with a PiM service that abides by a highly transparent code of conduct to re-socialize alienated fellow humans.

Figure 3.2 shows all the stages before violent extremism. The first two are normal and familiar, but on the relatively seldom occasions that they are not addressed (properly), recruitment becomes possible into whatever alternative institution finds a socially alienated person. In Belgium, these alternative institutions are mostly drug-trafficking related but for a time, ISIS usurped this prime recruiter position. At the time of writing, the Coordination Unit for Threat Analysis (CUTA) increasingly warned about 'threats of right-wing ideologies'.[22]

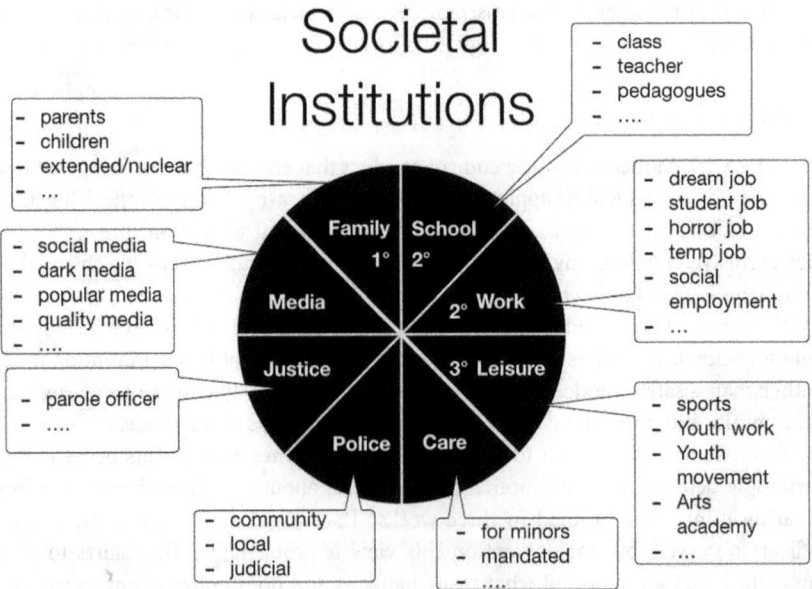

Figure 3.1 Societal institutions as discerned in the Mechelen Model.

Positive Identity and Societal Resilience (*Positieve identiteit en Maatschappijvorming, PiM*)

When an individual falls through the cracks of society, the PiM service at the city council should be the first port of call. PiM stands for Positive identity or getting rid of frustrations in identities and Societal resilience or repairing the safety net. The team is anchored within the city prevention service and consists of a diverse group of outreach personnel, called coaches. Each coach has a speciality. In total there are three. One specializes in the family institution, one in the school institution and another in care. Aside from the coaches, there is a large network of voluntary key figures to connect with several types of people who might be in need, two of whom are in permanent employment of the city. The team has a coordinator who spares the team from administrative work, lobbying for subsidies, press contacts, etc.

About thirty to fifty case referrals are made yearly, half of which are structurally related to drug trafficking, and the other half related to what is considered more ideological extremism.[23] Any kind of alienation can be referred. Consequently, it does not matter what kind of alternative institution could be recruiting. Also, referrals can be made after office hours. Flexibility and accessibility are very important.

Anybody can be a referrer. PiM discerns three kinds of referrals:

(A) *Concerned referral cases* occur where a professional consults her/his coordinator regarding a third person that seems to be disconnecting from institutions.

(B) A *prevention referral* can be made to the PiM-coordinator or a PiM-coach. There are two acts in this referral: first is the initial referral on the phone, by email or in person. This is followed within the week by a referral clarification with the whole team of coaches present. The referrer remains the owner of the case and no action is taken without her/his approval. The team will keep looking for solutions until approval is reached. In some cases it takes a long time to get there, but the team has always managed. Ideally, matters are discussed with the person concerned and this person takes ownership. However, persons dealing with social alienation are often not amenable to contact at the time of referral.

(C) A *safety referral* is when the PiM team and the referrer decide to involve the police. For this, there are strict and transparent rules, the most crucial of which is a judicial directive concerning the *management of judicial and administrative police information* which enables police to discard concerns that they rule out to be actual risks, based on their own data.[24] This possibility of discarding is a crucial aspect for PiM to gain the trust of potential referrers because they would not want to be responsible for putting a person on the list of violent extremist suspects without certainty.

The referral clarification discusses the degree of alienation from social institutions. Based on this, an assessment is made of the level of concern attached to the case (cf. Figure 3.2). The next stage generally involves appointing a key figure who can connect and sincerely engage with the person concerned. Preferably this is someone representing

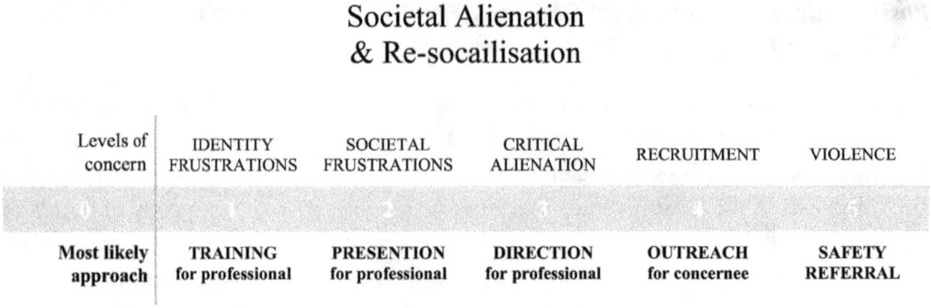

Societal Alienation
& Re-socailisation

Levels of concern	IDENTITY FRUSTRATIONS	SOCIETAL FRUSTRATIONS	CRITICAL ALIENATION	RECRUITMENT	VIOLENCE
0	1	2	3	4	5
Most likely approach	TRAINING for professional	PRESENTION for professional	DIRECTION for professional	OUTREACH for concernee	SAFETY REFERRAL

Figure 3.2 Societal alienation and re-socialization.

an institution, such as a school or a leisure association, but at higher levels of concern, this is oftentimes not possible, because one needs a professional 'outreacher' to re-establish contact with somebody who has experienced this Wacqantian broken social contact.[25] In this instance, the PiM-coaches step in. In some cases, it will be somebody who is for some reason close to the person concerned. It will be a committed person. He or she is mostly known as that coach who has helped all those others, instead of a prevention worker or PiM-coach. For this type of outreach and reconnecting, the professional needs to 'keep it real'.

On a weekly basis, the progress of re-socialization is discussed, based on the Penal Code laws on professional secrecy. Those laws allow for the possibility to discuss or share relevant information with those who are concerned.[26] If it comes to higher levels of concern, a safety referral will be made to the local police. Also, when there are doubts about the necessity for a safety referral, one can be made because in any case, the referral is made to a select group of information officers of the police, who have two weeks to check if the safety referral is justified. If it is not, they discard the information. Police never ask for sources. Transparency of this information flow is crucial to the Model and earning the trust of referrers. If word spreads that information on cases has been shared, PiM would lose all credibility.

Diversion in the Mechelen Model

The above section introduced Mechelen and the Mechelen Model. The current section ethnographically analyses this model, in which I have done extensive fieldwork and participant observation as coordinator and coach.[27] An ethnographic analysis allows for thick descriptions which place emphasis on the complexity of specific situations.[28] Case studies compiled using this approach enable an in-depth understanding of interpersonal interactions and as such lend themselves very well to insights on diversion in PVE.[29] This approach can inform PVE approaches but avoids making claims as to whether the PVE model under discussion is the 'right' one to use.

As the local coordinator of C/PVE, I have been heavily involved in operations relating to specific cases. This provides a privileged position but of course it requires critical reactions to be able to take an objective distance from the notes on and experience of the cases I am about to describe.[30, 31] These notes entail a weekly update on the interventions done to resocialize alienated persons into society. The selection of ethnographic case studies below is done to shed light on diversion as a recurrent set of interventions.

Positive identities

The very first prevention referral concerned a seventeen-year-old demanding a space to pray at school whilst starting to grow a beard and wear a *djellaba* (long robe). In the referral clarification, I understood the youngster desired to make amends for adolescent mischief by becoming a more pious Muslim. A lot of young Muslims go through a similar phase. Usually, an older Muslim will notice and suggest that this is not necessary. However, this particular youngster had fallen through the mesh of that safety net. I engaged a youth worker to reassure the young man that he was allowed to make mistakes and that learning from them sufficed as penance. The youth worker was able to successfully intervene, being a Muslim himself, and thus understanding what it is like to live as a Muslim in a region where expressions of Islamophobia are not insignificant.[32]

Mechelen has known numerous such referrals. The climate of Islamophobia and the marketing of ISIS have created a backdrop more conducive to adolescents inclined towards violent extremism. With a little bad luck, that prophecy becomes self-fulfilling. However, if such a case is referred to police services, it would incite disproportionate responses and overburden police capacity, as they become flooded with false positives. This clarifies why prevention should focus on social alienation and a safe and transparent influx towards the police.

Just over half of the cases that are referred to the Mechelen prevention service consist of social alienation in early stages. The solution mostly consists of supporting the key figures, volunteers or professionals, who are most capable of dealing with the underlying issues. These key figures do not go against or intentionally seek conflict with people with whom they engage. Rather, they help them to see a path that is feasible and safe.

Around 2015, the PiM-coaches started noticing that alienated youth were deliberately expressing sympathy towards violent extremism as a cry for help. They seemed outwardly to have become sympathetic to ISIS and would share their intentions of going to Syria. PiM sought out the right key figures, who were mostly professionals, but the main criterion was that they can establish a connection with a given youth. The selection can be based on still active connections, residual motivation of the concerned to strengthen a connection, or merely the connection skills of a PiM-coach. Therefore, a diverse group of key figures should be available. A key figure would have to present a trustworthy perspective. After referral clarification, it turned out they had all sorts of issues without any solutions in sight: family issues, addictions, debts, school problems, conflicts, intimidation, etc.

The mother of all cases

One case had all the elements that informed the Mechelen case flow. The referrer was a daughter of migrants and a mother of two adolescent minors. She was insecure about her knowledge of Dutch, which is the language of the public sphere, administration, etc., in the Flemish community. As the family had recently moved from Brussels and both parents still worked there, they were more used to speaking French. But she was committed to supporting her sons who showed problematic behaviour and she brought the younger son to us for a referral clarification.

She was very worried about her younger son's online interest in jihadi violence. Listening carefully, I noticed the youngster seemed obsessed with the matter. He proved very passionate and expressive about all of his interests by nature, but sadly the passions did not last long. At that point, I overconfidently thought I had 'cracked the code' and resolved to engage a key figure to put major support into advancing and consolidating the youngster's next passion: photography.

I found an exceptionally talented youth worker capable of engaging with the youngster and his first results exceeded all expectations. Knowing how to guide passionate youth and link them to predominantly white leisure institutions was an invaluable skill this youth worker possessed. Quite soon the mother thanked the youth worker for his service and asked him to focus on the elder brother instead, who was being solicited by drug dealers and needed a lot of community support to resist recruitment.

A few months later, the younger brother was arrested, accused of terrorist plotting. What had happened? While we had stopped our engagement with the younger brother, he was recruited by a youth gang known in Antwerp mostly for drug trafficking, showed interest in his photography and presumably recruited him into the ranks on a need-to-know basis. Together they made YouTube content praising general and jihadi violence. This was not noticed by anyone in the Mechelen community but it was noticed by the national security authorities who started tailing the youngster until he was in a public chat space joking about terrorist plots. At that point, he was arrested and PiM was notified through the local police service.

Psychologically, this was a heavy blow for the youngster, then seventeen years of age, and eventually sentenced to two years on probation. This boy had completely lost trust in anyone who claimed to help him. His probation came with a long list of terms and conditions. One condition was getting a job or schooling but his school had expelled him fearing negative publicity, so we found a programme for him with committed teachers. Another condition was to get religious counselling, but from the moment he heard his charges, he instantly stopped praying and in doing so renounced his religion. We then had to find a counsellor who would develop a programme that would not talk about Islam until he was ready for it, which ultimately took longer than two years.

We also worked on the family situation. It turned out the parents had always been well intentioned towards their sons and they assumed good Islamic training would protect the sons in life. That is true in general; yet, they had their sons schooled in Islam at the Great Mosque in Brussels, which was until recently Wahhabi-led. These specific teachings made the violent propaganda that the younger son was asked to film for the gang seem less problematic.

Diversion goes both ways. It can be made by the right people in the right place or conversely, by malicious people in the absence of legitimate institutions. Nobody forced the youth to take on photography or to support violence. But in engaging with him, everybody has an idea in mind of how things need to progress. So a coach acknowledged his ambitions and frustrations by talking them through at the pace he set. The process does *not* continuously involve deep conversation. The youth is recognized for who he is and that includes subjects other than his problems. Coaches and key figures will clearly take a stance on what he has done wrong and why albeit not overzealously – because what is done is done and they cannot change matters. Conversations must emphasize what is possible and how it is possible.

For success, there must be a genuine connection with a person for whom there is concern. To that end, the PiM-coach is transparent about her/his intentions. S/he empathizes with the individual who has made bad choices because it is a human thing to do. Hence, the coach/mentor makes sure the person concerned is so occupied with positive activities that s/he has no time or energy for illegal alternatives. The coach/mentor is not secretive about these plans: it merely needs to be shown that they are feasible and that he/she will be genuinely available for support.

Alternatives presented to the individual in question must be convincingly trustworthy. At first, the younger son did not go to the school we selected for him. He first spent a semester at a school that he knew to be wrong for him, but where he was at least familiar with the challenges. He knew we were still patiently waiting and reaching out to him, no matter what. Ultimately, he selected an even better school than we had previously tried to convince him of, and he did so entirely on his own. We had a good relationship with this new school because we had previously worked with them when some of their students became proselytizers. Based on this experience we had the necessary network in the school to stay informed without having to tell the whole staff what their new student was trying to forget and move past.

At a later point, there was a family crisis around a new problem of the elder son. This was something the younger son could just not deal with. Without any prior planning, three professionals were engaged throughout the weekend to give support to the family. It did not really matter what background these professionals had. It mostly mattered that they were prepared to devote themselves to the issue hands-on for an entire weekend.

These interventions ought to be executed transparently. Coaches and key figures are constantly planning the way forward and thinking about expected scenarios. At this point, they must mind the balance, because it would be an insurmountable breach of trust if we proved to be operating behind the youngster's back. In any case, it cannot be forced upon him: not the school we envisaged or the religious mentoring the judge envisaged when giving probation, nor the new friends we would have liked him to make in the community house where we provided him with a computer to work on his audiovisual products.

Societal resilience

When different people fall through the same meshes in the safety net, our welfare state must take remedial action. In the following section, two projects that use diversion are elaborated on.

Based on feedback from professionals that there was a dearth of programmes that could offer youth training that might enable the youth to walk away from recruitment into gangs and extremist organizations, the city council granted the development of a tailored resilience training programme.[33] This differed from ongoing trainings on two levels. One is that it was a very physical training, inspired by a PhD study in medical anthropology and based on the idea that through psycho-physical training, new methods could be internalized more quickly than through cognitive lecturing.[34]

Another difference was that it was designed in a 'train-the-trainer' format, so a range of key figures could implement resilience training in their daily operations and activities. We went through three waves: we successively trained prevention workers, teachers and youth workers. Together they formed a team of experts on the matter. The prevention workers would mostly organize sessions for youth, leading to the next project discussed further on.

Youth workers and physical education teachers would incorporate the training in regular activities, such as insanity training which is a form of endurance training of which youth are fond. Or they would adapt the rules of a soccer game so as to disadvantage a team or a few players, in order to playfully learn that they can survive these setbacks. Imagine a kid about to score a beautiful goal. Unfortunately, at that moment, the referee blows her/his whistle so, abiding by the adapted rules, the kid has to freeze all movement. Imagine her/his frustration after building up to this glorious moment, for all is lost. The kid shouts abuse and swears. But immediately s/he bursts out in laughing, realizing her/his own overreaction. The idea is that this experience is transferrable to incidents like racist vitriol.

Rather unexpectedly, the teachers experienced personal growth through the training, as they learned to find more personal stability in their confrontation with students who enter classrooms with too many problems on their minds.[35] This can be very stressful for teachers who have to keep a session on track and cannot interrupt teaching for social assistance. However, through the training, they completely changed the appeal they make to their students, inciting in turn more positive reactions from those students.

As Nadia Charkaoui attests from a long ongoing professional career in civil rights advocacy, resilience does not suffice if not supplemented by an adequate coping method.[36] This has been manifest in Mechelen too. Many of the youth in Mechelen report how social institutions continue to fail them, and they cannot keep laughing just because these failures do not kill them. For some time, I had felt that youth trained in resilience should be given support in taking on a project of their own. This could be a little business project or learning how to organize activities for younger kids. After a while, those experiments merged together as Jongeren BuurtZorg (Youth Neighbourhood Care). Youngsters are employed for three months,[37] with a possible extension of another three months, while tasked to keep their neighbourhood clean and repair incidental damages. It keeps them close to us, which is not the case when support is given to them to find employment elsewhere. Wages are kept very low, but it is not the money that appeals to them. It is the esteem they get from being selected by the city and mostly from showing leadership in their neighbourhood. After six months, they organize a neighbourhood barbecue and move on to other challenges. Some find regular employment, while others become youth leaders in sports or leisure activities.

This project did amazing things for one youngster. Before the summer of 2017, the police service signalled that this young man was causing a lot of nuisance and would presumably do a lot more over the summer. So first we engaged the Mayor himself to invite the youngster and his parents to the town hall for a talk. The Mayor said this would either be a difficult summer for all of us or the youngster could decide to refrain from trouble and the city would provide any support needed. The youngster, impressed by the engagement of the city and the Mayor himself, accepted the extended hand.

And so the youngster joined Jongeren BuurtZorg and later told one of the PiM coaches that while cleaning his neighbourhood, he earned sustainable esteem, as opposed to the volatile esteem of informal networks. Encouraged by a key figure, the youngster started organizing sports events in his community and earned nationally recognized certificates for it. The next year he participated in a European exchange programme, co-facilitating (with a PiM-coach) a youth leadership course in Northern Macedonia.

For this individual, the restoration of his broken social contract was all he needed. It showed him that he would be able to fulfil his ambitions legitimately. Now people are saying that he maybe was not such a bad kid. The coaches and key figures never doubted that. Such a moral judgement would have meant destructive forcing as opposed to diversion. Rather, the right people needed to stick around and give this youngster a nudge in a direction enabling the development of the potential he always had.

Conclusion and policy recommendations

This chapter has introduced the Mechelen PVE Model, illustrating the workings of the model through ethnographic case studies. In these cases, diversion is used to counteract the effects of social alienation, which is the aim of the Mechelen Model. Within the Mechelen Model, diversion takes the form of sets of tailored interventions to support and guide those who have given up on institutionalized interventions. This PVE provides for outreach to those who have given up on the very idea of help, as opposed to many forms of social work which can only help those who want to be helped.

Dos and don'ts of diversion

In Belgium, many politicians have fallen prey to the idea of introducing interventions against the spectre of violent jihadism, which in turn leads to anti-Muslim sentiments.[38] In the Northern regions, ingrained Islamophobia within public discourse exacerbates the problem: many intellectuals argue that there are too many Muslims in order to maintain a sustainable country.[39] An understanding of PVE as Muslim management is problematic, does not give us any useful insights and is seen by many as a post-colonial attempt to control Muslims.[40]

A moralizing and othering way of framing a problem does not drive solutions.[41, 42] It stigmatizes the concerned.[43] When it comes to social alienation, social institutions offer far more insightful ways of solving a case and preventing escalation to violence.[44, 45] Moreover, the effect of an anti-Muslim understanding of PVE is that interventions do not care for the identity development that is at the core of concerns and they push a person further away from institutions towards illegal groups.

Secondly, in the early stages of concern, radical thinking is normal. Growing through adolescence, brain development does not yet allow for very nuanced thinking.[46] Consider the youths described in the case studies. One thought he should become a very pious Muslim to make amends for all the mischief he managed. Another made dangerous decisions on a whim. This is very adolescent behaviour, whether there is a religious aspect or not.

Discussing this in training sessions for professionals,[47] they often respond that these feelings and frustrations accompanying identity formation are not limited to adolescence. To have radical thoughts or expressions is very normal although most of us do not fall through the net. The key for a coach or key figure is to look beyond extremist expressions and tap into her/his professional expertise (e.g., youth work, social work or teaching) to address the cause of frustrations.

Thirdly, and crucially, the role of the accidental hit of recruitment becomes clear. Whether someone is recruited into an alternative institution and which alternative institution is based on coincidence. That process is described by Stef Christiaensen and Amy-Jane Gielen as how continuous frustrations in identity formation and the ongoing failure of society to ensure welfare for all create a cognitive opening for radical and subsequently extreme thought.[48, 49] Which radical and/or extreme thought is a matter of chance or accidental hit. Muslims who are socially alienated need not necessarily be recruited by ISIS, just as native Flemings who are alienated need not become Flemish nationalists. Everything depends on who they will encounter when at risk of disconnection from supportive institutions. This challenges the prevailing idea that ideologies create extremism. Just as a fire needs more than fuel, violent extremism needs more than ideas.

In the cases described above, youth were looking for a certain something. A recruiter was able to offer this something in a very manipulative way, but the coach/key figure was able to offer a pathway out. Or (as in the case of the first youth) the vulnerable individual was found by a key figure before any recruiters found him. The key figure expressed empathy for his course of action but managed to gradually support him to take another path. The youth is now a happy and successful man. The second youth was looking to express himself when he was led to believe these alleged new friends would finally be the ones to make that possible. He now produces legitimate videos and has started to ask for some religious counselling. The third youth wanted to be a role model. The informal economy was the first to offer him a dream of esteem. Fortunately, he discovered a better path. In the end, I would say they all made their own way back, even though there was a brilliant catalyst (the key figure or coach) to guide them on their path.

Last, diversion requires engagement. This is the secret weapon of the case worker. If one succeeds in building trust, being there when needed, then the youth concerned will believe the message. In the first case, a youth worker, who has been around for decades and has quite a reputation, approached the youth after school on the very day the referral was made.

Policy recommendations

So far, the Mechelen City Council has allowed space for effective prevention. Other levels of government have had issues with radicalization as a problematic signifier.[50] Consequently, youth workers have had to negotiate the subsequent policies to retain even basic funding.[51] So a first and foremost policy recommendation should be to rid ourselves of counterproductive concepts and narratives.

Secondly, there is the role of the media. As Thomas Frissen suggests, a jihadi is first and foremost a marketeer.[52] Violence is a method whereby the end justifies the means. That end is to increase influence and control through the recruitment of a population. The targets group of these marketers are our policymakers who, provoked by the jihadis' violent acts, respond fiercely towards Muslims, ultimately making the latter socially alienate towards the point of recruitablity. This is a media-terror ecosystem.[53]

Going forward we must recognize the role that media plays in so-called new phenomena as well. We must understand how right-wing extremists get their discourse into mainstream media and subsequently normalized.[54] We cannot make villains of youth who develop far-right thoughts. So thirdly, the lessons learned about the nature of becoming recruitable into violent extremism must be applied to the increasing threat of the far-right in Belgium. We must not consider every socially alienated Flemish person. Rather, we should recognize that our current society is confusing and threatening in many ways,[55] for example, the climate crisis, economic crises, Covid-19 pandemic, unsolved issues of poverty and diversity, abundance of choices and decisions to make, etc. This makes reactionary ideologies like the far-right appealing to those who are socially alienated from society.

Two observations in Mechelen support this claim. It is not uncommon to hear that social care and youth work are only directed at youth from migrant backgrounds. Possibly the far right is the only one to take notice of the fact that a number of (non-Muslim) Flemish youth are structurally falling through the welfare net and the policies towards that issue remain insufficient. This needs to be looked into and addressed. There is also a popular extreme-right wing and Flemish-nationalist youth organization, Schild & Vrienden, appealing to youth with energetic speeches in social gatherings.[56] These talks are given by charismatic people. This charisma on the part of the speakers outweighs, or to some degree masks, their anti-Muslim vitriol. But these youth acknowledge this but want to pretend it is not there, because they feel so good. The youth in the audience also feel that the media also over-hypes the racism of these far-right speakers.

Last but not least, policies must account for a (the) perspective of a major stakeholder: youth. PVE policies are made in negotiations between policymakers and practitioners. The former want resolute responses to the safety issue and the latter try to acquire projects to compensate for ever-decreasing basic funding.[57] Simultaneously, PVE studies are piling up; yet, they include but a handful of studies with professionals and virtually none with youth. So we are making policies about the youth, but we do not ask them how they experience it all. Their brains might still be developing; yet, they can certainly contribute to improving policies and practices. Therefore, my next research project aims to develop insights for policymakers as to how the voice of youth can improve their politicizing.

As a certified youth worker, I must admit that the only thing that youth in Mechelen have ever asked me is for their voice to be heard. This is a blind spot in policymaking. For the feasibility of any efforts towards the socially alienated and PVE, the youth concerned must have a seat at the table as the third major stakeholder next to professionals and policymakers.

Notes

1　　Maarten De Waele, 'Belgium: Preventing Radicalisation on a Local Level and Working for an Inclusive Society', in *Terrorism, Radicalisation and Countering Violent Extremism. Practical Considerations and Concerns*, S. Jayakumar, ed. (Singapore: Springer, 2019).

2　　This was very apparent when a separatist minister of the Flemish region discontinued working with accomplished Civil Society Organisations (CSO), dealing them a financial blow and replacing them with novel CSOs, who would in turn need to request the benevolent support of the accomplished CSOs in terms of expertise. The minister also withheld previously granted subsidies, because the CSOs in question were too critical about the political push factors on radicalization. See Vlaanderen, Agency for the Interior, 'Positive Identity Development in Young People' (2021), available at: https://preventie-radicalisering-polarisering.vlaanderen.be/project/ positieve-identiteitsontwikkeling-bij-jongeren (accessed 30 June 2021), and Stef Arends, 'Homans stopt project tegen radicalisering om ideologische redenen', *apache*, 25 April 2019, available at: https://www.apache.be/2019/04/25/homans-stopt-project- tegen-radicalisering-om-ideologische-redenen/ (accessed 30 June 2021).

3　　U. Beck, 'The Terrorist Threat', *Theory, Culture & Society* 19, no. 4 (2002): 39–55; T. Eriksen, *Overheating: An Anthropology of Accelerated Change* (London: Pluto Press, 2016).

4　　A. Zijderveld, *The Waning of the Welfare State: The End of Comprehensive State Succor* (New Brunswick: Transaction, 1999).

5   Nadia Fadil and Martijn de Koning, 'Turning "Radicalization" into Science. Ambivalent Translations into the Dutch (speaking) Academic Field', in *Radicalization in Belgium and the Netherlands: Critical Perspectives on Violence and Security*, Nadia Fadil, Martijn de Koning, and Francesco Ragazzi, eds. (London: I.B. Tauris, 2019).

6   Plan M and Plan R are official plans drawn up by intelligence analysts of the anti-terror unit CUTA. See https://cuta.belgium.be/what-do-we-do/#Plan_R for more details.

7   Silke Jamine and Nadia Fadil, '(De-)Radicalization as a Negotiated Practice: An Ethnographic Case Study in Flanders', in *Radicalization in Belgium and the Netherlands: Critical Perspectives on Violence and Security*, Nadia Fadil, Martijn de Koning and Francesco Ragazzi, eds. (London: I.B. Tauris, 2019).

8   Thomas Hegghammer from the Norwegian Defence Research Establishment in Oslo reports estimations of 100–300 Belgians on a total of 1,100 to 1,700 Europeans: See Van Lommel, S., 'Belgen in koppeloton Syriëstrijders', *De Morgen*, 29 November 2013, available at: https://www.demorgen.be/nieuws/belgen-in-koppeloton-syriestrijders~b0c5ca23/ (accessed 30 June 2021).

9   T. Frissen, *(Hard)Wired for Terror: Unraveling the Mediatized Roots and Routes of 'Radicalization* (PhD dissertation, Institute for Media Studies, Faculty of Social Sciences, Katholieke Universiteit Leuven, Leuven, 2019).

10 Federal Public Service Home Affairs of Belgium, *Royal Decree on the Granting of a Security and Cohabitation Contract Allowance for Municipalities That Previously Had a Security and Cohabitation Contract in the Context of the Implementation of a Local Security and Prevention Policy for the Year 2013* (Brussels: Board of the Belgian Official Gazette, 2013).

11 This concept makes an analogy with the famous Aarhus model, which was developed in Copenhagen to serve all of Denmark on PVE. (Indeed, one would start tohypothesize PVE policies are children of Chaos.)

12 J. Van Baelen and R. Putzeys, 'Criminaliteit in Mechelen hoger dan in Antwerpen', *Archief Gazet van Antwerpen*, 21 April 1999, available at: http://www.archiefgazetvanantwerpen.be/vw/article.do?id=GVA-19990421-01003005&lm=mechel%2Ccriminaliteit&lm2=mechelen%20criminaliteit (accessed 30 June 2021).

13 B. Somers, *Mechelen: Bouwstenen voor een betere stad* (Antwerpen: Houtekiet, 2012).

14 Stef Christiaensen (ed.), *Een lokaal integraal veiligheidsplan: voor en met Mechelaars* (Mechelen: Stad Mechelen, 2007).

15 A. Van Leuven, 'Radicaliseringsbeleid als de blijvende en actieve strijd om het vertrouwen. De Mechelse integrale aanpak in radicaliseringsprocessen: een antropologische kijk', in *Cahiers politiestudies: 42. Aanpak van gewelddadige radicalisering*, M. De Waele, H. Moors, A. Garssen and J. Noppe, eds. (Antwerpen: Maklu Uitgevers, 2017).

16 Ibid.

17 A. Gielen, *Radicalisering en identiteit: Radicale rechtse en moslimjongeren vergeleken* (Amsterdam: Amsterdam University Press, 2008).

18 A. Zijderveld, *The Institutional Imperative: The Interface of Institutions and Networks* (Amsterdam: Amsterdam University Press, 2000).

19 J. Bardoel and J. van Cuilenburg, *Communicatiebeleid en communicatiemarkt: Over beleid, economie en management voor de communicatiesector* (Amsterdam: Cramwinckel, 2003).

20   Loïc Wacquant, *Urban Outcasts: A Comparative Sociology of Advanced Marginality* (Cambridge: Polity Press, 2008).

21   F. Buijs, F. Demant and A. Hamdy, *Strijders van eigen bodem: Radicale en democratische moslims in Nederland (Solidariteit en identiteit)* (Amsterdam: Amsterdam University Press, 2006); Van Leuven, 'Radicaliseringsbeleid als de blijvende en actieve strijd om het vertrouwen'.

22   OCAM (2020), 'La menace extrémiste de droite en recrudescence', *OCAM*, 18 May, available at: https://ocam.belgium.be/la-menace-extremiste-de-droite-en-recrudescence/ (accessed 30 June 2021).

23   Personally, preferring to maintain informal economy to a legal job is ideological enough for me.

24   Federal Public Service of the Interior of Belgium, *Information Management for Judicial Police and Administrative Police* (Brussels: Federal Public Service Interior, 2002).

25   Wacquant, *Urban outcasts*.

26   Anne-Sofie Versweyvelt, Johan Put and Tim Opgenhaffen, *Wegwijzers beroepsgeheim*, 2018, available at: https://www.law.kuleuven.be/isr/alle-wegwijzers (accessed 30 June 2021).

27   The role of the coördinator is mainly to keep things going: a hands-on approach, communication between stakeholders, engagement of partner organizations, reports to the Mayor and the transparent info flux with police.

28   C. Geertz, *The Interpretation of Cultures: Selected Essays* (New York: Basic Books, 2000).

29   methodsMcr, 'What Is the Case Study Method (as Used in Anthropology) by Karen Sykes', 18 August 2014, available at: https://www.youtube.com/watch?v=XkYflDloR8g&t=3s

30   C. A. Davies, *Reflexive Ethnography: A Guide to Researching Selves and Others* (Routledge: New York, 2009).

31   H. Powdermaker, 'A Woman Going Native', in *Ethnographic Fieldwork: An Anthropological Reader*, A. Robben and J. Sluka, eds. (Malden, NJ: Wiley-Blackwell, 2008).

32   Alexander Van Leuven, Stefan Mertens, Leen d'Haenens and Abdelwahed Mekki-Berrada, 'Debating the Political and Intellectual Discourse on Islam and Muslims in Flanders', in *Islamophobia, Extremism and Radicalism: Exploring the Nexus*, A. Mekki Berrada and L. d'Haenens, eds. (Leuven: Leuven University Press, forthcoming, 2023).

33   This training was developed by Kristof Everaerts and Bram De Grootte. For more information, see www.kernkracht.be

34   D. Vercammen, *The Way of Qi* (Antwerpen: TASK, 2000).

35   I. El Hadioui, *Hoe de straat de school binnendringt: Denken vanuit de pedagogische driehoek van de thuiscultuur, de schoolcultuur en de straatcultuur* (Amsterdam: Van Gennep, 2015).

36   Nadia Charkaoui, *Racisme: Over wonden en veerkracht* (Berchem: Uitgeverij EPO, 2019), 183.

37   Participants work three hours on Wednesdays, Saturdays and Sundays. That is when public places are busiest. They are payed a volunteer's wage and enter the service of the local government. They (proudly) send (an abundance of) pictures of their work to prevention workers via WhatsApp. The budget allows for twelve participants every year.

38   Frissen, *(Hard)Wired for Terror.*
39   Van Leuven, Mertens, d'Haenens and Mekki-Berrada, 'Debating the Political and Intellectual Discourse on Islam and Muslims in Flanders'.
40   Fadil and Koning, 'Turning "Radicalization" into Science'.
41   Rik Coolsaet, *All Radicalisation Is Local: The Genesis and Drawbacks of an Elusive Concept* (Brussels: Academia Press for Egmont – The Royal Institute for International Relations, 2016); Sahana Udupa and Matti Pohjonen, 'Extreme Speech and Global Digital Cultures: Introduction', *International Journal of Communication* 13 (2019): 3049–67.
42   P. Werbner, 'Essentialising Essentialism, Essentialising Silence: Ambivalence and Multiplicity in the Constructions of Racism and Ethnicity', in *Debating Cultural Hybridity. Multicultural Identities and the Politics of Anti-Racism. Critique, Influence, Change*, P. Werbner and T. Modood, eds. (London: Zed, 2015).
43   Fadil and Koning, 'Turning "Radicalization"'; Arun Kundnani, *The Muslims Are Coming! Islamophobia, Extremism and the Domestic War on Terror* (London: Verso, 2014).
44   Wacquant, *Urban Outcasts*; Buijs, Demant and Hamdy, *Strijders van eigen bodem*; Van Leuven, 'Radicaliseringsbeleid als de blijvende en actieve strijd om het vertrouwen'.
45   Zijderveld, *The Institutional Imperative.*
46   Michelle K. Jetha and Sidney J. Sagalowitz, 'Structural Brain Development in Late Childhood, Adolescence, and Early Adulthood', in *Adolescent Brain Development*, authors Michelle K. Jetha and Sidney J. Sagalowitz (Cambridge, MA: Academic Press, 2012).
47   Over the years I have trained many professionals in dealing with social alienations. These professionals worked in all the relevant social institutions: schools, employment mediation, youth work, welfare service, civil service, management, etc.
48   Belgium, *Beheersen van moslimradicalisering, Handreiking voor beleid en praktijk* (Antwerp: Tom Meeuws, 2013).
49   Gielen, *Radicalisering en identiteit.*
50   Fadil and Koning, 'Turning "Radicalization"'.
51   Debruyne, P., 'Jeugdwerk en radicalism: Dromen van een andere wereld', *sociaal.net*, 25 November 2015, available at: https://sociaal.net/opinie/jeugdwerk-en-radicalisme/ (accessed 30 June 2021); B. Van Boechaute, R. Göröz, T. Vanhove, T. Debaene, and D. Kerger, *Deradicalisering als uitdaging voor het jeugdwerk* (Ghent: Artevelde Hogeschool, 2018).
52   Frissen, *(Hard)Wired for Terror.*
53   A. Hoskins and B. O'Loughlin, 'Media and the Myth of Radicalization', *Media, War & Conflict* 2, no. 2 (2009): 107–10.
54   I. Maly, *Nieuw rechts* (Berchem: Uitgeverij EPO, 2018).
55   Beck, 'The Terrorist Threat', 39–55.
56   Schild and Vrienden, or "Shield and Friends", is a name that is has connotations of nationalism or xenophobia. It is a revival of a proverb used in the 1302 Battle of the Golden Spurs (sometimes referred to as the Battle of Courtrai) unexpectedly won by the Flemish during the Franco-Flemish War. At the battle, Flemish used this proverb as a password to distinguish the Dutch speaking Flemings from the francophone French (the French would pronounce "Schild and Vrienden" as "Skild and Vrienden").

57   S. Jaminé and N. Fadil, *Tussen Preventie en Veiligheid. De Belgische aanpak in de strijd tegen radicalisering* (Leuven: Faculty of Social Sciences, Katholieke Universiteit Leuven, 2019).

Bibliography

Bardoel, J. and van Cuilenburg, J. *Communicatiebeleid en communicatiemarkt: Over beleid, economie en management voor de communicatiesector.* Amsterdam: Cramwinckel, 2003.

Beck, U. 'The Terrorist Threat'. *Theory, Culture & Society* 19, no. 4 (2002): 39–55.

Belgium. *Beheersen van moslimradicalisering, Handreiking voor beleid en praktijk.* Antwerp: Tom Meeuws, 2013.

Buijs, F., Demant, F. and Hamdy, A. *Strijders van eigen bodem: Radicale en democratische moslims in Nederland (Solidariteit en identiteit).* Amsterdam: Amsterdam University Press, 2006.

Charkaoui, N. *Racisme: Over wonden en veerkracht.* Berchem: Uitgeverij EPO, 2019.

Christiaensen, S. (ed.). *Een lokaal integraal veiligheidsplan: voor en met Mechelaars.* Mechelen: Stad Mechelen, 2007.

Coolsaet, R. *All Radicalisation Is Local: The Genesis and Drawbacks of an Elusive Concept.* Brussels: Academia Press for Egmont – The Royal Institute for International Relations, 2016.

Davies, C. A. *Reflexive Ethnography: A Guide to Researching Selves and Others.* Routledge: New York, 2009.

De Waele, M. 'Belgium: Preventing Radicalisation on a Local Level and Working for an Inclusive Society'. In *Terrorism, Radicalisation and Countering Violent Extremism. Practical Considerations and Concerns*, S. Jayakumar, ed., 69–78. Singapore: Springer, 2019.

El Hadioui, I. *Hoe de straat de school binnendringt: Denken vanuit de pedagogische driehoek van de thuiscultuur, de schoolcultuur en de straatcultuur.* Amsterdam: Van Gennep, 2015.

Eriksen, T. *Overheating: An Anthropology of Accelerated Change.* London: Pluto Press, 2016.

Fadil, N. and Koning, Martjin de. 'Turning "Radicalization" into Science. Ambivalent Translations into the Dutch (speaking) Academic Field'. In *Radicalization in Belgium and the Netherlands: Critical Perspectives on Violence and Security*, Nadia Fadil, Martijn de Koning and Francesco Ragazzi, eds., 53–80. London: I.B. Tauris, 2019.

Federal Public Service Home Affairs of Belgium. *Royal Decree on the Granting of a Security and Cohabitation Contract Allowance for Municipalities that Previously Had a Security and Cohabitation Contract in the Context of the Implementation of a Local Security and Prevention Policy for the Year 2013.* Brussels: Board of the Belgian Official Gazette, 2013.

Federal Public Service of the Interior of Belgium. *Information Management for Judicial Police and Administrative Police.* Bruxelles: Federal Public Service Interior, 2002.

Frissen, T. *(Hard)Wired for Terror: Unraveling the Mediatized Roots and Routes of 'Radicalization'.* PhD dissertation, Institute for Media Studies, Faculty of Social Sciences, Katholieke Universiteit Leuven, Leuven, 2019.

Geertz, C. *The Interpretation of Cultures: Selected Essays.* New York: Basic Books, 2000.

Gielen, A.-J. *Radicalisering en identiteit: Radicale rechtse en moslimjongeren vergeleken.* Amsterdam: Amsterdam University Press, 2008.

Hoskins, A. and O'Loughlin, B. 'Media and the Myth of Radicalization'. *Media, War & Conflict* 2, no. 2 (2009): 107–10.

Jamine, S. and Fadil, N. '(De-)Radicalization as a Negotiated Practice: An Ethnographic Case Study in Flanders'. In *Radicalization in Belgium and the Netherlands: Critical Perspectives on Violence and Security*, Nadia Fadil, Martijn de Koning and Francesco Ragazzi, eds., 169–93. London: I.B. Tauris, 2019.

Jamine, S. and Fadil, N. '*Tussen Preventie en Veiligheid. De Belgische aanpak in de strijd tegen radicalisering*'. Leuven: Faculty of Social Sciences, Katholieke Universiteit Leuven, 2019.

Jetha, M. K. and Sagalowitz, S. J. 'Structural Brain Development in Late Childhood, Adolescence, and Early Adulthood'. In *Adolescent Brain Development*, Michelle K. Jetha and Sidney J. Sagalowitz authors, 1–18. Cambridge, MA: Academic Press, 2012.

Kundnani, A. *The Muslims are Coming! Islamophobia, Extremism and the Domestic War on Terror.* London: Verso, 2014.

Maly, I. *Nieuw rechts.* Berchem: Uitgeverij EPO, 2018.

Powdermaker, H. 'A Woman Going Native'. In *Ethnographic Fieldwork: An Anthropological Reader*, A. Robben and J. Sluka, eds., 65–75. Malden, NJ: Wiley-Blackwell, 2007.

Somers, B. *Mechelen: Bouwstenen voor een betere stad.* Antwerp: Houtekiet, 2012.

Udupa, S. and Pohjonen, M. 'Extreme Speech and Global Digital Cultures: Introduction'. *International Journal of Communication* 13 (2019): 3049–67.

Van Boechaute, B., Göröz, R., Vanhove, T., Debaene, T., and Kerger, D. *Deradicalisering als uitdaging voor het jeugdwerk.* Ghent: Artevelde Hogeschool, 2018.

Van Leuven, A. 'Radicaliseringsbeleid als de blijvende en actieve strijd om het vertrouwen. De Mechelse integrale aanpak in radicaliseringsprocessen: een antropologische kijk'. In *Cahiers politiestudies: 42. Aanpak van gewelddadige radicalisering*, M. De Waele, H. Moors, A. Garssen and J. Noppe, eds., 91–108. Antwerp: Maklu Uitgevers, 2017.

Van Leuven, A., Mertens, S., d'Haenens, L. and Mekki-Berrada, A. 'Debating the Political and Intellectual Discourse on Islam and Muslims in Flanders'. In *Islamophobia, Extremism and Radicalism: Exploring the Nexus*, A. Mekki Berrada and L. d'Haenens, eds.. Leuven: Leuven University Press, forthcoming.

Vercammen, D. *The Way of Qi.* Antwerp: TASK, 2000.

Wacquant, Loïc. *Urban Outcasts: A Comparative Sociology of Advanced Marginality.* Cambridge: Polity Press, 2008.

Werbner, P. 'Essentialising Essentialism, Essentialising Silence: Ambivalence and Multiplicity in the Constructions of Racism and Ethnicity'. In *Debating Cultural Hybridity. Multicultural Identities and the Politics of Anti-Racism. Critique, Influence, Change*, P. Werbner and T. Modood, eds., 226–55. London: Zed, 1999.

Zijderveld, A. *The Waning of the Welfare State: The End of Comprehensive State Succor.* New Brunswick: Transaction, 1999.

Zijderveld, A. *The Institutional Imperative: The Interface of Institutions and Networks.* Amsterdam: Amsterdam University Press, 2000.

4

BURO ZEND-UIT, a pilot study on co-creating resilience in the Netherlands

Stijn Sieckelinck

Contemporary extremist groups such as the Islamic State in Syria and Iraq (ISIS) operate as semi-professional employment agencies for frustrated young people.[1] They do not exploit only vulnerabilities but also talents and ideals.[2] In a programme that was piloted in Arnhem, vulnerable youngsters follow five simple steps to become more aware of their inner capacities and opportunities for personal growth. The programme was co-created by youth, youth workers, social designers and social researchers. Preliminary findings suggest that the programme in effect mirrors elements of the rites of passage evident in the journeys of foreign fighters.[3] Following this pilot, the programme was rebuilt into an online tool that can be downloaded free of charge by youth workers and policymakers in PVE. The findings have implications for the construction of programmes that aim to support young individuals in the development of their identity (and to divert them away from extremist ideology). These programmes should, as the saying goes, keep it simple and keep it real. Programmes should create a temporary safe space, avoid overly complicated constructions that distract or demotivate, approach youth as authentic as possible, and offer sufficient space for their input.

Introduction

In the Netherlands, there is no place outside the densely populated Western urban cities where more cases of jihadism have been detected in recent years other than Arnhem.[4] In the past decade, a city that never made headlines in the field of at-risk youth has become one of the breeding grounds for supporters of Islamic extremist ideology. More specifically, the Presikhaaf neighbourhood made the national news several times as a recruiting ground for Islamic extremist groups.[5] Only a small minority of young people were eventually recruited and travelled to participate in the armed struggle in Syria and Iraq, but many others struggle with feelings of alienation and are still exposed to antisocial temptations to this day.

When in 2016 the local youth workers (JW) and the youth they worked with (both predominantly from ethnic minority backgrounds[6]) were asked how they experienced growing up and what difficulties they encountered, two elements kept recurring in the answers: growing up can best be compared to an obstacle course and the greatest frustration lies in the misrecognition of their talents. The metaphor of the obstacle course was illustrated by adverse experiences at school, when applying for jobs or at internships. Sometimes there were short-lived successes, but they again created new obstacles, for example, through their parents' clashing expectations. The image emerged of an endless road full of obstacles where it is less and less clear what purpose overcoming them would eventually lead to. Moreover, one gets the impression that because of the difficulties in making progress, the talents one possesses remain unnoticed. Teachers and parents are particularly interested in school performance and good behaviour. As a result, they do not always recognize what else a child has to offer. This goes at the cost of the youth's motivation and that is why local youth workers started a remarkable initiative with the goal to build resilience by better attending to their youth's talents and ideals.

The pilot for the programme was carried out with support of the municipality of Arnhem. The research was funded by a scientific grant for social innovation and involved close collaboration with the local policymakers and co-creation with social professionals and their youth at all stages of the project. The locus of action was the youth work service provider, Presikhaaf University (PU).

The civil non-profit organization Presikhaaf University in Arnhem was founded when two mothers reported that they could not afford commercially offered homework assistance. The Presikhaaf neighbourhood has a reputation in terms of crime[7] and more specifically radicalization.[8] Many families live in poverty, in broken households, and their children are more likely to have lower educational qualifications and attainments than their peers elsewhere in Arnhem. In one of the many interviews we did, the youth workers who initiated PU – which is not an institute for higher education, but suggests quality and good prospects – presented themselves as advocates of these youth. In general, youth workers have access to groups of young people, some of whom may be susceptible to social alienation, who are more difficult to reach and approach due to their inadequate connection to the institutions. These professionals are active in the world of young people, know their way around 'the street' and have a good idea of possible locations such as where young people gather in their leisure time; they have the know-how and expertise to be able to intervene at the level of young people, and as such connect the world of institutions with their environment. The founders of PU disagree when they are called just another educational service provider. Yes, they do homework support, but 'what we do is not what we are'. Their goal is clear: the children deserve more than they are getting right now. They are not given the opportunities they should be given. This seriously influences their self-image. Through PU, they want to build resilience by tackling identity issues at the core, in a holistic manner that involves the entire environment of children and young people. In one of the founder's own words: 'There should be room to work with the hope and anger that comes with the formation of identity'. PU has co-developed Buro Zend-Uit[9] (BZU) as its mentoring programme. For youth workers, working with BZU is a way to get closer to the young people in a short time and to gain more insight into their talents and opportunities.

To capture this process scientifically, an intensive action research design was used, making use of a partnership approach in which every member was asked to fulfill a clear role.[10] From the beginning, there was awareness of the ethical dimensions of this undertaking. How can a data collection tool be used to benefit not only the researcher but also the professional and his or her relationship with the young person? Early attempts to standardize data to increase comparisons and generalizability were re-evaluated. It should be noted that the effect of standardized questionnaires was particularly confrontational: the young people suddenly found themselves in a much more school-like position vis-à-vis the youth worker than they were used to. It was decided to use the standardized questionnaire only as a 'talking paper' (guide). In our opinion, this not only provided a much more natural situation but produced many valuable insights about the youth's experience of life challenges, as we will show further.

Challenges

BZU was borne out of experiences with structural discrimination: the acute threat of radicalization that has repeatedly been identified in the biographies of many Arnhem youth from Presikhaaf.

Structural condition: Discrimination in the labour market. Recent research shows that applicants with a migrant background were 30 per cent less likely to receive a positive response from employers than identically qualified applicants with a Dutch background.[11] Some sources suggest that the labour market gap between people with and without a migrant background is greater in the Netherlands than in most other European countries.[12] The public TV station ran the headline: 'Who is going to solve this? The short-term employment agencies] are apparently unable to put things in order.'[13] Time and time again, it is revealed that temporary employment agencies select for characteristics that should not matter by law. This persistent discrimination is experienced by young people from ethnic minority backgrounds who are distanced from the labour market. While Prime Minister Rutte agreed that discrimination in the labour market played an important role in the lack of equal opportunities, he contended that the government cannot solve this problem, 'The paradox is that the solution lies with Mohammed. Immigrants have always had to adapt and have always faced prejudice and discrimination. You have to fight.' Researchers, however, have concluded that applicants from ethnic minority groups cannot in fact do a great deal themselves to increase their chances on the labour market as Rutte suggested. For many young people there is frustration but also acquiescence. In others, it leads to combativeness and/or to further social alienation, increasing the attractiveness of the criminal/extremist milieu.

Acute condition: Several young inhabitants of Arnhem have travelled to foreign conflict areas. At the end of 2018, the number of radicalized young people with extremist Islamic ideas in Arnhem was twenty-nine.[14] Of the twenty-nine, six actually travelled to participate in *jihad* and at least one of these has died. Five have returned from the war zone. Eighteen others considered participating in the conflict. Reports show that jihadists are better organized than before and recruit more professionally. Judging by the interviews we did, they developed into a semi-professional employment agency for frustrated young people: they exploit not only vulnerabilities but also hidden talents. Vulnerabilities and talents are abundant among the young people who are reached by the youth workers. Our analysis of the risks associated with leaving these vulnerabilities and talents unseen is consistent with the characterization of terrorism scholar Scott Atran who encapsulates terror group ISIS's recruitment strategy as 'For all frustrated and suicidals: We have a job for you!'[15] Hence, both sides are appealing to some aspect of the individual that is usually not seen ('talents'). Moreover, the reality is that an extremist group like ISIS can present itself as the only employment agency where young people with a non-Dutch name are not discriminated against or might even have an advantage.

From the above, it is clear that the unseen talents due to unequal labour market conditions may be noticed and empowered by the antisocial milieu. Therefore, the programme's goal was to appeal to some aspect of the individual that is usually not seen ('talents').

Almost all young people who 'study' at PU find themselves in a position of vulnerability around their talents. The major obstacles they experience in their development arise not so much because of a lack of capacity but have to do with the environment in which they are brought up, go to school and are socialized. In a number of cases, there is so much pressure on the young person from different sides that they withdraw or show flight behaviour in order not to be constantly confronted with their hardships. Their resilience is therefore put to the test, which increases the need to find resources in the area.[16]

First, their families suffer from loss. In one of the interviews, we met a fifteen-year-old girl, Dorien. Behind her friendly smile, the interview revealed a lot of pain and sorrow. Dorien, it turns out, cries herself to sleep as the daughter of a single mother in a family of four children, of whom the youngest is placed outside of the home. The father, who was born in one of the Carribean ex-colonies of the Netherlands, has left the family and Dorien indicates that she no longer has any illusions about his role. 'She does not expect anything more from him, ever again', said the youth worker. For several respondents, their relationship with their fathers has been seriously disrupted, broken or is complicated. The youth workers signal that without help, the family seems incapable of addressing this grief. Therefore, they got in touch with the mother and invited Dorien to benefit from extra after-school activities.

Second, the interviews indicate that school is usually not the place where these young people can leave their sorrows from home behind, due to a lack of counselling services, missing credible role models, or a mismatch in what is offered to and what is desired by the pupil. Nor is the formal educational space a place where they experience growth. This lack of connection makes them very vulnerable because there is on the part of many of these young individuals a great will to grow and to prove themselves. In the interviews, almost all references to education were negative, with only a few exceptions. For instance, a sixteen-year-old boy actively helps his mother in the household at home and is described by his loved ones as extremely helpful but is constantly in trouble at school and on his internship. Like him, most of the young people have very few positive experiences at school and they do not achieve the results one would expect based on the talents they managed to display in the BZU programme.

For every individual participating in this programme, the two key areas of socialization and identity development, home and school, are sources of stress rather than resilience. Take as a final example, a seventeen-year-old young lady, Esther. Her childhood was marked by some far-reaching events. She moved to the Netherlands at the age of six, obviously with a considerable language delay, and lost her father at a very young age. In addition, she recently had to deal with a number of serious setbacks: she was not allowed to take a certain test to pass her education, her veil (*hijab*) was made into a problem in one grade, and on top of that she was recently a victim of racism on the street. Her invitation to BZU came 'at the right moment' as it helped her to examine her own capacity in times of uncertainty. It also inspired her to (re)formulate goals and take part in prosocial actions. This exercise helped her to rebuild trust and regain strength in times of high pressure on her identity and 'made her grow as a person'.

The practice

We click on the file of the second interview. The download takes a while before the images appear. The first thing we see from Michel[17] is the crown of his head above an Adidas sports suit. While carefully inspecting the completed forms, he is bending so much over that the famous three stripes on the shoulders seem to come out of his ears. Here sits a boy who wants to know what people have written about him and plans to get the most out of it. Then he finally straightens up and a radiant smile appears. 'My mother has written beautiful things.' A full two hours and seven minutes later, all the forms are carefully examined and an unseen journey has been made in the head above the three stripes. We have witnessed how this boy, persistently looking for the right words, had the courage to turn himself into a study object and has 'come out' as a more talent-aware youngster.

In BZU, young people help each other to work towards an examined and visualized self-portrait. In five well-defined steps, their inner world and the expectations of the outside world are explored. Following (1) an invitation and (2) an informal 360° review by their closest elders and peers, the youth is invited by the youth worker for (3) a one-on-one interview about his or her capacities, and subsequently intensively supported and assisted in (4) upgrading his or her life goals. This process, finally, is reported by the youth worker who is (5) filmed with the youth's phone camera, highlighting the young person's talents: What is his/her capacity? Who is to his/her support? What steps can (s)he take? BZU is aimed at all young people who want to work on their growth and is extra relevant for young people who are unaware of their talents and how they could develop these in relation to the wider society.

The main inclusion criterion is the extent to which a young person appears to be aware of vulnerabilities and talents in the eyes of youth workers. It is striking that both a lack of awareness and high awareness make young people less eligible to participate. The programme seems to work best for kids who are uncertain about but not totally unaware of their capacities. Moreover, young people who go through hard times affecting their basic safety or functioning are (temporarily) excluded from participation. This leads us to describe the target group of BZU as young people with low awareness of their vulnerabilities and talents, who are minimally capable of engaging in self-examination.

The following steps were taken by the research participants.

Step 1: Recruiting youth

In the first step, there was mutual consultation between youth workers about which young people from the vulnerable group would be selected for the project. This involved looking at fifteen individuals who could benefit from it. The selection was carefully made on the basis of the knowledge that the youth workers have about the personal situation of the young people. Based on the PVE literature,[18] we asked them to select individuals who do not really know who they are, in what positive direction they can go, or are unsure about themselves and their role in society. The selected young people were then approached one-on-one by the youth workers. The youth workers provided substantive information about the project and why they thought the youth could benefit from it. A couple of days later the youth were asked (via the app or face-to-face) whether they had given it some thought and whether they wanted to participate. In this, the youth workers also asked why they did or did not want to participate, so that the motivation was clear to them. This first step created a first shared commitment to the project.

Step 2: The 360 forms

The youth worker handed out five 360° review forms to twelve individuals who confirm participation. The form was accompanied by a brief explanation and a consultation about which five persons could be suitable as personal 'talent scouts'. Once the forms were handed out, the youth workers contacted the youth to remind them of the forms and ask them if they were able to reach out to their self-picked talent scouts and if not, what could be done to facilitate this. In some cases, this led to a personal conversation in which the youth workers went further with the young people in search of why he/she found it difficult to ask these people as talent scouts. Subsequently, all the completed forms were collected. The youth workers analysed the forms and looked for patterns or surprises. Again, the youth workers kept their own knowledge of the young people in the back of their mind to see whether they recognize things or not at all. The two youth workers discussed this analysis at length with each other, as preparation for the interview that would soon follow.

Step 3: Interview

The interview is held between one youth worker and one young person in a darkened, closed room that creates an intense, penetrating atmosphere. During this interview, the youth worker talks to the young person about the findings in the talent forms. The youth worker uses a (semi) open interview style in which use was made of a pre-prepared questionnaire and the completed talent forms. However, the youth worker takes plenty of time to ask follow-up questions or to alter and add questions based on the course of the interview. The interview is fully recorded on the youth's personal phone. The young person is told in advance that they are the owner of the images and that they can show them to others (including the youth workers) only if they want to. At the end of the interview, it is revealed which vulnerabilities and talents of the young person had emerged in the conversation. When the interview is done, the youth worker invites the young person to come by no later than a week later to complete the process.

Step 4: Debriefing and reflection

After conducting the interview with the young person, the two youth workers have a conversation (debriefing) about how the interview went (only one youth worker conducts the interview). The youth workers consulted with each other about what emerged in the interview as being the talent of the young person and what this means for the future in the coaching of the young person. In several cases, the discovered talent could be used in assigning other tasks and roles to the young person or in helping to find a suitable course of study or internship.

Step 5: Turning the tables

From the interview and the reflection on the interview, the youth worker obtains information that provides insight into the vulnerabilities and talents of the young person. With this information in mind, the youth worker invites the young person to review the process one last time. When the young person arrives, the youth worker places himself in front of the screen and asked the young person to turn on her/his phone. Then the youngster filmed the youth worker in which he reported about the process – based on his reflection – which talents he noticed and what is worth telling about the youngster. A maximum of five minutes is filmed in total. The video material is not edited, as sharing the experience rather than exact wording is judged important. The recording of the short follow-up where the youth worker reports from the in-depth interview is now on the young person's phone and can be used to introduce themselves in situations where this may be useful. This introduction may be suitable for sending to (potential) employers as an attachment to an application; alternatively, the young person may prefer to keep her/his personal introduction movie close as a souvenir and only show it to those who are trusted.

A couple of weeks later, a final discussion takes place between the youth workers and the participant. In this final interview, the young person is asked in which situations the introduction video on their own phone could come in handy. The intervention ends with a celebration of the achieved goals. Also during this conversation, an evaluation takes place: the young person is asked what he/she thought of the programme, what he/she learned from it and, in particular, what this means for the future. During this final interview, new plans are made in close collaboration with the young person to make the most of his/her talent.

We click on the next file. The video starts with a 'behind the scenes' spectacle. Muttered words as cameras are positioned, and a lot of teenage noise seems to come from the room next door. After a few minutes, the chaos is gone, and the camera is fixed on a young Black boy, Arie. We were told he is the silent force, not only on the soccer pitch but also at his fatherless home. What we see is that Arie is clearly too old for a child but still too young for an adult. He shows a big yawn, a clenched fist going to the mouth and the lips being moistened. Arie gives a somewhat tired impression in the first images, although it can also be nerves. With his black sweater and dark pants, he almost completely disappears into the decor. Maybe that's why he looks around a bit hesitantly. Once the conversation starts, it is clear that Arie and the interviewer know each other quite well. In this moment of mutual trust, Arie takes all questions seriously. Every now and then he looks down and seems to drift a bit away in his mind. But that is only appearance – this boy does not lose focus. When he cannot find the right words, he turns to gesticulating to avoid misunderstanding. Still, there is a lot of uncertainty in Arie, reinforced by some questions, such as: 'What side of yourself do you not show outside of the family?' 'And what does it mean when people see a natural leader in you?' These are the type of questions that are not asked every day. The interview clocks in at one hour and forty-three minutes. Meanwhile, fatigue and nerves have given way to a look that radiates confidence and relief. Arie pays attention until the finale. He speaks of a 'liberation' and the fragment ends as it started: behind the scene with what is most certainly a big hug.

Theory

The Buro Zend-Uit programme aims to support the search for young people who are at risk of losing faith in their own capacities. In the programme, 'identity' is considered an interaction between self-image ('Who am I?'), presentation ('What do I show to the world?') and attribution ('How does the world see me?').[19] In order to develop resilience, these three dimensions must be more or less in line with each other. Unfortunately, due to discrimination and polarization, this cohesion is frequently disrupted in socially painful confrontations and too rarely do educators manage to stimulate congruence. The programme, therefore, intends to support professionals so they can better guide this identity-formation process. A threefold theory of change was formulated: (1) anyone who gains insight into how he or she is perceived as a person by his or her close environment will find it easier to find his own talents[20]; (2) those who become more aware of their talents will do their best to show them and those who use their talents are more appreciated[21]; and (3) those who feel valued are less susceptible to destructive solutions to problems and thus better able to cope with the temptations of crime and extremism.[22]

Growing up is sometimes accompanied by strong feelings and beliefs. In the transition from childhood to adulthood, young people are sensitive and unpredictable. Because their lives actually take on a new shape, they are sometimes drawn to extremes. They can be manic one day and depressed the next. When the environment has little regard for this, frustration can increase and sometimes the only thing left is to run or fight in the eyes of the young person. For some, a fascination arises for the sacrificial spirit of heroes or for eternal life. In this way feelings of emptiness, invisibility and deep loneliness can be negated. The tragedy is that the young person is often only noticed by the adults around him when he falls into some excess. This applies to both boys and girls, although the excesses of girls are usually more harmful to themselves than to their environment.[23] Initiation of young people and guidance in adulthood are crucial opportunities for society to instil the values that preserve rather than destroy (the meaning of) life and the world. This meaning always has a social, spiritual and possibly religious character.[24] In any case, rituals of change help us to better understand the unstable period of adolescence.

Three phases can be derived from the literature surrounding *rites de passage*: first, distance yourself from existing (self) laws; second, endure a period of uncertainty (no man's land); third, find a new 'home' where other laws apply to eventually find acceptance of the new self in the old context. The structure of successful *rites de passage* unambiguously portrays the importance of boundaries and perspectives, in short of adult involvement. Recent research on young people who have migrated to the Caliphate from the Low Countries has shown strongly that they lacked confidence and were looking for something bigger to be part of. They organized their own rite of passage: they wanted to make a new start at the expense of everyone and everything,[25] including cutting off strong ties with relatives and (critical) friends, and/or destroying prospects of promising professional careers. The (absence of a guided) rite of passage also appears regularly in research into the backgrounds of crime and addiction.[26] The idea is that evolving consciousness requires certain structures, anchor points in time that mark change and point the way to the future.

In many conventional settings, however, rites of passage are no longer part of the youthful world and have largely been replaced by ceremonies that have a ritual function for some youths but seem very implausible to many. What happens then is that young people create their own rites. But because adolescents alone cannot fully determine what is of value to themselves, this actually always ends in disaster.[27] Certainly, when one comes from a less warm nest or is seen as a social burden, one can become particularly susceptible to a destructive lifestyle. Everywhere where 'normal' life threatens to end, where people no longer see a way out, young people can become caught in addiction, become obsessed with destructive images, engage in violent behaviour, or feel torn by grief and loss. It is precisely at such moments that the need for rites appears on the surface, but if one is left to that end, it remains unsuccessful attempts to give one's own life a new direction. Hence the importance of a strong pedagogical environment: without any adult guidance and limitation, adolescents cannot impart meanings to their experiences, feelings and beliefs necessary to grow internally.

Social initiatives aimed at combating criminal recruitment or violent radicalization not only fire counter-narratives but provide a space in which two elements are equally represented: an element of responsiveness and an element of restriction.[28] Desired characteristics of talent-oriented projects are described in a similar way by Kooijmans[29]: social and robust. Young people prefer to end up in a path where they really have to do their best, but where the atmosphere is inclusive and inviting and thus leads to better performance. Informal sports and artistic projects, for example, appear to have a protective effect on participants who have not yet come into contact with crime, but who run an increased risk. For these young people, the talent-oriented projects not only have a preventive effect, but they also have a 'promotional' effect on their identities: beneficial and stimulating.[30] Young people who immerse themselves in these projects will make better efforts and gradually show more constructive and pro-social behaviour. BZU's interventions in this respect are especially useful in the case of young people who are attracted by the norms and values of the 'street', but for whom other routes are also open. Effectiveness revolves around touching and appealing to certain dimensions that reflect the internal dynamics (backstage) and the external dynamics (frontstage) of the interactions: the emotions, aspirations, relationships and behaviour of young people. Kooijmans describes well how young people should be subtly unbalanced in order to successfully complete a talent development process. It is always about providing young people with the right support in their loops of confusion and wonder (both backstage) and connection and embodiment (both frontstage). This knowledge comes together in the model given in Figure 4.1:

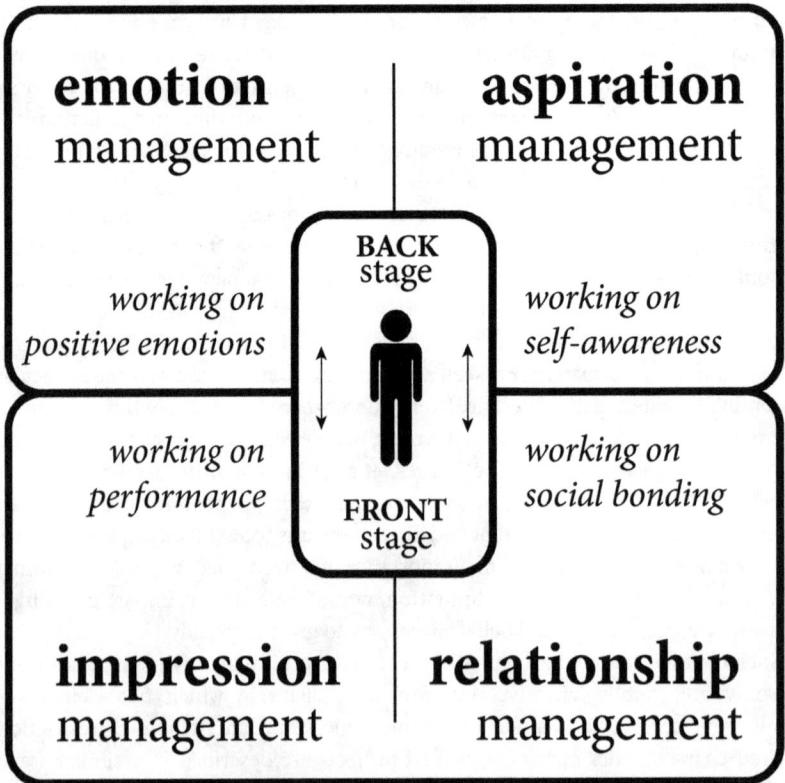

Figure 4.1 Kooijmans' model, translated (2017).

Outcomes

Youth Worker1 You ask what happens in the interviews?

Youth Worker2 You really start to understand

YouthWorker1 What kind of youth do I have here before me now?

Youth Worker2 You also start from things that come out of the forms

Youth Worker1 But you also give it a twist

Youth Worker2 Make it practical

YouthWorker 1 This is coming forward!

Youth Worker2 But could it also mean that?

BZU's main aim was to empower boys and girls in socially vulnerable positions to master their own search for talent in order to better withstand the call of antisocial temptations and to help young people to see and create a path for the future. The reason for the programme was the appeal of criminal networks and extremist groups to young people in search of identity. The programme invites young people to express their experiences and feelings in unexplored ways. Through the programme, a majority of participants experienced growth, development and self-realization, acquiring a more defined idea of their life goals. Some also showed more awareness of how to develop their talent(s) and how to deal better with discouraging situations (rejection or negative feedback), feelings of exclusion and antisocial temptations. This provides motivation and a sense of purpose. In one of the last interviews, the youth workers gave the following explanation: 'I guess it's how it makes them feel. Look, with us they are made a little bit immortal. They get the feeling that they can handle anything. This makes them fly, they start to believe in it and they will actually do it. Generally speaking, at school, they are more often addressed for what they are not doing well.'[31]

It is striking to hear how often the participants mention the significance of the mere act of setting self-dictated goals. It turns out this attitude is in strong contrast with the way they are used to setting goals in daily life. As one of the participating youth said in one of the concluding focus groups,[32] 'We (say street culture) cannot easily admit it: I am in need of this; I'm going to see how I can develop myself; can find myself.' According to another participant, the programme helps them focus on discovering a better version of themselves and positive goals would never have been formulated without the in-depth discussions with youth workers: 'Knowing your talents will help you gain confidence. I would never have realized my goals without in-depth conversations with Youth Worker1 and Youth Worker2.' According to him, this is closely linked to the problem of crime and the lure of extremism: 'I know a super smart boy in the second year, he gets recognition by extremist Muslims, was really part of it, appreciated him for what he was good at. In his eyes, these were cool guys, but they set harmful goals. So you need people who help you set positive goals. BZU can help with that.'

The programme invites youth to think about improving their selves in myriad ways. For example, another participant reflected in the same session on what the answers to the talent form did to him, 'If this is the image you want to give, it is positive. But if this is not the image you want to see of yourself, it is also positive, because then you can work on it.' Formulating goals for the future offers young people perspective and helps young people to make the right choices and pursue their dreams with more confidence. '[Here] it is not certain in advance what you will do. On Snap [chat] and on Insta[gram] you know what will happen, same when applying for a job. But here, you don't know. [It's] not about most likes, not about being seen. [This is also] not a school assignment. Motivation comes from elsewhere: being your own boss "about your self-image"'.[33]

In one of the many conversations we had with the youth workers,[34] the low ambition that some young people show in places where they are judged was discussed. Youth Worker2 said, 'If they want [a grading of] 6, the boy shows a 6. But we [expect to] see a 10.'; 'We place them super high, but do not let it be accompanied by pressure.' Youth Worker1 said, 'We want to let the youngsters get the most out of themselves. If you get that engine going.' High expectations are essential, but there is also an interesting role for vulnerability on the part of the youth workers. Looking back at the programme, the pioneers – the first youth to participate in the pilot – indicated that this programme differs from other pathways in that it forces them to be vulnerable. This positive form of vulnerability is made possible because the youth worker's attitude is one of vulnerability as well: 'I show myself as a person. Many young people think that I am perfect, that I was the ideal son-in-law, but I want to show them my pitfalls, my grief.' Youth Worker1 makes an effort to adjust the perfect image that young people (want to) have of him. 'Sometimes young people see professionals as superheroes.' He then tells them about his own identity crises, his peaks and troughs. Also, about the demanding task of being a good husband and father as well as a good youth coach, so that young person understands, 'He (the youth worker) is only human.' According to Youth Worker1, vulnerability requires that one is willing to show a picture of oneself that others initially do not (want to) see, because they want to look up to someone. Vulnerability paradoxically appears here as a strength, as a quality that makes one more credible in the eyes of the young people and helps to open up hearts and minds. As one of the youngsters said, 'Youth Worker1 shows something of himself, so then I dare to expose myself as well.'

Overall, the young persons seem to have gained a better idea of how they are viewed and are left with a tangible instrument that may be really helpful on various occasions: a video to introduce themselves in difficult situations, or a souvenir to recall the journey in which the relationship was deepened or to just be reminded of how they are valued by significant others. The video also serves a purpose to remind the individual about the goals they have set to pursue, tangible proof of the increased awareness of how their talents can help them in daily life, and if desired it is possible to use these in fighting for a better position in society, for example, during applications, job selections or auditions.

The Theory of Change was corroborated: youth who gain insight into how they are perceived by their significant others will find it easier to trace their own talents. Those who become more aware of their talents will do their best to show or live by them. Those who use their talents are valued more socially. Those who feel valued are less

Context	⇨	Talents	⇨	Person	⇨	Life goals	⇨	Straight path

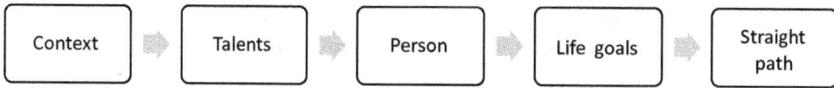

Figure 4.2 Phases in BZU.

susceptible to destructive solutions to problems and are thus better protected against the criminal and/or extremist milieu. At the same time, the programme reflects the three components known from the rite of passage literature (initiation, transformation and reintegration), as explained above. In other words, the fragility inherent to important life transitions is structured and supported. Schematically, the programme looks like the one mentioned in Figure 4.2:

	Phase 1: Initiation	**Phase 2: Transformation**	**Phase 3: Re-integration**
Time	4 weeks	4 weeks	1 week
Instrument	360° review form	Pop-up studio	Introduction
Place	Network	Safe Place	Youth Centre
Youth	Contact scouts	Self-examination	A new start
Youth Worker Actions	Reflection	Go in-depth	Concluding
Youth Worker Attitude	Non-judgemental	Vulnerable	Support and direction

The programme was co-developed with youth, youth workers, social designers and social researchers. For PU, youth participation is not just a perspective, but an everyday practice. The development of the programme has benefitted greatly from the contributions of young people as junior researchers to their own situation. Not only was the content of their ideas often ingenious, but the young people also brought an energy to the table that kept the whole team going. Moreover, it was the youth who put together a technical support team, aimed at troubleshooting challenges with ICT equipment, recording, video editing and the development of the programme's website interface. It shows that young people can be approached not only as a target group but also as a 'resource group' of intervention ideas.

A final finding concerns the position of the professionals: the two central youth workers used to be under contract with a large regional welfare organization, but no longer felt supported in their efforts to develop and run new and better-tailored services for their youth. Their move away from their employer obviously had an unanticipated impact on the research practice. More fundamentally, this event raises a question: What does it mean if none of these professionals (who consciously try to innovate their programmes to the needs of their target group) see a place in the regular welfare organizational structures to develop their activities? For PU, this was a clear signal that it was time to stop following directives from above and to reach out more to other organizations for building a strong pedagogical alliance on an equal footing. Since then, they have become active in various inter-professional forums where discussions take place about the themes that hit the youth the hardest in a district like Presikhaaf.

They started partnering with other services and have gained a lot of credit amongst policy and field actors in record time, as this confident quote from one of the founders shows: 'In a municipality like Arnhem, people work with a Local Educational Agenda. They meet every so often. But why are there only formal educational professionals involved? We can speak to all teachers.'[35]

Discussion

The BZU mentoring programme of Presikhaaf University, it seems, helps young people in socially vulnerable positions use their talents elsewhere than in an extreme or criminal group. In the mentoring programme, young people from vulnerable positions with hidden talents gain more insight and grip on their strengths (talents), opportunities and possibilities, and learn to expose themselves to the outside world in a more resilient way. One conclusion of this action research on BZU suggests that the programme in effect mirrors elements of the rites of passage evident in the journeys of foreign fighters.[36] Another conclusion is that programmes that aim to support young people in their identity development should 'keep it close, keep it simple, and keep it real'. One should ensure proximity to create a temporary safe space; complicated constructions that distract or demotivate should be avoided. The approach to the youth is kept as authentic as possible and offers sufficient space for their input. An equal dialogue between partners beyond ages is a catalyst for genuine dialogue and improvement.

Meanwhile, the complexities of participatory action research require attention to certain limits: the first limitation is the small scale on which the pilot was run. While the initial idea was to run the programme in several places in the Netherlands, it was eventually decided to keep the focus of the research very local. The decisive factor was the already-established bond between local professionals, designers and researchers. Also, as we were in a phase of trial and error, it was considered unwise and unethical to try our programme at this preliminary stage on more young people in vulnerable positions. The two main features of the chosen research strategy were 'depth' and 'precision' and, above all, shared step-by-step insights through a partnership approach. Whereas initially the question 'Does the programme work?' led, the focus increasingly shifted to the question: 'How does it work for these young people in Arnhem?' We realize that this may go against generalizability, but it does not change the value of the outcomes of the programme for the young people in this pilot.

As for validity, the question is: 'Did we register what we intended to register and measure what we wanted to measure?' We believe the following three elements add to the validity: We have obtained very personal, intimate data from young people in serious situations of vulnerability, in a municipality that used to be a recruitment area for extremist groups. Throughout the process, talents were discovered in the youths that had barely been noticed or developed before. Regarding reliability, we have to ask ourselves the question: Is this research reproducible? If one investigated the same phenomena again and the circumstances had not changed, then we indeed expect to find more or less the same result as shown in the results. The research can therefore be called reliable. But caution is necessary: even though we are convinced that certain insights are worthwhile for activities that transcend the Arnhem context, an elaborate transfer, an intelligent translation adapted to specific contexts that differ from the original, is always necessary.

Following the pilot, the programme was rebuilt into an online tool that can be downloaded free of charge by youth workers and policymakers in PVE: Burozend-uit.nl. On this website, aimed at both pedagogical professionals and young people, the visitor is taken on five clear steps along the route of the programme. Each step is introduced with a short video in which two youth workers explain what needs to be done. In each step, in addition to instructions, viewers will also find materials that are necessary for the implementation of the programme. The implementation is as simple as possible and the requirements are minimal to make the barriers to participation as low as possible. In addition to an 'IKEA-style' manual, five attachments are available free of charge to guide the user through the programme. The website is designed in such a way that autonomous use is possible. However, it is recommended that users contact the project team via s.sieckelinck@hva.nl, so that an experienced professional can assist with set-up and instruction. Upscaling is also to be expected across sectors. Where the programme was able to arise within the framework of youth work, there is now a lot of interest from colleges and municipalities outside of Arnhem, creating a huge potential for highly needed follow-up research.

Notes

1   S. Atran, 'The Youth Need Values and Dreams'. United Nations Address to the Security Council on 23 April 2015, at youtube.com/watch?v=qlbirlSA-dc.

2   S. Sieckelinck, *Reradicaliseren. Ronselen voor een betere wereld* (Leuven: Lannoo Campus, 2017).

3   M. Van San, *Kalifaatontvluchters [Escaping the Caliphate]* (Amsterdam: Prometheus, 2019).

4   NCTV. *Dreigingsbeeld Terrorisme* [Overview of terrorist threats] Vol. 49, February 2019.

5   C. Rosman, 'Alle lijntjes wijzen weer naar Arnhem, even dé jihadstad van Nederland' [All signs point to Arnhem again, the jihadi capital of the Netherlands], *Algemeen Dagblad*, 28 September 2018.

6   The youths' names in this chapter have been fictionalized for privacy purposes. On request of the respondents, we opted for typical native Dutch names.

7   See https://arnhem.incijfers.nl/jive/report/?id=kernwijkact&input_geo=wijk_4.

8   Since 2013, sixty-nine individual cases have been registered in Arnhem. Of these, thirty-six were still ongoing. Of these, ten have left for Syria and seven have been detained. Of the seven suspects of a big plot foiled in 2018, six had links to the Presikhaaf neighbourhood.

9   The name Buro Zend-Uit is a reference to the Dutch word for 'short-term employment agency', *uitzendbureau*, where the focus, more than in the English term, is on the act of 'sending', similar to 'broadcasting'.

10   I was involved as an academic in this empirical research on location, working together with the practitioners and the youth to come up with a better solution for

the problems some of the youth were dealing with. This process was observed and analysed by me and two colleagues Saskia Wernaart and Maike Kooijmans.

11 As we learn from research by the Universiteit van Amsterdam and Universiteit Utrecht, July 2019: https://www.uu.nl/nieuws/gediscrimineerde-sollicitant-kan-weinig-doen-om-baankans-te-vergroten

12 De Volkskrant, *Allochtoon erg slecht af op Nederlandse arbeidsmarkt* [Allochtoneous Citizens Worse off in Dutch Job Market] https://www.volkskrant.nl/economie/allochtoon-erg-slecht-af-op-nederlandse-arbeidsmarkt~bf882e77/?akamaiType=FREE (2015).

13 NOS, *Wie controleert of uitzendbureaus discrimineren? Nou, niemand* [Who Sees to It That the Employment Agencies Do Not Discriminate? Well, No One], 31 January 2018.

14 A. Kouwenhoven, 'Hoe een clubje uit Arnhem de jihad ging omarmen' [How a Club from Arnhem Came to Embrace the Jihad], *NRC Handelsblad*, 28 September 2018; B. Winters, 'Waarom Arnhem een jihadnest is.' [Why Arnhem Is a Jihadi Breeding Ground], *De Gelderlander*, 29 September 2018, available at: https://www.gelderlander.nl/arnhem/waarom-arnhem-een-jihadnest-is~a93f54e2/?referrer=https://www.google.com/ (accessed 1 December 2018).

15 See https://www.human.nl/onbehagen/kijk/interviews/scottatran.html

16 Michael Ungar (ed.), *The Social Ecology of Resilience: A Handbook of Theory and Practice* (New York: Springer, 2012).

17 For privacy purposes, all names of the youth have been fictionalized. In accordance with the youth, who are structurally discriminated against due to their foreign-sounding names, we decided to change their original names into typical Dutch names for this report.

18 For example, A. R. Feddes, L. Mann, and B. Doosje, 'Increasing Self-esteem and Empathy to Prevent Violent Radicalization: A Longitudinal Quantitative Evaluation of a Resilience Training Focused on Adolescents with a Dual Identity', *Journal of Applied Social Psychology* 45, no. 7 (2015): 400–11.; A. Kruglanski, J. Bélanger, and R. Gunaratna, *The Three Pillars of Radicalization: Needs, Narratives, and Networks* (Oxford University Press, 2019).

19 N. Heinich, *Wat identiteit niet is* [What Identity Is Not] (Amsterdam: Prometheus, 2019).

20 M. Ungar, *I Still Love You: Nine Things Troubled Kids Need from Their Parents* (Hamilton: Dundurn Group, 2014).

21 Kooijmans, M. *Talent van de straat. Hoe we jongeren kunnen verleiden uit de criminaliteit te blijven* [Talents from the Streets. How Youth Can Be Seduced to Stay Away from Crime] (Amsterdam: Van Gennep, 2017); I. Van Hoorik. (Hoe) Werkt talentontwikkeling bij 'risicojongeren'? [How Does Talent Development Work for Youth-at-risk?] Nederlands Jeugd Instituut, 2011.

22 J. L. Marret, A. R. Feddes, L. Mann, B. Doosje, and H. Griffioen-Young, 'An Overview of the SAFIRE Project: A Scientific Approach to Finding Indicators and Responses to Radicalization', *Journal EXIT-Deutschland: Zeitschrift für Deradikalisierung und demokratische Kultur [Journal for Deradicalization and democratic culture]* 2 (2013): 123–48; M. De Winter, *Verbeter de wereld, begin bij de opvoeding* [Improve the World, Start by Educating] (Amsterdam: SWP, 2013).

23 As is generally known in psychology, girls show more internalizing problem behaviour while boys generally externalize their problems more.

24 J. Campbell, *Hero with a Thousand Faces. The Collected Works of Joseph Campbell* (New York: New World Library, 1949).

25 Read how they distanced themselves from close relatives in, for example, Van San, *Kalifaatontvluchters*.
26 L. C. Mahdi, N. G. Christopher, and M. Meade, *Crossroads. The Quest for Contemporary Rites of Passage* (London: Open Court, 1998).
27 Campbell, *Hero with a Thousand Faces*.
28 Sieckelinck (in review), 'van Talent van de straat. Hoe je jongeren kunt verleiden uit de criminaliteit te blijven. [Review of Talents from the Streets. How Youth Can Be Seduced to Stay Away from Crime]', *Journal of Social Intervention: Theory and Practice* 26, no. 2: 64–9.
29 Kooijmans, *Talent van de straat*.
30 Ibid.
31 Interview, 21 February 2019.
32 Focus Group interview, 14 January 2019.
33 Ibid.
34 Interview, 27 March 2019.
35 Interview, 2 December 2019.
36 cf. Van San, *Kalifaatontvluchters*.

Bibliography

Campbell, J. *Hero with a Thousand Faces. The Collected Works of Joseph Campbell.* New York: New World Library, 1949.

De Winter, M. *Verbeter de wereld, begin bij de opvoeding [Improve the World, Start by Educating].* Amsterdam: SWP, 2013.

Heinich, N. *Wat identiteit niet is [What Identity Is Not].* Amsterdam: Prometheus, 2019.

Kooijmans, M. *Talent van de straat. Hoe we jongeren kunnen verleiden uit de criminaliteit te blijven [Talents from the Streets. How Youth Can Be Seduced to Stay Away from Crime].* Amsterdam: Van Gennep, 2017.

Kruglanski, A., Bélanger, J. and Gunaratna, R. *The Three Pillars of Radicalization: Needs, Narratives, and Networks.* Oxford University Press, 2019.

Mahdi, L. C., Christopher, N. G. and Meade, M. *Crossroads. The Quest for Contemporary Rites of Passage.* London: Open Court, 1998.

Sieckelinck, S. *Reradicaliseren. Ronselen voor een betere wereld.* Leuven: Lannoo Campus, 2017.

Ungar, M. (ed.). *The Social Ecology of Resilience: A Handbook of Theory and Practice.* New York: Springer, 2012.

Ungar, M. *I Still Love You: Nine Things Troubled Kids Need from Their Parents.* Hamilton: Dundurn Group, 2014.

Van Hoorik, I. *(Hoe) Werkt talentontwikkeling bij 'risicojongeren'? [How Does Talent Development Work for Youth-at-risk?].* Nederlands Jeugd Instituut, 2011.

Van San, M. *Kalifaatontvluchters.* Amsterdam: Prometheus, 2019.

Part Three

Schools, society and beyond

5

Early prevention with workshops at schools in Aarhus

Christian Damgaard Kristoffersen
and Anne Sofie Skare Rasmussen

Introduction

The purpose of this chapter is to provide an insight into the dialogue-based workshops in schools in Aarhus, Denmark, aimed at preventing radicalization, violent extremism and discrimination. These workshops are part of the larger PVE (prevention of violent extremism) work carried out within what is commonly called the 'Aarhus Model'. The Aarhus Model is a collaboration between East Jutland Police and the Municipality of Aarhus. These efforts are naturally a part of a broader CVE (countering violent extremism) and PVE framework with an important historical context. Readers interested in the historical development of the Aarhus Model are encouraged to contact the Municipality of Aarhus or East Jutland Police.

The Aarhus Model had its beginnings sometime before it rose to fame. The municipality and police had in fact been working closely together since 2007 regarding white supremacists who used to have a significant presence in Aarhus (with the police starting their efforts in this regard even earlier, from 2004). During the period of the Syrian conflict, which saw numbers of young men from Aarhus travel to Syria to join groups such as ISIS, the municipality did not have a standing start: it had in place the building blocks of an approach for individuals with extreme views and was able to build on this to develop approaches for people who returned from Syria having fought for various groups.

The Syrian conflict brought attention to bear on the core inter-agency work underpinning responses to returnees, with media portrayals making it seem as if these CVE efforts represented the Aarhus Model in its entirety. However, while CVE work with returnees and individuals who partake in extremist milieus or groups naturally is of vital importance, in reality the Aarhus Model consists of a wide variety of PVE efforts.

The Aarhus Model has at its core prevention as a concept. A prevention triangle (Figure 5.1) is used to illustrate the Model's parts and mechanisms. Figure 5.1 illustrates the interaction between the CVE work in the smallest ('Intervention') and middle

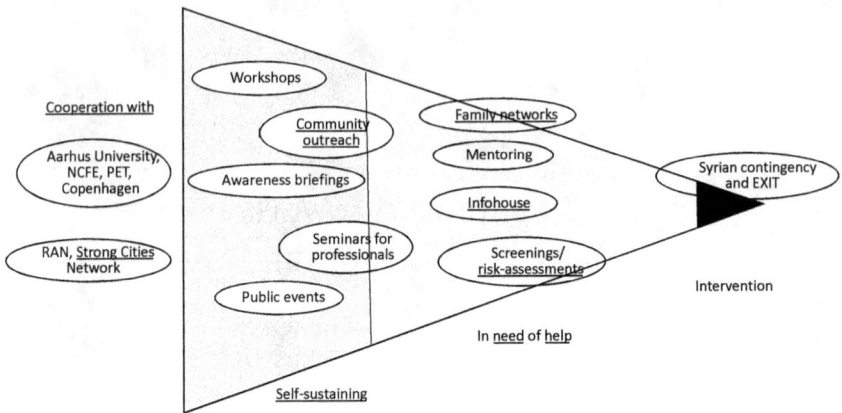

Figure 5.1 The Aarhus Model.
(Source: Internal Framework used by Aarhus Municipality and Police.)

('In need of help') areas of the triangle and the PVE work in the largest (in the 'Self-sustaining') and middle ('In need of help') areas. While it is important to work with individuals in the 'Intervention' area, it is equally important to prevent new individuals from going into this area in the future. Thus, as Figure 5.1 shows (in the largest and middle areas), the Aarhus Model has a wide variety of PVE efforts which deal with what might be termed the pre-radicalization space.

This chapter focuses specifically on the workshops for school students in the 'Self-sustaining' area in Figure 5.1. These workshops, which could be termed early-stage PVE, are managed by the Department of Children and Youth in the Municipality of Aarhus. The workshops attempt to address what might be *future* issues: well before any radicalization process has set in. The basis for these workshops (which also extends to crime prevention work in general in Aarhus) is to engage with children and young people to create reflection, dialogue and understanding to prevent risk behaviour. In many respects, the aim is *diversion* from what down the line might have been risky or pre-radicalized behaviour.

The purpose of the workshops

Some important points should be borne in mind before we address the structure and content of the workshops. The workshops are offered to *every* public school in Aarhus. Visits from the workshops are voluntary. No specific racial or religious groups or neighbourhoods are targeted. The workshops centre on inclusive dialogue about specific themes, and they are, as mentioned, the most upstream part of the overall Aarhus prevention effort. Therefore, they are for *everyone*. We believe that all children and young people can benefit from getting knowledge and having a dialogue in the classroom about topics like this. The schools which agree to hosting the workshops tend to want us to come back again every new school year. Our assessment is that this is because the schools understand (first) that they need not necessarily have existing problems to work on these topics; second, because working on these topics does not carry a stigma of being a 'problem school' and third, because there are benefits to be had from working with these topics. These benefits include better understanding, tolerance and strengthening of the social bonds within the class as well as in relation to the world outside.

It is also helpful for the understanding of our work to note exactly what it is we aim to address with our workshops. Scholars of the research field regarding radicalization and extremism are familiar with push and pull effects, risk factors, protective factors, etc. Therefore, we will not go into detail with this but a comment on protective factors (which is what the workshops aim to strengthen) might at this point be appropriate. The workshops are intended to strengthen and work with community, understanding, empathy and a broader perspective on the world, among other things for the students. In a nutshell, we try to give the students the tools to understand themselves, their classmates and the world they live in, as well as tools with which to interpret their experiences. It is important to note that we do not give them a specific worldview – we take them on a journey and give them the tools to figure things out for themselves as democratic citizens.

The academic foundation of the workshops

The workshops build on and draw inspiration from several sources. These can be divided into two groups: sources that provide the foundation for our workshop methodology and facilitation, and sources that provide the necessary knowledge about radicalization and extremism.

Sources on methodology and facilitation

Regarding the first group of sources, we will start by mentioning the Danish Primary School Act.[1] It states that the public school(s) must prepare students for participation, co-responsibility, (civil) rights and duties in a society with freedom and democracy. In a general sense, this is our mandate. As it is mandated by law that students must receive democratic education, we tap into this with our workshops and create a democratic dialogue about topics that have consequences for democratic societies.

A second source is 'Teaching Controversial Issues' (TCI) developed by David Kerr and Ted Huddleston.[2] TCI provides both a theoretical framework and applicable tools to facilitate working in dialogue with children and young people about controversial issues, which radicalization and extremism can be categorized as. TCI gives professionals exact instructions and a context for how to approach and address these topics when working with students. Both authors of this chapter have attended a course on TCI and how to apply it conducted by David Kerr, co-author and co-editor of "Living with Controversy. Teaching Controversial Issues through Education for Democratic Citizenship and Human Rights".

A third source is the vast amount of pedagogical and didactic knowledge that has been accumulated for decades. This includes practical experience – each of our own and within the Danish school system in general – along with academic works in this field. We cannot refer to one specific source, but one of the key focal points of our workshops is to create an inclusive space and dialogue in which all opinions and views are welcome. This is a space for dialogue where no one (and no view) is frowned upon, ridiculed or condemned, no matter what is brought to the table. The process takes time, patience and empathy. To guide the process, we use all we can from the existing body of pedagogical work. This is vital to the success of the workshop and an indispensable source.

Sources on radicalization and extremism

The second group of sources concerns the scholarly body of knowledge that is part of the workshops' foundation. To address the subject of radicalization and extremism in a professional manner, it is crucial that our material is in accordance with the science within this field.

One of the theoretical perspectives that captures the Aarhus Model in its entirety is *Life Psychology* as formulated by Professor Preben Bertelsen from Aarhus University. We will not account for the theory in its entirety here,[3] but one of Bertelsen's key points is that an individual needs to master a variety of life skills to be in proper control of their own life. Otherwise, that person is in a vulnerable position of which radical groups can take advantage. The workshops build on this perspective in the sense that we try to provide the students with some of the cognitive tools that can help them get closer to mastering some of the necessary life skills.

When it comes to the terms radicalization and extremism and how we understand them, the workshops use the following definitions:

> *Radicalization:* A process leading to a person's gradual acceptance of the use of violence or other illegal means to further political and religious agendas.

> *Extremism:* The use of violence or other illegal means to further political or religious agendas.

When working with young students, it is important for us to underline to students that radicalization is a non-linear process. Although the speed of the process varies from case to case, it is not something that happens overnight. Also, it is important to debunk myths such as radicalization has more to do with certain political or religious beliefs. By creating a common understanding of these key terms, we level the playing field so that everyone can participate within the same structures during a workshop.

Since 2016, we have started focusing on *online radicalization* using this definition:

> Online radicalisation is here conceived as a process whereby individuals, through their online interactions and exposure to various types of Internet content, come to view violence as a legitimate method of solving social and political conflict.

The issue of whether online radicalization in and of itself is sufficient to radicalize an individual or whether there needs to be some kind of offline interaction as well has been a subject of debate among experts. The understanding on the part of the municipality and police has favoured the latter. However, some of the more recent, namely far-right, cases cast doubt over this. A comprehensive examination is beyond the scope of this chapter but this issue is worth highlighting, as it is frequently debated.

It makes sense to address the term 'online radicalization' in a Danish context, given that young Danes are among the most connected online globally. It is imperative to give them the tools to navigate the online world in a qualified manner. One nuance is our preference to view this phenomenon as 'radicalization online', as it is the same kind of process that takes place online as well as offline. In Aarhus, we have chosen to work with this phenomenon offline. Creating and maintaining online interventions is often costly and the results are ambiguous (so far at least). Creating online counter-narratives is one example of this. Instead, we have chosen to draw upon our own experience with offline face-to-face dialogue through workshops. We have taken the framework and methodology from existing material and adapted it with content about online life. Research on online radicalization is still a fairly new field and thus there are limits to how much we can say with certainty at this point. Therefore, like everything else we do, these workshops are being developed continuously.[4]

Rounding off this section about sources, we would like to highlight the collaboration between the Aarhus Model and Aarhus University. The University has been pivotal in supporting the municipality and the police in our work. This is also the case with the workshops. The University has provided academic knowledge, intellectual sparring and general support, for which we are most grateful.

Description of the workshops

The workshops all consist of the same elements: presentation of central concepts, dissemination of knowledge, exercises, dialogue as well as (personal and group) reflection. These elements help us structure the workshops in a way that is informative, exploratory, and fun for the students participating. Every element serves its own purpose. First, it is important to present and discuss concepts that are central to the subject with the students. It is necessary to have a common understanding of what (for example) 'radicalization' means because otherwise the rest of the workshop would make little sense.

Second, it is imperative to provide for dissemination of knowledge within the workshop setting. Meeting a class for the first time, we can never be sure how much the students know about the topic beforehand. Thus, it is necessary that we provide a base of knowledge, as is the case with the central concepts, so the students can work with and discuss the subject. Therefore, each workshop starts with a basic introduction to the central concepts, typologies and historical examples. However, this must not take up too much time because we know that simply providing the students with information is insufficient when it comes to prevention. It may even be counterproductive. In addition, our aim is the students' dialogue (with us and each other) and their reflection, so as little as possible should come from us during the timeframe of a workshop.

Third, exercises are a cornerstone in the workshops. We pose questions, tasks and dilemmas for the students to answer in order to get their hands properly into the subject matter. During the exercises the students get to examine the different facets of the subject from multiple angles and perspectives, but they also get the opportunity to express their own thoughts and opinions. Thus, the exercises are a vessel that facilitates the dialogue and reflection in the workshops.

Fourth, this brings us to the critical aspect: the dialogue. Dialogue between the workshop instructors and the students as well as among the students themselves is the main pedagogical tool used in the workshops. It cannot be emphasized enough that the dialogue is a tool to create a setting where every opinion is welcome and where all are equal. Students who normally speak out and engage, as well as those who do not, are all on a level plane.

The final and fifth element is reflection. The aim is not so much for the students to learn to differentiate between specific types of extremism nor for them to account for the historical background of certain groups. Instead, we are interested in having them reflect upon what all this means for us as a society, us as smaller social groups and themselves as individuals. To have them pose the questions, 'How does this relate to me?' and 'What is my role in all of this?' In our experience, the collective and individual reflection is what brings the student closer to an understanding of the subject as a whole, of each other in the classroom, and of the world in which radical individuals and groups operate, which will bolster them and make them resilient against such influence and behaviour.

In addition to these elements, the workshops each have their own overarching theme. Radicalization and extremism in general have a wide variety of aspects, which makes it impossible to cover everything when working with a class for two and a half to three hours. Thus, as Table 5.1 shows, we have differentiated the workshops according to which themes are the most relevant and comprehensible in relation to the age of the students.[5]

The focus of the workshop for ninth and tenth grade (in primary school) and first grade (in secondary education) is the prevention of radicalization and discrimination. We find that these two topics are closely connected, as discrimination or at least perceived discrimination is often an element in radicalization processes. Therefore, it

Table 5.1 Workshop themes.

	4th grade (primary school)	8th grade (primary school)	9th + 10th grade (primary school) and 1st grade (secondary education)	2nd grade (secondary education)
Age	10	14–15	15–17	17–18
Duration (with breaks)	3 lessons, approx. 3 hours	3 hours	9th and 10 grade: 2.5 hours 1st grade: 3 hours	3 hours
Topics/themes	Digital literacy, digital footprints, online behaviour, democratic education	Critical thinking online, online mechanisms (algorithms, echo chambers, etc.), online behaviour, polarization, effects of images and video	Radicalization, extremism, discrimination, radicalization processes, constructive/empathic dialogue, law, online behaviour	Online radicalization, critical thinking, source criticism, propaganda, conspiracy theory, recruitment
Year Launched	2018	2019	2012	2017

is important for us to address both. The City Council decided in 2016 that the other three workshops (for fourth and eighth grades in primary school and second grade in secondary education) should have a focus on online radicalization. This has made it important to integrate the perspective of the students' social life and behaviour online in our work. The workshop for fourth grade (in primary school) is different from the other workshops, in focusing more on early intervention where we aim to teach children how to navigate online platforms with an emphasis on good online behaviour. This workshop for the fourth grade is handled by a team of schoolteachers who travel to all the schools in Aarhus. Therefore, the observations in the rest of this chapter do not apply directly to this workshop.

Materials for the workshops

To facilitate the workshops under the themes shown in Table 5.1, we have developed specific sets of materials for each workshop. Thus, every workshop has a slideshow, an instruction booklet and different materials that are used for the aforementioned exercises. The workshop instructors must use these, but it is important that they do it with their own 'take' or style. Therefore, the instruction booklet is *not* a manuscript. It conveys *what* to do but not *how* to do it. These materials are being developed continuously, as is the case with the workshop content, which we will discuss later. Therefore, it is not a finished, static product but rather a product that is regularly updated to stay as new and relevant as possible.

Supplementary materials for before and/or after the workshops

In addition to our visit with the workshop and the material that we present, we provide the teachers with supplementary material regarding the subject at hand. This is intended for use either before or after (or both) we visit the class. The aim is to provide teachers and students with tools to explore the subject further. Since the duration of a workshop is two and a half to three hours, we are not able to cover all facets of the given theme. The students might also discuss or take interest in a particular subtheme during the workshop which makes it relevant to continue the work after the workshop. This is encouraged, given that the workshops are not intended to be standalone events. What is envisaged instead is continuous reflection and engagement even after a workshop has been concluded – and in this ongoing process, we try to support teachers in facilitating supplementary materials.

Workshop instructors

Recruitment and introduction to the workshops

Not everyone can facilitate a workshop. We have two teams of instructors who have been trained in facilitation, but they also must have a certain background knowledge of the subject as well as a personality that matches the task. In our experience, personality matters a great deal. Not everyone is or can be trained to be comfortable with facilitating workshops about such controversial subjects. The suitability of the individual is difficult to assess without having seen them in action, which is why recruitment and training are important.

We recruit most of our instructors from academic milieus such as the university. An academic background is by no means a requirement, but we have learned that it is imperative for new instructors to have some background knowledge about the subject that they are going to work with in the workshops and they must understand the basic tenets of the field to be able to facilitate dialogue about it. Aarhus University is a longstanding collaboration partner and understands our prevention work as well as our methods. Thus, the University helps us find university students that could fit the instructor role.

Another advantage of recruiting university students is that the workshops embrace a youth-to-youth approach. Thus, we are able to recruit young instructors who can engage in dialogue with young students at the primary and secondary school levels. In our experience, this approach is the best way to facilitate the dialogue that we want, because the students can see themselves in the instructors when the age difference is minimal. In addition, it makes it easier for the instructors to understand and relate to the students and their world and way of thinking.

We aspire to include as much professional (as well as other types of) diversity among our instructors as possible. Therefore, we collaborate with several different institutes, namely – in no particular order – Political Science, Psychology, Religious Studies, Arabic and Islamic Studies, and Anthropology. We invite potential candidates for short interviews and based on that we invite them to become a part of one of the teams. Being an instructor is only a part-time job, which resonates well with university students.

Training

Training instructors to facilitate workshops is a step-by-step process. The first step is for instructors to get acquainted with the workshop material. After reading the workshop script, we give them a thorough walkthrough of the material and present it, explaining how it would play out in the workshop situation.

Second, the new instructors take part in two workshops as observers, watching experienced instructors facilitate. This helps considerably when it comes to getting an understanding of dynamics and how things can play out.

Finally, the new instructor partners with an experienced instructor and attempts to facilitate a workshop. This is done incrementally. The new instructor starts out with facilitating small chunks of the material, backed up by their experienced co-instructor. Gradually, the new instructor takes on more and more of the material until they are finally comfortable with being an instructor on level with the rest of the instructor team.

Throughout the entire process, we ask them if they are comfortable being where they are – both in the process and physically when they get to go into the classrooms themselves. It is important to ease them in and for them to feel that they are on top of the situation. It is acceptable at any time for a new instructor to back out if they feel that the job is not for them after all. We also reserve the right to stop the training at any time if we, as mentioned above, do not feel that the match between the new instructor and the workshop is good. This rarely happens, however.

Competence development

As mentioned above, it is important that new instructors have some background knowledge of the subject matter. But beyond this, an important part of the instructor's job is having the pedagogical and didactic skills to be able to facilitate dialogue and exercises in the workshops. University students rarely possess those skills to the required extent beforehand. In practice, we have found that it is easier to help train them and for them to learn these skills, compared to recruiting new instructors *with* these skills but who lack the aforementioned background knowledge. Where possible, we also try to recruit instructors with experience in working with children or young people, e.g., as a volunteer in an NGO or a substitute teacher in a school or kindergarten.

Notable experiences from the workshops

Feedback from students

Feedback from the students is crucial. A wide variety of different feedback has been given over time. Some of the key points are presented below.

(i) Students appreciate the chance to voice their opinions. We create a space that belongs to the students where they get the opportunity to dive into a subject and explore their classmates' and their own opinions thoroughly. From what we have seen, this is something that few students experience during their time at school.

(ii) The variation between dissemination of knowledge, exercises, dialogue, etc., resonates well with the students. This structure presents a different way of working with a subject from what they are used to. The interaction between the different elements makes it interesting and relevant to the students. This is a crucial parameter because students evaluate what we do based on whether it is boring or not – among other things. They *can* be a picky audience, which is a constructive thing for us, as it forces us to always optimize our practice to the best possible.

(iii) Another point worth bearing in mind in relation to feedback from students is the fact that we work with the explicit aim to hear from every participant during a workshop (this is dealt with further below in the discussion of the workshops' success at drawing out students who tend to be more withdrawn). The point is that it feels good for the individual student to be in a setting where there is a genuine interest in hearing what is on their mind. This is done without any evaluation as to right or wrong, positive or negative, which is what often happens in an academic setting such as the school.

(iv) We also receive a great deal of feedback from students saying that it was a great experience hearing what their classmates think and feel and that they have learned many new things about each other, even though they go to school together every day. Thus, the workshop setting provides a common neutral safe space for sharing that which does not normally come up during day-to-day interaction. In addition, it is an ideal setting for creating and nurturing common understanding, empathy and fostering community in the classroom.

As society develops so must the workshops

As mentioned, the workshops and their material are dynamic in their nature. As society develops, it is essential for us to develop what we do. It is necessary for us to provide the students with some background knowledge, examples and key terms but we aim to use the newest examples possible – with the proviso that for some examples it is not possible to use them right away because they are too close in space and time. Anders Breivik has been an example of that,[6] though he, as an example of right-wing extremism, is also a testament to why we have to develop our material continuously. A couple of years after his horrific attack in Oslo and Utøya, almost every public-school student knew who he was when shown a picture of him. Breivik's attacks were close to Denmark and targeted young people so the impression of these attacks hit hard. It might have been too soon if this was used as a case study within one to two years of his attacks. But by now, only one or two students on average in a classroom can recognize him from a picture (just as many students nowadays describe the 9/11 attacks in the United States of America as 'that event with the towers').

We do not judge whether students should be more familiar with these specific events, but it does pose an interesting question about when something has become a historic event and when enough distance has passed for it to be included as a discussion topic within a workshop. It also highlights why we need to update our material frequently. When we only work with the student for two to three hours, it is important that we establish a common baseline of knowledge and understanding quickly, and this is best done by using recent cases that they are more likely to have heard about.

In the same vein, we continuously work to improve the pedagogical methodology in the workshop. Drawing inspiration from a wide variety of sources, the aim is to constantly be on the forefront of how we engage children and young people in the best possible way. A part of this is also to ensure that the academic content of the workshops has the right level of difficulty. We aim to keep it on the easier side as the purpose of the workshops is not teaching per se. For example, we present some cases of political and religious extremism so that the students are able to distinguish them. We also present cases to help the students distinguish between subtypes such as left- versus right-wing extremism. However, we do not venture deeply into the ideological foundation and arguments of these typologies. That would be setting the bar too high for some students. Instead, the purpose is the dialogue where it is important that we do not exclude anyone, for example, if a student feels that the academic level is too high.

Forming students who are discovering and exploring society

The workshops see the older students (fifteen to seventeen years) at an interesting time in their lives. At this point, they are starting to orientate themselves towards the broader society. They go from being children to young adults, which is accompanied by a beginning interest in what happens in the world. In other words, they are being shaped as adults and therefore we have a responsibility to nurture this when we work with the students.

Our workshops at this stage are designed to encourage and inspire democratic participation in society (as noted above, preparing the students for participation in a democratic society is mandated by the Primary School Act), while also being aware of the pitfalls of radicalization and extremism. In our experience, schools address this to various degrees. We see no pattern in which some schools perform better or worse, but we can see that it is uneven across schools how much students are taught when it comes to democratic participation.

Learning lessons

In what follows some of the key learning lessons are covered.

Evaluation of the workshops

We evaluate the workshops with student and teacher questionnaires and general feedback from them as well, but there is the issue of evaluation of the prevention intervention. The perennial question is: How can you prove something that does not happen? Our workshops are no exception. We argue, however, that it is not impossible and that the purpose of prevention efforts could benefit from redefinition when they are subject to evaluation. Instead of asking 'Does it work or not?' a lot more could be gained from posing questions such as '*How* does it work?' or 'What do the participants gain from the experience?' All the work we have done up to this point means that we have had countless experiences with students who have had their eyes opened to a whole new way of understanding themselves, their classmates and the world around them – but evaluations seldom focus on researching and understanding these experiences and their mechanisms.

Teachers becoming aware of new things

We often experience teachers becoming aware of certain conditions, mechanisms, tensions, relationships, etc., in the class – things that they were unaware of even though they are together with the class every day.[7] Most teachers are deeply dedicated to their work and care about their students and classes. But it can be almost impossible to grasp everything that goes on in the classroom, and missing even seemingly small things and events can mean a world of difference for an individual student. TCI and the methods applied in our workshops create a space where it is possible to dive into these things, bring them to the surface and address them. Doing this in a systematic and stringent way does require training, but that training can be undertaken by any individual who is interested in furthering understanding, tolerance and healthy class environments with their students. Even without training in TCI, everyone can start by taking an interest in and asking directly how their students are doing – not just academically.

Success in including vulnerable or low-activity students

The workshops have been highly successful in getting the students who are ordinarily less forthcoming to participate.

Students can have a low activity level for a number of reasons. They may doubt themselves, feel academically inadequate, be intimidated by classmates, or they may simply be tired of going to school. Within the space of a workshop, the instructors create a safe zone where there are no rights or wrongs. The instructors are trained in creating trust, encouragement, positive reinforcement, nurturing those students who need it most and being genuinely interested. Therefore, one of the workshops' greatest achievements is that almost every student participates actively during a session. How much each student actually participates varies and we never force anyone into participation, but we do everything we can to encourage participation and we have often received feedback from surprised teachers telling us that a given student who participated eagerly in the workshop is normally quiet and reserved. Thus, a significant point from our work is that the open-minded, welcoming, encouraging, nurturing and genuinely interested approach is a key tool when it comes to ensuring that quiet and potentially vulnerable students also get the chance to participate on equal terms with everyone else.

The way forward

For the final part of this chapter, we would like to suggest two important perspectives for future diversion work – perspectives coming from our own experiences and challenges faced.

The first relates to the notion that while it is important that children and young people learn about and discuss the themes from our workshops, it is also of paramount importance (as our own experience has shown) that professionals who work with children and young people know about these issues too. In addition, they should possess the proper tools and competencies to engage with students in a qualified manner. Thus, the dissemination of TCI and the methodology along with knowledge from the workshops should preferably be something that all professionals who work with children and young people are able to apply in their work.

The second perspective is about whether this type of diversion work and dialogue should be mandatory in school. It could be an advantage for the students if it were a bigger part of an everyday life in school, notwithstanding the difficulties in realizing this. First, the proper framework has to be in place. This means that schools should have a clear plan for how they are going to work with diversion. In addition, authorities must have the same plan and be prepared to support schools in this work. Second, as mentioned above, professionals must have the proper training and be qualified to work with diversion or PVE. Third, the school system as a whole must be structured in a way that gives actual space and time for this work. In Denmark, it is not a school subject on its own, nor is it an integrated part of another specific school subject such as Social Studies. As a consequence, no one is responsible for carrying out this work and it is more or less a matter of luck whether or not students encounter it during their school life. As mentioned before, the Danish Public School Law does mandate that schools must prepare students for participation, co-responsibility, (civil) rights and duties in a society with freedom and democracy. However, it is up to the individual school to decide how this is done – and often this does not include diversion work, TCI or PVE.

Thus, the road ahead can seem long, but we strongly suggest that decision-makers and leaders, at their respective levels, work to ensure that the proper structures, conditions, and knowledge are in place and that TCI and PVE are prioritized in school curricula.

Notes

1   See https://www.retsinformation.dk/eli/lta/2019/823
2   See Ted Huddleston and David Kerr (eds.), *Living with Controversy. Teaching Controversial Issues through Education for Democratic Citizenship and Human Rights* (EDC/HRE). Training Pack for Teachers (Strasbourg: Council of Europe, 2015). It can be downloaded here: https://theewc.org/resources/living-with-controversy-teaching-controversial-issues-through-education-for-democratic-citizenship-and-human-rights-edc-hre/
3   See for example Preben Bertelsen, *Tilværelsespsykologi [Life Psychology]. Et godt nok greb om tilværelsen* (Copenhagen: Frydenlund, 2013), Preben Bertelsen, 'Danish Preventive Measures and De-radicalization Strategies: The Aarhus Model', *Panorama: Insights into Asian and European Affairs* 1 (2015): 241–53, and Simon Ozer and Preben Bertelsen, 'Countering Radicalization: An Empirical Examination from a Life Psychological Perspective', *Peace and Conflict: Journal of Peace Psychology* 25, no. 3 (2019): 211–25.
4   It is up for debate whether online radicalization can stand alone, so to speak, or if there has to be some kind of offline interaction as well. Thus far, our understanding has been based on the latter. However, some of the more recent, namely far-right, cases cast doubt over this. It is possible that the thesis that one can be solely radicalized through online means does hold some merit on its own. The workshops do not address this point directly, but we do note within the workshops that this is a contested area.
5   We will not go further into the specific content here as our focus is on the workshop *methodology* and the lessons that we have learned from the workshops. To learn more about the workshops' content, we encourage the reader to contact the Aarhus Municipality Department of Children and Youth.
6   Anders Behring Breivik is a Norwegian right-wing extremist and terrorist. In 2011, he committed an act of domestic terrorism in Norway when he bombed a government building in Oslo, killing eight people, and shot and killed sixty-nine people on the island Utøya during a camp for the Worker's Youth League.
7   The teachers have to be present during the workshop because they know the class, but they are prohibited from participating, given that the workshops are exclusively for the students.

Bibliography

Bermingham et al. *Combining Social Network Analysis and Sentiment Analysis to Explore the Potential for Online Radicalisation*, Advances in Social Networks Analysis and Mining, 20–22 July 2009, Athens. (In the workshop we use a Danish translation.)

Bertelsen, Preben. *Tilværelsespsykologi [Life Psychology]. Et godt nok greb om tilværelsen.* Copenhagen: Frydenlund, 2013.

Bertelsen, Preben. 'Danish Preventive Measures and De-radicalization Strategies: The Aarhus Model'. *Panorama: Insights into Asian and European Affairs* 1 (2015): 241–53.

Huddleston, Ted and Kerr, David (eds.). *Living with Controversy. Teaching Controversial Issues through Education for Democratic Citizenship and Human Rights* (EDC/HRE, 2015). Training Pack for Teachers. Strasbourg: Council of Europe. Available at https://

theewc.org/resources/living-with-controversy-teaching-controversial-issues-through-education-for-democratic-citizenship-and-human-rights-edc-hre/

Law of the Danish Primary Schools. Available at: https://www.retsinformation.dk/eli/lta/2019/823

Ozer, Simon and Bertelsen, Preben. 'Countering Radicalization: An Empirical Examination from a Life Psychological Perspective'. *Peace and Conflict: Journal of Peace Psychology* 25, no. 3 (2019): 211–25.

6

Early intervention and the challenge of radicalism in the Indonesian school system

Muhammad Abdullah Darraz

Increasing intolerance has become an entry point for the development of radicalism in Indonesia, which in some cases leads to violent extremism. Few places are more vulnerable to these concerning trends than the nation's school system, where a battle for hearts and minds is playing out through the instrumentalization of policy, outside influence and the contents of extracurricular activities. Prevention initiatives have emerged to counter these forces and divert the school community away from the infiltration and penetration of radical groups.

This chapter aims to explain the role of schools in disseminating and preventing radicalism in Indonesia. It will outline the ways in which intolerant views and instruction have been cultivated in schools, particularly since the process of regional decentralization following the nation's reform era from the late 1990s. Then it will discuss some of the strategies and mechanisms in place for countering these trends through school management, regional government policy and decisions at the national level.

One organization heavily involved in this space is the Maarif Institute,[1] which has facilitated a series of programmes in several problematic areas known as 'red zones' (*zona merah*) for radicalization in Indonesia, including Sukabumi, West Java and Padang, West Sumatra. In addition, since 2017, the Maarif Institute has become an important part of a large joint project between NGOs and various campus research institutions initiated by the Centre for Studies of Islam and Society (PPIM) Syarif Hidayatullah State Islamic University Jakarta as part of an umbrella programme called CONVEY Indonesia (Countering Violent Extremism for Youth), which targets the younger generation.[2]

Background and problem statement

After the fall of the Suharto regime in the late 1990s, Indonesia entered an era of increasing basic freedoms, including the freedoms of speech and association, and the freedom to express opinions openly. However, this positive new reality following what is known as the *Reformasi* (reform) era has been misused and exploited in some circles. Reform has created challenges that are not new but have become crucial issues for the journey of this nation. According to Frans Magnis Suseno, there are at least two important issues that challenged the Indonesian people during this period of reform: the collapse of national tolerance and the strengthening of religious extremism.[3] Suseno argued that while Indonesians were once able to live together peacefully in diversity, this harmony has been gradually eroded and risks complete collapse.

The national motto of *Bhinneka Tunggal Ika* (Unity in Diversity) is increasingly limited to symbols and tag lines, and at the grassroots level of society, it is now often undermined by mutual hatred and the rejection of diversity. This is caused by the strengthening of religious extremism, which is growing and spreading throughout Indonesian society. The phenomenon of intolerance towards difference, whether religious, ethnic or racial, has become a crucial problem in Indonesia,[4] because intolerant attitudes have become the main entry point for radicalism, which in some cases evolves into violent extremism.

The prevalence of intolerant attitudes has possibly become the most pressing problem amongst Indonesian youth. Prior research by the Maarif Institute (2011), LAKIP (2011) SETARA Institute (2015) and the Wahid Foundation research (2016) clearly shows this.[5] More recently, a survey conducted by the Center for the Study of Islam and Society (PPIM) on youth attitudes regarding issues of intolerance, radicalism and violence, with a sample base of 2,181 people (high school students, university students, and teachers), has shown that intolerance has acutely affected young people in Indonesia.[6] The research found that 33 per cent of respondents supported acts of intolerance towards minority groups; 34 per cent agreed that people who leave Islam (apostates) must be killed; and 68 per cent of students would refuse to acknowledge the authority of a non-Muslim local government (e.g., a non-Muslim governor, mayor or regent).[7] This research was especially revealing when it came to the views of young people towards groups outside their religion (i.e., non-Muslims). As many as 21 per cent of students considered Christians to be the enemies of Muslims, while 24 per cent thought that Christians hated Muslims.[8] Intolerant attitudes in the form of anti-Jewish sentiment were also present among respondents. As many as 54 per cent of students believed that Jews are the enemies of Muslims, while 53 per cent claimed that Jews hate Islam.[9]

Intolerance towards different ideologies or groups within the majority Muslim community is also a problem in Indonesia. Mainstream majority groups often reject the existence of minority groups, such as the Ahmadiyya and Shia groups, which they consider to be incompatible with the views of the majority in Islam. PPIM's research also confirms the intolerant views of the young Muslim generation towards groups within Islam which they consider as having deviated from the teachings of Islam. The findings show that almost 87 per cent of students would support the Government prohibiting the existence of minority religious groups. As many as 31 per cent of students cited Shiites as the most disliked group, while 20 per cent of students cited Ahmadis as the second least preferred group.[10]

Parallel with the intolerant attitudes above, there is a connection with the attitude of those inclined to resort to violence in dealing with difference. As many as 38 per cent of students agreed that the real struggle (*jihad*) was fighting non-Muslims or those whom they accuse of being infidels; however, this was defined. A worrying 23 per cent of students believed that suicide bombings in the name of religion are a true form of *jihad*. At least 31 per cent of students thought that attacks on the state apparatus, considered to be *thogut* (infidel), was justified. As many as 62 per cent of students believed that the caliphate (*khilafah*) system was a form of government that is recognized in Islamic teachings. And in perhaps the most striking finding, almost 91 per cent of students agreed that Islamic sharia law should be universally applied in Indonesia, while 76 per cent thought that all government policy must be based on Islamic law.[11]

These research findings reinforce the central argument of this chapter: intolerance is linked with radicalism and it can be the main entry point for the development of an extremist or even violent extremist ideology. Therefore, early attempts to prevent the growth of radicalism/extremism should target the spread of intolerance in the community.

The various research findings outlined above show that intolerance and radicalism are increasingly prevalent among students in Indonesian secondary and tertiary education institutions.[12] The question is, how do these young people form the alarming views outlined above? Social media certainly plays a role, as information can be posted and spread so easily, but in Indonesia, offline environments are equally important for the development and transmission of extremism among young people.

Based on research conducted by the Maarif Institute in 2011, there are at least three main issues that facilitate and exacerbate the proliferation of extremist views in schools. The first is the unregulated content of organized extracurricular activities. The next is the actual teaching curricula in class, and finally, the school principals' permissive policies on the inclusion of radical movements and neglect in strengthening the values of tolerance, diversity and anti-discrimination.[13]

The challenges of radicalism in schools and some early interventions

In this chapter, I will focus more on examining the role of extracurricular activities and their internal regulation, both as a means of spreading the ideas of radical groups and religious political groups (Islamists), as well as a bastion for strengthening the values of tolerance, diversity, and at the same time as an effort to prevent radicalization among the young generation.

In the West Java district of Sukabumi, extremist groups have been developing quite rapidly. During the past fifteen years, the sociopolitical system has been conducive to a homogeneous religious life by prioritizing the majority group. For ten years, a regent named Sukmawijaya, who came from an Islamist political party, the Social Justice Party (PKS), led Sukabumi.[14] Throughout his time in power, Sukmawijaya produced policies informed by religious interpretation prioritizing the majority, thereby marginalizing the minority.[15] There were also some policies with religious nuances, which marginalized minorities in educational institutions, especially government-affiliated public schools.

Among such policies were the Sukabumi District Head Instruction No. 4/2004 concerning Muslim Clothing for Students in the Sukabumi Regency, District Head Regulation No. 6/2006 concerning the Compulsory Religious Education Programme, Regent Regulation no. 33/2008 concerning the 'Ten Habituation of Noble Morals' in Schools, and District Regulation no. 8/2009 concerning Compulsory Religious Education. These regional regulations have become instrumental in encouraging educational institutions in Sukabumi to compete in creating a system of religious education learning outside curricular and co-curricular activities in the classroom. The school implements these regulations by activating various extracurricular activities which bolster religious education in schools.[16] However, the strengthening of religious education carried out through extracurricular activities is only limited to that of the majority's interpretation of Islam. The development of non-Islamic religious education does not receive adequate attention.

There is nothing wrong with the existence of extracurricular activities in schools which have been recommended by education legislation.[17] The problem emerges when these activities are exploited for the benefit of certain groups, including their politicization as an entry point for the penetration of radical groups in high schools.

Based on the findings of several previous research projects, of the many extracurricular activities in schools, religious extracurricular activities are those with the greatest potential to promote intolerance and further problems.[18] The Islamic Spirituality Division, Kerohanian Islam (commonly known as Rohis), is the most prominent and popular religious extracurricular organization throughout the Indonesian school system. Structurally, it is part of a student organization, the Intra-School Student Organisation (Organisasi Siswa Intra Sekolah, OSIS).[19] However, the Rohis system is better known and more influential than its parent OSIS because in some regions, Rohis has a strong network with other Rohis-linked organizations outside the schools. In many cases, Rohis in schools have an umbrella organization at the city/district level or even at the provincial level even though Rohis regulations are not supposed to be affiliated with organizations outside the schools.[20]

A case of intolerance involving Rohis activists occurred from mid-September to December 2019 and emerged in early 2020. This happened at a state high school in the city of Sragen, Central Java. A female student was intimidated and terrorized by a Rohis activist because she did not wear a headscarf (*jilbab*). He intimidated the victim into immediately wearing a headscarf, especially when attending school. This terror and intimidation was carried out through various messages conveyed through the WhatsApp platform. The perpetrator threatened the victim not to report the messages of terror and intimidation to the school. This terror and intimidation continued for four months, until the victim finally reported the incident to her parents. After that, the victim's parents reported the problem along with proof of the WhatsApp chat to the school management. After mediation, the perpetrator finally apologized to the victim and the problem was resolved, but there was a deep trauma in the victim which made her reluctant to go back to school. Eventually, the victim's parents moved her to a private school in accordance with her wishes. It turned out that the individual who carried out the intimidation imbibed the intolerant teachings from the Rohis study network outside the school – a network that involved mentors from radical groups outside the school.[21]

Of course, we cannot just criminalize or blame Rohis as the hive of radicalization among school students because Rohis is only a forum for activities at school and student participants are nothing but victims of radical movements, which use the platform to influence young people from outside the school. But the important point is how to fortify students against this influence, especially students who are active in Rohis extracurricular activities, in order to prevent radicalization.

In 2017, the Maarif Institute, through Phase I of the Countering Violent Extremism for Youth (CONVEY) programme, conducted qualitative research to explore the extent to which radical groups can reach students through extracurricular activities. In the district of Sukabumi, the study found some Rohis alumni were incorporated in an association called the Qur'anic Club (QC), which was established by the Regent of Sukabumi from 2005 to 2015 as a forum for 'developing student morals' in Sukabumi (a regency which has the motto 'Save the Heir of the Country!'). However, QC is a movement underlined by the conservative *tarbiyah* ideology and its establishment was allegedly the realization of a political contract between the regent and his supporting political party.[22]

In addition to being assembled in QC, some Rohis alumni in Sukabumi are also networked with an exclusivist Islamic boarding school and Islamic college (with a two-year academic programme) affiliated with the Saudi-Wahhabi movement, which teaches Arabic and Islamic studies but also conducts anti-diversity propaganda. The alumni were connected to the foundation because they continued their education at the Islamic college. So far, through the role of students and community service institutions, the exclusive Islamic college spread their radical and intolerant views in the Cikembar and Cibadak areas, two heterogeneous sub-districts of Sukabumi.[23]

Another interesting finding in the district of Sukabumi is the strong influence of religious-based vigilante groups among students who become '*santri kalong*' in Salafi (traditional) *pesantren* (Islamic boarding schools). This group is known as the Islamic Defenders Front (FPI) and was a prominent presence during the mobilization of mass actions for the 2016 Defending Islam Movement (*Aksi Bela Islam*) in Jakarta.[24] The movement was the largest protest ever held in Indonesia. Hundreds of thousands of people inundated the streets protesting the alleged blasphemy against Islam by Basuki Tjahaya Purnama (commonly known as 'Ahok'), a prominent Chinese-Indonesian candidate in the 2017 Jakarta gubernatorial election. The journey of students from Sukabumi to Jakarta in the context of the Defending Islam Movement was facilitated by *pesantren* and public high schools. Apart from the Defending Islam Movement, this group is attractive to students due to its values of solidarity, militancy, firmness and blessings from their *ulama* (*habaib*).

So far, there is no clear evidence of radicalism that has led to violent extremism in the student council (OSIS) and Rohis in Sukabumi but their views are coloured by these three different patterns of intolerant and Islamist groups: Tarbiyah, Wahhabi and the Sharia NKRI.[25]

The influence of alumni on extra-curricular activities has been particularly pronounced in the West Sumatra city of Padang. Salafi-style and puritan religious attitudes tend to exclusively colour the OSIS, given the impact of alumni indoctrination through the mentoring programme outside the school. In some regions, including around Padang, school alumni have played a role in the penetration of radicalism among both OSIS and Rohis activists. The alumni itself has a strong connection with the Tarbiyah group and some puritan activists affiliated with Salafi-Wahhabi thought.

This puritanism is more influential among students' religious attitudes, which are drawn from the ideas taken from Muhammad ibn Abdul Wahab and Ibn Taymiyah and were later influenced by Sumatran Saudi-Wahhabi network activists in West Sumatra.[26] The puritan movement in West Sumatra has its roots in the nineteenth century, when the Sumatran *hajj* returnees led the Padri movement. They were influenced by the teachings and practices of the Wahhabis who conquered Mecca in the early nineteenth century.[27]

Other methods of introducing radicalism into schools include the interactions with several religious teachers from the exclusive Islamic boarding schools (*pesantren*). One of the boarding schools in question has formal middle and high school institutions and claims to provide the best religious education in Padang. The religious character of this *pesantren* is Salafi-Wahhabi, where most of the teachers are alumni from the Institute of Arabic and Islamic Studies (LIPIA), an Islamic College in Jakarta founded in the 1980s as a branch of Ibn Saud University in Saudi Arabia.[28] Politically, this *pesantren* has a close relationship with the Tarbiyah group.

The involvement of the Tarbiyah group among students is increasingly visible through the association of OSIS Nusantara Forum (FON) and Rohis (Assalam). The OSIS Nusantara Forum (FON) is a national-level OSIS association that has political associations with the Tarbiyah group. Assalam is an Islamic student association and represents a gathering place for Rohis activists throughout West Sumatra. Assalam was formed by the Muslim Student Development Institute (LPPM) through the Middle School and Senior High School Rohis forum in West Sumatra in late 1999 at the Nurul Iman Mosque in Padang City.

In terms of religious orientation, Assalam activists are closer to Tarbiyah and Salafi groups. By political affiliation, Assalam is closer to the *tarbiyah* group because it is supported by activists from the Campus Propagation Organisation (LDK).[29] Even Assalam's activities are facilitated by one of their seniors by using a place in a tutoring institution initiated by the *tarbiyah* movement.

The Assalam activists acted in solidarity with Muslims in Syria by collecting donations from students through the Rohis network and channelling them through the Indonesia Care for Shams Forum (FIPS) based in Jakarta. FIPS is an association concerned with channelling assistance to conflict zones in the Middle East.[30] Some FIPS leaders are known as prominent puritans and Salafi-Wahhabi figures such as Fahmi Salim, a young Egyptian Al-Azhar alum who is active in a prominent young Islamic intellectual and religious scholar organization as well as MUI.[31]

Early intervention from within

To erode radical and intolerant views among students, school institutions need to expose students to and familiarize them with diversity. The problem is in several public schools in Indonesia, including homogeneous regions such as Sukabumi and

Padang; schools are dominated by students from religious majority backgrounds and homogeneous tribes. However, we find that some of these schools are aware of the importance of countering the radicalization that afflicts their schools, seeking to promote diversity and tolerant attitudes towards differences in their school environment.

Some school communities consciously intervened from within to maintain resilience against various ideological penetrations that could erode their roles as guardians of the Indonesian identity for the younger generation. They are also aware that the interventions were carried out as an effort to maintain the school's image. They recognize that acts of violent extremism stemming from radicalism and intolerance must be kept away from their school. Therefore, the school's management is aware of its responsibility to intervene to prevent radicalization in the school environment and this is also the responsibility of the state and society in general.

An example is one public high school in Sukabumi Regency called SMAN 1 Cikembar, which has around fifteen non-Muslim students on its roll – a significant number compared to other public schools in this homogeneous region. The school applies the principles of togetherness and equality, always involves minority students in school activities, and celebrates all religious holidays, including those of the minority. A Christian student who became a correspondent in this study stated:

> I sang Islamic songs because I joined the choir. If I'm not mistaken, it was one of GIGI's (a famous band in Indonesia) songs at the event or Maulid Mi'raj. I am happy to sing the songs.
>
> AL, Christian student in SMAN 1 Cikembar[32]

To instil the values of diversity and nationalism among students, the school usually cooperates with the Indonesian military (TNI) and police (Polri), especially through their community development divisions, to strengthen Pancasila and national values. TNI and Polri are two elements of the nation, which since independence have been symbols of the guardians of the national identity and have played an active role in maintaining the unity and integrity of the nation and state from various external ideological threats. Almost all schools invite the TNI and Polri to oversee their flag-raising ceremonies, which are usually held every Monday. In addition, they often involve the TNI as speakers in LDKS (Student Leadership Basic Training) activities. The principal and other school management staff view the TNI and police involvement positively as they strengthen the state ideology among students, in contrast with radical or Islamist groups with an interest in replacing state ideology.[33]

In order to reinforce the resilience of the school community from exposure to radicalism, some schools have enacted specific policies and programme initiatives. For example, in MAN 3 Sukabumi, the school formed an Islamic boarding school with a moderate Islamic vision, which is intended for students majoring in Islamic Studies.[34] One of the main objectives of the establishment of the Islamic boarding school is to present a more moderate, tolerant and inclusive religious authority, which becomes a reference for Muslim students active in extracurricular organizations who may well be exposed to the influence of radical groups.

Another significant approach for preventing radical groups from infiltrating the school environment is to openly invite moderate community groups and religious organizations in for discussions. In Sukabumi, this is done by the Fopulis group (Youth Interfaith Forum) through a programme called 'Fopulis Goes to School', which tries to involve students in getting to know and understand diversity issues. Interestingly, they have an encounter programme between inter-religious and inter-cultural student communities. The majority group (Muslim students) are persuaded to be more aware and open towards their friends who come from minority groups, whether religious, ethnic or cultural.

An important role of these moderate groups has also been played by Nahdlatul Ulama (NU) and Muhammadiyah, the two largest Muslim mass organizations in Indonesia. The NU and NU-affiliated Student Association (PMII) has a *tawasut* programme to influence life in public schools, so students are not only exposed to ideologies brought by radical groups such as Hizb ut-Tahrir, Wahhabis and *tarbiyah* groups. Muhammadiyah, through the role of the Maarif Institute as one of its cultural networks, has carried out various programmes in schools over the past ten years, through policy formulation, capacity-building for principals, teachers, supervisors and the students. Every year, the institute holds a meeting that presents 100 students from various schools in a programme called *Jambore Pelajar Teladan Bangsa*. This is a one-week training programme to internalize the values of moderate Islam, 'Indonesian-ness' and humanity. Maarif also actively facilitates various meetings for school principals, teachers and supervisors in an effort to raise awareness of attempts by radical groups to infiltrate the school environment.[35] This is possible because some schools have the initiative to open themselves to intervention and prevention efforts to counter the radicalization that occurs in their communities.

Policy intervention and extracurricular activities

The role of groups outside the school should be to encourage and facilitate the intervention so they are conducted in a participatory manner by the school, based on a thorough needs assessment. Maarif Institute has attempted to facilitate this type of self-intervention on various occasions. In some cases, Maarif Institute has done this in collaboration with the Indonesian Ministry of Education and Culture, facilitating meetings involving key stakeholders. These include key individuals within the school, such as the principal, vice principal for student affairs, the mentor of school extra-curricular activities and the school supervisor, who are asked to speak more deeply to strengthen the resilience of the school community. The idea of this intervention is to fortify schools from the infiltration of radical groups through school policy and strengthen students' critical thinking and resilience against extremist arguments.[36]

In relation to the school policy, Maarif is concerned with three distinct levels. First is the level of internal school policy. Some internal school policies have actually led to a process of radicalization in schools. As a concrete example, some schools invite radical groups to speak at their monthly religious meetings. These meetings have become part of the school's programmes. Instead of strengthening diversity, they often come with study materials that are ideologically charged with radical, exclusive, sectarian, anti-Pancasila and anti-democratic themes, while rejecting the concept of Indonesia as a republic because it is considered a *thogut* (infidel) state. This was the case in some state high schools.

Maarif Institute started from the premise that mainstreaming diversity is one thing that can fortify students from the propaganda of radicalism. If school policies that stem the tide of radicalism can be implemented consistently and there is an effective monitoring mechanism, schools will be able to prevent radicalization among students.

Before actual interventions that might change school policy, Maarif specifically conducted a study related to internal school policies for strengthening diversity, especially through extra-curricular activities. The results found that in seven cities/districts (Banda Aceh-Aceh Province, Makassar-South Sulawesi, Mataram-West Nusa Tenggara, Surakarta-Central Java, Cianjur-West Java, Sukabumi-West Java and Lebak-Banten), there were no specific policies at the regional or school level specifically aimed at strengthening diversity.

This research found efforts to replace the flag-honouring ceremony – which should be carried out once a week – with religious activities in the form of religious lectures (on Islam), *dluha* prayers and *tadarus Quran*. These religious activities that replace the flag-honouring ceremony were routinely carried out by a public school in Sukabumi Regency in the second and fourth week of each month. This effort was carried out to implement the principle of faith and piety contained in the National Education System Law no. 20 of 2003.

Through certain processes, the radical groups want to lay down a radicalization agenda that this author contextually interprets based on the definition given by Della Porta and LaFree in an effort to change in beliefs, feelings and behaviours in directions that increasingly justify intergroup violence and demand sacrifice in defence of the group.[37] So it creates the phenomenon of people embracing opinions, views and ideas which could lead to forms of conflict rather than acts of terrorism.

In a different sub-district of Sukabumi, radicalization has strategically and structurally involved the village-level government apparatus. A foundation affiliated with a transnational radical group has established an Islamic and Arabic Studies College where youths are recruited to become preachers for mosques in local Sukabumi villages. They are also sent to be mentors in schools, especially public high schools. Through a village head, they built a mosque in a public school in Cibadak area. This is part of the '1,000 mosques' construction programme.[38]

Beyond mosques, they are building clean water management facilities for residents. Alongside the construction of this mosque, they require that their preachers conduct religious mentoring activities at the school and that they should manage the new mosques (i.e., imams, preachers and the mosque management must come from their circles).[39] Through this strategy, they can penetrate their radical ideologies through the school and surrounding community. The key is to meet the basic needs of the local community by providing clean water and a new place of worship, and then to entrench their influence through ideology.

The second level is that of implementing policy among local or regional governments which tends to be discriminatory and anti-diversity. Since the period of decentralization following the fall of Suharto's New Order regime, each regional government, in this case the provincial education department, has managed high school institutions. Many regions have implemented their own regulations with religious nuances, which have ultimately encouraged school policymakers to formulate discriminatory school regulations. For example, the regencies of Pandeglang and Banyuwangi have implemented discriminatory policies requiring all female students, Muslim and non-Muslim, to wear the hijab. In Banda Aceh, on the basis of local regulations, a state school has even prohibited the enrolment of non-Muslim students.

The third level concerns policy at the national level. A 2017 Maarif Institute research project revealed that central government policies related to strengthening diversity and inclusiveness (Minister of National Education Regulation No. 39/2008 on Student Development, and Minister of Education and Culture Regulation No. 23/2015 on Growth of Character) could not be implemented or articulated at the school level, even though the existing policies would protect students from extremism if implemented and articulated effectively. Although the Ministry of Education provides guidance for the two Ministerial Regulations, individual schools have the power to translate and implement the policy as they see fit, even if it then becomes contrary to the spirit of the regulation. As mentioned earlier, this condition has been further exacerbated by decentralization since the regional autonomy legislation was enacted in 2004. The spirit of regional autonomy in practice greatly influences the worldview of a student's education in each region.

Based on the above findings, Maarif Institute facilitated a meeting of school principals and committee members from twenty-five public high schools in seven cities/districts (Banda Aceh, Makassar, Mataram, Surakarta, Cianjur, Sukabumi, Lebak) in May 2017. One common finding was the fading authority of the teachers – especially classroom religious teachers. This happens because of the increasing influence of mentors from outside the school, the student council and those involved with Rohis extra-curricular activities. Students trusted external mentors more than their teachers,[40] so they tended to become the main reference points for students seeking religious knowledge and understanding. This warns schools to be more selective in choosing and inviting outside mentors who usually enter the school as alumni. The central government, local governments and internal school parties need to think about the existence of mentoring standards to accompany extra-curricular activities in schools.

Another issue is the importance of selecting various resource persons for monthly meetings and study sessions, which then become routine monthly school programmes. Often the school institution invites lecturers or resource persons who have narrow religious views, monolithic styles and anti-diversity positions, with the school having limited knowledge about the actual views of the person in question. The school's gap of knowledge when it comes to the landscape of radicalist movements in Indonesia contributes to this ignorance.

To encourage efforts to strengthen schools in countering radicalism, the Maarif Institute initiated a programme called 'Strengthening School Institutions through Internal School Policies That Strengthen Diversity'.[41] The idea is that internal school policies can foster diversity within the school, which is the best way to safeguard against intolerance and extremism. In addition, it is also necessary to formulate an early warning system and an oversight mechanism at the school level that can stem potential processes of radicalization. The Maarif Institute hopes the public high schools that are part of this programme will strengthen diversity and eliminate radicalization.

An associated workshop has helped twenty-five public high schools in seven areas to formulate school policies appropriate for their respective needs. The principals agreed to prevent radicalization in schools through specific policies aimed at counter-radicalization and by increasing human resources, strengthening curriculum and learning processes, developing facilities and infrastructure that support the strengthening of diversity in school life, early detection systems, supervision of extracurricular activities, control systems and activity filters, increasing activities to maintain diversity at school and improving student media literacy.[42]

Reinforcing human resource capacity is done through various training courses that enrich the insights of diversity for teachers and students. In addition, they agreed to insert diversity values in the curriculum of each subject. In the learning process, the school is committed to creating spaces for encounters with different communities (religious, ethnic and cultural backgrounds) by learning about one another's differences, so students become interested and develop deeper understandings of their communities. This is in line with the Ministry of Education and Culture's policy that encourages learning not only in classrooms but witnessing real life in the field, such as through religious lessons conducted in inter-religious houses of worship, to create deeper recognition and better knowledge of other religions.

School principals have also been assisted in creating an early warning system in their respective schools. In this system, they formulate rules for the selection of every religious activity (especially extra-curricular ones) by providing signs in accordance with the vision and mission of the school to prevent threats to diversity. In addition, the school creates guidelines to detect the symptoms of intolerance among students, displayed through ways of thinking, attitudes towards others and behaviour in school. Signs of deviation include refusal to attend flag-raising ceremonies, anti-social attitudes in association and accusing people who disagree of being infidels. Detection of intolerance and radicalism is important for conducting prevention initiatives as early as possible, to ensure extremism does not take root in the school's community.

Building critical thinking on social media

Another important approach is strengthening students' resilience when exposed to radicalism and intolerant views on the internet. This is done by improving critical thinking among students. Young people are exposed to torrents of information through social media and it is vital that they learn how to carefully consider what they see and read online. With increasing engagement through mobile phones, violent extremism and intolerant religious views are among a number of harmful influences facing young internet users in Indonesia. Digital literacy and the development of critical perspectives when browsing through posts are a pressing issue for students, especially those who are exposed to offline extra-curricular activities. Equally important is the creation of more positive content encouraging harmony and diversity, which young people will ideally design themselves.

Based on research conducted by CONVEY Indonesia in 2017, social media is one of the main sources of radicalization among youth in Indonesia. More than 50 per cent of the respondents in the research stated that the propaganda on radicalism that they had received so far came from social media.[43] They also receive content containing hate speech, intolerant views and various types of misinformation such as hoaxes, which can trigger misunderstandings and lead to conflict. Exposure to misinformation is often taken for granted without adequate criticism, even if this only involves asking about the origin and validity of the information.

In 2017, the Maarif Institute collaborated with Google Indonesia to initiate a training programme aimed at increasing critical thinking skills among young people, when facing the flow of information they receive on various social media platforms. The training was also intended to strengthen students' skills in using social media as a medium to spread positive content to campaign for the values of peace, tolerance and diversity. The project involved 2,000 participants from 130 high schools (SMA) in five major cities in Indonesia, namely Jakarta (DKI Jakarta Province), Bandung (West Java), Yogyakarta (DI Yogyakarta Province), Semarang (Central Java) and Surabaya (East Java).

Observers noted a number of positive outcomes. The students became increasingly aware that social media is used as a propaganda tool for radicals and if they find such radical content, they should follow up through reporting mechanisms to the moderators of social media providers such as Facebook, YouTube and Twitter. Organizers were encouraged by the enthusiasm for creating positive content to counter negative content on social media, including those containing radicalism. Participants were also challenged to disseminate their created content as widely as possible to inspire the public to maintain a life of harmony and peace and not to be provoked into committing acts of violence.

Conclusion

It cannot be denied that extremists in Indonesia, since the reform era of the new millennium, have targeted young people and especially school students. Awareness of these dangers must belong to all elements of the nation's citizens. During the past five years, the nation's education community has begun to realize the extent of the challenges and threats to their students. They are learning that their role of instilling national and humanitarian values is being displaced by those brandishing ideologies in conflict with the state philosophy of Pancasila and the nation's core principle of *Bhinneka Tunggal Ika* (Unity in Diversity). Schools can and should represent a bulwark against extremism by sowing values of tolerance, peace and respect for diversity among the younger generation. If they fail to carry out this noble task and instead let schools become institutions of radicalism, there will be no hope for a better future in Indonesia.

Intervention efforts to prevent the wave of radicalization targeting schools are emerging from initiatives within the school system, which are then facilitated by moderate groups outside the school. Through the Ministry of Education and Culture, the central government also has a significant role to play. Intervention efforts have been carried out based on needs analyses for each school in various regions in Indonesia. Of course, these efforts need to be carried out consistently, as we strive towards a more peaceful, harmonious, tolerant society, which respects our nation's rich diversity.

Notes

1   Maarif Institute was established in 2003 to respond to the humanitarian crisis after the 11 September 2001 tragedy in the United States of America. This institution was inspired by the role and thoughts of Ahmad Syafii Maarif, former Chairman of the Central Board of Muhammadiyah, the largest modernist Islamic civil society organization in Indonesia. Since the beginning, Maarif Institute has had a focus on strengthening the issues of democracy, human rights, pluralism and peace in Indonesia. They rolled out the issue as a counter to religious narratives that were intolerant, sectarian, conservative, exclusive and extreme among Indonesian people. Their main focus is on education and the young people. This institution believes that education is the main vehicle for transformation to create a civilized nation. Considering the challenges of extremist groups that are getting stronger and that have entered the educational system in Indonesia, since 2011 they have been involved in counter-violent extremism and prevention of extremism among young people in various educational institutions in Indonesia. They also conducted a series of research projects in an effort to map the roots of radicalism-extremism and its development in Indonesia. From the results of that research, Maarif Institute conducted several interventions to minimize and prevent radicalization among youth in Indonesia.

2   The Centre for Studies of Islam and Society (PPIM) UIN Jakarta is an autonomous research institution under Syarif Hidayatullah State Islamic University (UIN) Jakarta. PPIM UIN Jakarta was established in 1994 and has been continuously conducting research, advocacy and publication on issues of religious life and education in Indonesia. In collaboration with UNDP Indonesia, PPIM UIN Jakarta has since 2017 conducted Countering Violent Extremism for Youth (CONVEY) Indonesia, a programme which aims to build peace in Indonesia based on the religious education potential by addressing tolerance, diversity and violence issues among youth. In addition, since its establishment, PPIM UIN Jakarta has published the internationally acclaimed *Studia Islamika* journal, which focuses on Islamic studies in Indonesia and Southeast Asia.

3   Frans Magnis Suseno, 'Strengthening the Moral Dignity of Indonesia's Politics', *MAARIF Journal* 9, no. 1 (2014): 29–31.

4   Zachary Abuza, *Political Islam and Violence in Indonesia* (London and New York: Routledge, 2007), 81.

5   Qualitative research conducted by the Maarif Institute in 2011 has confirmed that the view of intolerance and radicalism has infiltrated students in schools through the role of alumni in mentoring and extra-curricular activities influenced by radical groups

from outside the school. See Ahmad Gaus, 'Mapping the Problem of Radicalism in Public High Schools in 4 Regions', *MAARIF Journal* 8, no. 1 (2013), 174–91. While the 2011 LAKIP research states that 50 per cent of students agree on radicalism-based actions, 84.8 per cent of students agree on the application of Islamic Sharia in Indonesia. In this research, they also found that 52.3 per cent of students agreed to acts of violence for religious solidarity. The SETARA Institute's research confirms the strengthening of intolerance among students in public schools with patterns of dissemination that are almost the same as those in previous Maarif Institute findings, namely through mentoring activities. See Wargadireja, A.T., 'Lampu Kuning Meningkatnya Radikalisme di Sekolah-Sekolah Indonesia', *Setara Institute for Democracy and Peace*, 5 September 2017, available at: http://setara-institute.org/lampu-kuning-meningkatnya-radikalisme-di-sekolah-sekolah-indonesia/ (accessed 3 March 2020). Whereas survey research conducted by the Wahid Foundation (2016) on the potential of radicalism and support for extremism among Rohis activists (with 1,626 respondents) found that 78 per cent of respondents supported the idea of the Caliphate; 33 per cent of respondents interpret *jihad* as a war against non-Muslims; 60 per cent of respondents expressed readiness to fight in Muslim countries in conflict. See the Wahid Foundation, *Research Report on the Potential of Radicalism among Rohis Activists in Public Schools* (2016), p. 12.

6   Rangga Eka Saputra, 'A Fire in the Husk: Religiosity of Generation Z', *Convey Report* 1, no. 1 (2018): 5; see also Didin Syafruddin and Ismatu Ropi (eds.), 'Islamisme, Intoleransi, dan Radikalisme', in *Gen Z: Kegalauan Identitas Keagamaan* (Jakarta: PPIM, 2018), 56.

7   Ibid., 70.

8   Ibid., 81.

9   Ibid., 82.

10   Ibid., 85–6; see also Saputra, 'A Fire in the Husk', p. 14.

11   Syafruddin and Ropi (eds.), 'Islamisme, Intoleransi, dan Radikalisme', p. 77.

12   Jamhari Makruf, *Incubator for Extremists? Radicalism and Moderation in Indonesia's Islamic Education System* (Center for Indonesian Law, Islam, and Society (CILIS), 2014); see also A. T. Wargadireja, 'Is Radicalism on the Rise in Indonesia's Public Schools?' *Vice*, 6 May 2017, available at: https://www.vice.com/en_asia/article/nz8b9x/is-radicalism-on-the-rise-in-indonesias-public-schools (accessed 17 March 2020).

13   Gaus, 'Mapping the Problem of Radicalism in Public High Schools in 4 Regions', 174–91.

14   Khelmy K. Pribadi and Pipit Aidul Fitriyana (eds.), 'Sukabumi', in *Maintaining the Fortress of Diversity in Schools: A Study on Student Council (OSIS) Policies in Padang, Cirebon, Sukabumi, Surakarta, Denpasar, and Tomohon* (Jakarta: PPIM & MAARIF Institute, 2019), 58–9.

15   In some schools, school management does not provide any teachers for Christianity, Catholicism, Hinduism, Confucianism or Buddhism for students with these minority religious backgrounds. Students are asked to go to priests or religious leaders who were in the church or house of worship near their homes outside school hours to get lessons about their religions. This is partly due to the absence of regulations in the regions that require schools to fulfil the obligation to provide religious education for minority groups (such as Christian students, Hindu students, Catholic students and students from other minority religions). The technical reason is because they are too few to create a learning group (study group). See Hayadin, 'Religious Education Service According to Student's Religion at School', *Edukasi Journal* 15,

no. 1 (2017), 13–31. Another process of marginalization that often occurs inside schools is injustice against minorities in celebrating religious holidays. Both in terms of regulations and practices in schools there is no attention and support from school management towards celebrating religious days for minority groups, whereas when there are Islamic holidays, the school holds events that involve all school members. See Fahmi Syahirul Alim, *Research Report on Strengthening the School Institution Through Internal Policies Which Mainstreaming Diversity in Sukabumi District,* 2017 [unpublished, archived at Maarif Institute].

16   Pribadi and Fitriyana (eds.), 'Sukabumi', 79.

17   See National Legislation No. 20 of 2003 concerning the National Education System, Article 3, Article 4 paragraph (4) and Article 12 paragraph (1b). See also Ministry of Education's Regulation number 81A 2013 about Curriculum Implementation wherein there are rules regarding extra-curricular activities; see also Ministry of Education's Regulation no. 39 of 2008 concerning OSIS and Student Development.

18   See Ahmad Gaus et al., *Research Report on the Problem of Radicalism in Public High Schools (Kab. Pandeglang, Kab. Cianjur, Kota Yogyakarta, dan Kota Surakarta,* 2011 [unpublished, archived at Maarif Institute]; see also Muhammad Abdullah Darraz, 'Radicalism and the Weak Role of Citizenship Education', *MAARIF Journal* 8, no. 1 (2013): 154–73.

19   OSIS is an organization located at the school level in Indonesia that starts from junior high schools and senior high schools. OSIS is administered and managed by the students chosen to be student councillors. Usually, this organization has a mentor from the teachers chosen by the school management. OSIS's members are all students who are in one school where the OSIS is located. OSIS is the only legitimate student organization in schools. Therefore, each school is required to form an Intra-school Student Organization (OSIS) which has no organizational relationship with the other OSIS at other schools and is not part of other organizations that exist outside of schools. For further information, see Ministry of National Education's Regulation no. 39 of 2008 on Student Development.

20   Formally, Rohis is part of the internal school student organization (OSIS) in each school in Indonesia. As part of OSIS, as stipulated in the Ministry of National Education's Regulation No. 39 of 2008 on Student Development, Rohis should not have organizational relations with any organizations or NGOs outside the school. But in reality Rohis in several schools have quite strong links with several organizations outside the school established by its alumni. Some of these organizations become extension of radical and Islamist groups such as Hizbut Tahrir Indonesia and Tarbiyyah group affiliated with PKS. These organizations are usually at the city/ district, provincial and national levels. This is the entry point for the penetration of radicalism in Rohis at school. See Ministry of National Education's Regulation No. 39 of 2008 on Student Development.

21   Further information see A. Tarmy, 'Begini Kronologi Siswi SMA Sragen yang Diteror Gegara Tak Berjilbab', *Detiknews,* 20 January 2020, available at: https://news.detik. com/berita-jawa-tengah/d-4866820/begini-kronologi-siswi-sma-sragen-yang-diteror-gegara-tak-berjilbab (accessed 10 July 2020).

22   The Tarbiyah movement or Jamaah Tarbiyah is an Islamic movement in Indonesia that has developed a process in understanding Islam among society in Indonesia since the 1980s. Tarbiyah movement is inspired by the Islamic thought of Hasan al-Banna (1906–49), the founder of the organization al-Ikhwan al-Muslimun, the Muslim Brothers of Egypt. The Tarbiyah movement developed its influence

among students in certain state universities, in campuses in Java and in various universities in the outer Islands like Sumatra, Sulawesi, Maluku and Kalimantan. Later they were also concerned with school students, especially in public schools, as a basis for their regeneration. In 1998, the Tarbiyah movement transformed itself into the political party known as the Justice Party (Partai Keadilan, PK), and then in 2003 it changed its name to the Prosperous Justice Party (Partai Keadilan dan Kesejahteraan, PKS). See Yon Mahmudi, *Islamising Indonesia: The Rise of Jemaah Tarbiyah and the Prosperous Justice Party* (Australia: The Australia National University E Press, 2006).

23 Pribadi and Fitriyana (eds.), 'Sukabumi', 82–3.

24 Muhammad Abdullah Darraz and Zuly Qodir, 'OSIS Rowing between Two Reefs: School's Policy, Radicalism, and Nationalistic Inclusivism', *CONVEY Report* 1, no. 4 (2018): 15; see also Pribadi and Fitriyana (eds.), 'Sukabumi', 86.

25 Sharia NKRI is the idea that the Republic of Indonesia needs to implement Islamic laws through sharia regulations, bureaucratic Islamization, schools and all but remain under the auspices of the Republic of Indonesia. Pancasila would remain the basis of the state, but its contents would be local sharia regulations and Islamic law would replace positive and civil law.

26 See Delmus Puneri Salim, *The Transnational and the Local in the Politics of Islam: The Case of West Sumatera Indonesia* (Switzerland: Springer, 2015).

27 See Sumanto Al Qurtuby, *Saudi Arabia and Indonesian Networks: Migration, Education, and Islam* (London: I.B. Tauris, 2019).

28 Khelmy K. Pribadi and Pipit Aidul Fitriyana (eds.), 'Latent Radicalism: Padang', in *Maintaining the Fortress of Diversity in Schools: A Study on Student Council (OSIS) Policies in Padang, Cirebon, Sukabumi, Surakarta, Denpasar, and Tomohon* (Jakarta: PPIM & Maarif Institute, 2019), 112.

29 Ibid., 112–3; see also Darraz and Qodir, 'OSIS Rowing between Two Reefs', 17.

30 When sending humanitarian aid to Syria through Turkey, FPIS had a misunderstanding with the Turkish government because FPIS is considered to be pro-ISIS (Islamic State of Iraq-Syria). Another figure in FPIS is Ustadz Abu Harits, who is also active in HASI (Hilal Ahmar Society Indonesia) or the Indonesian Crescent Societies, a non-profit organization working in the humanitarian field, similar to the Indonesian Red Cross (PMI). The only difference between HASI and PMI is that HASI is more dedicated to humanitarian issues affecting national and international Muslims. See Pribadi and Fitriyana (eds.), 'Latent Radicalism: Padang', 127.

31 There is Ustadz Bahtiar Nasir (UBN), who is considered pro-caliphate and one of the leaders of PP Muhammadiyah. There is also Achmad Miqdan, a member of the Muslim Lawyers Team (TPM), who was the defence attorney for the former leader of Jamaah Islamiyah, Abu Bakar Baasyir. See Pribadi and Fitriyana (eds.), 'Latent Radicalism: Padang', 127.

32 Ibid., 102.

33 Ibid., 69, 103.

34 Ibid., 102–3.

35 See Cameron Sumpter, 'Countering Violent Extremism in Indonesia: Priorities, Practices, and the Role of Civil Society', *Journal for Deradicalization* Summer volume, no. 11 (2017): 12–147.

36 These two things are the main parts that have been carried out by the Maarif Institute with the Indonesian Ministry of Education and Culture to systematically

prevent the penetration of radical groups in schools. Another thing that is also done is to strengthen the capacity of teachers and school supervisors in other different programmes. See Muhammad Abdullah Darraz, 'Radicalism and the Weak Role of Citizenship Education', *MAARIF Journal* 8, no. 1 (2013): 159.

37 See A. P. Schmid, 'Radicalisation, De-Radicalisation, Counter-radicalisation: A Conceptual Discussion and Literature Review', *ICCT Research Paper*, March 2013, available at: https://icct.nl/app/uploads/2013/03/ICCT-Schmid-Radicalisation-De-Radicalisation-Counter-Radicalisation-March-2013_2.pdf (accessed 16 December 2020).

38 Based on information received from the research respondents, the mosque, which was built at Public High School 1 Cibadak, is part of the '1,000 mosques' construction programme provided by the Arroyah Foundation, an umbrella foundation for the Arroyah Islamic and Arabic Studies College. The '1,000 Mosque' construction programme is a programme of da'wah and islamization carried out by the Arroyah Foundation for the Sukabumi district. See Fahmi Syahirul Alim, *Research Report on Strengthening the School Institution through Internal Policies Which Mainstreaming Diversity in Sukabumi District,* 2017 [unpublished, archived at MAARIF Institute] at pp. 13 and 19.

39 Fahmi Syahirul Alim, *Research Report on Strengthening the School Institution through Internal Policies Which Mainstreaming Diversity in Sukabumi District,* 2017 [unpublished, archived at MAARIF Institute] at 8.

40 Many reasons can be found for why students have more trust in their mentors from outside the school as the main reference for religious knowledge than their own religious teachers at school. First, the mentors come with religious material that is more interesting than what their teachers deliver. The mentors use religious and political discourse in their own modules. The mentors from Islamist groups usually provide a critical discussion on the conditions and systems of the country, which they view as a *thogut* or infidel state, and they offered the concept of the Caliphate as the only solution. For students this seems reasonable, more heroic and more in line with their Islamic vision. Second, mentors also offer academic assistance to help students with their assignments at school. They provide additional free courses with the requirement that students are willing to be actively involved in their study groups. The mentors also promise to help students apply for university. See Fahmi Syahirul Alim, *Research Report on Strengthening the School Institution through Internal Policies Which Mainstreaming Diversity in Sukabumi District,* 2017 [unpublished, archived at Maarif Institute]; see also Gaus, 'Mapping the Problem of Radicalism in Public High Schools in 4 Regions', 174–91.

41 The programme was initiated through a joint workshop involving principals and student coaches from twenty-five public high schools in seven areas. At the end of the workshop, the principals declared a joint agreement to strengthen diversity in schools. In addition, the output of the workshop was the formulation of internal policies in each school that strengthened diversity and specific programmes that strengthened the policy. Among the programmes they have initiated are (1) capacity building for human resources; (2) curriculum enrichment and renewal of learning methods that encourage diversity in schools; (3) building some facilities and infrastructure; (4) formulating an early detection and warning system; (5) providing extra assistance for extra-curricular activities and student organizations; (6) creating control systems and observing activities; and (7) strengthening media literacy in schools. In addition, this programme involves school supervisors from the Education

Office at the city and district level to more actively monitor school developments in an effort to strengthen diversity in school life.

42　See Fithri Dzakiyyah Hafizah, *MAARIF Institute's Narrative Report of Workshop on Strengthening the School Institution through Internal Policies Which Mainstreaming Diversity,* 2017 [unpublished, archived at Maarif Institute].

43　Saputra, 'A Fire in the Husk', 31.

Bibliography

Abuza, Zachary. *Political Islam and Violence in Indonesia.* London and New York: Routledge, 2007.

Al Qurtuby, Sumanto. *Saudi Arabia and Indonesian Networks: Migration, Education, and Islam.* London: I.B. Tauris, 2019.

Alim, Fahmi Syahirul. *Research Report on Strengthening the School Institution through Internal Policies Which Mainstreaming Diversity in Sukabumi District,* 2017 [unpublished, archived at Maarif Institute].

Darraz, Muhammad Abdullah. 'Radicalism and the Weak of Citizenship Education'. *MAARIF Journal* 8, no. 1 (2013): 154–73.

Darraz, Muhammad Abdullah and Qodir, Zuly. 'OSIS Rowing between Two Reefs: School's Policy, Radicalism, and Nationalistic Inclusivism'. *CONVEY Report* 1, no. 4 (2018): 5–37.

Gaus, Ahmad. 'Mapping the Problem of Radicalism in Public High Schools in 4 Regions'. *MAARIF Journal* 8, no. 1 (2013): 174–91.

Gaus, Ahmad et al. *Research Report on the Problem of Radicalism in Public High* Schools *(Kab. Pandeglang,* Kab. *Cianjur,* Kota Yogyakarta, *dan Kota Surakarta,* 2011) [unpublished, archived at Maarif Institute].

Hafizah, Fithri Dzakiyyah. *MAARIF Institute's Narrative Report of Workshop on Strengthening the School Institution through Internal Policies Which Mainstreaming Diversity,* 2017 [unpublished, archived at Maarif Institute].

Hayadin. 'Religious Education Service According to Student's Religion at School'. *Edukasi Journal* 15, no. 1 (2017): 13–31.

Mahmudi, Yon. *Islamising Indonesia: The Rise of Jemaah Tarbiyah and the Prosperous Justice Party.* Australia: The Australia National University E Press, 2006.

Makruf, Jamhari. *Incubator for Extremists? Radicalism and Moderation in Indonesia's Islamic Education System.* Center for Indonesian Law, Islam, and Society (CILIS), 2014.

Pribadi, Khelmy K. and Fitriyana, Pipit Aidul (eds.). 'Latent Radicalism: Padang'. In *Maintaining the Fortress of Diversity in Schools: A Study on Student Council (OSIS) Policies in Padang,* Cirebon, *Sukabumi,* Surakarta, *Denpasar, and Tomohon,* 107–34. Jakarta: PPIM & Maarif Institute, 2019.

Pribadi, Khelmy K. and Fitriyana, Pipit Aidul (eds.). 'Sukabumi'. In *Maintaining the Fortress of Diversity in Schools: A Study on Student Council (OSIS) Policies in Padang,* Cirebon, *Sukabumi,* Surakarta, *Denpasar, and Tomohon,* 51–104. Jakarta: PPIM & Maarif Institute, 2019.

Salim, Delmus Puneri. *The Transnational and the Local in the Politics of Islam: The Case of West Sumatera Indonesia.* Switzerland: Springer, 2015.

Saputra, Rangga Eka. 'A Fire in the Husk: Religiosity of Generation Z'. *Convey Report* 1, no. 1 (2018): 3–48.

Sumpter, Cameron. 'Countering Violent Extremism in Indonesia: Priorities, Practices, and the Role of Civil Society'. *Journal for Deradicalization* Summer volume, no. 11 (2017): 112–47.

Suseno, Frans Magnis. 'Strengthening the Moral Dignity of Indonesia's Politics'. *MAARIF Journal* 9, no. 1 (2014): 7–13.

Syafruddin, Didin and Ropi, Ismatur (eds.). *Gen Z: Kegalauan Identitas Keagamaan.* Jakarta: PPIM, 2018.

The Wahid Foundation. *Research Report on the Potential of Radicalism among Rohis Activists in Public Schools*, 2016.

7

Individually targeted preventions in Indonesia: Effective in theory, tricky in practice

Cameron Sumpter

Introduction

Dating back to a long wave of arrests following the bombing attacks on the island of Bali in 2002, Indonesia has had considerable practice with initiatives to prevent violent extremism. Much of this has come through engaging individuals convicted of terrorism offences and more expansive programmes that seek to build societal tolerance and unity. Yet the nation has far less experience with programmes aimed at 'diversion' – defined here as identifying people becoming involved with violent extremism and attempting to steer them towards more positive pursuits before they commit a crime.

A useful means for conceptualizing this particular approach to intervention is illustrated by the *public health model* of prevention, which was repurposed in the early 1980s to curb the prevalence of violent crime and has more recently informed approaches to preventing and countering violent extremism (P/CVE).[1] The model divides interventions into three stages of requirement, from structural prevention systems to individually targeted programmes and reintegration assistance following prison sentences. The Indonesian government has not adopted this model to formulate its prevention policies, but the framework remains a pertinent resource for considering efforts to date and identifying possible gaps.

Upstream strategies to prevent extremism from burgeoning, which are discussed in detail throughout Muhammad Abdullah Darraz's chapter in this edited volume, are beginning to take shape in the Indonesian education system. The present chapter considers the bigger picture with a specific focus: first, by outlining the benefits of the public health model for P/CVE policy and analysing Indonesia's experience with the associated practices, and then discussing the difficulty of implementing individually targeted programmes.

As in other contexts, the main problem is accurately identifying individuals who may pose a future threat and could benefit from a personalized intervention programme. Further issues include suboptimal coordination between state security agencies and civil society organizations, resistance from Islamic associations concerned about stigmatizing religion, and the sheer scale of the issue. While only a few extremists ultimately become violent in Indonesia, the number of those who could take this path is likely to be in the thousands.

Given the global travel restrictions imposed by the Covid-19 pandemic, interviews for this chapter were conducted by phone, video applications and email correspondence between Singapore and Indonesia. Respondents included researchers, civil society P/CVE practitioners and former government officers.[2]

Preventing violence through public health

Public health methods have been applied to the prevention of societal violence for almost forty years. In 1983, the United States Centers for Disease Control and Prevention (CDC) set up a Violence Epidemiology Branch to focus on addressing violent behaviour through a public health lens.[3] The approach developed into a 'relay race' of four stages, involving an array of contributing stakeholders with each phase informed and empowered by its predecessor.

First, the aim was to define the particular problem and to gather as much data as possible. Next, indicators that both increase and potentially decrease the likelihood of violence were identified before specific prevention strategies were established and assessed. Finally, initiatives thought to mitigate the problem were rolled out with training and close coordination among stakeholders.[4]

In 2002, the World Health Organization (WHO) released a landmark report on violence and health, emphasizing the structural drivers of violence and a collective action response. The document divided preventions and interventions into three levels. Primary, secondary and tertiary preventions respectively focused on avoiding violence, immediately responding when it does occur, and ensuring long-term care in its wake.[5] *Universal* interventions were aimed at the general population, such as through public messaging campaigns; *selected* interventions considered individuals deemed to be at risk of involvement in violence and *indicated* interventions dealt with those who had already displayed violent behaviour.[6]

The public health model has been embraced by researchers and practitioners working to prevent gang membership and violence, particularly due to its emphasis on risk and protective factors associated with joining gangs and the expectation of a multi-disciplinary response.[7] The WHO's terminology is present but adapted, with the three stages of intervention delineated as primary, secondary and tertiary.[8] Primary preventions/interventions are considered particularly important as they target the structural conditions conducive to young people gravitating towards gang affiliation.[9]

An important difference between joining a criminal gang and a terrorist organization is that the former is generally motivated by money and power, and the latter will have ideological goals underlying its identity. While this adds a layer of complexity when considering how to prevent affiliation with violent extremist groups, the public health strategy is nonetheless deemed a useful framework for structuring efforts.[10] Similar to benefits for general violence and gang membership prevention, the rigours of public health methods require P/CVE initiatives to involve multi-disciplinary input and community partnerships, and to identify risk and protective factors.[11] The three divisions of focus also provide methodological clarity and are outlined in the following discussion.

Primary preventions for violent extremism

The goal of primary prevention is to stop the initial emergence of violent extremism before it takes root.[12] Programmes in this broad space are often informed by the structural and societal conditions thought to drive radicalization. Issues of focus can vary widely depending on context. Initiatives may seek to address problems at the societal level, such as governance and injustice, but many primary preventions addressing violent extremism are directed towards communities or sections of society considered vulnerable to extremism, whether it be a particular age group, geographic location or other markers identified by pre-design mapping research.

A broad complication for primary interventions to prevent violent extremism is the difficulty of identifying precise risk factors. Whereas criminal street gangs largely operate in communities suffering from identifiable structural problems, extremist organizations tend to be more diffuse, and their drivers are a more convoluted array of push and pull factors. In Western nations, this has sometimes induced the targeting of whole migrant communities. Potentially constructive social programmes are thus tarnished with a national security brush, resulting in stigmatization and erosion of trust.[13] Governments on different continents also tend to emphasize the role of ideology as the key driving force of violent extremism, as it precludes the acknowledgement of thorny grievances regarding governance and other structural issues.[14]

On the civil society side, a rush for lucrative P/CVE funding streams has generated initiatives that may hold broad benefits if delivered effectively, but either fail to address specific risk factors or fall short by engaging only accessible sections of society. For example, independent monitoring teams have observed non-governmental organizations in Kenya 'rebranding' themselves from development to P/CVE in order to secure funding, which adversely impacts buy-in from local stakeholders and creates conceptual problems.[15] Activists in the southern Philippines island of Mindanao have also spoken of the myriad small organizations that suddenly emerged to exploit the P/CVE donor 'gravy train' following the siege of Marawi in 2018.

Some argue that primary preventions for P/CVE should be fundamentally all-of-society, in order to address structural issues without stigmatizing certain communities.[16] But while promoting human rights, good governance, education and societal tolerance are all necessary endeavours where they are lacking, primary interventions for violent extremism ultimately require more particular targeting than initiatives aimed at general criminality and gang membership.

Secondary preventions for violent extremism

Secondary interventions are those specifically targeting individuals who are displaying signs of 'radicalization' or deemed as being vulnerable to extremist recruitment.[17] The idea is to provide people with an 'off-ramp' from the pathway they may be following and divert them towards more positive endeavours.[18] In the UK, and to a lesser degree the United States of America and Australia, the strategy has involved identifying likely participants and channelling them into social programmes, usually conducted by civil society organizations.[19] Denmark perhaps has one of the more effective initiatives, involving appropriately selected mentors who work with participants to build trust and break barriers over an extended period of time.[20]

People become involved in (violent) extremism for different combinations of reasons and at varied paces, so personalized secondary interventions provide a suitably nuanced method for conducting P/CVE. But the approach also raises a number of issues and complications. As with primary preventions, the identification of target candidates is a significant obstacle.

The UK's Prevent Duty includes a statutory requirement for educators and public health professionals to report suspicious behaviour or views among their students and patients. But while teachers may be well placed to spot concerning attitudes, drivers are often too complex to observe, particularly with the limited training teachers receive. Well-publicized false positives have provoked controversy, and observers believe the requirement may hinder healthy classroom discussion.[21]

More clear-cut referrals come from law enforcement, when individuals are found on the peripheries of an investigation; yet, this strategy has its own challenges. A 2019 guidebook on referral mechanisms in the Western Balkans noted the role of police in secondary interventions hinges on a number of issues, such as levels of trust between police and the communities they serve, the transparency of relevant information-sharing mechanisms, and whether an inclusive community policing model is favoured over more repressive approaches.[22] Where institutional trust is high, law enforcement may provide constructive contributions to the process. But in post-conflict or authoritarian states, policing methods may be unconducive to working with social service providers and civil society.

Trust deficits can also lead practitioners working on primary and secondary prevention initiatives to resist partnerships with state agencies, for fear of losing credibility by association. In the United States of America, a number of civil society organizations working on community initiatives declined CVE funding from the federal government in early 2017 because of disagreements with the Trump administration's policies and public comments from the president.[23] Organizations involved with P/CVE in Australia have also been hesitant to sign on to a government 'directory of services', to which police-led assessment panels refer when deciding particular courses of intervention for individuals of concern.[24]

Occupying the so-called 'pre-crime' space, secondary interventions court controversy and attract legitimate criticism in different contexts. However, if frameworks and processes are designed sensitively with substantial input (if not leadership) from civil society, individually targeted prevention initiatives can play an important role in any comprehensive P/CVE strategy.

Tertiary preventions for violent extremism

The third area of focus in the public health model concerns individuals who have been convicted of terrorism-related offences and who are either serving prison sentences or reintegrating with society. Tertiary preventions would also cover those who have returned from abroad after involvement with violent extremist organizations in other nations, where there is insufficient evidence to prosecute them in court.

A primary distinction here is whether the initial aim is to 'de-radicalize' or 'disengage' the individual in question.[25] The former involves a process of modifying an individual's ideological convictions, so that they no longer support the cause, while the less ambitious goal of disengagement is to change the person's behaviour, so that they do not seek to commit violent or illegal acts, while still perhaps endorsing the ideological movement. Some observers believe that maintaining a distinction between the two goals is counterproductive, as focusing on both beliefs and behaviour is important in equal measure, and a balanced approach is necessary, depending on the individual and context in question.[26]

Others have argued convincingly that the relationship between extremist ideas and violent behaviour is nonlinear and complex, so ideological debate or a guided process of de-radicalization may not be a constructive function of managing convicted terrorists.[27] Recent empirical studies have shown that 'push factors' such as disillusionment are more important influences among individual decisions to disengage from an extremist organization.[28]

Tertiary interventions for violent extremists face a number of other more practical challenges. Chief among them is whether to separate inmates convicted of terrorism into specialized sections or to disperse them among the general prison population, both of which present problems.[29] Another issue is the incentive structure of rehabilitation and reintegration initiatives for violent extremists. An excessive example is in Saudi Arabia, where de-radicalization programmes have involved participants receiving cars, accommodation, stipends and even help in finding a wife.[30] But even when an initiative simply leads to more comfortable conditions in prison compared with those for other inmates, questions are raised regarding the possible moral hazard of rewarding extremism over regular criminality.

In the post-9/11 world, initiatives to counter violent extremism mostly began in prisons, before attempts to mitigate recidivism travelled further upstream to prevention efforts in communities and among individuals flirting with involvement. Indonesia's experiences have largely followed this path, first with tertiary interventions and then with the development of more primary preventions. However, individually targeted secondary preventions have remained few and far between. The next sections outline these experiences in order.

The origins of P/CVE in Indonesia

Islamist extremists have emerged in Indonesia through subsequent waves since the nation's struggle for independence in the 1940s. However, contemporary counterterrorism practices mostly date back to the October 2002 Bali bombing attacks, which were conducted by the regional terrorist organization Jemaah Islamiyah and killed over 200 people.[31] The tragedy fast-tracked new anti-terrorism legislation in early 2003, which defined the associated crimes, extended powers of investigation and surveillance, and allowed suspects to be held for seven days without charge.[32]

Despite an effective operational response from law enforcement, the nation's long-neglected prison system, with its overcrowded cells and culture of corruption, was not an ideal environment in which to place regular batches of dangerous militants and ideologues. Police were concerned about their influence on regular inmates but also saw the convicted extremists as a potential wealth of information on operatives connected to the bombings and the broader jihadi movement in Southeast Asia. Officers knew that once their prisoners were transferred to the anarchic prison system they would lose the ability to work with them regularly, so they aimed to hold detainees in police cells for as long as possible.[33] Police began to develop relationships with the detained extremists, and it was in this context that Indonesia began experimenting with de-radicalization.

Tertiary preventions: From relationships to ideology

While Indonesian government stakeholders have long employed the term *deradikalisasi* (de-radicalization) to describe their tertiary interventions, early efforts bore more resemblance to disengagement strategies. The aim was to slowly build trust with the detainees by treating them respectfully, which was often met with surprise. Officers gradually developed dialogue by finding areas of mutual interest, such as religious faith and family dynamics.

A central figure in the approach was Brigadier General Surya Dharma, a former head of police counterterrorism unit Special Detachment 88 (*Densus 88*). BG Dharma stressed the importance of police showing the detainees that they, too, were devout Muslims by leading prayer sessions and even staying overnight in cells. Initiatives were sometimes controversial, such as in 2007 when the Densus head invited around twenty convicted terrorists to his house for an *Iftar* (breaking of the fast) event, which sparked anger in Australia.[34]

During this period, civil society actors also conducted programmes within prisons aimed at piecemeal disengagement. One example was the Indonesian chapter of the US-based Search for Common Ground, which had a project aimed at 'conflict management training', encouraging prisoners to engage more constructively with other inmates.[35] Confined to only eight prisons, the initiatives were somewhat limited, but the organization's creative team-building and role-play activities were reportedly well received.[36] Another NGO called *Yayasan Prasasti Perdamaian* (YPP) has also worked to build personal relationships with prisoners and supported their reintegration following release, either by starting their own business or working at the organization's two restaurants.[37]

While these 'personal' approaches have ostensibly remained a prominent feature of interventions in Indonesia, the establishment of a national counterterrorism agency in 2010 led to a greater focus on counter-ideological argument. The new *Badan Nasional*

Penanggulangan Terorisme (BNPT) served as a platform for the Indonesian military (TNI) to secure a counterterrorism foothold and tertiary interventions developed a more nationalist complexion. The agency's 2013 Blueprint for Deradicalisation laid out a new approach that would target the 'radical ideology of terrorism'.[38] Indonesia's foundational philosophy of *Pancasila* began to feature in tertiary interventions, which have included flag-raising ceremonies in prison yards and pledges of loyalty to the republic.[39]

Civil society organizations were largely left out of the BNPT's tertiary interventions, but have more recently found space following the forced repatriation of hundreds of extremists who attempted to join the Islamic State in Syria and Iraq. Starting from late 2017, waves of so-called 'deportees' were accommodated in shelters run by the Ministry of Social Affairs (Kemensos) for one month before reintegrating into society.

Stakeholders such as Civil Society against Violent Extremism (C-SAVE) and YPP then developed the capacity of Kemensos social workers to engage the new recalcitrant residents. Success was patchy and not helped by a lack of distinct funding and deficient coordination among the various agencies and organizations involved. But the approach evoked memories of early police efforts, as the general goal was to slowly build relationships with the intention of diminishing exclusivist views and possibly broadening their acceptance of perceived outsiders.

Primary preventions: Good intentions and complex problems

Structural risk factors for violent extremism can be confounding in Indonesia. The militant organization Jemaah Islamiyah (JI) was established in the 1980s and 1990s by veteran Islamist activists who had developed a particular hatred for the repressive New Order regime of President Suharto. JI's founding leaders sent several batches of Indonesian militants to train with the Afghan *mujahideen* at camps in Pakistan during the 1980s, where they began to internalize the Salafi-Jihadi ideology of Abdullah Azzam and Osama bin Laden.[40] When communal violence broke out in the Indonesian islands of Maluku and Sulawesi in the years following Suharto's fall in 1998, jihadi organizations exploited religious dimensions to fan the flames, recruit new members and gain conflict experience.

Beyond the history of regional militant jihadi organizations, commentators have also pointed to the influence of Wahhabi interpretations of Islam through Saudi outreach efforts over the past thirty years, leading to the increased popularity of Salafism and possibly greater exclusivity and societal intolerance.[41] But while this may have facilitated more of an enabling environment, links between purist Salafi practice and militant Islamism have never been uniformly established in Indonesia.[42]

Democratic reforms over the past twenty years and the resolution of conflict in the outer islands surely helped dampen extremist activity, as did effective law enforcement operations, but the militant jihadi movement in Indonesia is stubbornly resilient and the rise of ISIS in 2014 reinserted considerable amounts of energy. However, the diffuse movement of splintered networks has no socio-economic profile, no assumed educational background or a geographic centre. Instead, a number of 'hot spots' called *zona merah* ('red zones') have been classified as being vulnerable to recruitment and extremist activity. One identifiable feature of the post-ISIS period is the increased involvement of women in every aspect of the militancy, while another longstanding theme is the prevalence of family connections – sometimes going back generations.

The most purpose-built primary prevention initiative from the government has been the *Forum Koordinasi Pencegahan Terorisme* (FKPT), which was set up by the BNPT in 2012 to coordinate efforts at the regional level. Now encompassing thirty-two of the archipelago's thirty-four provinces, FKPT involves occasional meetings between provincial governments and security officials, former senior police officers, academics, and religious scholars from the Indonesian Ulama Council (MUI).

While the associations serve to raise awareness among regional elites and may sometimes lead to constructive local initiatives, observers believe the events and seminars often held at upmarket hotels are too high level to be effective.[43] The forums would be useful for addressing provincial structural issues that may fuel extremism but instead, they appear to be mostly generic talk shops for discussing concepts and recent incidents.

The government has also worked with civil society associations on PVE-type initiatives, particularly those connected to the nation's largest Muslim organization, Nahdlatul Ulama (NU). An example is the Wahid Institute (now the Wahid Foundation), which was founded in the mid-2000s to address extremism and communal conflict in Indonesia through research, advocacy and public education.[44] In 2013, the Foundation conducted baseline studies on intolerant views among high school students and began a project in collaboration with BNPT, where practitioners engaged students through issues such as multiculturalism and pluralism using specially designed board games, which were left at each school for further use.

One initiative involves a board game that teaches students about the principles and positive values of Pancasila. The Gusdurian Network is another organization working on primary prevention-type activities and like the Wahid Institute was named after former president Abdurrahman 'Gus Dur' Wahid. Operating in over 100 cities throughout the country, the Network tackles exclusivism by building narratives of national pride and encouraging parents to foster openness and curiosity among their children.

Dozens of smaller grassroots associations have emerged with similar programmes in recent years, often funded by international donors and the aid agencies of national governments. As in other settings, some organizations have modified their focus from issues such as development to P/CVE to access funding streams and sometimes feel the need to follow models prescribed by the donor agencies, rather than using local knowledge.[45]

Yet the major issue with primary prevention programmes for violent extremism is their generality. The landscape of intersections where politics and religion meet in Indonesia is complex. Some exclusivist organizations are non-violent but considered subversive, such as the now outlawed Hizbut Tahrir Indonesia (HTI). Others, such as the hard-line Front Pembela Islam (FBI), have supported the Indonesian state in the past (depending on those in power) but have also encouraged and conducted acts of political violence. Indonesia has a problem with creeping intolerance, which is important for civil society to address, but specifically preventing *violent* extremism requires a more targeted approach.

Secondary interventions: The double-edged sword of identification

In 2016, the nation's Chief Security Minister General Wiranto said, 'In Indonesia, [a potential extremist] cannot be caught. We have to wait for him to act before we can act. We can catch him only after he has already claimed a life. To prevent such a situation and to ensure the authorities can apprehend the person before he pulls off such nefarious act, the law must be immediately revised.'[46]

After years of stalled discussion, the 2003 terrorism legislation was finally updated in mid-2018, fast-tracked following shocking suicide bombing attacks on churches in Indonesia's second city of Surabaya, conducted by parents with young children in tow. The new law included a controversially broad definition of terrorism and extended periods of pre-charge detention quite significantly, but also roughly outlined the government's approach to preventing terrorism, which was to be fleshed out by subsequent regulations.[47]

Government Regulation (*Peraturan Pemerintah*) Number 77 was eventually issued in November 2019.[48] As with de-radicalization initiatives, counter-radicalization is to be coordinated by BNPT and carried out by the 'relevant ministries/institutions', including possibly regional governments, given the statutory provisions. The approach involves three similar and overlapping categories: counter-narratives (*kontra narasi*), counter-propaganda (*kontra propaganda*) and counter ideology (*kontra ideologi*).[49] The latter is focused on strengthening nationalism and a subject's understanding of Pancasila, while the first two encompass online and offline messaging campaigns, monitoring online content, religious instruction, and 'training activities, seminars and discussions on the dangers of radical terrorism'.

A subsequent presidential regulation issued in early 2021 expanded the strategy further by instituting a national action plan to prevent violent extremism, known by its Indonesian acronym RAN PE.[50] The broad plan covers a range of counterterrorism activities, from target hardening and professionalizing law enforcement practice, to witness and victim protection, and legislative oversight.[51] The second of the plan's three 'pillars' covers counter-radicalization, which is consistent with the approach established through previous regulations.

RAN PE promises to provide a greater role for local governments in terms of implementing programmes relevant to their context, but it remains unclear how individual participants will be identified, selected and incentivized to join associated programmes. BNPT has worked with the families of people convicted of terrorism offences, offering financial support and attempting to build relationships. However, such efforts come under Regulation 77/2019's stipulations on de-radicalization, which apparently provide people 'exposed to radical terrorism' with religious and nationalist instruction and assistance with starting a small business.[52]

There are no mechanisms for targeting appropriate individual candidates for the activities and discussions mentioned in the regulations. Instead, the state-led counter-radicalization approach would be more accurately defined as primary intervention, as it involves strategies such as online counter-messaging and public outreach events.

One attempt to create a localized mechanism for identification that precludes direct input from law enforcement, initially at least, was a programme known as the *Early Warning System*. Established by a consortium of non-state organizations called Civil Society against Violent Extremism (C-SAVE) in 2019, the pilot included sixteen villages across Java, following research into vulnerable areas and consultation with sub-district and village leaders. Not every village was receptive to the idea, however, and organizers suspect the communities that rejected the proposal may well be those in greater need of intervention.[53]

Within villages that agreed to participate, the organization attempted to raise awareness of violent extremist networks and ideology in Indonesia and to discuss potential signs of radicalization. People were then encouraged to report suspicious behaviour to a 'village team', which was pre-elected by local popular vote. Neighbourhood police and the military district command were informed of the system and played an advisory role but were not involved in any participant engagements (an attempt to remove the security dimension). The initiative was not meant to be a surveillance instrument, but rather a tool for alerting people to potential issues and for providing a 'safe space' to address problems locally.[54]

While the initiative's intentions were almost certainly constructive and pure, Indonesia has a murky history of co-opting local level authority for state surveillance. During President Suharto's New Order Regime (1966–98), the Army stationed non-commissioned officers in villages throughout the country, where they worked with respective local leaders from the nationwide network of neighbourhood associations, or *rukun warga* and *rukun tetangga* (RW/RT), to collect information on political/cultural/economic gatherings in their communities.[55]

During the 1980s, police began coordinating private neighbourhood security patrol posts, which provided information to police on local gangs and potential criminality.[56] In the current climate, RT/RW heads have been instructed to keep an eye on their neighbourhoods for possible terrorist activity, which has also led to the surveillance and targeting of people from religious minorities and the LGBT community, for example.[57] Moreover, the RAN PE national action plan includes provisions on community policing, which have renewed debates over whether the practice is intended to be a genuine collaboration with local residents or more of an intelligence collecting exercise.[58]

In some Western nations, attempting to pinpoint individuals on pathways to violent Islamist extremism has led to the alienation and stigmatization of ethnic minority communities. In Indonesia, it has been organized Islam that has felt targeted by counter-radicalization strategies. Groups with connections to violent extremist networks have unsurprisingly cried foul, but so too have representatives of the nation's highest clerical body, the Indonesian Ulama Council (MUI), and other mainstream associations, which have argued that de-radicalization efforts weaken faith and threaten the unity of the Muslim community.[59]

Critics have asserted in the past that the government's emphasis on ideology as a driver of violent extremism panders to Western donor nations and ignores structural problems such as corruption and injustice.[60] More recently, this debate has become embroiled in political polarization, as the Widodo administration is seen as taking a resolute position against Islamists, who largely supported his opponent in 2019's general election.[61]

One way around the problems associated with identification (and stigma) is to find people online, where they may be more open to revealing their views. Activists behind an online initiative called *ruangobrol.id* began such attempts in mid-2019 as part of an eighteen-month pilot project to engage people on Facebook, with a view to meeting up for offline interventions. As they were under the cover of pseudonyms, it was not difficult to find people espousing concerning views and following observation and scrutiny of their 'likes' and 'friend' lists; the individuals were placed on a spectrum from the simply curious to the possibly dangerous.[62]

Practitioners then reached out to those considered to be on a potential pathway to violence, firstly by praising their analysis of a post or article, then trying to point them towards constructive endeavours such as educational scholarships. But while the initiative provided insight into the online networks, those involved found that building trust online is even harder than offline, and after a year and a half, not a single person had been engaged in the real world. Ruangobrol has other innovative and positive initiatives, but its foray into secondary interventions further highlights the challenges involved.

A further notable effort was established by an organization called the Maarif Institute, which has run outreach programmes for young people thought to hold intolerant views.[63] Since 2011, Maarif has held an annual youth camp called the National Jamboree, involving students from dozens of high schools across the country. Hundreds of applications are narrowed down to around 100 participants per year, who are selected on different criteria, including the extent to which they display exclusivist or sectarian religious attitudes. The institute developed a curriculum for the camp, covering concepts such as social justice, democracy, tolerance, empathy and faith.[64] Facilitators take the young people through a range of immersive community activities and inter-faith lessons, such as visits to places of worship.

While such engagement is highly promising, perhaps the most directly effective approach towards targeted intervention in Indonesia has involved communities recapturing local mosques that had come under extremist influence. The Institute for Policy Analysis of Conflict (IPAC) has outlined particular cases where astute strategies and careful operation have had successful outcomes. One took place at the Muhammad Ramadhan Mosque, southeast of Jakarta, which had gradually developed a militant jihadi constituency over several years but was unpopular with many surrounding residents.

Following discussions, a sub-district government official, the local police chief and neighbourhood religious leaders devised a plan to use the Prophet's birthday (an occasion not observed by Salafi Jihadists) to stage a strategically deft community intervention, while a land claim was concurrently issued to legally wrestle the property from the mosque's governing board.[65] With many moving parts, IPAC is clear that such schemes require prudent sensitivity, as any hint of vigilantism could quickly descend to violence.[66] But handled correctly, community mosque takeovers present a pertinent example of a grassroots, multi-stakeholder P/CVE initiative with tangible outcomes.

This type of initiative again raises the question of the distinction between primary and secondary interventions and probably exists somewhere in between. The majority of individual community interventions in Indonesia are tertiary efforts involving ex-inmates recently released from prison. BNPT regularly sends people to engage with these 'formers', who are often given modest grants of a few hundred dollars to set up a small business such as a street food cart or clothing shop. Assistance is almost always greatly appreciated and allows BNPT officers to stay in contact with the former prisoners, but the individuals are generally spread throughout the nation, so it is not always easy for the Jakarta-based officers to meet them regularly, which diminishes the programme's effectiveness.

For this reason, grassroots organizations doing similar work are likely more successful, as they can draw on local knowledge and community support networks for more consistent engagement. A good example is a programme run by a former JI bomb-maker named Ali Fauzi, who has been working to disengage extremists from their networks in his hometown of Lamongan in East Java for several years.[67] With the foundation he established, *Lingkar Perdamaian* (Peace Circle), Ali Fauzi conducts various initiatives, from helping former prisoners start new lives and working with young people in his community to organizing events where victims of terrorism share their stories and experiences. The BNPT's involvement in supporting such grassroots efforts has been scattered in the past, but the agency has recently become more open to working with civil society, which would be a hugely positive development moving forward.[68]

Conclusion

The public health model for prevention holds value for both informing comprehensive strategies to prevent violent extremism and highlighting the difficulties of their implementation in practice. Particularly helpful is the emphasis on (and input from) a diverse range of stakeholders in programmes aimed at preventing the lure of extremism and diverting people from pathways to violence.

Civil society organizations are now widely considered to be crucial components of P/CVE efforts; yet, a number of practical challenges present obstacles. The operational cultures and worldviews of national security and law enforcement agencies are usually quite different from those focused on social services and community development. In some contexts, trust deficits are bottom-up, where community actors are wary of the state's blunt instruments. In others, a lack of respect comes from top-down and government agencies view civil society as a possible resource to be used on their own terms, but not as an equal partner. Often, both sentiments are present.

But the main problem with realizing the intentions of the public health model for P/CVE is the need to identify clear-cut risk and protective factors associated with involvement. While this evidence-based approach is crucial for addressing the appropriate issues and the right people, the unfortunate truth is we still do not have a secure handle on what exactly drives individuals to commit violence for an ideological cause.

Sometimes the pathways are obvious in hindsight, but countless people embrace a violent ideology without committing violence, while others carry out attacks without really understanding the intended end. Attempting to identify people before they become terrorists may be possible, but only if we are to accept an accompanying number of false-positive cases, which can be damaging to each individual concerned and potentially their wider communities.

Ideally in Indonesia, the police would identify individuals on the peripheries of their counterterrorism investigations and incentivize their engagement with intervention programmes conducted by civil society organizations. This may have happened in isolated cases in certain areas, but the police would probably prefer to use such individuals as sources of information rather than specific candidates for reform.

Given the scale of the issue and complex dynamics between stakeholders, it may be unrealistic for a secondary prevention mechanism to be formalized in Indonesia. Individually targeted P/CVE interventions are still possible, but they will more likely emerge organically in particular settings where strong communities, charismatic personalities and other favourable conditions create genuine opportunities for diversion.

Notes

1   See, for example, Organisation for Security and Cooperation in Europe (OSCE), *Understanding Referral Mechanisms in Preventing and Countering Violent Extremism and Radicalization that Lead to Terrorism: Navigating Challenges and Protecting Human Rights; Guidebook for South-Eastern Europe* (Vienna: Organization for Security and Cooperation in Europe (OSCE), 2019).
2   The project obtained ethics approval from the Institutional Review Board (IRB) at Nanyang Technological University in Singapore.
3   Centers for Disease Control and Prevention (CDC) (last reviewed: 28 January 2021), 'Timeline of Violence as a Public Health Problem', *Centers for Disease Control and Prevention (CDC)*, available at: https://www.cdc.gov/violenceprevention/ publichealthissue/timeline.html (accessed 14 May 2020).
4   Centers for Disease Control and Prevention (CDC) (last reviewed: 28 January 2021), 'The Public Health Approach to Violence Prevention', *Centers for Disease Control and Prevention (CDC)*, available at: https://www.cdc.gov/violenceprevention/ publichealthissue/publichealthapproach.html (accessed 14 May 2020).
5   Etienne G. Krug, Linda L. Dahlberg, James A. Mercy, Anthony B. Zwi and Rafael Lozano, *World Report on Violence and Health* (Geneva: World Health Organization, 2002), 15.
6   Ibid.

7   Dawn Delfin McDaniel, 'Risk and Protective Factors Associated with Gang Affiliation among High-risk Youth: A Public Health Approach'. *Injury Prevention* 18, no. 4 (2012): 253–8.

8   Tamara M. Haegerich, James Mercy and Billie Weiss, 'What Is the Role of Public Health in Gang-membership Prevention?' in *Changing Course: Preventing Gang Membership*, Thomas R. Simon, ed. (Washington, DC: National Institute of Justice, 2013), 31–49.

9   Erika Gebo, 'An Integrated Public Health and Criminal Justice Approach to Gangs: What Can Research Tell Us?' *Preventive Medicine Reports*, no. 4 (2016): 376–80; For associated discussion on violent extremism in Indonesia, See Muhammad Abdullah Darraz's chapter in this volume.

10   Tore Bjorgo, *Lessons from Crime Prevention in Preventing Violent Extremism by Police* (European Commission: RAN Centre of Excellence, 2020).

11   Kamaldeep S. Bhui, Medlyn H. Hicks, Myrna Lashley and Edgar Jones, 'A Public Health Approach to Understanding and Preventing Violent Radicalization'. *BMC Medicine* 10, no. 16 (2012): 1–8; Jonathan Callgren, Ted Kenyon, Lauren Kervick, Sally Scudder, Micah Walters, Kate Whitehead, Jeffrey Connor and Carole Rollie Flynn, 'Countering Violent Extremism: Applying the Public Health Model', *Georgetown Security Studies Review* (special report) (2016): 1–38.

12   Steven Weine and David Eisenman, 'How Public Health Can Improve Initiatives to Counter Violent Extremism', *START*, 5 April 2016, available at: https://www. start.umd.edu/news/how-public-health-can-improve-initiatives-counter-violent-extremism (accessed 12 May 2020).

13   See Faiza Patel and Meghan Koushik, *Countering Violent Extremism* (New York: Brennan Center for Justice, 2017), 1–80.

14   Eric Rosand, Emily Winterbotham, Michael Jones and Franziska Praxl-Tabuchi, *A Roadmap to Progress: The State of the Global P/CVE Agenda* (London: The Prevention Projects and Royal United Services Institute, 2018), 23.

15   Royal United Services Institute (RUSI), *STRIVE Horn of Africa Lesson Learned: Strengthening Resilience to Violence and Extremism* (London: Royal United Services Institute, 2017), 6.

16   Callgren, Kenyon, Kervick, Scudder, Walters, Whitehead, Connor and Flynn, 'Countering Violent Extremism', 14.

17   Shandon Harris-Hogan, Kate Barrelle and Andrew Zammit, 'What Is Countering Violent Extremism? Exploring CVE Policy and Practice in Australia', *Behavioral Sciences of Terrorism and Political Aggression* 8, no. 1 (2016): 10; Judy Korn, 'European CVE Strategies from a Practitioner's Perspective', *ANNALS AAPSS* 668, no. 1 (2016): 183; Weine and Eisenman, 'How Public Health Can Improve Initiatives to Counter Violent Extremism'.

18   George Selim, 'Approaches to Countering Violent Extremism at Home and Abroad', *ANNALS AAPSS* 668, no. 1 (2016): 96.

19   The respective programmes are Prevent and Channel in the United Kingdom; Empowering Local Partners to Prevent Violent Extremism in the United States; and the Living Safe Together Grants Programme in Australia.

20   Preben Bertelsen, 'Danish Preventive Measures and De-radicalization Strategies: The Aarhus Model', *Panorama*, no. 1 (2015): 242–3.

21   Owen Bowcott, 'Prevent Strategy 'Stifles Debate and Makes Teachers Feel Vulnerable', *The Guardian*, 9 March 2016, available at: https://www.theguardian.com/uk-

news/2016/mar/09/prevent-strategy-stifles-debate-and-makes-teachers-feel-vulnerable (accessed 19 May 2020).

22 Organisation for Security and Cooperation in Europe (OSCE), *Understanding Referral Mechanisms*, 43–4.

23 Amy B. Wang, 'Muslim Non-profit Groups Are Rejecting Federal Funds because of Trump', *The Washington Post*, 12 February 2017, available at: https://www.washingtonpost.com/news/post-nation/wp/2017/02/11/it-all-came-down-to-principle-muslim-nonprofit-groups-are-rejecting-federal-funds-because-of-trump/ (accessed 20 May 2020).

24 Australian National Audit Office, *The Design of, and Award of Funding under, the Living Safe Together Grants Programme* (Canberra: Australian National Audit Office, 2016), 8.

25 John Horgan, 'Deradicalization or Disengagement? A Process in Need of Clarity and a Counterterrorism Initiative in Need of Evaluation', *Perspectives on Terrorism* 2, no. 4 (2008): 3–8.

26 Sam Mullin, 'Rehabilitation of Islamist Terrorists: Lesson from Criminology', *Dynamics of Asymmetric Conflict* 3, no. 3 (2010): 162–93; Tinka Veldhuis, 'Designing Rehabilitation and Reintegration Programmes for Violent Extremist Offenders: A Realist Approach', *The International Centre for Counter-Terrorism – The Hague* 3, no. 2 (2012): 1–23.

27 John Horgan and Tore Bjorgo, *Leaving Terrorism Behind* (London: Routledge, 2009), 19.

28 Mary Beth Altier, Emma Leonard Boyle, Neil D. Shortland and John G. Horgan, 'Why They Leave: An Analysis of Terrorist Disengagement Events from Eighty-seven Autobiographical Accounts', *Security Studies* 26, no. 2 (2017): 305–32.

29 Mark Hamm, *The Spectacular Few* (New York: New York University Press, 2013), 163–78.

30 Christopher Boucek, 'Extremist Disengagement in Saudi Arabia: Prevention, Rehabilitation and after Care', in *Terrorist Rehabilitation and Counter Radicalisation*, Jerard, Gunaratna and Rubin, eds. (New York: Routledge, 2011), 70–90.

31 *BBC News*, 'Bali Death Toll Set at 202', 19 February 2003, available at: http://news.bbc.co.uk/2/hi/asia-pacific/2778923.stm (accessed 22 May 2020).

32 Lindsey, Timothy, 'Indonesia's New Anti-Terrorism Law: Damned If you Do, Damned If You Don't', *Asian Law Centre*, 2003, available at: https://law.unimelb.edu.au/__data/assets/pdf_file/0008/1546316/Indonesias_new_Anti_Terrorism_Law_Damned_if_you_do_Damned_if_you_dont1.pdf (accessed 22 May 2020).

33 Milda Istiqomah, '*De-radicalization Program in Indonesia Prisons: Reformation on the Correctional Institution*' (Conference Proceeding delivered at the 1st Australian Counter Terrorism Conference at Edith Cowan University, Perth, Western Australia, 5–7 December 2011), Security Research Centre, Edith Cowan University, Perth, Western Australia, 29–34.

34 Peter Smith, 'Indonesian Terror Party Angers Australians', *Financial Times*, 13 October 2007, available at: https://www.ft.com/content/d7521160-7908-11dc-aaf2-0000779fd2ac (accessed 22 May 2020).

35 Search for Common Ground, 'Program Evaluation Report: Countering and Preventing Radicalization in Indonesian Prisons', *Search for Common Ground*, February 2011, available at: https://www.sfcg.org/wp-content/uploads/2014/07/INA_EV_Feb11_Countering-and-Preventing-Radicalization-in-Indonesian-Prisons.pdf (accessed 22 May 2020).

36   Wahyudi Soeriaatmaadja, 'Conflict Resolution, Prison Style', *The Straits Times*, 12 July 2010, available at: https://www.sfcg.org/articles/semarang%20prison.pdf (accessed 31 July 2020).

37   Ben Bland, 'Indonesian Scheme Serves Up a New Life for Reformed Militants', *Financial Times*, 10 June 2014, available at: https://www.ft.com/content/f9992764-e700-11e3-aa93-00144feabdc0 (accessed 31 July 2020).

38   Badan Nasional Penanggulangan Terorisme (BNPT), *Blueprint Deradikalisasi', Deputi Pencegahan, Perlindungan dan Deradikalisasi, Badan Nasional Penanggulangan Terorisme* (West Java: Badan Nasional Penanggulangan Terorisme, 2013), 64.

39   Institute for the Policy Analysis of Conflict (IPAC), 'Prison Problems: Planned and Unplanned Releases of Convicted Extremists in Indonesia', *IPAC Report*, no. 2 (2013).

40   Solahudin, *The Roots of Terrorism in Indonesia* (Singapore: NUS Press, 2013), 126–44.

41   Michael Vatikiotis, *Blood and Silk: Power and Conflict in Modern Southeast Asia* (London: Orion Publishing Group, 2017), 233–6.

42   See International Crisis Group, 'Why Salafism and Terrorism Mostly Don't Mix', *Asia Report*, no. 83 (2004).

43   See Cameron Sumpter, 'Countering Violent Extremism in Indonesia: Priorities, Practice and the Role of Civil Society', *Journal for Deradicalization*, no. 11 (2017): 121–2.

44   See http://wahidfoundation.org/eng/index.php/page/index/About-Us.

45   Kate Grealy, 'Challenges to Countering Violent Extremism in Indonesia', *New Mandela*, 7 March 2019, available at: https://www.newmandala.org/the-problems-of-countering-violent-extremism-in-indonesia/ (accessed 26 May 2020).

46   Tempo, 'Gov't Encourages De-radicalization Program', *Tempo Co.*, 19 November 2016, available at: https://en.tempo.co/read/821489/govt-encourages-de-radicalization-program (accessed 24 May 2020).

47   Human Rights Watch, 'Letter on Indonesia's New Counterterrorism Law', *Human Rights Watch*, 20 June 2018, available at: https://www.hrw.org/news/2018/06/20/letter-indonesias-new-counterterrorism-law (accessed 26 May 2020).

48   Peraturan Pemerintah Republik Indonesia Nomor 77 Tahun 2019 Tentang Pencegahan Tindak Pidana Terorisme dan Pelindungan Terhadap Penyidik, Penuntut Umum, Hakim, dan Petugas Pemasyarakatan.

49   Ibid., Article 23.

50   The full name is: The National Action Plan for Preventing and Countering Violent Extremism That Leads to Terrorism (Rencana Aksi Nasional Pencegahan dan Penanggulangan Ekstremisme Berbasis Kekerasan yang Mengarah pada Terorisme).

51   Peraturan Presiden Republik Indonesia Nomor 7/2021 Tentang Rencana Aksi Nasional Pencegahan dan Penanggulangan Ekstremisme Berbasis Kekerasan Yang Mengarah Pada Terorisme Tahun 2020–2024, 6 January 2021.

52   Ibid., Article 47.

53   Interview of Mira Kusumarini, former Director of C-SAVE (13 May 2020).

54   Ibid.

55   Richard Tanter, *Intelligence Agencies and Third World Militarization: A Case Study of Indonesia, 1966–1989, with Special Reference to South Korea, 1961–1989* (PhD thesis, Monash University, February 1991), 245.

56   Joshua Barker, 'State of Fear: Controlling the Criminal Contagion in Suharto's New Order', *Indonesia*, no. 66 (1998): 8–9.

57 Sana Jaffrey, 'Civic Structures and Uncivil Demands in Indonesia', *New Mandela*, 23 April 2018, available at: https://www.newmandala.org/civic-structures-uncivil-demands-indonesia/ (accessed 24 May 2020).

58 A. Muh. Ibnu Aquil, 'New Antiterror Policy Sparks Fears of Witch Hunt', *The Jakarta Post*, 18 January 2021, available at: https://www.thejakartapost.com/news/2021/01/18/new-antiterror-policy-sparks-fears-of-witch-hunt.html.

59 Masdar Hilmy, 'The Politics of Retaliation: The Backlash of Radical Islamists to Deradicalization Project in Indonesia', *Al-Jāmi'ah* 51, no. 5 (2013): 144.

60 Sihbudi, Riza, 'Will Deradicalization Lead to De-Islamization?' *The Jakarta Post*, 14 October 2011, available at: https://www.thejakartapost.com/news/2011/10/14/will-deradicalization-lead-de-islamization.html (accessed 29 May 2020).

61 Quinton Temby, 'Terrorism in Indonesia after "Islamic State"', *ISEAS Trends in Southeast Asia*, no. 3 (2020): 19.

62 Interview of Rasyid Nurul Hakim, Editor-in-Chief of Ruangobrol.id (3 June 2020).

63 For further information on the Maarif Institute's work, and a more detailed discussion of the associated issues, see the chapter by M. Abdullah Darraz in this volume.

64 See: Cameron Sumpter, 'Countering Youth Radicalisation in Indonesia', *Lowy Interpreter*, 12 March 2018, available at: https://www.lowyinstitute.org/the-interpreter/countering-youth-radicalisation-indonesia (accessed 31 July 2020).

65 Institute for Policy Analysis of Conflict, 'Countering Violent Extremism: Need for a Rethink', *IPAC Report*, no. 11 (2014): 9–11.

66 Ibid., 13.

67 Rebecca Henschke and Endang Nurdin, 'Crossing Divides: The Bomb Maker Turned Peacemaker', *BBC News*, 28 May 2020, available at: https://www.bbc.com/news/world-asia-51907603 (accessed 28 May 2020).

68 Interviews with Insp. Gen. Benny Mamoto, Head, Research Centre of Police and Terrorism Studies (PRIK-KT), University of Indonesia (17 May 2020) and Dete Aliah, Director, Society against Violent Extremism (SeRVE) (6 June 2020).

Bibliography

Altier, Mary Beth, Boyle, Emma Leonard, Shortland, Neil D. and Horgan, John G. 'Why They Leave: An Analysis of Terrorist Disengagement Events from Eighty-seven Autobiographical Accounts', *Security Studies* 26, no. 2 (2017): 305–32.

Australian National Audit Office. *The Design of, and Award of Funding under, the Living Safe Together Grants Programme*. Canberra: Australian National Audit Office, 2016, 1–56.

Badan Nasional Penanggulangan Terorisme (BNPT). *Blueprint Deradikalisasi', Deputi Pencegahan, Perlindungan dan Deradikalisasi, Badan Nasional Penanggulangan Terorisme*. West Java: Badan Nasional Penanggulangan Terorisme, 2013.

Barker, Joshua. 'State of Fear: Controlling the Criminal Contagion in Suharto's New Order'. *Indonesia*, no. 66 (1998): 7–42.

Bertelsen, Preben. 'Danish Preventive Measures and De-radicalization Strategies: The Aarhus Model'. *Panorama*, no. 1 (2015): 241–53.

Bhui, Kamaldeep S., Hicks, Medlyn H., Lashley, Myrna and Jones, Edgar. 'A Public Health Approach to Understanding and Preventing Violent Radicalization'. *BMC Medicine* 10, no. 16 (2012): 1–8.

Bjorgo, Tore. *Lessons from Crime Prevention in Preventing Violent Extremism by Police*. European Commission: RAN Centre of Excellence, 2020, 1–13.

Boucek, Christopher. 'Extremist Disengagement in Saudi Arabia: Prevention, Rehabilitation and after Care'. In *Terrorist Rehabilitation and Counter Radicalisation*, Jerard, Gunaratna and Rubin eds., 70–90. New York: Routledge (2011).

Challgren, Jonathan, Kenyon, Ted, Kervick, Lauren, Scudder, Sally, Walters, Micah, Whitehead, Kate, Connor, Jeffrey and Flynn, Carole Rollie. 'Countering Violent Extremism: Applying the Public Health Model'. *Georgetown Security Studies Review* (special report), 2016, 1–38.

Gebo, Erika. 'An Integrated Public Health and Criminal Justice Approach to Gangs: What Can Research Tell Us?' *Preventive Medicine Reports*, no. 4 (2016): 376–80.

Haegerich, Tamara M., Mercy, James and Weiss, Billie. 'What Is the Role of Public Health in Gang-Membership Prevention?' In *Changing Course: Preventing Gang Membership*, Thomas R. Simon, ed., 31–49. Washington, DC: National Institute of Justice, 2015.

Hamm, Mark. *The Spectacular Few*. New York: New York University Press, 2013.

Harris-Hogan, Shandon, Barrelle, Kate and Zammit, Andrew. 'What Is Countering Violent Extremism? Exploring CVE Policy and Practice in Australia'. *Behavioral Sciences of Terrorism and Political Aggression* 8, no. 1 (2016): 6–24.

Hilmy, Masdar. 'The Politics of Retaliation: The Backlash of Radical Islamists to Deradicalization Project in Indonesia'. *Al-Jāmi'ah* 51, no. 5 (2013): 130–58.

Horgan, John. 'Deradicalization or Disengagement? A Process in Need of Clarity and a Counterterrorism Initiative in Need of Evaluation'. *Perspectives on Terrorism* 2, no. 4 (2008): 3–8.

Horgan, John and Bjorgo, Tore. *Leaving Terrorism Behind*. London: Routledge, 2009.

Institute for the Policy Analysis of Conflict (IPAC). 'Prison Problems: Planned and Unplanned Releases of Convicted Extremists in Indonesia'. *IPAC Report*, No. 2 (2013): 1–26.

Institute for the Policy Analysis of Conflict (IPAC). 'Countering Violent Extremism: Need for a Rethink'. *IPAC Report*, No. 11 (2014): 1–22.

International Crisis Group. 'Why Salafism and Terrorism Mostly Don't Mix'. *Asia* Report, no. 83 (2004): 1–58.

Korn, Judy. 'European CVE Strategies from a Practitioner's Perspective', *ANNALS AAPSS* 668, no. 1 (2016): 180–97.

Krug, Etienne G., Dahlberg, Linda L., Mercy, James A., Zwi, Anthony B. and Lozano, Rafael. *World Report on Violence and Health*. Geneva: World Health Organization, 2002, 1–346.

McDaniel, Dawn Delfin. 'Risk and Protective Factors Associated with Gang Affiliation among High-risk Youth: A Public Health Approach'. *Injury Prevention* 18, no. 4 (2012): 253–8.

Mullins, Sam. 'Rehabilitation of Islamist Terrorists: Lesson from Criminology'. *Dynamics of Asymmetric Conflict* 3, no. 3 (2010): 162–93.

Organisation for Security and Cooperation in Europe (OSCE). *Understanding Referral Mechanisms in Preventing and Countering Violent Extremism and Radicalization That Lead to Terrorism: Navigating Challenges and Protecting Human Rights; Guidebook for South-eastern Europe*. Vienna: Organization for Security and Cooperation in Europe (OSCE), 2019, 1–111.

Patel, Faiza and Koushik, Meghan. *Countering Violent Extremism*. New York: Brennan Center for Justice, 2017, 1–73.

Rosand, Eric, Winterbotham, Emily, Jones, Michael and Praxl-Tabuchi, Franziska. *A Roadmap to Progress: The State of the Global P/CVE Agenda.* London: The Prevention Projects and Royal United Services Institute, 2018, 1–65.

Royal United Services Institute (RUSI). *STRIVE Horn of Africa Lesson Learned: Strengthening Resilience to Violence and Extremism.* London: Royal United Services Institute, 2017, 1–29.

Selim, George. 'Approaches to Countering Violent Extremism at Home and Abroad'. *ANNALS AAPSS* 668, no. 1 (2016): 94–101.

Solahudin. *The Roots of Terrorism in Indonesia.* Singapore: NUS Press, 2013.

Sumpter, Cameron. 'Countering Violent Extremism in Indonesia: Priorities, Practice and the Role of Civil Society'. *Journal for Deradicalization*, no. 11 (2017): 112–47.

Tanter, Richard. *Intelligence Agencies and Third World Militarization: A Case Study of Indonesia, 1966–1989, with Special Reference to South Korea, 1961–1989.* PhD thesis, Monash University, Melbourne, 1991.

Temby, Quinton. 'Terrorism in Indonesia after "Islamic State"'. *ISEAS Trends in Southeast Asia*, no. 3 (2020): 1–21.

Vatikiotis, Michael. *Blood and Silk: Power and Conflict in Modern Southeast Asia.* London: Orion Publishing Group, 2017.

Veldhuis, Tinka, 'Designing Rehabilitation and Reintegration Programmes for Violent Extremist Offenders: A Realist Approach'. *The International Centre for Counter-Terrorism – The Hague* 3, no. 2 (2012): 1–23.

Part Four

Diversion/disengagement as official strategy

8

Upstream interventions with individuals and building resilience in communities: The UK's Prevent Strategy

Sean Arbuthnot

Since 2013, I have been involved with the UK government's Prevent Strategy in a variety of different roles – first, as a police Prevent Officer managing caseloads and working directly with individuals who had been referred to the programme, then as an independent training consultant advising organizations how to effectively embed Prevent as part of their safeguarding responsibilities, and now as a Prevent Coordinator responsible for the strategic implementation and oversight of all aspects of local Prevent delivery in one of the most multicultural parts of the country. This diverse range of experiences at the heart of Prevent has equipped me with a comprehensive, practical understanding of how its different elements work in practice and how they fit within the wider counter-terrorism landscape.

A key aspect of Prevent delivery centres on diversion and early intervention in order to safeguard people against radicalization – the process by which a person comes to support terrorism and extreme ideologies associated with terrorist groups. The implications of these upstream interventions will be the focus of this chapter.

The UK government's strategy to counter-terrorism, CONTEST, was first developed in 2003. Initially a 'slender document', it was a response to the emerging terrorist threat in the aftermath of the 9/11 attacks in the United States of America.[1] Since then, the threat from terrorism has evolved, new risks have materialized and the capacity of terrorism to inflict harm and inspire fear has grown. As a consequence, CONTEST has been regularly revised and strengthened in order to combat these threats.

The CONTEST framework is multi-faceted.[2] It promotes a joined-up approach involving coordination between government and the wider public sector to strengthen infrastructure and protect the UK from attack, to stop attacks from taking place and to mitigate the impact of terrorist incidents. Of the four elements that comprise CONTEST – Protect, Prepare, Pursue and Prevent – there is undoubtedly one that has attracted the most attention and controversy in recent years. The Prevent strategy aims to stop people from becoming terrorists or supporting terrorism. It does this by identifying individuals who are vulnerable to radicalization and extremism and offering voluntary care and support to divert them away from a path that could lead to violence. The UK's most senior counter-terrorism police officer, Assistant Metropolitan Commissioner Neil Basu, has called it the most important pillar of the CONTEST strategy.[3]

The human cost of terrorism is palpable and heartbreaking. In 2017, the UK suffered five terrorist attacks at Westminster, Manchester, London Bridge, Finsbury Park and Parsons Green, resulting in the loss of 36 civilian lives and over 200 injuries. Media fervour and public interest, both online and offline, may contribute to wider fears and amplify the terrorist threat. The financial cost is significant. Data shows that the 2017 terror attacks potentially led to a loss in economic output of over £3 billion.[4] It is therefore beyond debate that stopping people from becoming terrorists in the first instance should be a vital aim. The question is how to achieve this. How can people be identified and diverted from such a violent path?

Put simply, the Prevent strand of CONTEST aims to support people who are vulnerable to radicalization or extremism and, with their consent, provide wraparound care from a variety of different agencies and professionals to dissuade them from following a route that could lead towards terrorism and violence.

Prevent has been surrounded by controversy and debate since its inception. Some critics within academia or linked to activist organizations such as Cage have vilified it for stigmatizing Muslim communities, spying on or criminalizing people, suppressing freedom of speech and promoting a 'conveyor belt' process of radicalization, meaning that radicalization is perceived as a simplistic, linear process whereby having a radical ideology automatically leads to violence, regardless of other factors such as grievance or the wider political/social context. However, these perceptions do not represent the reality of Prevent delivery.

Prevent does not have an exclusive focus on Muslim communities because it deals with all forms of extremism – it is not limited to Islamist-inspired ideologies. In 2018–19, only 24 per cent of individuals brought to the attention of Prevent were referred for concerns related to Islamist radicalization.[5] With regard to the myth around spying, the Prevent Duty aims to be open and transparent and clearly states that it 'must not involve any covert activity against people or communities'.[6] Rather than criminalizing people, it aims to keep people out of the criminal justice system. Rather than undermining free speech, it tries to create safe spaces and promote open debate, particularly in education. The Duty states, 'Schools should be safe spaces in which children and young people can understand and discuss sensitive topics, including terrorism.'[7] As for the 'conveyor belt' theory, I have never met anyone within the Prevent network who promotes such a process. Research has consistently indicated that there is no single socio-demographic profile of a terrorist in the UK and no single pathway of radicalization leading to involvement in terrorism.

One common but significant misconception is that Prevent is a *deradicalization* programme. It is not. In fact, the aim of Prevent is to 'safeguard and support those vulnerable to radicalisation, to stop them from becoming terrorists or supporting terrorism'.[8] In other words, Prevent aims to engage people as far upstream as possible, whilst they are on a path to radicalization, *before* they are actually radicalized or criminalized. Its aim is to turn people away from violence. To do this, it takes a pro-social, public health approach of support and early interventions with vulnerable people, and resilience building in communities through projects, workshops and social programmes. Prevent may be part of the counter-terrorism landscape but at its heart, it is a safeguarding strategy that works with a variety of agencies including police, local authorities, education, health, communities and civil society organizations to ensure that individuals are not exploited or groomed into following a path of violent extremism.

Prevent as a strategy has evolved since its inception. The support offered to individuals and communities has become more effective, nuanced and responsive to risks. At times, the journey has been challenging and fraught with controversy. But it is fair to say that the current delivery model and working practices within Prevent are significantly different from what they were in the mid-2000s. In my view, it currently epitomizes an exemplar way of diverting people away from radicalization. It would be simplistic to say that this has been achieved through 'trial and error' because each Prevent initiative or review has been grounded in widespread consultations and in response to emerging risks. As a practitioner who has worked within Prevent in a variety of roles and locations, I feel that I have had a privileged position in observing and undertaking attempts to prevent radicalization – what has been tried, what has worked and why, as well as the shortcomings and lessons we have learned along the way. To understand some of these it would be helpful to briefly consider the journey that Prevent itself has taken since it was conceived.

History of Prevent

In the wake of the London Bombings of 7 July 2005 and the killing of fifty-two innocent people, the principal terrorist threat to the UK was perceived to be from radicalized individuals using a distorted, unrepresentative version of the Islamic faith to justify violence. Victims of the horrific attack hailed from eighteen different nationalities; yet, the tragedy highlighted the potential impact of homegrown terrorism – suicide attacks by British citizens. The UK government therefore sought to work in partnership with British Muslim communities to help prevent extremists from gaining influence and creating a divisive atmosphere resulting in conditions that incite hate and violence.

A community consultation exercise 'Preventing Extremism Together' was launched and additional resources were ploughed into counter-terrorism efforts.[9] Although it was acknowledged that Muslim communities themselves were not a threat and that British Muslims made an outstanding contribution to social, economic and cultural life in the UK, it is also fair to say that this early focus on Muslim communities has continued to shape public perceptions of Prevent despite its evolution since then. By 2009, much of Prevent's attention was focused on community cohesion efforts and the growing role played by the police in leading local Prevent delivery added to concerns around the securitization of the strategy.[10]

The Prevent Strategy was reviewed in 2011 under the Conservative and Liberal Democrat coalition government, marking a sea-change for the delivery of the programme. The review regarded the previous iteration of Prevent as flawed because it 'confused the delivery of Government policy to promote integration with Government policy to prevent terrorism'.[11] Crucially, the review formally acknowledged that Prevent should deal with all forms of terrorism. It found no evidence of Prevent spying on communities but acknowledged that trust in the strategy should be improved.

As Prevent focused on the ideological challenges of terrorism and the safeguarding of individuals from being drawn into violence, it also recognized the wide range of sectors and institutions that can work in partnership to tackle radicalization. An oft-repeated maxim within the UK security apparatus is that 'Communities Defeat Terrorism'. This led to another significant milestone in the history of Prevent. The Counter Terrorism and Security Act 2015, introduced by the UK government, included a requirement for specified authorities, including local government, criminal justice, education, health and social care, to have 'due regard to the need to prevent people from being drawn into terrorism'.[12] This meant that Prevent became a legal duty for a wide range of agencies and professionals, working in partnership to reduce risks and divert people from radicalization.

The fourth version of the CONTEST Strategy, released in June 2018, was the most expansive to date. It maintained the tried and tested framework of Protect, Prepare, Pursue and Prevent, but it had to respond to a higher number and greater variety of threats than ever before. For example, the prominence of ISIS/Daesh represented an increased risk given that the conflict in Syria had been in its infancy when the previous strategy was published. It also acknowledged the increase of lone actor attacks, which can be hard to detect and disrupt given their unsophisticated nature and the potentially rapid timescales of radicalization.

One of the strengths of UK counter-terrorism policy is its ability to respond promptly and adapt to meet emerging threats and risks. Therefore, over time Prevent has evolved into an increasingly effective, mature and well-functioning strategy. It has also become more open and transparent, as evidenced by the annual release of referral statistics, collaboration with academia and improved communications. At the time of writing, an independent review of Prevent is underway.[13] While not prejudging the outcome, it is anticipated that the review will look closely at the effectiveness of the government's strategy to protect vulnerable people from being drawn into terrorism and make recommendations for the future, thereby providing further opportunities for improvements and innovations in Prevent.

Structure

The current structure of Prevent enables it to work in similar ways to other safeguarding programmes designed to protect people from social harms such as gang culture, drug abuse, knife crime and physical or sexual abuse. Its three main objectives are to tackle the causes of radicalization and respond to the ideological challenge of terrorism, to safeguard and support those most at risk of radicalization through early intervention, and to enable those who have already engaged in terrorism to disengage and rehabilitate.

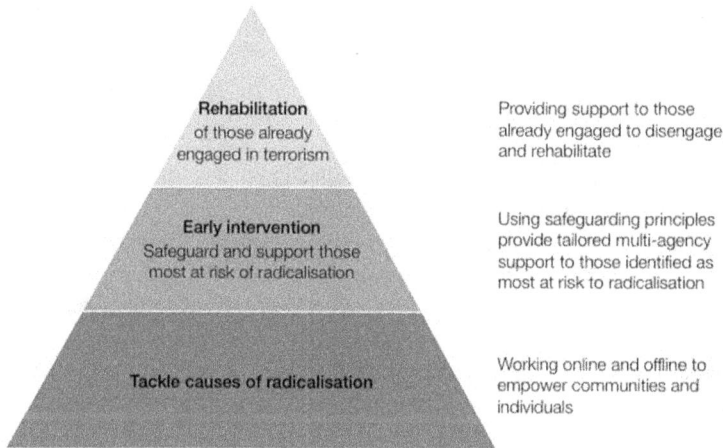

Figure 8.1 The Prevent Delivery Model.
U.K. Home Office.

The 2018 CONTEST review added the third tier of disengagement and rehabilitation. This involves providing support to those who have already engaged in terrorism through a Desistence and Disengagement Programme. However, this is evidently not an upstream intervention, and this chapter will only focus on the elements of intervention and resilience-building that comprise the majority of Prevent delivery at a local level.

Early intervention

A well-known quote attributed to Archbishop Desmond Tutu states, 'There comes a point where we need to stop just pulling people out of the river. We need to go upstream and find out why they're falling in.'

The most important and well-developed strand of Prevent involves identifying individuals who are most at risk of supporting terrorism and providing positive diversionary support and interventions. To do this effectively, practitioners need to ensure not only that this takes place as early as possible but also that risks have been correctly identified. The mechanism by which this takes place is known as 'Channel' and it is one of the key elements of the entire Prevent Strategy.

Channel is a multi-agency programme that aims to identify people at risk, to assess the nature and extent of that risk, and to develop the most appropriate support plan for the individuals involved.[14] If a member of the public or a frontline worker has a concern about someone who they think might be vulnerable to radicalization, they can refer them to Channel for appropriate support or intervention. Such referrals can be made to the local authority or a local police force.

Channel panels meet monthly. They are chaired by local authorities/municipalities and include partners from agencies such as education, police, health and probation who collectively share information, assess the extent of a referral's vulnerability and decide on a support package that is suited to their needs. It applies a vulnerability assessment framework built around three factors – *engagement* with a group, cause or ideology, *intent* to cause harm, and *capability* to cause harm – resulting in a holistic view of a person's issues, grievances and needs.

Participation in Channel is voluntary and whilst it may seem fanciful that someone on the cusp of supporting terrorism would consent to intervention from authorities, my experience indicates that individuals rarely decline support once they understand the implications and benefits of Channel intervention.[15] This is because Channel support is largely positive, it is tailored to the individual needs of the referral and it often provides them with opportunities that ordinarily wouldn't have been open to them. Typical examples of support include life skills, mental health support, anger management, career advice and educational support. But by far the most potent, powerful and widely utilized form of support is mentoring. As one former Channel referral recently told me, 'The main reason I left the far right was because of my mentor's guidance.'[16]

Channel panels regularly call upon a cadre of mentors, often called 'intervention providers' to work with referrals on a one-to-one basis and support them however they can. Equipped with experience, knowledge and most crucially, credibility, they are drawn from a range of backgrounds and paired with referrals to provide a bespoke mentoring programme.

Intervention providers can include religious scholars, trained Imams, psychologists, counsellors, youth workers and mental health practitioners. Some have worked with gangs, others are former extremists, with direct personal experience of radical right or Islamist-inspired extremism. They know only too well the reality of extremism and can provide a powerful counter-narrative to those on the fringes of political violence.

Of course, there are risks and moral questions around working with 'formers' in the diversion space and I, like many practitioners, have often reflected on whether some of these individuals have really changed. Are their views compatible with our values, or are we rewarding or endorsing their previous, possibly illegal, activities? For my part, I am reassured that Channel intervention providers have undergone a rigorous Home Office application and vetting process. I have met many 'formers', witnessed their transformative work first-hand and have been greatly inspired by and appreciative of their efforts. They have been an indispensable part of Channel's success.

In 2020–1, 688 individuals were adopted as Channel cases (compared to 697 in the previous year). The majority of these individuals was male (88 per cent) and aged twenty years or younger (49 per cent). For the first time since recorded data became available there were more extreme right-wing referrals to Prevent (25 per cent) than concerns related to Islamist radicalization (22 per cent). An emerging theme has been referrals of individuals with a mixed, unclear or unstable ideology (51 per cent). 'Mixed' cases may demonstrate an interest in several (sometimes disparate) ideologies, often simultaneously. For example, a joint interest in extreme right-wing content and incel subcultures is not uncommon. In 'unclear' cases, ideological influences are less coherent, but individuals may be fixated with mass violence, such as school attacks, or the hatred of a perceived 'other', such as women. 'Unstable' cases refer to those who initially appear to adhere to one ideology but then switch to another. Unlikely as it may seem, I recall a number of individuals referred to Prevent for right-wing extremism, only to be re-referred months or years later for violent Islamist-inspired ideologies – and vice versa.

The vast majority of Channel cases (85 per cent) resulted in individuals successfully exiting the process with no further radicalization concerns.[17] The remaining 15 per cent either withdrew from the programme or intervention was no longer deemed appropriate. In such cases, support from some services may remain in place but ultimately, if any terrorism risk remains it is managed by the police. For example, if offences are committed or an individual continues to pose a risk of violent extremism, it may be more appropriate to pursue a criminal investigation.

Referrals to Prevent come from a variety of sources. In recent years, the primary and secondary education sector has consistently accounted for approximately one-third of all cases. Other contributors included police, local authorities, health, the prison service, friends and family, and communities.

Case study: Channel referrals

In presenting the following case studies, the intention is not to provide a formal evaluation of Prevent support. At best they can be seen as a snapshot of wider Channel activity. But they reflect genuine, practical experiences and by showcasing the reality of local delivery, including the human stories behind diversion, they may help to paint a more vivid picture of how upstream interventions can work in practice.

One of the first Prevent cases I ever encountered related to a teenage boy. He originally attracted police attention when he abused officers with racist language and threatened them with a hunting knife. Chillingly, at the time of the incident he was wearing a hockey mask that he had decorated with Nazi swastikas and a toothbrush moustache (commonly associated with Adolf Hitler). In fact, he had scrawled various sinister signs and slogans all over the mask. These included 'white pride', 'SS', a Star of David with a cross through it, and the numbers '14' and '88'.[18] Concerned police officers ultimately referred the boy to Prevent.

The boy openly espoused racist views associated with white supremacist narratives. When I first met him, he startled me by shaking my hand but refusing to shake the hand of my colleague. He casually remarked that this was because my colleague wasn't white. During our initial conversations, he openly declared that white people were the 'master race', threatened by extinction and that a race war was on the horizon. He confidently predicted that my colleague and I would find ourselves on opposite sides of such a war.

The extreme, racist views of the boy, his violent behaviour both at home and school, and his call to action for a race war raised significant concerns. But rather than criminalizing him or vilifying him for his ideology, he was treated with respect, even empathy, throughout the Channel process. This is not to say that his views were condoned or unchallenged, but they were dealt with in a productive, powerful manner. To be truly successful, a multi-agency partnership approach was required.

In this particular case, most of Channel's partner agencies played a key role in a support plan for the referral. For instance, he received mental health support and was diagnosed with a behavioural disorder that accounted for much of his erratic, violent conduct in school. Health professionals worked with teachers to support him and offer reasonable adjustments that resulted in improved attendance and behaviour.

Social services provided insights into the boy's background and discovered that a close family member was a negative influence in his life. He had essentially been radicalized by his own father who had indoctrinated him with racist, anti-Semitic views and allegedly took him, blindfolded, to secret radical right group meetings. In many ways, given such an ugly influence since his early childhood, the boy was arguably a victim himself.

As stated earlier, mentoring can be a hugely effective support mechanism. In this case we introduced the boy to a youth worker, a skinhead, with a background in far-right culture. In fact, the mentor's appearance and smart casual clothing that had a far-right aesthetic immediately gave him credibility and helped him to connect with the boy. They developed a close bond and the mentor encouraged the boy to engage in new ways of thinking about race and ethnicity based on DNA, evolution and deconstructing racism. The encouragement of critical thinking is a vital part of upstream interventions and in this case the boy's own research led him to learn that the advancement of DNA testing shows that a '100% pure race' is a myth, that all humans are essentially related and that it can be argued that the concept of race is an artificial, human construct.

One of Channel's strengths is that its upstream interventions can be creative and tailored to the individual. Diversionary activities may tap into a referral's interests or provide them with skills and qualifications that enhance their career prospects or life skills. It can offer unique, personal experiences that have lasting, positive impacts. In this case, the boy displayed an avid interest in military history. He was also obsessed with conspiracy theories. He openly maintained that 9/11 was a US government plot and he denied that the Holocaust took place. The boy's mentor took him to visit the National Holocaust Centre and Museum in Nottinghamshire. Not only did the museum tour provide primary evidence of the horror and scale of the atrocity, but the boy was also introduced to a Holocaust survivor who shared his experiences of life in a concentration camp. The fifteen-year-old self-declared white supremacist could hardly deny the reality of the Holocaust as he shared lunch and a cup of tea with a living witness to its inhumanity. It is not an exaggeration to say that this experience was life-changing.

As with all Channel cases, this boy was not criminalized or forced to take part in the programme. The positive interventions he received were tailored to his individual needs. The racist ideology that he was once so proud of effectively dissipated. In fact, not only did he shake my colleague's hand at the end of the process, he hugged him and thanked us profusely for the support he received.

Another former Channel case that I was involved with was a potentially violent Islamist who came to the attention of authorities after a family argument during which he hinted that he wanted to join ISIS. When I first spoke to him, during a lengthy conversation he openly stated to me that he felt obliged to travel to Syria and fight because it was his religious duty. He said that Michael Adebolajo, one of the killers of Fusilier Lee Rigby in Woolwich in 2013, was his 'brother in Islam'.

As a young, Black male and a recent convert to Islam he had convinced himself that was not welcome in the UK. He did not feel that he had a stake in society. He strongly asserted that Muslims are discriminated against and treated with suspicion. Unable to practise his faith in the West, he felt that the only place where he could be a 'true' Muslim was in the so-called Caliphate of the Islamic State. He claimed that he had to make a choice because the 'end of days' was fast approaching and he was obliged to be present in Dabiq, Syria when the second coming of the Messiah took place.

Hatred of the other, a 'them against us' mentality, Islam vs. the West, an apocalyptic race war/end of days vision, a clear, important choice to make, a call to action – all of these warning signs were present and yet the boy had not committed a crime by this point. But he was showing clear signs of being on a path to radicalization and the consequences of extremist travel to Syria could have been catastrophic.

Although this boy was well versed in the apocalyptic propaganda perpetuated by ISIS, he actually possessed very little knowledge about faith itself. He had never read scripture and had never attended a *masjid* (mosque). He received Channel support from a variety of agencies but once again, mentoring was the key that diverted him from violence. His intervention provider was an Imam. Weekly religious discussions began to foster a more positive outlook on his faith. He was taken to a local mosque and introduced to local community members who welcomed him warmly. Over a very short period, he came to understand that ISIS propaganda was not a true reflection of mainstream Islam and his desire to travel to Syria abated.

There is no single method of upstream diversion that can be successfully applied across the board. But the above examples demonstrate that an empathetic, human-focused support system can achieve positive results in certain cases. I have found that mentoring is the most commonly effective form of intervention, often based on the establishment of trust and empathy, supplemented by the development of critical thinking skills and facilitated by strong partnership working at a local level.

It may feel counter-intuitive to build a personal relationship with someone who aspires to hurt others or holds extreme views that are not compatible with basic human rights. But building a rapport and establishing a simple human connection is the key to successful mentoring. It is about listening, not condoning, and showing respect. Extremists often dehumanize 'the other' and it is easier to give in to hate when they are part of a gang of like-minded individuals. Mentoring relies on fostering positive, personal connections with others, particularly if they are individuals from different faiths, ethnicities and backgrounds, or positive role models like intervention providers.

Effective mentoring is usually supplemented by the promotion of critical thinking. Extremists often view the world in clear-cut, black and white terms, offering simplistic 'them against us' narratives. I think that there is great value in introducing shades of grey. The world is a complex place. Therefore, a common theme of support under Channel revolves around encouraging dialogue, research and critical thinking. For example, one former referral told me that Prevent really 'picked apart' his extreme right-wing views by encouraging him to undertake detailed, objective research on them. In this case, it was to study controversial passages from the Qur'an quoted by far-right groups and to read them in context.

The journey of a Prevent referral can be quite inspiring and I am fortunate to have witnessed many troubled young people turn their lives around for the better with the help of Channel support and early intervention. It is humbling to reflect that during my twelve-year police career in a variety of roles and specialist teams, I feel like I made more of a difference and witnessed more positive transformation in Prevent than any I did in other area of policing.

Tackling the causes of radicalization

In order to tackle the root causes of radicalization, Prevent works with a host of civil society organizations (CSOs) to develop programmes, workshops and projects that raise awareness and build resilience against extremist narratives. These initiatives work as far upstream as possible and reach wide audiences. In the UK during 2018–19, over eighty CSOs delivered 226 Prevent-funded projects reaching over 141,000 participants.

In this context, a local delivery model is key. Activity and resources are directed to areas where the threat from terrorism and radicalization is highest. It is insufficient for projects to produce good work if it is not targeted or nullifying genuine risk. They cannot simply aim to promote integration. There must be a specific, risk-based rationale for them. They should be driven and enhanced by community engagement and tailored to local threats and vulnerabilities related to radicalization and terrorism.

There is sometimes a perception that Prevent is a 'top-down' securitization strategy. But as a local coordinator I can attest that each authority or municipality is responsible for their own local strategy, risk assessment and action plan. Effective delivery is driven by trusted partnerships, community engagement and local knowledge. This is important to increase the transparency of Prevent and increase trust and confidence in each local area. In addition, all project activity should be targeted to locally identified threats and risks; otherwise, we would risk blindly following a scattergun, ineffective approach. One of the ways that compatibility is achieved is by linking project delivery to Counter Terrorism Local Profiles.

A Counter Terrorism Local Profile (CTLP) is a strategic document, revised at least annually, that outlines the threat from and vulnerability to terrorism-related activity within a specific area.[19] It is developed by local policing teams in partnership with the local authority and other agencies from the public sector, local businesses and community organizations. By taking account of a range of crime and terrorism data, local intelligence and community sentiment, it provides an up-to-date, rich picture of the local context, outlining key risks and tensions to target activities and resources as effectively as possible. When shared with partner agencies, it becomes a useful tool in identifying where to focus proactive intervention and resilience-building.

Case study: Real talk

A 2017 collaboration between Prevent and Streetvibe, a Leicester-based youth service, resulted in the development of a workshop called Real Talk which responded to emerging local and national threats that had been highlighted by effective community engagement.

UK Home Office figures for 2017–18 indicated a 36 per cent spike in extreme right-wing-inspired referrals to Prevent nationally.[20] This reflected an upward trend that had seen such referrals rise significantly in recent years as the number of individuals with a radical right ideology who received Channel support almost doubled. At a local level, I witnessed first-hand the swell of far-right referrals at our Channel panel whilst in late 2016 the neo-Nazi group National Action was the first extreme-right group to be proscribed by the UK government as a terrorist organization under the Terrorism Act 2000.[21]

Against this backdrop, a Streetvibe youth worker identified a clear, local groundswell of support for extreme-right activists in the wake of the Westminster Bridge attack in London on 22 March 2017. One particular incident involved a group of teens gathered round a tablet, engrossed by a YouTube video featuring Tommy Robinson (real name Stephen Yaxley-Lennon, a far-right, anti-Islam activist and former leader of the English Defence League) recorded in the aftermath of the horrific incident wherein he declared, 'We are at war … Our government have failed us … This is an Islamic jihad attack … It's got everything to do with Islam.'[22] The youth worker knew that this was a group of young people that had hitherto displayed no regard for politics or current affairs but the slickly produced video clearly resonated with them. They were captivated and angry.

In response, and in partnership with local Prevent practitioners, Streetvibe developed RealTalk – an interactive workshop that uses innovative technology to raise awareness of right-wing extremism, to challenge ethnic and religious stereotypes, and to encourage debate and critical thinking skills. The aim was to provide a positive counter-message that resonated with its target audience to respond to the hate-filled videos that captured their imaginations.

A central strand of RealTalk's workshop uses augmented reality, a mixture of real-life and virtual reality viewed through a tablet or smartphone, whereby life-size banners of various individuals effectively come to life to share their personal experiences. Participants hear directly from diverse voices including a former gang member, a former English Defence League organizer, a former football casual hooligan and a former recruiter for the neo-Nazi paramilitary group Combat 18. Their stories run directly counter to the preconceptions that people may have had about them based solely on their appearance.

During a pilot RealTalk session at the youth centre where the YouTube video had been so popular, young people had to be coaxed into taking part with the promise of free pizza. However, from such an inauspicious start, participation and engagement soon grew. The technological element of the workshop sparked the curiosity of participants, and the debates that followed were challenging and productive. One young person pointed at the banner showing a Muslim female wearing a niqab and remarked, 'Spot the terrorist.' This disturbing comment was challenged and undermined as soon as the augmented reality element of the workshop began because the interactive video showed that the person on the banner is a friendly blogger and tech enthusiast with a passionate outlook on life. This completely refuted the stereotype of a conservative, veiled Muslim female that the participants assumed from the initial image. The workshop demonstrated that religious observance or conservatism is not a sign of extremism, even if many people resort to lazy prejudices. RealTalk challenges these generalizations head-on, encouraging people to see beyond them.

To date, RealTalk has reached over 2,000 participants in a variety of settings within the local area, selected in accordance with perceived threat, consultation with partner agencies and communities, and CTLP data. It is but one example of how Prevent projects can provide positive interventions as far upstream as possible, mitigate local threats and build resilience by addressing risk factors, and providing the skills and confidence to resist the threat posed by extremist influences.

Challenges and lessons

For all the successes of Prevent and upstream intervention, it is not a panacea to the scourge of radicalization. Even with good practice and best intentions, it will not work in all cases. For example, practitioners who work in this field must always be cognizant of the potential for disguised compliance. In other words, an individual receiving support may give the appearance of cooperation and progress to allay professionals' fears and divert attention away from their continued immersion into an extreme ideology.

In March 2019, Lewis Ludlow was sentenced to life imprisonment having pleaded guilty to preparing acts of terrorism. An ISIS supporter, he planned to launch a 'spectacular multi victim attack' in London using a 'bomb-laden truck'.[23]

It came to light during his trial the previous year that whilst he was undertaking hostile activities, he was engaging with Prevent. In fact, since 2008 when he was found carrying a knife at college, Prevent had made several attempts to engage with him. In 2017 and 2018, he met with an assigned intervention provider seventeen times. The prosecution revealed that an associate told him, 'Even if u don't believe it, fake it' and advised him to 'be polite' with Prevent officers.[24]

Thankfully, the scale of the threat was ultimately acknowledged and prior to his arrest, Ludlow had been placed under twenty-four-hour police surveillance. This demonstrates the need for various strands of CONTEST, in this case Prevent and Pursue, to share information when the need arises. If Prevent support is not working, other options may be considered. It also highlights the inherent complexities and difficulties regarding risk management.

Preventing terrorism is controversial and hard to measure. Of course, that does not mean that we should not try. Therefore, for upstream intervention to be successful, I would suggest that the following lessons increase the chances of positive outcomes.

Focusing on integration, cohesion and community engagement is not sufficient. Prevention needs to be targeted towards threat and risk. Reputationally, the Prevent strategy still suffers from the legacy of well-intentioned but ultimately misguided attempts to engage Muslim communities during its early implementation. It is important that upstream intervention programmes tackle all ideologies and forms of extremism.

Linked to this is openness and transparency. An intervention programme that is perceived to be secretive or securitized will have difficulty achieving widespread support within communities. Accepting that confidential matters of safeguarding and national security may be at stake and that referrals' anonymity should be protected, it is nonetheless recommended to share as much information as is reasonable, particularly regarding processes and data.

Interventions should be driven by a local, multi-agency approach as opposed to a top-down, government-directed process. Effective partnerships are vital. Building relationships and working closely with other local agencies ensure that the many skills and insights from other professionals can be utilized. This encourages greater information sharing as well as creative solutions or support measures, like sports engagement or cultural visits, that may not ordinarily be considered. Also, intervention should not be a solely police-led initiative.

That said, even early intervention should have the capacity to escalate a case if it appears that support is not having the desired effect or mitigating risk. If an individual crosses the threshold into criminality or continues on a path of radicalization despite our best efforts, as in the Ludlow case described above, a counter-terrorism investigation may be more appropriate than a programme of mentoring and support. The four elements of the UK CONTEST strategy have become increasingly interconnected in recent years. In practice, this means that whilst the strands of Prevent and Pursue (investigation and disruption of terrorist activity) are separate, there may be occasions when a Prevent case needs to be managed by Pursue if the risk is assessed to be too great.

Consistency with other forms of safeguarding helps to achieve understanding and participation from partner agencies and other professionals. The word 'terrorism' can be intimidating and sound melodramatic. It can lead partners to assume that cases are beyond their expertise. But ultimately, we are dealing with human beings who are vulnerable, and the warning signs of radicalization can be strikingly similar to those of other social harms such as gang culture and so-called 'county lines' (transporting illegal drugs across police and local authority boundaries).

Most importantly, interventions need to be personally tailored to each case. People are individuals and there is no set path of radicalization. Every referral I have ever dealt with is unique and oftentimes the grievances that fuel radicalization, whether real or perceived, are very personal. Their journey away from extremism should be equally personal. Obtaining the consent of individuals concerned is also very important so that they can embark upon the process with their eyes fully open.

Practitioners who are responsible for interventions should be willing to have uncomfortable and difficult conversations. Engagement has to be meaningful. We have to listen to people and show respect and empathy even if the views we are seeking to challenge are profoundly disturbing. I remember a Channel referral once said to me, 'I'm not a Nazi, but if everyone keeps calling me a Nazi, then I'm just going to say all right, I'll show you what a Nazi looks like.' This is not a particularly mature or sophisticated justification for his ugly behaviour, but it was that his reality. We had to be cognizant of that. His views were challenged but in a respectful way that didn't alienate or undermine him. Following Prevent support, he said that the only people who listened to him and showed him respect were from Prevent and that is what kept him out of prison.

Conclusion

Not only is early intervention one of our best weapons in the fight against terrorism, it is also one of the most cost-effective. Counter-terrorism spending equates to over £2 billion per year in the UK.[25] Meanwhile, the budget for the Prevent strategy in 2018/19 was £47.3 million.[26] Put simply, the entire Prevent strategy, including Channel intervention, accounts for approximately 2–3 per cent of the total counter-terrorism budget. We already know that the economic cost of a terrorist attack is huge, and of course the human cost is incalculable. But in cold stark financial terms, upstream intervention simply represents exceptional value for money.

It may not be perfect, but on a personal level I have seen plenty of cases where early intervention has changed peoples' lives for the better. More than one individual has told me that Prevent saved their life. But the journey is not over. Prevent is not a silver bullet that will work in 100 per cent of cases. I have no doubt that elements of our diversion can be improved. The ongoing independent review of Prevent and its recommendations will undoubtedly have a significant impact on the future of the strategy. Alongside this, new risks and threats will surely emerge in the coming years. But I have every confidence that our response will continue to evolve and that innovative, tailored, upstream interventions will continue to be one of the most effective ways to protect communities and build resilience against terrorism.

Notes

1   House of Commons, Home Affairs Committee, *Project CONTEST: The Government's Counter-terrorism Strategy: Ninth Report of Session 2008–9* (Chair: Rt Hon Keith Vaz MP, July 2009), 4.

2   United Kingdom, Home Department, *CONTEST: The United Kingdom's Strategy for Countering Terrorism*, CM9608 (United Kingdom: APS Group on behalf of the Controller of Her Majesty's Stationery Office, 2018).

3   UK Counter Terrorism Policing, 'Neil Basu Leads Prevent Conversation at ICT Summit', *UK Counter Terrorism Policing*, 9 September 2019, available at: https://www. counterterrorism.police.uk/neil-basu-leads-prevent-conversation-at-ict-summit/ (accessed 28 May 2020).

4   Caitlin Morrison, 'Terror Attacks Cost the UK Economy £3bn Last Year, New Research Shows', *Independent*, 6 June 2018, available at: https://www.independent. co.uk/news/business/news/terror-attacks-uk-economy-cost-manchester-arena-westminster-london-bridge-a8385661.html (accessed 14 September 2020).

5   United Kingdom, Home Office, *Individuals Referred to and Supported through the Prevent Programme, England and Wales, April 2018 to March 2019* (United Kingdom: Statistical Bulletin 32/19, 19 December 2019) at 10.

6   Home Office, 'Revised Prevent Duty Guidance: For England and Wales', *Home Office*, 10 April 2019, available at: https://www.gov.uk/government/publications/prevent-duty-guidance/revised-prevent-duty-guidance-for-england-and-wales (accessed 28 May 2020).

7   Ibid.

8   United Kingdom, Home Department, *CONTEST: The United Kingdom's Strategy for Countering Terrorism*, CM9608 (United Kingdom: APS Group on behalf of the Controller of Her Majesty's Stationery Office, 2018) at 10.

9   United Kingdom, Home Department, *Countering International Terrorism: The United Kingdom's Strategy*, CM6888 (United Kingdom: The Stationery Office Limited on behalf of the Controller of Her Majesty's Stationery Office, 2006) at 14.

10   John Bahadur Lamb, 'Preventing Violent Extremism: A Policing Case Study of the West Midlands', *Policing* 7, no. 1 (2012): 88–95.

11   United Kingdom, Home Department, *Prevent Strategy*, CM8092 (United Kingdom: The Stationery Office Limited on behalf of the Controller of Her Majesty's Stationery Office, 2011) at 1.

12   Counter Terrorism and Security Act 2015, 2015, c 6, s 26.

13   Home Office, 'Independent Review of Prevent. Documents Related to the Review of Prevent', *Home Office*, 16 September 2019, available at: https://www.gov.uk/government/collections/independent-review-of-prevent (accessed 14 September 2020).

14   United Kingdom, Home Office, *Channel Duty Guidance: Protecting Vulnerable People from Being Drawn into Terrorism: Statutory Guidance for Channel Panel Members and Partners of Local Panels* (United Kingdom: APS Group on behalf of the Controller of Her Majesty's Stationery Office, 2015) at 5.

15   All individuals who receive support through Channel must be made aware that they are receiving this as part of a programme to protect people from being drawn into terrorism. People who do not consent to receive support through Channel, or who decide to leave the programme before the Channel panel decides they are ready, may be offered alternative forms of support by the local authority or other providers, and any terrorist risk is managed by the police. In the case of a child, there may be certain circumstances when a parent/guardian does not give consent for their child to be supported through Channel, particularly if some of the vulnerabilities present are in the home environment. If the child is thought to be at risk from significant harm, whether that is physical, emotional, mental, intellectual, social or behavioural harm (as defined by Section 31(9) of the Children Act 1989), then social services for the relevant local authority area must be involved in decisions made about the child.

16   Sean Arbuthnot, 'Mentoring the Radical Right: Talking to a Channel Referral and His Mentor', *CARR Insights Blog*, 25 June 2019, available at: https://www.radicalrightanalysis.com/2019/06/25/mentoring-the-radical-right-talking-to-a-channel-referral-and-his-mentor/ (accessed 24 July 2020).

17   United Kingdom, Home Office, *Individuals Referred to and Supported through the Prevent Programme, England and Wales, April 2020 to March 2021* (United Kingdom: Statistical Bulletin 33/21, 18 November 2021).

18   '14' references the 'fourteen words', a popular white supremacist slogan: 'We must secure the existence of our people and a future for white children.' This slogan was coined by David Lane, a member of the white-supremacist terrorist group known as The Order (Lane died in prison in 2007) and derives from the eighth chapter of Hitler's political autobiography Mein Kampf. '88' references the eighth letter of the alphabet, giving 'HH' standing for Heil Hitler. Reference to 88 was popularized by David Lane's '88 Precepts' and also alludes to a famous 88-word statement of intent from Mein Kampf. See United Kingdom, Centre for Analysis of the Radical Right (CARR), *A Guide to Online Radical-right Symbols, Slogans and Slurs* (United Kingdom: Centre for Analysis of the Radical Right (CARR), 2020).

19   United Kingdom, Home Office and Association of Chief Police Officers in partnership with the Welsh Government, *Counter Terrorism Local Profiles: An Updated Guide* (United Kingdom: Home Office, 2012).

20   United Kingdom, Home Office, *Individuals Referred to and Supported through the Prevent Programme, April 2017 to March 2018* (United Kingdom: Statistical Bulletin 31/18, 13 December 2018).

21   Home Office and The Rt Hon Rudd, Amber, 'National Action Becomes First Extreme Right-wing Group to Be Banned in the UK', *gov.uk*, 16 December 2016, available at: https://www.gov.uk/government/news/national-action-becomes-first-extreme-right-wing-group-to-be-banned-in-uk (accessed 11 September 2020).

22   YouTube/Rebel News, 'London Attack: Leftists Laugh at Tommy Robinson', 23 March 2017, available at: https://www.youtube.com/watch?v=ZhrhLovaFs8.

23   BBC News, 'Oxford Street Terror Plotter Lewis Ludlow Jailed', *BBC News*, 6 March 2019, available at: https://www.bbc.co.uk/news/uk-england-kent-47466625 (accessed 14 September 2020).

24   BBC News, 'Oxford Street Terror Plotter "Resisted" De-radicalisation', *BBC News*, 3 January 2019, available at: https://www.bbc.co.uk/news/uk-england-kent-46750782 (accessed 14 September 2020).

25   HM Government, 'CONTEST: The United Kingdom's Strategy for Countering Terrorism', CM9608, June 2018, 86, https://assets.publishing.service.gov.uk/government/uploads/system/uploads/attachment_data/file/716907/140618_CCS207_CCS0218929798-1_CONTEST_3.0_WEB.pdf.

26   U.K. Parliament, 'Counter-terrorism: Expenditure. Question for Home Office', 13 May 2019, available at: https://questions-statements.parliament.uk/written-questions/detail/2019-05-13/253602.

Bibliography

Bahadur Lamb, John. 'Preventing Violent Extremism: A Policing Case Study of the West Midlands'. *Policing* 7, no. 1 (2012): 88–95.

Centre for Analysis of the Radical Right (CARR). *A Guide to Online Radical-right Symbols, Slogans and Slurs*. United Kingdom: Centre for Analysis of the Radical Right (CARR), 2020.

Home Department. *Countering International Terrorism: The United Kingdom's Strategy*. United Kingdom: The Stationary Office Limited on behalf of the Controller of Her Majesty's Stationery Office, 2006.

Home Department. *Prevent Strategy*. United Kingdom: The Stationary Office Limited on behalf of the Controller of Her Majesty's Stationery Office, 2011.

Home Department. *CONTEST: The United Kingdom's Strategy for Countering Terrorism*. United Kingdom: APS Group on behalf of the Controller of Her Majesty's Stationery Office, 2018.

Home Office. *Channel Duty Guidance: Protecting Vulnerable People from Being Drawn into Terrorism: Statutory Guidance for Channel Panel Members and Partners of Local Panels*. United Kingdom: APS Group on behalf of the Controller of Her Majesty's Stationery Office, 2015.

Home Office. *Individuals Referred to and Supported through the Prevent Programme, April 2017 to March 2018*. United Kingdom: Home Office, 2018.

Home Office. *Individuals Referred to and Supported through the Prevent Programme, England and Wales, April 2018 to March 2019*. United Kingdom: Home Office, 2019.

Home Office and Association of Chief Police Officers in partnership with the Welsh Government. *Counter Terrorism Local Profiles: An Updated Guide*. United Kingdom: Home Office, 2012.

House of Commons, Home Affairs Committee. *Project CONTEST: The Government's Counter-terrorism Strategy: Ninth Report of Session 2008–09*. London: The Stationery Office Limited, 2009.

9

Independent/hybrid P/CVE youth work in the UK: Grassroots work beyond Prevent

Fernán Osorno Hernández

In the UK, early intervention approaches to Prevent/Counter Violent Extremism (P/CVE) are guided by the Prevent Strategy.[1] The Prevent policy has been under public scrutiny since its inception due to its focus on ethnic and religious minorities,[2] particularly Muslim youth.[3] Understandably, much of the scholarly research in the UK has focused on P/CVE efforts under the Prevent framework. This chapter contributes to the gap in the literature by providing primary data on independent and hybrid youth work[4] approaches in the UK beyond Prevent-funded P/CVE work. These approaches, independently and partially funded by Home Office and private/charitable sources, adapt and reinterpret P/CVE policies, such as Prevent, to fit pre-existing holistic approaches[5] and localized needs. The aim of studying independent and hybrid P/CVE work is to demonstrate how alternative knowledge rooted in localized expertise can raise resilience against violent extremism while avoiding social stigmatization.

First, a conceptual clarification. Although in P/CVE work 'preventing' and 'countering' are often used interchangeably in the literature, a distinction should be addressed as the latter can be associated with security-led frames of intervention, similar to counter-terrorism strategies (deradicalization, for example). A 2020 report by the UN Human Rights Council argues: 'Addressing "pull factors" has broadly fallen into the domain of countering violent extremism. Interventions relevant to preventing violent extremism are most usefully defined as those that seek to address the structural drivers of violent extremism, or "push factors". Where preventing and countering violent extremism includes both security and development, there is a need to ensure a balanced approach that does not privilege the former over the latter.'[6]

This chapter follows the UN's guidance to highlight small but meaningful distinctions between state-funded P/CVE work focused on interventions seeking to *counter* pathways to violent extremism through the identification of individualized risk factors (pull factors), on the one hand, and, on the other, *prevention* or 'diversion', efforts that tackle structural of drivers of radicalization (push factors). Work focused on structural drivers (as discussed further below) integrates violent extremism prevention work with pre-existing intersecting complex social issues (such as gang violence and knife crime), also regarded as 'wicked problems'.[7]

This distinction between interventions focused on pull/risk factors and push/ structural factors helps unpack the nuances behind P/CVE work, particularly when making a distinction between state-led (Prevent) and independent/hybrid interventions in the UK. Interventions focused on disrupting the structural conditions which enable grooming for violent extremism and wider social harms are defined in the diversion literature as secondary-level initiatives aiming to 'remove individuals from at-risk environments or negative influences through forms of meaningful engagement and activities that inculcate alternative ways of thinking and acting'.[8] Throughout this chapter, similar distinctions are drawn in the field when state-funded P/CVE work, such as Prevent-funded programmes, focuses exclusively on risk factors as predictive tools to *counter* radicalization processes, and independent P/CVE work seeks to incorporate efforts to prevent violent extremism within localized and holistic approaches tackling wider complex social issues with intersecting root (structural) causes. This chapter seeks to expand our understanding of grassroots youth work, highlighting how it adapts state-led whole of society approaches, such as the Statutory Duty,[9] to refer individuals at risk of radicalization, to their pre-existing practices and traditions.

Youth workers engaged in the field of upstream interventions have the benefit of context-based experiences and they often point to differences between *countering*, *preventing* and *diverting* violent extremism. For example, Azim, project manager for the independently funded Resilience Project[10] in Wales, highlighted an ontological difference in how they approach the problem of radicalization, in contrast to Prevent-funded programmes:

> We do not think it is possible, I do not think it's possible, to predict who is going to be a terrorist. Full on. I do not think that social sciences are there or will ever be there. It is not a predictive model. So you know you can take two individuals, one of whom is a part of a radical group and one of whom isn't, and they can have exactly the same social and biological factors, [and] one will become a terrorist and one won't. It might not even be the one who is part of a radical or extremist group.
>
> Azim, The Resilience Project[11]

Preventing radicalization, Azim further argued, is not about predicting who is at risk and vulnerable but rather about identifying the different factors that may make someone fall into criminality or violence, not exclusively terrorism.[12] It should also be noted that although some youth workers included in the sample, such as Azim, share a critical view of aspects of the Prevent model of intervention, the data does not necessarily show that this is a binary or ideological position against Prevent. In fact, organizations such as the Resilience Project have a close collaborative relationship with local Prevent officials, notwithstanding the fact that the controversy over Prevent has led to the politization of the P/CVE field in the UK.[13]

The three phases of the Prevent strategy and its critiques

Since its origins in 2003, the UK's counter-terrorism (CT) strategy, CONTEST, included the Prevent Strategy as an innovative response to the threat of domestic radicalization. Unlike other CT policies worldwide, P/CVE efforts such as Prevent in the UK sought to identify and interrupt early stages of radicalization as a pre-emptive model[14] which relied on whole of society efforts to govern security threats.[15] However, it was not until 2006/7 that Prevent took a prominent role within the overall CONTEST strategy in the UK through the Preventing Violent Extremism Pathfinder Fund in 2006.[16] The 2006 'Pathfinder' pilot project funded 261 projects from 2007 to 2008 with an initial £6 million investment. The Department for Communities and Local Government (DCLG) detailed that funding was focused on local authorities with 'sizeable Muslim communities' meaning those areas with 'populations of 5 per cent or more' Muslims,[17] which became an area of contention.

Since the rollout of the pathfinder fund to the announcement of an independent review of Prevent, this policy had been under public scrutiny due to its focus on ethnic and religious minorities,[18] particularly Muslim youth,[19] undermining community cohesion policies in the UK.[20] Due to the contested practice of Prevent within local communities, most P/CVE research and mass media in the UK has focused on analysing the design and implementation of Prevent policy and its Statutory Duty (2015), leaving unexplored the practices and contributions of independent/hybrid P/CVE work. Criticisms to the design of the policy follow the evolution of Prevent in each of its three phases:

- Prevent Phase One (2007–11): The conflation of surveillance and community cohesion policies targeting Muslim-dense communities defined as Prevent Priority Areas (PPAs), leading to interventions focused on Muslim youth.[21]
- Prevent Phase Two (2011–15): The centralized management of Prevent which reduced the number of PPAs used to map out communities at risk of radicalization, and the incorporation of non-violent extremism into the Counter-terrorism strategy. This played a role in increasing the focus of Prevent's early intervention work within front-line settings during the second phase of Prevent.[22] This led to the central role of local Channel panels[23] for the evaluation of potential radicalization of individuals through the use of assessment tools such as 'ERG 22+' (Extremist Risk Guidance) and the 'Vulnerability Assessment Framework', which came under scrutiny due to their exclusive focus on jihadist radicalization factors, weak empirical evidence and the contested nature of radicalization as a guiding concept;[24] and
- Prevent Phase Three (2015–present): The Counter-terrorism and Security Act (2015) strengthened Prevent's presence in public authorities through the introduction of the Prevent Duty. Among its key components are Prevent training and the use of Fundamental British Values (FBV) by Ofsted as guidelines (Prevent Guidelines) for schools to tackle (non-violent) extremism and to identify members in their community who are vulnerable to radicalization and refer them to their local Channel panels. This led to concerns over the definition of

FBV, as well as the possible 'chilling effects' in higher education, and concerns over compromising confidentiality and incompatibility between pre-existing safeguarding models in front-line practices, particularly in education and health sectors, and safeguarding practices superimposed by Prevent's Statutory Duty.[25]

Some of the most common criticisms of Prevent focused on its design and implementation and how these intersect with criticisms towards the overall counter-terrorism strategy (CONTEST) have prevailed throughout the three phases of Prevent.[26] At the core of these politicized debates are concerns over 'the balance between state security and human rights, the compatibility between Islam and "western values", and the legitimacy of Muslim citizenship in predominantly non-Muslim western states'.[27]

The existing literature has shown how Prevent and wider CT policies have contributed to social stigmatization, Islamophobia and the reproduction of suspect communities due to their focus on ethnic and religious minorities in the UK,[28] particularly targeting Muslim youth.[29] Although these approaches have been valuable in highlighting how CT and P/CVE strategies apply security frameworks to grassroots, and community and public sector professional work to counter the threat of radicalization with the outcome of imposing policy frames that stigmatize ethnic/religious minorities in the UK, they often do not provide the complete picture of front-line implementation. This is because there is a predominant characterization of P/CVE policy implementation as a top-down versus bottom-up binary.[30] Furthermore, the implication of these studies is that the Prevent policy is being cascaded down into the front line without much contestation,[31] as they argue that Prevent's framework has securitized the public sphere, with front-line workers and civil society being made responsible for identifying and referring anyone vulnerable to radicalization.[32]

A *Decentred* framework for the study of P/CVE grassroots work

A Decentred Security Governance approach proposed by Bevir (2016) provides a different take on power that goes beyond binary understandings of policy compliance versus policy contestation or a 'top-down versus bottom-up' divide.[33] As discussed above, the predominant picture of the study of Prevent has reproduced such binaries between those who support Prevent policy and those who oppose it on the ground. Instead of framing government policy as either cascading down or being challenged on the front line, Bevir believes that policy outcomes actually rely on co-production, meaning that there are co-dependencies between multi-layered sectors of society and government in order to solve complex policy problems, also regarded as 'wicked problems'[34] such as violent extremism.[35] These are problems that are not amenable to bureaucratic expertise alone; therefore, there is a need to partner with public sector professionals, local stakeholder and service users to try to figure out the nature of the problems and to harness their expertise to deliver solutions.[36]

Bevir (2016) also argues that wicked problems are usually 'interrelated', meaning that 'any response to a wicked problem has an impact on other wicked problems' (230). The literature reviewed in the previous section provides evidence that tackling radicalization and terrorism has brought on additional issues around stigmatization and racism/islamophobia, which in youth can intersect with and enhance other complex social issues such as gang grooming, domestic violence and knife crime, to name a few. This makes evident the 'interrelated' dimension of those social issues, perhaps some but not all of them holding 'wicked' dimensions of their own or in their collective relationships. The last two sections discuss how youth work is both at the centre of this due to the UK's P/CVE approach and pre-existing practices and context-based knowledge.

My work is situated within research which has analysed first-hand experiences from front-line workers and local communities in their engagement with the Prevent Strategy.[37] Such important work has detailed how governance through Prevent policy is not merely passively implemented from the top-down by public service professionals and community members, particularly in education and health settings. Such research focused on practices under the frame of Prevent has expanded its focus on policy implementation, mainly on the experiences and practices of front-line workers in the health, education and community work sectors, providing nuanced understandings of P/CVE implementation. A wide range of responses to Prevent policy, particularly to the Statutory Duty, show that Prevent policy does not simply cascade down into the front line, as instances of agency where P/CVE policy is contested, challenged, re-interpreted,[38] as well as complied with[39] on the front line are all documented by research.

In addition, although there is important research problematizing youth work and Prevent policy,[40] there is little data on how independent youth work intersects with P/CVE efforts beyond Prevent policy.[41] This is because, as discussed above, most of this research on youth work has maintained a Prevent policy focus, providing an incomplete picture of how non-state-led P/CVE is delivered on the front line. There is therefore an existing need to understand the role of youth workers and practitioners in P/CVE efforts in the UK from beyond the scope of Prevent policy.

My research addresses this need by integrating independently and hybrid-funded youth work practices into existing understandings of Prevent-funded work, revealing the existing tension between policy design and policy outcomes and between state-funded and independent P/CVE work, and how these tensions are resolved on the front line. One key contribution is to demonstrate how independent/hybrid P/CVE youth workers/practitioners incorporate P/CVE work with their pre-existing practices in safeguarding against gang violence, knife crime, Female Genital Mutilation (FGM) and other complex local issues through holistic models. Such models aim to tackle the intersecting root causes of these complex social issues ('wicked problems') such as socio-economic marginalization, exposure to violence, social stigmatization, racism/Islamophobia, with the aim of developing youth empowerment, employment and social/political agency.

P/CVE youth work in the UK

In each of Prevent's distinctive phases (2007–11; 2011–15; 2015–present), this policy has relied on local communities, public sector professionals and grassroots organizations in the private and public sectors to tackle signs of radicalization within communities.[42] This section discusses the continued role of youth workers under the current iteration of the Prevent Strategy, highlighting firstly the outcome of collaboration between Prevent and grassroots organizations and secondly, the alternative P/CVE approaches stemming from independent/hybrid youth work.

For the first decade at the turn of the century, youth work safeguarding practices in the UK played a key role during the 1997–2010 Labour government's 'social exclusion' policy agenda '... including the drive to reduce teenage pregnancies, efforts to educationally re-engage so-called "NEETs" (Not in Educational, Employment or Training), and roles within formal education doing preventive work with individuals at risk of educational disaffection and school expulsion ...'.[43] Furthermore, Durose (2009) in her study in Salford found that the New Labour 'network community governance' approach relied on decentred networks of front-line workers, including youth workers, for policy delivery. Durose's findings showed that 'front-line workers were able to act to reconcile policy demands – around public health – with community priorities – about tackling financial exclusion – through their understanding of the micro context of the neighbourhood they worked within'.[44] These are examples of decentred frames of intervention, where the government relied on front-line workers and communities to co-design and co-implement potential solutions to complex, 'wicked', social problems,[45] similar to the current approach to tackle radicalization in the UK.[46]

My fieldwork, carried out between June 2018 and April 2019 in England and Wales, included a sample of youth workers and practitioners and Prevent Coordinators. In a conversation with a Prevent Coordinator located in the Midlands, there is evidence of a continued aim of encouraging grassroots collaboration (and therefore the *responsibilisation*) of P/CVE work under the current third phase of Prevent:

> *What we do [in Birmingham] is all of our programmes know each other. We encourage all of our programmes to work together, even though they may be in different areas. Look, if you're doing diversionary activity work with this program that does intervention activity because you may not be good at intervention, but they are, but they don't engage with the people, you engage with me. So rather than you trying to create the same, or duplicate what they are doing, create a system in which you refer to each other.*
>
> Waqar, Prevent Coordinator

As the quote suggests, there are continued efforts to align grassroots work and its safeguarding responsibilities with P/CVE work supervised by local Prevent Coordinators. My study includes in the sample an organization which shows the outcome of embedding safeguarding duties through grassroots collaboration between Prevent practitioners and local stakeholders. A group operating in the same locality as the Prevent Coordinator above, KIKIT Pathways to Recovery CIC (KIKIT), confirmed their involvement in leading 'community safeguarding panels' under the guidance of local Prevent Coordinators. Mohammed details how these panels work:

> *So why [did] we set up the community safeguarding panel? It's for all the practitioners to come together and basically take referrals from the community, assess every case ourselves and then provide the right interventions for that case collectively, together.*

We do that as part of the Prevent Project and then sometimes if that individual or that family need Channel help we will work with Channel together. The community safeguarding panel and the Channel panel will work together. Statutory and voluntary.

Mohammed, KIKIT

Mohammed describes here one of the outcomes of KIKIT's close work with Prevent in local communities, by participating in the creation of 'community safeguarding panels'. A key distinction of these panels is that the Channel panels are part of the Statutory Duty introduced in 2015, which encouraged front-line workers to refer anyone they assessed as being vulnerable to radicalization. For clarification, front-line workers incorporate into their pre-existing safeguarding practices the additional responsibility of referring for potential radicalization cases. The actual statutory duty therefore falls on their institution rather than on the individuals. However, a lack of clarity on who is bounded by the Statutory Duty can have negative effects on pre-existing practices, and referral processes, for example, have shown to compromise trust and confidentiality on the front line.[47] The potential consequence of creating voluntary safeguarding panels with local grassroots organizations is further overlapping the Statutory Duty to refer to Prevent Channel panels and voluntary participation in safeguarding panels within communities.

The description of how these 'community safeguarding panels' mimics the Prevent's Channel panels,[48] suggesting a 'whole of society' approach that 'favours polycentric or nodal approach to security governance'.[49] These panels are the outcome of the partnership of local organizations, such as KIKIT and local Prevent Coordinators, as an opportunity to increase local collaboration between grassroots organizations to expand P/CVE safeguarding work. In the view of Mohammed, such community safeguarding panels are an opportunity to improve local P/CVE work and to increase the likelihood of funding from the Home Office as they would demonstrate their value through the number of referrals being processed in that particular Prevent Priority Area. Later in the interview, Mohammed argued that these panels should be coordinated within communities, saying they should have 'similar functions as Channel but its run from the community ... not statutory'.[50] The potential outcome here is creating the infrastructure for P/CVE referrals, combining statutory compliance due to the Prevent Duty (for public sector professionals) and a safeguarding culture (from the voluntary sector). Previous research and my data show that state-led policies which increase the focus of P/CVE work on the front line can compromise existing resources and efforts to tackle wider social issues with intersecting root causes such as gang violence, racism, Islamophobia, domestic violence, knife crime and education disengagement.

However, early studies showed the challenges for youth workers in their incorporation of Prevent funded work to their practices: '... the increasing interest in youth workers' abilities to connect can create a tension: between the need for trust and credibility with communities and young people fundamental to youth work, and the extent to which to engage with the often stigmatising policies and practices of state security'.[51] These community-based approaches can provide some benefits for local organizations as argued by Mohammed. However, as McDonald argued, and more recent research has proven in education and health sectors[52] and as youth workers in this sample also noted, it can also provide greater challenges on the front line in balancing trust, wider safeguarding responsibilities and P/CVE work.

Back in my interview with Azim from the Resilience Project in Cardiff, there is evidence of an extended compliance with the referral processes designed by Prevent:

> *In terms of our relationship with Prevent, we will of course refer, if we get a case where it is extremely clear that this is a kid that is on the path to violence and needs to be referred on to Prevent, we will refer them on. Very often it's not because of the fact that we are looking at different factors. Someone who's been referred to Prevent needs deradicalisation, someone who has been referred to us, even the most severe cases where we're talking about building resilience, that is not an overlap in that kind of scenario.*

Azim, Resilience Project

This quote is evidence that for youth workers, developing working relationships at the grassroots level with local Prevent officers is a commitment to pre-existing safeguarding practices. Furthermore, Azim shows here that these partnerships are viewed as opportunities to support local stakeholders on cases which might have intersecting social issues that do not exclusively require P/CVE work led by Prevent.

As Azim continued in the interview, the collaborating relationship between the Resilience Project and Prevent is influenced, in part, by the presence of Prevent officials in localities (PPAs) and through polices such as the Statutory Duty: 'But we do keep in touch with the local council and Prevent leads. We will always know who the Prevent leads are in schools because it is such, it's such a big part of the state sector at the moment. Prevent is unavoidable, it's massive, it's huge, and we're always in its shadow, to be completely honest.'[53] This quote further supports the perception that Prevent is prevalent in the field, particularly in PPAs. As Azim states here, partial compliance with referral processes is rooted in Prevent's 'huge' presence in his locality. As a result, identifying who are the local Prevent bodies is a useful tool for this independent grassroots organization.

The perception of an increasing presence of Prevent in PPAs has potentially led to an increased focus of grassroots work on P/CVE. The framework of interventions supports the claim being made here that Prevent-led interventions often are more targeted at *countering* pathways to radicalization through security frames. As mentioned above, Prevent increasingly has relied on whole of society approaches through the *responsibilization*[54] of intervention on the front line through community-led programmes and the Statutory Duty (2015) of public sector professionals to refer anyone identified as vulnerable to violent extremism. However, this framework of intervention relies on the unproven link between radicalization and terrorism.[55] As a result, their targeted interventions result in making distinctions between those at risk and those who are not.[56]

Alternatively, independent/hybrid P/CVE youth work suggests that broad interventions, when co-produced and co-designed by front-line workers, can better integrate P/CVE work into holistic safeguarding practices. Such practices acknowledge the multi-layered and often intersecting root causes of complex/'wicked' social issues, such as gang violence, knife crime, domestic violence, FGM, racism, Islamophobia, etc., which often predate and intersect with P/CVE work. The final section highlights the characterization of P/CVE from the practices of independent/hybrid youth workers/practitioners in the UK.

Heterogeneous practices in the frontline: Safeguarding beyond P/CVE

A recurring aim for the participants in this study is to raise awareness in schools and within communities of the possible *pathways* to radicalization and to promote a wider understanding of vulnerability. Revealing these pathways to young people often requires reviewing case studies of radicalization/grooming and engaging with the stories of 'former' extremists. It also involves talking about religion, racism, violent and non-violent extremism and socio-economic contextual factors such as access to education, employment and housing. The first task for youth workers in such conversations is often to debunk the idea that violent extremism grooming is something that happens to other people (far away), or that it is an issue prevalent in Muslim populations. RP2,[57] from Hybrid Organisation, offered a practical insight into the benefit gained from reviewing hypothetical pathway scenarios with their young participants:

> *I think that our job is to show how easy it is to get sucked into something. So it's more about their protection rather than their responsibility, and I think we start with that. [Then] you can move on to ... ok protect yourself, what do you do when you think a friend is at risk or radicalised, where would you go, what would you do?*
>
> RP2, Hybrid Organisation.

Efforts to keep local communities safe require raising awareness about VE and the safety measures available for youth and members of the community, as illustrated by RP2 further in our conversation. Although this organization is located in a local authority persistently labelled a PPA throughout the existence of Prevent, their work is not primarily funded by Prevent. They are a hybrid model of P/CVE and most of their revenue comes from the work they deliver, as argued by a colleague from Hybrid Organisation: 'The reason we are an independent organisation is because we wanted to keep independent offer' (RP 1, 2018). They therefore have the flexibility to work with the partners they want to engage with, which they find is key to breaking myths about radicalization and creating wider understandings of vulnerability.

Odd Arts is another hybrid organization which aims to dispel misconceptions around radicalization and violent extremism through critical debates. They implement critical thinking as a tool to tackle VE through theatre and arts, as Rebecca described:

> *The bit I'm interested in is giving people an increased sense of belonging, increasing critical thinking, increasing empathy and holding challenging conversations around difference and allowing people to see that we can disagree, we can be different, we can*

discuss it and not hate. What is interesting to me is what people understand about radicalisation. It's actually the understanding of what I am interested in [that] the workshop explores: where do our values come from, where does hate come from, and are you ok with the values and views you hold? Have you ever considered where they come from and have you considered the impact of that?

Rebecca, Odd Arts

Odd Arts practitioners aim to establish safe spaces in their workshops where people can disagree and discuss without feeling there is a right or wrong answer. Rebecca provides insights into how Odd Arts seeks to develop critical thinking and contributed to P/CVE work by challenging belief systems often charged with strong emotive pre-dispositions. In her experience, it is more likely that participants will walk away with a broader understanding of a topic through a critical discussion. Debate pushes participants to engage with opposing viewpoints, which helps to create empathy towards different views, resulting in bringing people together and increasing a 'sense of belonging'.

Similarly, independent P/CVE grassroots efforts documented in this research aim to disclose the emergence of possible pathways to VE grooming through open dialogue with youth. For example, Khalil's work as the director of the Bristol Horn Youth Concern (BHYC) has increased his networks with local stakeholders in Bristol, such as police, city council, Somali community members and other grassroots organizations, because of his rapport with Somali youth and how he has used this trust to safeguard them from grooming. He provided an anecdote on how some of his interactions with local youth are used to expand safeguarding practices against vulnerability to radicalization:

We talked about the groups like the one in London, like the al-Muhajiroun. We talk about these groups. We talked about [how] these groups exist in Bristol, and someone says, 'Oh, I've seen someone like that who was here'. So when we talk about that, we talk about the group that is existent and everybody knows it, it's in the public eye so nothing to worry about, but do you know anyone who has seen it? And then they sometimes say: 'Somebody was last week here talking about them, and we just walked away, we don't want to relate to them'. And then (to) that person who said that, I tell them, 'Can we have a private meeting and have a coffee?' ... They sometimes ask the reason why I ask, and I say that I don't want [the person they saw] to harm anyone.

Khalil, BYHC director

Khalil, like other youth workers in this study, provides evidence here about the benefits of nurturing strong bonds at the grassroots level to safeguard the community from VE and wider social harms. Furthermore, it evidences the valuable work of independent organizations countering radicalization in non-PPAs, such as Bristol.

However, safeguarding practices are not just limited to raising awareness of VE grooming. There is important work being done at the grassroots level around vulnerability towards violence beyond P/CVE work as well. The work of Jawaab, an independent organization focused on Muslim empowerment based in London, illustrates this well. Rizwan, the director of Jawaab, discussed their focus on raising awareness of structures that reproduce cycles of violence, particularly those that target ethnic and religious minorities in the UK:

> *ISIS and the propaganda around airstrikes (are) creating a sense of stereotype and dehumanisation of Muslims in those countries and how those have impacts on young Muslims all together. Here, the interviews we do with young people and the research that we have done shows a constant focus on violence, whether it is on TV or in state counterterrorism policies, young people are just completely exposed to violence; whether it's the English Defence League or hearing about hate crimes, it is not creating a healthy environment for young Muslims to really become part of society. This builds a sense of powerlessness, and that is why we exist, building the power of Muslims. It is to impact and help dismantle that powerlessness that has been created by society.*
>
> Rizwan, Jawaab

Jawaab raises awareness about the structures of racism and Islamophobia that Muslim youth are exposed to on a daily basis that affect their sense of belonging. Similarly, Azim (Resilience Project) also pointed to the concern about the overexposure of youth to violence in general, which can lead to VE as much as it can lead to other social harms:

> *In the majority of cases, we've had young people being referred to us for that [watching ISIS propaganda], by schools in most cases, 90% of the time, so I'm talking about 14 or 15 cases we've had … in the majority of those cases it wasn't that much a person attracted to ISIS, it was a young person attracted to violence. So alongside the videos they are watching by ISIS, where people are getting killed and murdered, they are also watching snuff videos, which are online material videos where people are getting killed and murdered. So along with the videos which include ISIS killing people, there's also videos by Mexican cartels of an assassination being recorded, there's also videos of street fights in central Asia. The kind of materials online which are graphic and violent and that's what they are attracted to. That person still needs help because again, a person with the level of infatuation with violence needs support because if they are interested in violence on that level, then maybe they need to be intervened. But you wouldn't necessarily consider them potentially attracted to extremism as a form of violence.*
>
> Azim, Resilience Project

Azim argues that an exclusive focus on violent extremism would not necessarily tackle wider narratives of violence within communities. Therefore, tackling only violent *extremism* would not necessarily result in safeguarding an individual from other types of grooming (such as gang violence). Knowing the context of violence, Shahab agrees, is key in the design of a programme that tackles violence holistically in local communities:

> *The public policymakers need to be fully aware of all the variables, all of the other factors that might be contributing to someone doing crazy things, whether it's committing an act of violence, whether it's committing burglary or any other crime,*

or committing VE, and so forth. So this would be a holistic approach, you get much more buy-in from all of their communities, even Muslim communities, if it's coming across as well-researched, well-understood and it's a general problem. Honestly, I have not come across one individual since 9/11, I have not come across any individual I thought, 'Hey I'm a bit worried about you.'

Shahab, MEND *regional manager*

Shahab expressed in the interview concerns over an over-emphasis on P/CVE efforts, which undermines youth support in other areas. Furthermore, his saying that he has never encountered someone who seemed vulnerable to violent extremism in his experience is relevant, as he is in a locality in the North of England consistently labelled as a PPA since 2007. Similarly, RP3's work goes beyond P/CVE work with Hybrid Organisation, as he notes that daily violence can easily be transferred to youth:

Alongside [Hybrid Organisation], my full-time role is working within a serious youth violence and exploitation team within a hospital. So, I suppose that the violence thing stems throughout all of the stuff I do, whether it's countering violent extremisms, or whether its gangs and youth violence. Violence goes from people to young people.

RP 3, Hybrid Organisation

Although P/CVE programmes in the third sector do target awareness-raising around vulnerability to violent extremism and grooming, a wider approach to tackle 'violence' and other social harms often frames their interventions. In the search to understand the underlying issues or structures that contribute to youth grooming, these grassroots organizations often shift their focus solely from radicalization to include wider pathways into grooming processes.

Conclusion

My research has also provided a nuanced perspective to the polarizing understandings of Prevent policy at the grassroots level which go beyond simplistic binary divisions between those supporting Prevent and its critics, prompting the questions: What should the role of Home Office be in addressing issues around social stigmatization within the framework of P/CVE efforts? How can the current and future Prevent programmes address the personal grievances of those who were stigmatized during the early stages of Prevent? There are key themes which should be considered in the P/CVE field moving forward, particularly for the consideration of the 'independent' review of Prevent, to critically engage with these questions.

One suggestion is that critical views of Prevent on the front line are rooted in experiences of direct social stigmatization, such as Islamophobia, that occurred due to the framework of Prevent focusing disproportionately on Muslim communities. Though there has been a shift in recent years to include the increasing threat of far-right violent extremism in P/CVE work, these accounts persist on the front line. This is due to the intersection of Islamophobia and security-framed interventions in

Muslim communities, but also due to the notorious absence in the Prevent Strategy of any objectives to reconcile and (re)build relationships with Muslim communities, starting perhaps with the need to recognize its role in contributing to the wider social stigmatization suffered by these communities since its origin. This type of work requires reframing of intervention from a security focus aimed at predicting risk and vulnerability factors into holistic frames of intervention used in independent and hybrid P/CVE work, shown in this study to be valuable. One factor worth looking into in future research is analysing to what extent the current framework of Prevent is operationalized by personnel closely linked to police culture (e.g., ex-police officers). This could factor in a prevalent inclination to follow a pre-crime and risk mitigation logic. Potential reframes of state-led P/CVE work which are inclusive of localized forms of intervention would benefit from the expertise of front-line workers such as youth workers, social workers, teachers, and health professionals at an operational level of whole-of-society programmes such as Prevent.

Notes

1   Prevent's three aims are to 'tackle the causes of radicalisation and respond to the ideological challenge of terrorism; safeguard and support those most at risk of radicalisation through early intervention, identifying them and offering support; enable those who have already engaged in terrorism to disengage and rehabilitate' (Home Office, *Channel Duty Guidance: Protecting People Vulnerable to Being Drawn to Terrorism* (London: HM Government, 2020), 5).

2   For evidence-based work highlighting the unintended effects of Prevent's first phase; see: A. Kundnani, 'Spooked: How Not to Prevent Violent Extremism', Report, London: Institute of Race Relations, 2009; C. Pantazis and S. Pemberton, 'From the "Old" to the "New" Suspect Community: Examining the Impacts of Recent UK Counter-terrorist Legislation'. *The British Journal of Criminology* 49, no. 5 (2009): 646–66; Y. Birt, 'Promoting Virulent Envy? Reconsidering The UK's Terrorist Prevention Strategy', *The RUSI Journal* 154, no. 4 (2009): 52–8; and B. Spalek and L. Z. McDonald, 'Terror Crime Prevention: Constructing Muslim Practices and Beliefs as "Anti-social" and "Extreme" through CONTEST 2', *Social Policy & Society* 9, no. 1 (2010): 123–32.

3   L. Z. McDonald, 'Securing Identities, Resisting Terror: Muslim Youth Work in the UK and Its Implications for Security', *Religion, State and Society* 39, nos. 2–3 (2011): 177–89, and P. Thomas, 'Youth, Terrorism and Education: Britain's Prevent Programme', *International Journal of Lifelong Education* 35, no. 2 (2016): 171–87.

4   De St. Croix argues that youth work in the UK is: '... predominantly (but not only) in purpose-built youth clubs, community centres, village halls, religious buildings, parks, sports fields and on street corners ...' (2016: 4). The author also points out fundamental characteristics in youth work: 'Its key features are that young people's perspectives are central to the process; young people become involved by choice rather than being compelled to attend; and there is an element of informal education, of learning through conversation, relationships and activities (Davies, 2015)' (De St. Croix, 2016: 4).

5   As narrated by youth workers, the holistic approaches aim to build resilience to narratives of violence upskill and develop a sense of belonging in youth, thereby preventing youth from falling prey to grooming, including radicalization, while also countering any possible stigmatizing effects of P/CVE and CT policies. This brings to mind findings by Durose on front-line work in Salford under the New Labour's 'networked community governance' (1997), which showed that front-line workers '… can respond holistically to issues allowing them to be responsive to both national policy agendas and the priorities of the communities they work within' (Durose, 2009: 45).

6   UN Human Rights Council, 'Human Rights Impact of Policies and Practices Aimed at Preventing and Countering Violent Extremism', 20 February 2020, A/HRC/49/45, available at: https://digitallibrary.un.org/record/3872336?ln=en

7   H. W. J. Rittel and M. M. Webber, 'Dilemmas in a General Theory of Planning', *Policy Sciences* 4 (1973): 155–69.

8   Cherney, A., 'Designing and Implementing Programmes to Tackle Radicalization and Violent Extremism: Lessons from Criminology', *Dynamics of Asymmetric Conflict* 9, nos. 1–3 (2016): 82–94.

9   According to the Prevent Statutory Duty and Guidance published in 2015 (and updated in April 2019), local authorities are required to make sure front-line workers (such as those in public health and education) are fully trained to refer anyone they view as vulnerable to radicalization (HO, 2019). The duty was to be implemented in 'conjunction with other relevant safeguarding guidance' such as 'Working Together to Safeguard Children' (Prevent Duty Guidance, 2015: 7). However, the Prevent Duty's increased focus on front-line workers for the risk management of radicalization in communities renewed criticisms towards the state-led P/CVE strategy.

10   This project focused on far-right extremism was originally called The Think Project, developed by the Ethnic Youth Support Team (EYST) in Swansea and launched in 2011. It then expanded its work to other forms of radicalization, such as religious-inspired violent extremism, and is currently known as the Resilience Project. One of the purposes of the project was to provide evidence-based strategies that could be used by policymakers in the UK to counter violent extremism inspired by any ideology and therefore improve Prevent's practices (Cifuentes et al., 2013: 305).

11   All interviews were collected between June 2018 and April 2019. They were all one-on-one audio-recorded semi-structured interviews lasting between sixty and ninety minutes. The interviews were carried out in 'natural settings' (Carpenter, 2018: 36) such as local coffee shops or within the facilities of the organizations. The interviews consisted of eleven main questions, with twelve sub-questions that were mostly variations of the original question or related follow-up questions and were designed to follow four of the areas of inquiry: How they got involved into youth work and P/CVE work; descriptions of the work they do related to P/CVE; discussions around P/CVE policies, particularly the Prevent Duty; and discussion around their understanding of safeguarding, risk and vulnerability.

12   Azim at the time of the interview in October 2018 was a project manager at the Resilience Project.

13   A politization characterized by a recurring perception of binary divides between those who support Prevent and accept Prevent funding and its critics (Spalek and Lambert, 2011), which at the grassroots level implied a perceived division between those seen by Home Office as safe partners and those who are aligned with 'extremist' ideology (Ragazzi, 2014).

14   C. Heath-Kelly, 'The Geography of Pre-criminal Space: Epidemiological Imaginations of Radicalisation Risk in the UK Prevent Strategy, 2007–2017', *Critical Studies on Terrorism* 10, no. 2 (2017): 297–319, and T. Martin, 'Governing an Unknowable Future: The Politics of Britain's Prevent Policy', *Critical Studies on Terrorism* 7, no. 1 (2014): 62–78.

15   J. Froestad and C. D. Shearing, *Security Governance, Policing, and Local Capacity*. Hoboken: CRC Press. Advances in Police Theory and Practice, 2013, available at: https://search.ebscohost.com/login.aspx?direct=true&scope=site&db=nlebk&db=nlabk&AN=1763416, and M. Webber, S. Croft, J. Howorth, T. Terriff and E. Krahmann, 'The Governance of European Security', *Review of International Studies* 30, no. 1 (2004): 3–26.

16   Department for Communities and Local Government (DCLG), *Preventing Violent Extremism: Winning Hearts and Minds* (London: DCLG, 2007).

17   See page 6 in Department for Communities and Local Government (DCLG), *Preventing Violent Extremism Guidance Note for Government Offices and Local Authorities in England* (London: DCLG, 2017b).

18   For a complete scope of the evidence-based analysis of the first phase of Prevent, see the following literature: Kundani, 2009; Spalek et al., 2010; Pantazis and Pemberton, 2009; Birt, 2009.

19   Thomas, 'Youth, Terrorism and Education', 171–87, and L. Z. McDonald, 'Securing Identities, Resisting Terror: Muslim Youth Work in the UK and its Implications for Security', *Religion, State and Society* 39, nos. 2–3 (2011): 177–89.

20   Thomas, 'Between Two Stools? The Government's "Preventing Violent Extremism" Agenda', *The Political Quarterly* 80, no. 2 (2009): 282–91.

21   Thomas, 'Youth, Terrorism and Education', 171–87; P. Thomas, *Responding to the Threat of Violent Extremism: Failing to Prevent*. London: Bloomsbury Academic, 2012; B. Spalek, '"New Terrorism" and Crime Prevention Initiatives Involving Muslim Young People in the UK: Research and Policy Contexts', *Religion, State and Society* 39, nos. 2–3 (2011): 191–207; Kundnani, 'Spooked'; and page 46 of the Prevent Strategy (2008).

22   See page 21 in P. Thomas, M. Grossman, K. Christmann, and S. Miah, 'Community Reporting on Violent Extremism by "intimates": Emergent Findings from International Evidence', *Critical Studies on Terrorism* (2020): 1–22, and page 308 in C. Heath-Kelly, 'The Geography of Pre-criminal Space: Epidemiological Imaginations of Radicalisation Risk in the UK Prevent Strategy, 2007–2017', *Critical Studies on Terrorism* 10, no. 2 (2017): 297–319.

23   Channel Panels are piloted with Prevent since 2007; they were then rolled out in 2012 and made part of Prevent's Statutory duty in 2015. They come into effect once a Prevent referral of an individual is confirmed to be vulnerable to terrorist recruitment; this is an early state intervention as it is focused on individuals who have not directly engaged with terrorist-related activities. Its panel is made up of local multi-agency partnerships made of personnel from the following areas: Ministers of the Crown and government departments, local government, criminal justice, education and childcare, health and social care and the police. Its aims are to 'identify individuals at risk, assess the nature and extent of that risk, develop the most appropriate support plan for the individuals concerned' (Channel Duty Guidance, 2020: 7, 8, 50).

24   See page 19 in P. Thomas, M. Grossman, K. Christmann, and S. Miah, 'Community Reporting on Violent Extremism by "intimates": Emergent Findings from

International Evidence', *Critical Studies on Terrorism* (2020): 1–22; also Kundnani, 2012; Heath-Kelly, 2013.

25   Busher et al., 2019; Heath-Kelly and Strausz, 2019; OSJI, 2016.

26   Thomas, 2020; Kundnani, 2014.

27   See page 179 in L. Z. McDonald, 'Securing Identities, Resisting Terror: Muslim Youth Work in the UK and Its Implications for Security', *Religion, State and Society* 39, nos. 2–3 (2011): 177–89.

28   Extensive research on this topic is available: Abbas, 2018; Qureshi, 2017; Thomas, 2016; Heath-Kelley, 2013; Hickman et al., 2012; Spalek, 2011; J. Githens-Mazer and R. Lambert, 'Why Conventional Wisdom on Radicalization Fails: The Persistence of a Failed Discourse', *International Affairs* 86, no. 4 (2010): 889–901; Kundnani, 2009.

29   V. Coppock and M. McGovern, '"Dangerous Minds"? Deconstructing Counter-Terrorism Discourse, Radicalisation and the "Psychological Vulnerability" of Muslim Children and Young People in Britain', *Children & Society* 28, no. 3 (2014): 242–56.

30   Spalek, 2011; Durose, 2009: 47.

31   P. Thomas, 'Changing Experiences of Responsibilisation and Contestation within Counter-terrorism Policies: The British Prevent Experience', *Policy & Politics* 45, no. 3 (2017): 305–21.

32   Pilkington and Acik, 2020; Abbas, 2018; Qureshi, 2017; Heath-Kelly, 2013; Mavelli, 2013.

33   B. Spalek, 'New Terrorism' and Crime Prevention Initiatives Involving Muslim Young People in the UK: Research and Policy Contexts', *Religion, State and Society* 39, nos. 2–3 (2011): 191–207.

34   Originally described in H. W. J. Rittel and M. M. Webber, 'Dilemmas in a General Theory of Planning', *Policy Sciences* 4 (1973): 155–69.

35   N. Bouhana, 'The Moral Ecology of Extremism: A Systemic Perspective', UK Commission for Countering Terrorism, 2019, available at: https://assets.publishing. service.gov.uk/government/uploads/system/uploads/attachment_ data/file/834354/ Bouhana-The-moral-ecology-of-extremism.pdf, and L. Davies, 'Security, Extremism and Education: Safeguarding or Surveillance?' *British Journal of Educational Studies* 64, no. 1 (2016): 1–19.

36   The essential characteristics of wicked problems, Davies argues, apply to violent extremism due to three issues: definitions – 'a multiplicity of types of extremism' means there is not an agreed definition and therefore no clear target for CT and P/CVE strategies; causes – a search for 'root causes of extremist behaviour' varies as it is not a 'linear path' and 'idiosyncratic combinations predispose individuals', and targets – education focused on nurturing positive traits and moral virtues could also be found in the character of violent extremists (Davies, 2016: 33–4). However, Davies argues that 'wicked problems cannot in fact be solved at all – all that is possible is that the problem space is loosened so that a wider range of options for action emerges' (Davies, 2016: 32).

37   Pilkington and Acik, 2020; Busher et al., 2019; Silverman, 2017; O'Toole et al., 2016.

38   See H. Pilkington and N. Acik, 'Not Entitled to Talk: (Mis)recognition, Inequality and Social Activism of Young Muslims', *Sociology* 54, no. 1 (2020): 181–98; Busher et al., 2019; O'Toole et al., 2016.

39   See Matthew Guest et al., *Islam and Muslims on UK University Campuses: Perceptions and Challenges* (Durham: Durham University, London: SOAS, Coventry: Coventry University and Lancaster: Lancaster University, 2020), available at: https://www. soas.ac.uk/representingislamoncampus/publications/file148310.pdf; Clements et al.,

'Listening to British Muslims: Policing, Extremism and Prevent', Crest Advisory, March 2020, available at: https://www.crestadvisory.com/post/listening-to-british-muslims-policing-extremism-and-prevent; Busher et al., 2017.

40   Thomas, 2018; McDonald, 2011; Iacopini et al., 2011.

41   R. Cifuentes, G. R. Whittaker and L. Lake, 'The Think Project: An Approach to Addressing Racism and Far-right Extremism in Swansea, South Wales', *Democracy and Security* 9, no. 3 (2013): 304–25.

42   Thomas, 2020; Brown, 2019.

43   See page 371 in P. Thomas, 'The Challenges for British Youth Workers of Government Strategies to "Prevent Terrorism"', in *The SAGE Handbook of Youth Work Practice*, Alldred et al., eds. London: SAGE Publications, 2018, available at: https://sk.sagepub.com/reference/the-sage-handbook-of-youth-work-practice

44   See page 47 in C. Durose, 'Front-line Workers and "Local Knowledge": Neighbourhood Stories in Contemporary UK Local Governance', *Public Administration* 87, no. 1 (2009): 35–49.

45   See page 230 in Bevir, M., 'Decentring Security Governance', *Global Crime* 17, nos. 3–4 (2016): 227–39.

46   Davies, L., 'Security, Extremism and Education: Safeguarding or Surveillance?' *British Journal of Educational Studies* 64, no. 1 (2016): 1–19.

47   Busher et al., 2019; Heath-Helly and Strausz, 2019.

48   Channel panels are '... multiagency meetings, chaired by the Local Authorities designed to identify and provide support to individuals who are at risk' of radicalization (gov.uk). In other words, referrals from the wider community reach a Channel panel that determines the appropriate support required on an individualiszd case by case. About 40 per cent of these cases are not considered P/CVE cases and are therefore signposted for alternative support (Home Office Factsheet, 2019); this is a common practice even in traditional safeguarding due to the nature of safeguarding processes, which promote referring in the frontline even when in doubt of a potential safeguarding issue.

49   See page 2 in J. Froestad and C. D. Shearing, *Security Governance, Policing, and Local Capacity* (Hoboken: CRC Press, 2013. Advances in Police Theory and Practice), available at: https://search.ebscohost.com/login.aspx?direct=true&scope=site&db=nl ebk&db=nlabk&AN=1763416

50   Research participant Mohammed, 2018.

51   See page 180 in L. Z. McDonald, 'Securing Identities, Resisting Terror: Muslim Youth Work in the UK and Its Implications for Security', *Religion, State and Society* 39, nos. 2–3 (2011): 177–89.

52   Busher et al., 2019; Heath-Kelly and Strausz, 2019.

53   Research participant Azim, 2018.

54   Thomas, 2018; Sliwinski, 2013.

55   UN, 2020; Sageman, 2017.

56   C. Heath-Kelly, 'The Geography of Pre-criminal Space: Epidemiological Imaginations of Radicalisation Risk in the UK Prevent Strategy, 2007–2017', *Critical Studies on Terrorism* 10, no. 2 (2017): 297–319.

57   From my data set only one organization, hybrid in its funding sources, asked for full anonymity in the data. Its three members participating in this research were anonymized and identified as *Research Participant* (RP), and the organization is identified as *Hybrid Organisation*.

Bibliography

Abbas, M.-S. 'Producing "Internal Suspect Bodies": Divisive Effects of UK Counter-terrorism Measures on Muslim Communities in Leeds and Bradford'. *The British Journal of Sociology* (2018).

Abbas, T. 'Implementing "Prevent" in Countering Violent Extremism in the UK: A Left-Realist Critique'. *Critical Social Policy* 39, no. 3 (2019): 396–412.

Åm, H. 'Limits of Decentered Governance in Science-society Policies'. *Journal of Responsible Innovation* 6, no. 2 (2019): 163–78.

Amoore, L. and De Goede, M. 'Governance, Risk and Dataveillance in the War on Terror'. *Crime, Law and Social Change: An Interdisciplinary Journal* 43, no. 2–3 (2005): 149–73.

Asim, Q. 'Fight the Power: How CAGE Resists from within a "Suspect Community"'. Palgrave, 2017.

Bartlett, J. and Miller, C. 'The Edge of Violence: Towards Telling the Difference between Violent and Non-violent Radicalization'. *Terrorism and Political Violence* 24, no. 1 (2012): 1–21.

Bell, S. and Hindmoor, A. *Rethinking Governance: The Centrality of the State in Modern Society*. Cambridge: Cambridge University Press, 2009.

Bevir, M. 'Decentring Security Governance'. *Global Crime* 17, no. 3–4 (2016): 227–39.

Bevir, M., Bevir, M., Daddow, O. J. and Hall, I. *Interpreting Global Security*. Routledge advances in international relations and global politics. London: Routledge and Taylor & Francis Group, 2014.

Birt, Y. 'Promoting Virulent Envy? Reconsidering the UK's Terrorist Prevention Strategy'. *The RUSI Journal* 154, no. 4 (2009): 52–8.

Bouhana, N. 'The Moral Ecology of Extremism: A Systemic Perspective'. UK Commission for Countering Terrorism, 2019. Available at: https://assets.publishing.service.gov.uk/government/uploads/system/uploads/attachment_data/file/834354/Bouhana-The-moral-ecology-of-extremism.pdf

Brown, K. E. 'Gender, Governance, and Countering Violent Extremism (CVE) in the UK'. *International Journal of Law, Crime and Justice* (2019).

Brown, K. E. and Saeed, T. 'Radicalization and Counter-radicalization at British Universities: Muslim Encounters and Alternatives'. *Ethnic and Racial Studies* 38, no. 11 (2015): 1952–68.

Busher, J., Choudhury, T., Thomas, P. and Harris, G. *What the Prevent Duty Means for Schools and Colleges in England: An Analysis of Educationalists' Experiences*. London: Aziz Foundation, 2017.

Busher, J., Choudhury, T. and Thomas, P. 'The Enactment of the Counter-terrorism "Prevent duty" in British Schools and Colleges: Beyond Reluctant Accommodation or Straightforward Policy Acceptance'. *Critical Studies on Terrorism* (2019): 1–23.

Cherney, A. 'Designing and Implementing Programmes to Tackle Radicalization and Violent Extremism: Lessons from Criminology'. *Dynamics of Asymmetric Conflict* 9, no. 1–3 (2016): 82–94.

Christmann, K. *Preventing Religious Radicalisation and Violent Extremism: A Systematic Review of the Research Evidence*. London and Swansea: Youth Justice Board for England and Wales, 2012.

Cifuentes, R., Whittaker, G. R. and Lake, L. 'The Think Project: An Approach to Addressing Racism and Far-right Extremism in Swansea, South Wales'. *Democracy and Security* 9, no. 3 (2013): 304–25.

Coppock, V. and McGovern, M. '"Dangerous Minds"? Deconstructing Counter-terrorism Discourse, Radicalisation and the "Psychological Vulnerability" of Muslim Children and Young People in Britain'. *Children & Society* 28, no. 3 (2014): 242–56.

Davies, L. 'Security, Extremism and Education: Safeguarding or Surveillance?'. *British Journal of Educational Studies* 64, no. 1 (2016): 1–19.

De St. Croix, T. *Grassroots Youth Work: Policy, Passion and Resistance in Practice*. Bristol: Policy Press, 2017. Available at: https://doi.org/10.1332/policypress/9781447328599.001.0001

Department for Communities and Local Government (DCLG). *Preventing Violent Extremism: Winning Hearts and Minds*. London: DCLG, 2007a.

Department for Communities and Local Government (DCLG). *Preventing Violent Extremism Guidance Note for Government Offices and Local Authorities in England*. London: DCLG, 2007b.

Department for Communities and Local Government (DCLG). *PVE Pathfinder Fund: Mapping of Project Activities 2007/08*. London: DCLG, 2008.

Dudenhoefer, A. 'Resisting Radicalisation: A Critical Analysis of the UK Prevent Duty'. *Journal for Deradicalization* 14 (2018): 153–91.

Durose, C. 'Front-Line Workers And "Local Knowledge": Neighbourhood Stories in Contemporary UK Local Governance'. *Public Administration* 87, no. 1 (2009): 35–49.

Elshimi, M. 'De-radicalisation Interventions as Technologies of the Self: A Foucauldian Analysis'. *Critical Studies on Terrorism* 8, no. 1 (2015): 110–29.

Froestad, J. and Shearing, C. D. *Security Governance, Policing, and Local Capacity. Advances in Police Theory and Practice*. Hoboken: CRC Press, 2013. Available at: https://search.ebscohost.com/login.aspx?direct=true&scope=site&db=nlebk&db=nlabk&AN =1763416

Heath-Kelly, C. 'Counter-terrorism and the Counterfactual: Producing the "Radicalisation" Discourse and the UK PREVENT Strategy'. *The British Journal of Politics & International Relations* 15, no. 3 (2013): 394–415.

Heath-Kelly, C. 'The Geography of Pre-criminal Space: Epidemiological Imaginations of Radicalisation Risk in the UK Prevent Strategy, 2007–2017'. *Critical Studies on Terrorism* 10, no. 2 (2017): 297–319.

Heath-Kelly, C. and Strausz, E. 'The Banality of Counterterrorism "after, after 9/11"? Perspectives on the Prevent Duty from the UK Health Care Sector'. *Critical Studies on Terrorism* 12, no. 1 (2019): 89–109.

Hickman, M. J., Thomas, L., Nickels, H. C. and Silvestri, S. 'Social Cohesion and the Notion of "Suspect Communities": A Study of the Experiences and Impacts of Being "suspect" for Irish Communities and Muslim Communities in Britain'. *Critical Studies on Terrorism* 5, no. 1 (2012): 89–106.

Home Office. *Pursue Prevent Protect Prepare: The United Kingdom's Strategy for Countering International Terrorism*. London: HM Government, 2009a.

Home Office. *Delivering the Prevent Strategy: An Updated Guide for Local Partners*. London: HM Government, 2009b.

Home Office. *CONTEST: The United Kingdom's Strategy for Countering Terrorism*. London: HM Government, 2011.

Home Office. *Prevent*. London: Home Office, 2011.

Husband, C. and Alam, Y. *Social Cohesion and Counter-terrorism: A Policy Contradiction?* Bristol: Policy Press, 2011.

Iacopini, G., Stock, L. and Junge, K. *Evaluation of Tower Hamlets Prevent Projects*. London: Tavistock Institute, 2011.

Jerome, L., Elwick, A. and Kazim, R. 'The Impact of the Prevent Duty on Schools: A Review of the Evidence'. *British Educational Research Journal* 45, no. 4 (2019): 821–37.

Kundnani, A. *Spooked: How Not to Prevent Violent Extremism*, Report. London: Institute of Race Relations, 2009.

Kundnani, A. 'Radicalisation: The Journey of a Concept'. *Race & Class* 54, no. 2 (2012): 3–25.

Lloyd, M. and Dean, C. 'The Development of Structured Guidelines for Assessing Risk in Extremist Offenders'. *Journal of Threat Assessment and Management* 2, no. 1 (2015): 40–52.

Mavelli, L. 'Between Normalisation and Exception: The Securitisation of Islam and the Construction of the Secular Subject'. *Millennium: Journal of International Studies* 41, no. 2 (2013): 159–81.

McDonald, L. Z. 'Securing Identities, Resisting Terror: Muslim Youth Work in the UK and Its Implications for Security'. *Religion, State and Society* 39, nos. 2–3 (2011): 177–89.

OSJI. *Eroding Trust: The UK's Prevent Counter-extremism Strategy in Health and Education*. New York: Open Society Foundations, 2016.

O'Toole, T. 'Governing and Contesting Marginality: Muslims and Urban Governance in the UK'. *Journal of Ethnic and Migration Studies* (2019).

O'Toole, T., Meer, N., DeHanas, D. N., Jones, S. H. and Modood, T. 'Governing through Prevent? Regulation and Contested Practice in State–Muslim Engagement'. 50, no. 1 (2016): 160–77.

Pantazis, C. and Pemberton, S. 'From the "Old" to the "New" Suspect Community: Examining the Impacts of Recent UK Counter-terrorist Legislation'. *The British Journal of Criminology* 49, no. 5 (2009): 646–66.

Pilkington, H. and Acik, N. 'Not Entitled to Talk: (Mis)recognition, Inequality and Social Activism of Young Muslims'. *Sociology* 54, no. 1 (2020): 181–98.

Ragazzi, F. *Towards 'Policed Multiculturalism'? Counter-radicalisation in France, the Netherlands and the United Kingdom*. Paris: Sciences Po, 2014.

Rittel, H. W. J. and Webber, M. M. 'Dilemmas in a General Theory of Planning'. *Policy Sciences* 4 (1973): 155–69.

Roy, O. *Jihad and Death: The Global Appeal of Islamic State*. Translated by C. Schoch. Hurst, 2017.

Sageman, M. *Misunderstanding Terrorism*. Philadelphia, PA: University of Pennsylvania Press, 2017.

Silverman, T. 'U.K. Foreign Fighters to Syria and Iraq: The Need for a Real Community Engagement Approach'. *Studies in Conflict & Terrorism* 40, no. 12 (2017): 1091–107.

Sliwinski, K. F. 'Counter-terrorism – A Comprehensive Approach. Social Mobilisation and "Civilianisation" of Security: The Case of the United Kingdom'. *European Security* 22, no. 3 (2013): 288–306.

Spalek, B. '"New Terrorism" and Crime Prevention Initiatives Involving Muslim Young People in the UK: Research and Policy Contexts'. *Religion, State and Society* 39, nos. 2–3 (2011): 191–207.

Spalek, B. *Terror Crime Prevention with Communities*. London, UK: Bloomsbury Academic, 2013. Available at: http://site.ebrary.com/id/10735357

Spalek, B. and McDonald, L. Z. 'Terror Crime Prevention: Constructing Muslim Practices and Beliefs as "Anti-social" and "Extreme" through CONTEST 2'. *Social Policy & Society* 9, no. 1 (2010): 123–32.

Thomas, P. 'Between Two Stools? The Government's "Preventing Violent Extremism" Agenda'. *The Political Quarterly* 80, no. 2 (2009): 282–91.

Thomas, P. *Responding to the Threat of Violent Extremism: Failing to Prevent/Paul Thomas.* London: Bloomsbury Academic, 2012.

Thomas, P. 'Youth, Terrorism and Education: Britain's Prevent Programme'. *International Journal of Lifelong Education* 35, no. 2 (2016): 171–87.

Thomas, P. 'Changing Experiences of Responsibilisation and Contestation within Counter-terrorism Policies: The British Prevent Experience'. *Policy & Politics* 45, no. 3 (2017): 305–21.

Thomas, P. 'The Perception of Counter-radicalisation by Young People'. In *'De-radicalisation' Scientific Insights for Policy*, L. Colaert, ed., 119–35. Brussels: Flemish Peace Institute, 2017.

Thomas, P. 'The Challenges for British Youth Workers of Government Strategies to "Prevent Terrorism"'. In *The SAGE Handbook of Youth Work Practice*, Alldred et al., eds. London: SAGE Publications, 2018. Available at: https://sk.sagepub.com/reference/the-sage-handbook-of-youth-work-practice

Thomas, P., Grossman, M., Christmann, K. and Miah, S. 'Community Reporting on Violent Extremism by "intimates": Emergent Findings from International Evidence', *Critical Studies on Terrorism* (2020): 1–22.

UN Human Rights Council. 'Human Rights Impact of Policies and Practices Aimed at Preventing and Countering Violent Extremism'. 20 February 2020, A/HRC/49/45. Available at: https://digitallibrary.un.org/record/3872336?ln=en

Part Five

Interventions in and out of official strategy: The community

10

Butig: Where money talks and ideology balks – A case study

Justin Richmond and Reed Mikkelsen

Diversionary development

Diversion is one of the four pillars of Countering Violent Extremism (CVE) along with prevention, mitigation and resilience. The US Department of Homeland Security, the United Kingdom's Home Office, Australia's Department of Home Affairs and even the United Nations all have guidance for diversionary programmes employed by domestic law enforcement, to address radicalization, especially among Muslim youth. Drug abuse, gangs, family violence, sectarian violence and religious extremism all exist in communities that lack resilience. Resilience programmes focus on building capacity among individuals, groups, organizations and local communities to prevent recruitment to, or engagement in, extremist violence, and to restore social cohesion and public trust in government, following extremist attacks.[1] Effective diversion is a community-focused grassroots effort that attempts to off-ramp vulnerable population segments away from violence and crime.[2] Diversionary programmes, when executed correctly, are less costly and harmful than incarceration or military action. If executed properly, diversion creates net economic and community gains that benefit vulnerable communities.

Diversionary programmes are often studied within the context of domestic law enforcement operations: off-ramping youth from criminality, gang participation, de-radicalizing immigrant communities or countering online extremism. Despite the West's twenty-year Global War on Terror and counterinsurgency (COIN) efforts, there appears to be a dearth of study on Diversionary Programming implementation practised by international non-governmental organizations, militaries or governments. This is in part because effective diversionary programming usually cannot come from outside the community in which it is being implemented. Outside experts or occupying forces lack the correct cultural and language skills required to build trust in vulnerable communities, especially among those most vulnerable to radicalization. Indeed, the mere presence of foreign soldiers or NGOs may cause a tipping point that leads radicals to pursue violence.

Effective CVE should divert at-risk populations, meaning that programme beneficiaries are recruited from the exact demographic pool from which Violent Extremist Organizations (VEOs) recruit. How can donor nations assist partners in Diversionary Development when at-risk communities are likely to be the most remote and dangerous for outsiders? Can aid organizations reach the truly at-risk and still ensure the security of their staff? US-based public charity Impl. Project (implproject.org) developed a methodology for doing so by minimizing expatriate involvement, involving local stakeholders and venturing far from mainstream development operations locations or urban centres, to work in areas nominally controlled by VEOs. Crucially, Impl. Project addresses core grievances of vulnerable populations using local solutions.

Impl. Project is a 501(c)3 international non-governmental organization which focuses on building resilience among vulnerable communities through precise and holistic data mapping, focus group research, key informant interviews and project design based on these microdata inputs. Impl. Project receives funding from the United States Agency for International Development, the US State Department, the US military, private corporations and private donors. Impl. Project has worked in Libya, Cameroon, Azerbaijan, Niger, Nigeria and Chicago, Illinois, but most of our effort in CVE programming is in the southern Philippines. The Global Center on Cooperative Security, a security-focused think tank, evaluated CVE programmes and found that most Western government CVE implementers over-emphasized programme development and implementation and under-emphasized evaluation or results.[3] Impl. Project's data-driven methodology corrects this by placing a high level of effort on assessment and continuous evaluation before, during and after projects with local staff embedded in the community. Since 2015, Impl. Project has repeated this methodological cycle in the southern Philippines, improving each time. Iterative learning enabled our most successful programme to date, a Diversionary Development Programme conducted throughout 2020 in Butig, Mindanao, the heart of the recruiting pool, a safe haven and the staging ground of various militant elements, including the Maute Group, an Islamic State affiliate.

Background

The Maranao are an indigenous, Muslim people that live around Lake Lanao in the provinces of Lanao Del Sur and Lanao Del Norte on the island of Mindanao in the Philippines. Butig Municipality stretches from the southeast corner of Lake Lanao to Mount Makaturing. In this sparsely populated area live 20,000 people divided into sixteen barangays (roughly equivalent to a ward, district or neighbourhood). Butig is the traditional home of the Romato clan which, when joined by marriage to the neighbouring Maute clan, formed a formidable alliance. Brothers Omar and Abdullah Maute, along with a network of Maute and Ramato supporters, recruited, trained and fundraised to build the Philippine branch of the Islamic State movement.[4] The Maute brothers partnered with Abu Sayyaf leader Isnilon Hapilon and pledged allegiance to the Islamic State in 2017.[5] While the details of ISIS's relationship with its Philippine franchise are the subject of debate, the people of Mindanao widely believe that Hapilon and the Mautes represented ISIS and intended to establish a caliphate in Mindanao. When speaking with Impl. Project staff, residents referred to the group as 'Dawlah', meaning 'the State'. While Hapilon's pedigree as an insurgent is well-documented, his placement as emir caused significant strife amongst the Maranao people of the region. Hapilon's band, predominantly Yakan and Tausug fighters, and some foreign fighters of mostly Indonesian and Malaysian descent, originated from the Sulu Archipelago.

On 23 May 2017, the Armed Forces of the Philippines (AFP) launched a pre-emptive kill/capture mission on Hapilon, Omar and Abdullah Maute, and the other members of core Islamic State- Philippines (ISP) leadership in Marawi. This mission failed and led to a five-month siege in the city that decimated one-third of Marawi's infrastructure. The siege ended in October 2017 with hundreds of thousands of people without homes or jobs. More than three years later, the main battle area is littered with abandoned and condemned structures, with scant reconstruction progress taking place.[6]

Estimates of the number of ISIS fighters in Marawi range from a low of 300 to a high of 1,200. The real answer will never be known, but it likely sits in the 600–800 fighter range, including all part-time fighters, helpers and battlefield recruits that joined the movement once the fighting began.[7] Disturbingly, the AFP reported that most fighters were young boys between the ages of fourteen and nineteen years old.[8] While ISP leadership was small, it enjoyed outsized support among out-of-school youth (OSY) in remote corners of Lanao Del Sur, where Maute and Ramato family ties created an additional influx of boys who were promised free Islamic education but instead became unwitting jihadists.[9] These are the boys of the Marawi Siege, lured into dying for a cause they hardly understood or benefitted from. To prevent this from happening again, future diversionary programming must be designed to address the motivations and grievances of this demographic group.

Historically, Butig municipality was ignored and marginalized within the larger court of royal Maranao clans identified within each municipality and by the Philippine government. The Mautes and Romatos had blood feuds with clans that held political leadership roles within the province and region, depriving Butig of the support and development that other municipalities enjoyed. This political discrimination exacerbated feelings of resentment, creating the environment into which the scions of the Maute and Romato clans injected Salafist ideology, to upend the status quo. The Maute brothers educated recruits in Salafist Islam and trained them in military tactics in Butig from 2013 to 2015.[10] As demonstrated by the Marawi Siege, some elements of the extremist movement were effective enough to hold out against the AFP for five months, despite aerial bombardment and commando raids.

Julie Chernov-Hwang conducted interviews with twenty-five former ISP fighters and found that at the time of their recruitment, twelve were farmers, five were students, four ran small businesses, and the rest were teachers, unemployed addicts or criminals. Most recruits failed to attend school beyond the elementary level, with only six attending high school and three attending college. Fifteen of Hwang's subjects were recruited by a trusted relative or friend and they joined primarily for the promised salary equivalent to $400–$900. Only for the more educated did ideology play a part in their radicalization. The Maute brothers drew new recruits from Butig, Piagapo and Marawi, and members of the Maranao, Tausug and Maguindanao people.[11] This is the same population that long provided manpower for the Moro Islamic Liberation Front (MILF). The MILF grew out of the Moro National Liberation Front (MNLF) after the MNLF accepted a peace agreement with the central government in 1987. The MILF continued to fight for autonomy until it too accepted government reconciliation, which led to the creation of an autonomous region. Radical elements within the MILF again split off to produce the Maute Group and ISP.

Impl. Project's field research after the Marawi Siege confirms that radicalization among poor, rural youth occurred mostly among those that were non-religious. Youth from poor families cannot afford to send their sons to moderate madrassahs and lack the religious education to refute the radical ideology provided by Maute matriarch Farhana Romato Maute. 'Lack of faith' was a common reason given in focus groups for high levels of radicalization among poor, rural youth, the single largest contingent of foot soldiers for militant groups in the southern Philippines. When the Maute brothers selected Butig as their base of operations, it was not by chance that they were successful; rather, they exploited vulnerabilities of which they were aware and which their clans could effectively leverage for the benefit of the ISP movement. Extreme poverty and lack of education are enduring problems in Butig but the years since the Marawi Siege have only exacerbated Maranao youths' already desperate circumstances. It would not be difficult for another VEO to enter the scene and recruit youth by leveraging the same grievances and vulnerabilities on which the Mautes capitalized.

Abubakar 2015

If Impl. Project entered Lanao Del Sur for the first time in 2020 to conduct programming, we would have quickly failed without any type of social capital. Instead, we began to build trust with local communities beginning in 2015 in the tiny village of Abubakar, located 7 kilometres south of Butig. As we collected data, we were surprised by a peculiar dynamic: girls were attending middle and high school at twice the rate of boys. OSY boys committed cattle and horse theft, causing clan violence. Lack of livelihoods was overwhelmingly the primary grievance of the population. Our field team, during its vetting and validation phase, found that schooling, livelihoods and crime were deeply interconnected. Farmers had to quickly get their crops to market or their harvests would rot from heavy rains, due to a lack of agricultural preparation or storage infrastructure. Because of this rush to market, buyers could lowball farmers when negotiating crop sale prices. Failing farmers pulled their sons from school, hoping that extra hands would increase harvest volume and profits. The out-of-school youth, depressed about their bleak futures without proper education, would smoke methamphetamines at night, and steal horses and cattle from neighbouring villages to feed their drug habits and thereby instigate blood feuds between clans.

Impl. Project entered the village hoping to address violent extremism and its related issues. What we found instead was a problem of economic infrastructure. Our emphasis on data from day one saved us from misdiagnosing the problem and mistreating it. To address these multiple, interrelated issues, Impl. Project helped Abubakar stand up a livelihoods cooperative. Together with the co-op we designed a project to prevent farmers from pulling their sons out of school: a large concrete solar dryer to minimize crop rot. It cost only US$6,200. The outcomes were profound: 40 per cent of cooperative members used the solar dryer, resulting in five tons of corn sold for profit that would have otherwise rotted. At last measure in 2018, this infusion of capital via higher profits drove a 278 per cent increase in micro-enterprise, largely in the form of crop diversification to cacao. More importantly, since the founding of the Abubakar Siddique cooperative, not a single farmer within the cooperative pulled their sons out of school for financial reasons, leading to a 68 per cent increase in boys attending high school since Impl. Project began its programming. Cattle and horse rustling become a rare occurrence in this community due to the improved economic circumstances and gainfully employed youth.

The real test for Abubakar came in December 2016, when an AFP offensive pushed part of the Maute Group out of a neighbouring municipality. Militants sought safe haven in the vicinity of Abubakar, but the community turned them away, saying that they wanted no part of Maute's violence or ideology. When the Mautes appeared anyway, community leaders reported the incursion to the local MILF commander, whose men assaulted the Maute Group's position and drove them back into Butig. Abubakar was thriving and the presence of this group would have undermined the progress they were making. Impl. Project's main takeaway from this interaction is that VEO recruitment can be prevented without over-policing, deprogramming or direct-action operations. This is a success story of community resilience, in which Impl. Project interventions allowed the community to divert their youth away from VEOs by decreasing the conditions that foster vulnerability to radicalization. Impl. Project's more focused Diversionary Development would come two years later.

Pre- and post-Marawi siege data mapping 2017

Beginning in January 2017, Impl. Project gathered qualitative and quantitative data around Lake Lanao. The population could tell that ISP was a growing problem that was quickly reaching a tipping point. In April 2017, the AFP assaulted a large ISP training camp in Piagapo, where a disproportionate number of the fighters were males under eighteen years old.[12] When our staff interviewed AFP after the assault, officials expressed shock at the high levels of youth involvement. The AFP was not fighting hardened Salafist insurgents at all: ISP appeared to be comprised largely of OSY, with virtually no education in radical ideologies.[13]

This event was quickly followed by the Marawi Siege. AFP operations neutralized ISP leadership when Ipsilon Hapilon, Abdullah and Omar Maute were killed. The Duterte administration used strong kinetic counter-terrorism strategies, but not in prevention and de-radicalization. The seizure of the city was not surprising to Lake Lanao communities. There was a common refrain from citizens regarding the Marawi Siege and its effects. A Poctan community leader told Impl. Project staff, 'If only the government listened to our needs and desperation, I don't think the Marawi Siege would have happened.'[14] After the AFP retook Marawi City, Impl. Project conducted another data mapping of internally displaced persons (IDPs). Unsurprisingly, the conditions of vulnerability among OSY were even more pronounced because of the damage to communities and the loss of their meagre livelihoods. The destruction of ISP leadership did nothing to address OSY grievances and drivers of radicalization. Conditions were ripe for a charismatic leader to rise from within the Lanao community and recruit the next group of OSY.

Piagapo Community Construction Cooperative 2018

Many of the youth that fought for ISP in Marawi came from the upland areas of Gakap and Mama'an in Piagapo municipality, located 15 kilometres west of Marawi and geographically distant from Butig. Maute clan members married into some of the stronger clans in Piagapo, forming a traditional family alliance that created a pipeline of OSY to Butig for training and education.[15] Since most OSY fill labour or agricultural jobs their entire lives, ISP offered youth a path to wealth and respect that they are otherwise denied because of their desperate economic circumstances. ISP exploited this vulnerability effectively, paying recruits US$600 as a signing bonus.[16] That is more money than most of the boys' fathers earn in a year. The value proposition is obvious.

When surveyed about the biggest problem facing their community, the general Piagapo population and OSY identified the lack of livelihoods as their primary grievance. This response comprised nearly 50 per cent of all answers by youth. The obvious follow-on question to such a significant and agreed-upon problem would be: how should groups resolve this issue? Most answers focused on providing livelihoods, training, capital and other resources.[17] Our Theory of Change for this project was that if the boys could learn viable construction tradecraft and civic values through the teambuilding mechanism of the cooperative, then they could carry that socially positive mindset to their respective communities, showing a viable alternative to monetary ISP recruiting efforts.[18] In partnership with Piagapo Mayor Ali Sumandar, Impl. Project designed and implemented a construction cooperative pilot to train and place the OSYs in construction jobs to prevent them from radicalizing for economic or power-seeking incentives.

During the six-month construction cooperative pilot during the summer of 2018, the barangays of Mama'an and Gakap did not report a single instance of violent conflict or insurgent activity, despite being the site of a large training camp a year prior. By the end of the programme, thirty-two of the forty boys graduated, three secured jobs within the AFP and five dropped out. The municipal government promised to provide projects for the boys to work on for at least a year.[19] The municipality failed to deliver on these job projects despite the government's professed eagerness to rebuild the areas surrounding Marawi. The rebuilding effort should have provided many local labour jobs. Despite this setback, many of the cooperative beneficiaries were hired as apprentices around Lanao del Sur. Impl. Project staff reached out to our Piagapo graduates in January 2020 and found that most were employed on construction projects in their villages.

While the outcome of the project was positive, building enduring resilience requires time, connection and social capital. Unfortunately, the youth in Piagapo did not get the needed time to work together in construction crews on behalf of the Philippine government. This programme allowed Impl. Project to test the model and saw that it is successful. However, it is not sustainable without ongoing efforts from local stakeholders. Efforts at Diversionary Development are easily undone if participants' expectations are set high, and then not met because they cannot find continued purpose and employment.

The Butig opportunity – 2020

In January 2020, Impl. Project received funding to scale its construction cooperative pilot from Piagapo to Butig, the last bastion of support for the ISP movement. Before the Marawi Siege, Impl. Project identified Butig's vulnerability through its data mapping and flagged this vulnerability to the AFP, the Philippine government and US government officials. At that time, none were interested in pursuing immediate strategies to reduce Butig's vulnerability. Because of the danger of working in Butig, international development organizations and the Philippine government would not (and still do not) conduct programming there, further exacerbating the economic desperation, lack of education and perceived isolation of local youth fostering conditions which allow radicalization to grow unchecked.

The initial Impl. Project data mapping effort is entirely focused on framing local issues through the perspective of the community. International development is often fraught with implicit bias and pre-selected programmatic solutions based on what an organization does well, rather than community needs. These obstacles are mitigated by strong, clean and copious data, designed, and gathered in surveys, meant to amplify local voices to the donor community. Impl. Project core staff vet and validate the perception data through local site assessments, focus group discussions and key leader interviews. These efforts place a qualitative layer of data on top of the broad quantitative survey data, giving a richer view of the scope of local dysfunction and vulnerability, which drive susceptibility to radicalization. Diversionary programming entails vulnerability identification and intervention before these issues are effectively leveraged by malign actors.

The first step in identifying which diversionary programme is a good fit is a broad population survey. Impl. Project gathers qualitative and quantitative data to design projects and programmes to build resilience in communities. When we conduct data mapping, the quality and volume of our data often make Impl. Project's datasets the best available on those communities. The Butig baseline sample size is intentionally large for a rural municipality estimated at 15,000 residents. Impl. Project's survey of 1,520 people comprises roughly 10 per cent of the population. This large data scale allows us to maintain confidence in our data even as we begin disaggregating the data into sub-groups. For instance, if we disaggregate to find only responses of male youth aged fifteen to twenty-four, we have a count of 250 responses, which makes their responses more statistically significant and valid.

Table 10.1 Survey purpose and approach.

Purpose of baseline	To understand community resilience dynamics in Butig, Lanao del Sur, with respect to respondents' core community problems, potential solutions and to whom they go to for services and support.
Quantitative survey approach	Face-to-face, geo-tagged interviews with a man/woman on the street approach, with a particular focus on youth and women.
	Confidence level: 99 per cent, with ± 3 per cent margin of error. At least 50 per cent youth (15–24 years old or 25–34 years old age brackets).
	N = 1,520 over 15 days of data collection in January-February 2020 (pre-Covid-19)
Qualitative vetting and validation	Core team conducted eight facilitated focus groups, eleven key leader interviews and eleven site assessments to validate perception data.

The core purpose of the survey is to understand broadly how a community frames its problems, its local solutions to those problems and who the community trusts to solve these problems. We assess these three concepts through open-ended questions, the answers to which are enumerated on each survey via drop-down menus. The data collectors' ability to listen to answers and select an answer choice from an enumerated list is critical in bringing structure to complex, cross-sectoral issues. After each answer is coded, the surveyor follows up with 'Why?' questions, the answers to which are captured in the unstructured notes section of the survey. When we analyse cohort groups by answers (e.g., 'All women who identified a lack of potable water'), we can see the magnitude of the grievance in the structured answers and identify potential cause-effect dynamics in the unstructured notes of the survey subset. This surveying approach is the latest evolution of the District Stability Framework, a USAID logical framework for identifying and mitigating the drivers of instability.

Impl. Project data collectors or 'enumerators' are hired from local communities and trained in our methodology and technological toolkit. Enumerators help to refine our surveys, to specifically answer enumerations and to capture local issues precisely. They speak the local languages and follow local customs and norms naturally, thereby breaking down distrust and promoting honest data collection. Butig, being a rural and heavily clan-influenced area, is not a place to which unvetted or untrusted outsiders can simply show up and start conducting surveys or programming safely. It has long been a bastion of MILF base camps. The MILF organized itself at the grassroots level in Lanao del Sur, naturally integrating with local communities and seeking their support, thereby shielding the group from outsiders. This distrust of outsiders is even more prevalent today, with the stigma that comes from Butig's reputation as the home of the ISP movement.

To mitigate risks, Impl. Project's local staff local Maranao staff socialized our work with formal and informal leaders to gain their support. Involving local MILF at all phases of the process is key to keeping Impl. Project staff safe, as the AFP presence is non-existent in these far-flung barangays, as well as to demonstrating transparency in our purpose. MILF commanders approved of the project and used their influence in the community to facilitate and safeguard our staff. MILF helped secure focus group sites

Figure 10.1 Impl. Project Founder and Executive Director, Justin Richmond, conducts a Key Leader Interview with an elder and a former MILF base commander in Poctan, Barangay in Butig (photo by Impl. Project Staff, January 2020).

and public forums, allowing us increased access to speak to all facets of the Maranao population in Butig. Many outsiders distrust the MILF but for years, the MILF was and largely still is the most credible formal organization in Butig. Since the Bangsamoro Organic Law (BOL) was passed in 2018 and the MILF has been reintegrating into broader society, inclusive surveying and programming further support this source of resilience and credibility in Maranao society.

Close engagement and coordination with the MILF leadership ensured the safety of our staff. In turn, our data practices ensured the safety of Butig's residents. To ensure the safety and privacy of our partner communities, all Impl. Project data is anonymous and no personally identifying information is recorded on survey forms or in focus groups, site assessments or key leader engagements. Impl. Project prefers to conduct 'person on the street' surveys over household surveys since each survey is geotagged. Household surveys with geotags threaten anonymity for the respondents, so the default is often street discussions.

Butig baseline demographics

Once an Impl. Project enumerator gains informed consent from a survey participant, they record demographic data, as all of these factors contribute deeply to one's perspective. A common and justified criticism of data collected by civil society groups is that it lacks the quality and rigour of academic research. Impl. Project addresses these issues in part by gathering robust and relevant demographic information. The ability to drill down into answers by demographic sub-group allows implementers to craft strategies that address the sensitivities among community sub-groups. Once this demographic data is properly categorized, the formal survey questions begin.

Impl. Project strives for fair representation of women, youth and minority voices in its data collection. To avoid the over-representation of male voices, Impl. Project tries as much as possible to maintain at least a 50/50 split on gender inclusion. Butig data mapping differed by prioritizing male youth for this data collection because the programme aimed to address male OSY grievances and to deliver programming in construction skills. Within Maranao culture, only men engage in this sector.

As Impl. Project progressed with data mapping, demand signal from neighbouring barangays of Samer and Coloyan was significant enough to warrant their inclusion in our data mapping efforts. This increased the sample size by another 300 respondents from 1,200 to 1,500. Samer and Coloyan are rarely engaged by outsiders and therefore add tremendous value to our data sample, potential project impact and community insight. These remote, upland communities are also where ISP organized extensive training camps for its fighters prior to the Marawi Siege.

The data collected underscored what previous surveys elsewhere in Lanao del Sur revealed: young men felt deeply vulnerable and insecure regarding the precariousness of their livelihoods. Focus groups with these young men revealed that, far beyond ideological and religious motivations, young men in Butig face few choices and opportunities with which to have reliable, lucrative careers to raise families and to increase their socio-economic status. When ISP offered money, education and work to young men looking for money and purpose, the group leveraged ubiquitous vulnerability gaps within rural Maranao communities. Impl. Project data revealed extremely high levels of desperation among people in these outlying and last-mile communities. Most have not graduated from high school (87 per cent) and most were unemployed at the time of the survey (60 per cent). The data validated the overarching plan and objectives for Impl. Project's Butig Community Construction Cooperative (B3C) project: train vulnerable youth in key skills, organize them into work crews, mentor them in rebuilding and repairing their communities, and make them employable in the construction sector after the conclusion of the B3C project.

Butig Community Construction Cooperative (B3C)

During data mapping, the community expressed frustration with the government and international community regarding the lack of follow-through on development and aid commitments. To address their frustration and desperation, our local Impl. Project lead, Julius Suarez, set up beneficiary identification and registration appointments on the spot. If an interview subject met the beneficiary criteria (male, aged eighteen to thirty) and expressed a desire for vocational training, then enumerators gave him the chance to immediately enrol for training that had a definitive upcoming start date. This way communities could simultaneously observe the data mapping and the

Table 10.2 Selected out-of-school youth (OSYs) by barangay.

Barangay	Selected OSYs
Poctan	15
Ragayan	15
Sandab	46
MILF – Satellite Community	8
Samer	12
Coloyan	18

resulting action by a US non-governmental organization (NGO). Communities could immediately and tangibly connect the data mapping assessment with the forthcoming development project.

When registering students for B3C training, Impl. Project ensured that we registered participants from the same ethnic groups, age, education level and occupations from which ISP recruited. Our funding covered 100 students, but we enrolled 119 so that stand-by students could replace anyone that could not complete training. The educational make-up of our class was seven who attended college, forty-five high school, sixty-one elementary school, and five with no schooling at all. Only thirty-seven recruits were married. We found thirty-eight farmers, four MILF soldiers, two teachers, one retail worker, one quarry labourer and seventy-two with no occupation.

Unfortunately, just as we finished final preparations for training, Covid-19 arrived in the Philippines and Impl. Project suspended operations until August 2020. Manilla instituted travel restrictions under the Modified Enhanced Community Quarantine (MECQ). During the summer MECQ, 10 per cent of our registered OSY moved away from Butig and were replaced. The resulting travel restriction had a severe impact on the economy. Before restarting the project, we deployed enumerators for another round of data collection, as dynamics had shifted. This data collection was smaller in size and geography because of MECG travel restrictions. During analysis Impl. Project corrected for this discrepancy, only comparing barangays that were equally surveyed during both data mapping efforts.

Perception indicators showed that during Covid-19, residents were less confident in local job opportunities and that the money from their current jobs was insufficient to cover their needs. Half of our respondents said that they were worse off economically after Covid-19 began. When asked about the main problem facing their community, livelihoods remained the overwhelming response but Covid-19, lack of food and lack of security all saw increased responses. Lack of food was due to problems with agriculture and commercial logistics caused by movement restrictions. Concerns about security increased after an AFP clearing operation against the resurgent communist elements of the New People Army (NPA) northeast of Butig. The NPA is an enduring anti-government VEO that addresses many of the economic grievances that ISP exploited. Their presence in nearby communities meant that Diversionary Development was still needed. The survey question with the most significant positive change was 'Do you agree with the statement "I can easily access skills training in my barangay."' It is probable that the presence of Impl. Project staff and the promise of upcoming training caused this shift in perceptions. It appeared we had raised expectations at the same time economic conditions worsened. We could not afford to disappoint the community without seriously damaging their relationship with the world outside of Butig.[20]

Impl. Project enumerators also monitor a wide range of contextual indicators so that we can measure ground truth indicators and not simply perception indicators. Indicators include the number of businesses in a barangay, the price of a bag of rice, reports of violence, school attendance and health clinic activity. Because Impl. Project began gathering these indicators in January, we had a pre-Covid-19 baseline established and could measure actual changes in the municipality throughout the pandemic. This allowed us to see how bad the effects were, and when conditions appear to normalize. Covid-19 restrictions also meant that our US staff could no longer travel to the Philippines and the rest of the programme was managed by our very competent local staff.

B3C training

Rural, non-permissive locations are key operating, training and recruiting areas for radicalization in the southern Philippines, so this is where Impl. Project had to work to reach those at risk. Transporting at-risk youth to Marawi for training was not feasible, so we had to go to them. Impl. Project hired four Technical Education and Skills Development Authority (TESDA) trainers from Saguiaran, another municipality within Lanao del Sur. Trainers used the approved TESDA curriculum and training methodology: lecture, demonstration, hands-on practical exercises and certification exams. The 100-day TESDA course covers masonry, electrical wiring, carpentry, tile setting, pipe fitting, plumbing, painting and shield metal arc welding. Our community outreach and MILF support gave the trainers confidence that they would not be harmed while travelling to or working in Butig.

B3C did not involve deradicalization training per se, because political and religious radicalization was never the primary systemic cause of vulnerability within the population. Our theory of change was that poverty and lack of employment drove radicalization, not religious extremism inherent in the community. Even so, we felt that values and religious training should be a component of the programme. ISP recruits with education and jobs were more likely to join for ideological reasons, and we did not want our beneficiaries to follow that path. Every month, an imam from Lanao Del Sur gave participants a sermon in moderate Islam and values. He corrected their misconceptions about Islam, counselled against violence and emphasized the charitable aspects of the religion. Because of the position of authority that the imam holds, these sessions do not have much discussion or debate. Most of the boys have a bare minimum of religious understanding, so this is their only introduction to Islamic scholarship if their family lacks the money to pay for madrassah education. We hope this introduction to Islam by a respected local scholar will help to inoculate the boys from radicalization.

Some of our staff believe that disenfranchisement and alienation from the Philippine government were factors in the community's radicalization, and it was hoped that the creation of the Bangsamoro Autonomous Region of Muslim Mindanao (BARMM), led by respected local MILF commanders, would help alleviate this sentiment. However, OSY did not articulate if the creation of the BARMM changed their attitudes towards the Philippines government or made them feel less marginalized. Issues of their subsistence are more important than political activity.

Evaluation

OSY were given 3 kg of high-quality rice per day of training, to meet the nutritional needs of their family while they were away from the family farm in training. Throughout the programme, participants and one of their siblings or family members were weighed. If their individual BMI stayed the same or increased, then Impl. Project had confidence that they were not selling their rice allowances. Thanks to the rice allowances provided to beneficiaries, the BMI of OSY trainees increased from 22.25 to 23.48 and the BMI of family members increased from 16.76 to 18.69.

All B3C programme participants took our perception survey at the programme's start and end, so that Impl. Project can measure confidence in their job skills, perception of the job market and their confidence in finding alternate means of supporting their families. We compared these results to the same cohort that is not enrolled in the programme (the control group) to measure impacts on our recipients. On the endline survey, 64 per cent of B3C beneficiaries believe they now have adequate skills to find a job, as opposed to 53 per cent of their youth cohort. While this is an improvement, some students are still in need of training assistance. A small number of B3C participants did not feel confident enough to take the TESDA electrical assessment and opted instead for the masonry test. These participants would have preferred to take the Electrical Wiring Installation and Maintenance assessment because of the higher wages associated with it. Even more disappointing, we found that nine OSY beneficiaries were too scared to take any TESDA skill assessments because of their low reading comprehension levels. On average, the highest educational level attainment among the OSY beneficiaries is grade two. In the future, Impl. Project will request funding for Alternative Learning System (ALS) literacy training. In April 2021 graduates took their TESDA assessments – twenty-six tested in masonry, five in carpentry and seventy-two in Electrical Wiring Installation and Maintenance (EIM).

In addition to skills, we also gave OSY heightened expectations. To the question 'How hopeful are you for the future?' 82 per cent answered with 'Hopeful' or 'Very hopeful'. It falls upon Impl. Project and donor organizations to ensure that their expectations are met. Failure to do so could leads to further disillusionment among a population that is already vulnerable. The risk is illustrated in the responses to the question, 'If you cannot find a job with your construction skills, what will you do?', 16 per cent responded 'I don't know' or 'remain unemployed', which was a proxy answer designed to show the propensity of OSY to backslide away from society into crime or extremist

Table 10.3 'If you cannot find a job with your construction skills, what will you do?'.

Responses	Percentage
Find a non-construction job outside of Butig	30
Find a non-construction job in Butig	28
Remain unemployed	10
Farming	9
I don't know what I'll do	7
Find a job with MILF/BARMM	6
Business	3
Student/driver	2 per choice (4 per cent total)
Salesman/quarry/other/Join the security services	1 per choice (3 per cent total)

(Endline-B3C Beneficiaries Responses)

movements. Impl. Project uses some enumerations of the question 'Who do believe can solve your problem' as a proxy for hopelessness and cynicism. If respondents say they believe that 'No one', 'God' or 'Ourselves' can solve their problems, then they have lost hope in institutions. Proxy answers for hopelessness among the general population decreased from 13 per cent to 7 per cent. Among B3C trainees, only 4 per cent gave one of those answers.

Sustainability

These short-term impacts have a shelf-life, however. Without follow-on work and employment, OSY risk further marginalization from larger Filipino society, as evidenced by some responses in the endline survey. When asked to identify the biggest obstacle to finding employment, 45 per cent identified the lack of jobs in Butig. When asked to identify the biggest problem facing their community, 57 per cent answered 'lack of livelihoods'. Some of our graduates had college degrees, including one with two years of computer training, but Butig lacks the jobs to accommodate them. The skills that the participants acquired in B3C are inadequate in addressing vulnerabilities and resilience in Butig without jobs to accompany them.

Although they now have construction skills and certifications are forthcoming, the OSY understand that construction jobs are not readily available in Butig. Agricultural jobs are plentiful and are required to provide subsistence for the community. OSY informed Impl. Project team members of numerous required infrastructure improvements within Butig on which the B3C graduates can work. They requested assistance to improve irrigation infrastructure, seeds, fertilizer, agricultural equipment and specifically pest control, which was identified as a primary problem. Critical community needs also include improved irrigation and flood control mechanisms, which fall directly into the B3C graduate skillset. The B3C graduates are eager and

Table 10.4 'What is the biggest obstacle to finding employment after you finish this training?'.

Responses	Percentage
No jobs are hiring	31
There are no jobs in Butig	18
I will have trouble finding work	14
No vehicle/transportation to get to work	13
I don't know how to find a job	10
Covid movement restrictions	6
My family does not want me to leave	3
I don't know how to apply for a job	3
I cannot take the certification test	3

(Endline-B3C Beneficiaries Responses)

Table 10.5 'There are sufficient job opportunities in my community.'

Responses	Percentage
Strongly agree	17
Agree	22
Don't know	1
Disagree	18
Strongly disagree	43

(Endline-B3C Beneficiaries Responses)

motivated to work and although many obstacles stand in their way, very few stated that they would give up the search for work after completing the programme. Even now in Butig, most construction workers are from Iligan and Marawi. Once our graduates have a National Certification (NC1 and NC2) from TESDA, they can be hired to work in their own villages. Impl. Project is in discussions with international donors regarding funding for our OSY cooperative in Butig to repair basic infrastructure in their barangays, namely schools, canals, latrines and agriculture storage houses.

The Mautes exploited economic desperation, ineffective governance and ethnic marginalization. On a surface level, it may appear that Impl. Project is only addressing economic issues but throughout the project, Impl. Project connected community leaders to higher levels of government and we showed the Maranao of Butig that their people are not forgotten. In the background of the Butig project was the newly established BARMM. The OSY involved in the B3C are not politically engaged and did not appear to be affected by their new political status. They live subsistence lifestyles and want to provide for and feed their families. The BARMM is expected to generate more development projects that should help keep the boys employed. More importantly, the creation of the BARMM should undercut the grievances that MILF and NPA used to rally fighters. A third of the BARMM parliament is Maranao, so the group will finally have the political representation it deserves. Because this political grievance has decreased, positive conditions for the rise of the next 'Mautes' may decrease as well.

Until this point, Impl. Project did not have a formal procedure for a longitudinal study of programme recipients. Our programmes were small and infrequent. With this large group of recipients in Butig, we will institute a longitudinal monitoring programme to ensure that the Diversion Programme achieved its intended impact. We will compare our beneficiaries with their peers in rates of employment, responses to perception surveys and rates of incarceration.

Not only did the OSYs gain valuable construction skills, but Impl. Project's Filipino staff also did. To meet donor compliance, our staff had to professionalize and become familiar with international and US government accounting compliance protocols. We gave them classes in registration and regulations, administrative tasks, accounting, record keeping, banking requirements and using Google Drive systems. They became more capable and able to represent the organization to international donors. Because of our success working in the heart of the ISP movement, the Philippine government and military reached out to our Philippine Team Lead to conduct similar interventions in VEO hotspots throughout Mindanao. Impl. Project Philippines will have the longevity to continually assess Butig and the B3C graduates. Impl. Project grows by co-opting capable local staff and we will be able to identify future full-time employees from the Butig project that will allow us to maintain a footprint there. Local enumerators will continue to gather contextual indicators to see if our project has lasting positive effects. That is how Impl. Project monitors its effects on diversionary development in these communities.

Notes

1 RTI International, *Countering Violent Extremism (CVE) – Developing a Research Roadmap Final Report* (2017), prepared for Science and Technology Directorate, US Department of Homeland Security, at https://www.dhs.gov/sites/default/files/publications/861_OPSR_TP_CVE-Developing-Research-Roadmap_Oct2017.pdf
2 Ibid.
3 See Peter Romaniuk, 'Does CVE Work? Lessons Learned from the Global Effort to Counter Violent Extremism', Global Center on Cooperative Security (2015). https://www.globalcenter.org/wp-content/uploads/2015/09/Does-CVE-Work_2015.pdf.
4 See Raju Gopalakrishnanand Manuel Mogato, 'The Mautes of the Philippines: From Monied Family to Islamic State', *Reuters*, 23 June 2017, available at: https://www.reuters.com/article/us-philippines-militants-matriarch/the-mautes-of-the-philippines-from-monied-family-to-islamic-state-idUSKBN19E0A9
5 Maria Ressa, 'ISIS to Declare a Province in Mindanao?', *Rappler*, 10 January 2016, available at: www.rappler.com/nation/isis-declare-province-mindanao
6 Justin Richmond, *Butig Data Mapping, Focus Groups and Key Leader Engagements*, 2020.
7 Justin Richmond, *Marawi IDP Camp Data Mapping, Focus Groups and Key Leader Engagements*, 2017.

8   Richmond, *Marawi IDP Camp Data Mapping, Focus Groups and Key Leader Engagements*.
9   See Julie Chernov Hwang, 'Relatives, Redemption, and Rice: Motivations for Joining the Maute Group', *CTC Sentinel* 12, no. 8 (September 2019).
10   Hwang, 'Relatives, Redemption, and Rice'.
11   Ibid.
12   Richmond, *Marawi IDP Camp Data Mapping, Focus Groups and Key Leader Engagements*.
13   Ibid.
14   Ibid.
15   Justin Richmond, *Piagapo Data Mapping, Focus Groups and Key Leader Engagements*, 2018.
16   Richmond, *Marawi IDP Camp Data Mapping, Focus Groups and Key Leader Engagements*.
17   Ibid.
18   Ibid.
19   Richmond, *Piagapo Data Mapping, Focus Groups and Key Leader Engagements*.
20   Richmond, *Butig Data Mapping, Focus Groups and Key Leader Engagements*.

Bibliography

Gopalakrishnan, Raju and Mogato, Manuel. 'The Mautes of the Philippines: From Monied Family to Islamic State'. *Reuters*, 23 June 2017. Available at: https://www.reuters.com/article/us-philippines-militants-matriarch/the-mautes-of-the-philippines-from-monied-family-to-islamic-state-idUSKBN19E0A9

Hwang, Julie Chernov. 'Relatives, Redemption, and Rice: Motivations for Joining the Maute Group'. *CTC Sentinel* 12, no. 8 (September 2019). Available at Relatives, Redemption, and Rice: Motivations for Joining the Maute Group – Combating Terrorism Center at West Point.

Romaniuk, Peter. 'Does CVE Work? Lessons Learned from the Global Effort to Counter Violent Extremism'. Global Center on Cooperative Security (2015). Available at: https://www.globalcenter.org/wp-content/uploads/2015/09/Does-CVE-Work_2015.pdf

Ressa, Maria. 'ISIS to Declare a Province in Mindanao?', *Rappler*, 10 January 2016. Available at: www.rappler.com/nation/isis-declare-province-mindanao

Richmond, Justin. *Abubakar Data Mapping, Focus Groups and Key Leader Engagements*. 2015.

Richmond, Justin. *Marawi IDP Camp Data Mapping, Focus Groups and Key Leader Engagements*. 2017.

Richmond, Justin. *Piagapo Data Mapping, Focus Groups and Key Leader Engagements*. 2018.

Richmond, Justin. *Butig Data Mapping, Focus Groups and Key Leader Engagements*. 2020.

RTI International. *Countering Violent Extremism (CVE) – Developing a Research Roadmap Final Report* (2017), prepared for Science and Technology Directorate, US Department of Homeland Security. Available at: https://www.dhs.gov/sites/default/files/publications/861_OPSR_TP_CVE-Developing-Research-Roadmap_Oct2017.pdf

U.S. Department of State. *2019 Country Reports on Terrorism: Philippines*. Bureau of Counterterrorism. Available at: https://www.state.gov/reports/country-reports-on-terrorism-2019/philippines/

11

Bringing them home: Building a trusted support framework for the safe return of women and children associated with foreign fighters

Clarke Jones, Kamalle Dabboussy and Alasdair Roy

Introduction

At the time of writing, there were at least sixty-three Australian women and children stranded in dangerous conditions in the al-Hawl and al-Roj camps in Northeast Syria. In these camps, everyday survival is a struggle due to violence, poor sanitation, sickness and limited healthcare.[1] Of the sixty-three, there are forty-three children and twenty women, with thirty-four children under the age of seven.[2]

As time progresses and as more information becomes available, these numbers are likely to change. For instance, one seventeen-year-old boy was earlier moved to an adult prison. In the al-Roj camp, where most of the Australians are now held, there are approximately 3,500 people living in overcrowded conditions. While al-Roj is highly securitized and therefore more protected from external and internal hostilities than the al-Hawl camp, the camp's security is slowly destabilizing as more women are transferred in from other camps. What is more, conditions in the al-Roj camp are also dire, with the women and children living in tents exposed to the elements. The net result is that the health of several women and the large number of vulnerable children is deteriorating, meaning that urgent action should be taken by the Australian government to get them home to safety.

There have been many obstacles preventing their repatriation. This included restrictions around international travel due to Covid-19, which created impediments to their safe rescue and return. The International Committee of the Red Cross raised concerns that the camps are some of the most dangerous places in the world for Covid-19 due to their extremely high population density. While the true extent of virus infections in the camps was difficult to gauge due to lack of testing, as of 1 June 2021 there were positive cases in the areas where the camps are located. Even before the pandemic, both al-Hawl and al-Roj camps were already at breaking point, with al-Hawl built for 15,000–20,000 people but housing more than 70,000.

Despite the pandemic, at least nine other countries have so far repatriated women and children detained in Iraq, Libya and north-east Syria. In 2020, Norway, France, Russia and Kazakhstan repatriated their citizens with the help of the United States. The United States government recognizes the importance of getting the children, the parents and even the foreign fighters out of Syria and back home to their countries of origin. Late in 2019, the United States also offered to rescue the Australians[3]; however, as of May 2022, the Australian government had resisted efforts to bring them home. The United States's offer still stands.

There are several reasons why the Australian government resisted the repatriation of the women and children. They argued that 'the Covid-19 pandemic not only made it too dangerous to repatriate them due to the international travel situation' and that there was a lack of 'domestic resources' required to deal with 'radicalised people'.[4] Further, they argued that they did not have the resources 'needed to reintegrate, to monitor, to secure, and to de-radicalise people who are brought home'.[5] In making these statements, the common assumptions are around the perceived risk that some of the women and children could be 'radicalized', that they could radicalize others into committing violent acts, or commit violent acts themselves on their return. Others have said, 'The longer the children stay, and the older they get, the more likely they themselves may be to grow up into a new Islamic State generation.'[6] Therefore, we acknowledge they may pose serious risks and concerns. It is inappropriate, however, to make these assumptions without proper evidence-based assessments of the women and children, which are usually made by qualified mental health practitioners.

There are many risks in leaving them stranded in the camps. Our primary concern is around their safety and welfare. The children trapped in these camps 'are already suffering malnutrition, pneumonia, shrapnel wounds and other treatable medical conditions'. The NGO, Save the Children, which continues to work closely with the families, says that the 'conditions are deteriorating by the day'.[7] It is important to acknowledge that the women and children will face their own risks and challenges on their return. For example, in our efforts to divert them from the criminal justice system and reintegrate them safely and successfully, they are likely to encounter difficulties around stigma, marginalization and isolation from other Australians and within their own communities. The authors know that some communities do not want them back home again, despite the moral and legal obligations we have to look after our own Australian citizens.

The authors recognize the several concerns of governments and communities; however, our understanding of the women and children is more nuanced. The first author (Jones) has been conducting primary research with hard-to-reach[8] Muslim communities for several years. Stemming from this research, he was introduced through a community contact to the second author (Dabboussy) who advocates for the families of those who have daughters, grandchildren and other relatives stranded in the camps. The third author, Roy, is a clinical psychologist with over thirty years' experience promoting and protecting the rights of children and has contributed significantly to the modelling of the proposed support structure for the returnees. With the added input of lawyers and family members, the authors co-designed Changing Tides. Changing Tides is a community-led support framework that consists of a range of preventative interventions and other supportive mechanisms designed to assist the safe reunification and ongoing welfare of Australian women and children returning home from Syria. It recognizes the right of families as the fundamental group in society to be leading decision making, safety planning, and solutions to care for and support the women and children.

Through personal engagement with family members, we know that many, if not all, of the women were trafficked or coerced into travelling, and some left Australia as children but eventually married and had children of their own in Syria. The children certainly had no choice because they were either following their parents or were born in-country. Knowing these circumstances and having a more intimate understanding of the women and children, we argue that the risks can be mitigated through a carefully crafted support and diversionary framework that has now been developed specifically for them. We use the term 'framework' rather than programme to emphasize that our model consists of a range of supportive options rather than a one-size-fits-all 'programme' where participants must meet a number of set requirements to successfully complete it. We recognize that each woman and child will have different needs based on assessments they will undergo once home and therefore will require individualized types of support programmes, which sit within our framework. We also recognize that some of the women may face prosecution if proven in the courts to have committed offences and that some may be required to undergo control orders issued by the courts. Therefore, we anticipate that some will require more intensive support while others may require minimal intervention apart from close family support. Also included in the support mechanisms within the framework is the ability to work closely with existing government and police-led deradicalization or intervention programmes. Overall, we know that between the government and relevant communities there exists a wealth of capabilities and expertise to help safely manage their return.

So what does our support and diversionary framework look like and can this assure community safety?

Changing Tides is unique and according to our own research and engagement with similar family groups overseas, such a concept for returning women and children has not been developed in other countries to date. We have, however, shared our model with other families in similar situations in Belgium, Morocco and the United States to assist them to develop their own support structures. In Australia, the framework has yet to commence but will begin when the women and children start to be repatriated; however, this remains subject to all parties' active agreement, including the State and Federal Governments. The foundations of the framework were developed with several Muslim communities to capture cultural and religious sensitivities and the consequent needs of those communities. The model has since been re-designed in close cooperation with the immediate families of the women and children in the camps to ensure that it meets their specific needs, has their support and cooperation, and, most importantly, has their trust.

Our research shows that families who are strong in their culture and religion and who are connected to their communities will be more successful in raising resilient children who are proud of who they are. Bonding capital, through culture and religion, is a strength and not a risk in this framework. It also recognizes the importance of trauma-informed practices, which are also strength-based frameworks grounded on an understanding of, and responsiveness to, the impact of trauma. These practices emphasize physical, psychological and emotional safety for the families, and create opportunities for them to rebuild a sense of control and empowerment once home again.[9]

The key areas of support in our framework will include: pre-departure preparation, which would ideally occur before the return to Australia to help them cope with physical and emotional adjustments and the processes of what to expect with family reunification; the facilitation of appropriate accommodation for all of the women and children (including kinship care arrangements where necessary); child protection considerations; legal support; religious support and guidance; the provision of initial psychological first aid; health/mental health support; and the delivery of specific intervention services if and when required. Overall, the goals of Changing Tides are not just to support the women and children but are also to strengthen the health and welfare capacities in the receiving families and their associated communities, as well as improving social cohesion with broader Australian communities.[10]

Part of the impetus for the development of this different family- and community-centric support framework stemmed from consultation with several Muslim communities. They felt that existing government and police-led programmes for young Muslims were too narrowly focused, stigmatizing and primarily developed to counter violent extremism (CVE). As a result, the services were not achieving the desired responsivity or results for families and their children and, instead, were potentially aggravating the underlying issues driving risky behaviour. As an alternative, Changing Tides provides family and community ownership, with the focus on support, guidance and positive choices as part of a strength-based service delivery framework. However, the model also works to complement and cooperate with existing external services if required.

At its core, the framework recognizes the right of families as the fundamental group in society to be leading decision making around the planning for the safety and protection of the women and children and as co-contributors in the development of solutions for their care and ongoing support. As such, the framework is designed to address a range of complex issues with a range of multifaceted responses. What is more, it is adaptive and scalable to address a range of potential problems with culturally and religiously sensitive preventative solutions, as well as the provision of support to prison-based programmes, should anyone enter the criminal justice system. In this sense, also imbedded in Changing Tides is the need for accountability. We recognize that some situations may require close cooperation and support from law enforcement agencies and other government services.

Background

Changing Tides was conceptualized from four years of ethnographic research with Muslim community groups in Melbourne and Sydney, Australia. For confidentiality reasons, we do not name these organizations in this chapter. In this research, the first author found the need for alternative approaches to CVE. For those Muslim young people most at risk of committing anti-social or violent behaviour, a broader focus of crime prevention is more likely to generate active participation by families and communities than those programmes geared specifically at CVE. All too often, policies and solutions set up around CVE ignore much of the evidence about 'what works' and 'what works for whom'. It also clings to approaches where evidence tell us not to do and functions as if evidence is settled in areas, such as radicalization, where this is not the case.[11]

To reach these conclusions, the first author found that it was common for members of communities to express concerns about engaging in, or being directly associated with, CVE programmes. Often, they did not trust the intent of the programmes and perceived them to be mechanisms for state surveillance, intelligence collection and profiling. They were aware that government agencies funding or running CVE programmes dressed them as community outreach, community resilience or social cohesion initiatives, but were convinced that the programmes were largely dedicated to stopping Muslims from becoming violent extremists. While they all agreed that preventing violent extremism was an important objective, they felt that programmes were counterproductive because they lacked transparency, always conflated Muslims with terrorism, and therefore they viewed them as 'discriminatory and divisive'. This is largely due to the regular targeting of vulnerable young Muslims,[12] which can potentially worsen underlying issues like stigmatization, marginalization and discrimination that often lead to offending in the first instance. Overall, the research found that there was a significant lack of trust in the intent of government or police-backed programmes, which created significant obstacles for voluntary participation and was likely to impact heavily on the efficacy of such CVE programmes.

This initial research used a three-phase longitudinal strategy, which included trust and relationship building, participant observation and a community-based participatory design (or commonly referred to as a community-based participatory approach, CBPA).[13] The key to this strategy was trust, which resulted from successful long-term community engagement and relationship building. Through established trust, the author was able to develop a more nuanced understanding of the key challenges facing Muslim families and their communities. From this quasi-insider's perspective, and together with family and community members, a more tailored support programme was then developed to support them. An 'insider' researcher is usually defined as a member of the community under study, whereas an outsider researcher is generally a member of the majority in the group under study.[14] This differs from other interventions where the programme is developed by 'outsiders' with little or no consultation and then implemented, hoping that participants will take part openly and genuinely.

The first author also examined other programmes that had success in eliciting attitude and behaviour change across a range of risky behaviours (such as substance use and domestic violence). For example, research on youth interventions describes several critical elements in individual and social contexts important in positive young people's development. Families, schools, communities and increasingly religion have identified key elements and processes within these dimensions that, when present, increase the prevalence of healthy outcomes.[15] Culture and religion often have positive impacts on how children, their families and communities respond, recover and heal from a traumatic experience.[16] Research has also shown that 'family unity and harmony' can be a key cultural value, where there is a strong connection with family dynamics and mental health in 'children's narratives of adversity, risk, and resilience'.[17] These factors can moderate risk or adversity and promote healthy development in children and family well-being. They can also serve as safeguards to help parents 'find resources or supports and encourage coping strategies that allow them to parent effectively, even under difficult circumstances'.[18] What this suggests is that the social environment is an important factor in explaining and understanding how to produce attitude and behavioural change among young people, particularly when dealing with those at risk of antisocial or violent behaviours.[19]

In re-conceptualizing the model for Changing Tides, we have used the same CBPA and combined it with the relevant theory summarized above. In doing so, we have consulted with the families, relevant community members, religious leaders, professional health providers and academics. This approach can be described as a collaborative method of research that equitably involves all partners in the research process and recognizes the unique strengths that each brings.[20] Such co-design ensures the framework includes a range of expertise that can understand and support the potential complex individual and family needs. These needs may vary considerably, but it is crucial that whatever support is provided, it should be sensitive to cultural and religious differences.[21] Needs can revolve around housing and education, health and mental health, social engagement, religion, sport and recreation, racism and Islamophobia, family and extended family, individual criminogenic needs, and language and cultural practices. Overall, the co-design ensures that the framework can appropriately address a range of sensitive, multi-faceted issues that could arise on their return to Australia.

Framework

The framework is evidence-based and grounded on the 'what works' principles that have been found successful in other interventions, such as those conducted with Indigenous young people, street and prison gangs (desistence models), drug and alcohol offenders, domestic violence offenders and other young people involved in antisocial and violent behaviours.[22] Evidence indicates that effective programmes contain a range of factors including that they are:

- tailored to individual needs;
- focus on treatment readiness and the participants' capacity to engage;
- involve community, multi-agency and specialist collaborations;
- build a therapeutic alliance between case workers, participants, and other relevant parties;
- harness the value of peer role models and mentoring;

- foster the development of a pro-social community and replace antisocial associates; and
- provide a stable, ongoing contact in a participant's life.[23]

Other research shows that programmes are comprehensive if they can include a variety of factors such as different teaching methods, sufficient dosage, appropriate theory, opportunities for positive relationship development, appropriately timed, culturally (and religiously) relevant, have evaluations, and involve well-qualified and relevant volunteers and professionals.[24] The theory that supports this framework also takes into consideration many of the push-pull factors and different dynamics that can lead to negative behaviours, and the support mechanism to help build resilience to address these behaviours.

Our framework also aligns with the central philosophy of the Good Lives Model (GLM) where we focus predominantly on strengths, not risks. The GLM is a contemporary strengths-based approach to offender rehabilitation where 'treatment aims to equip offenders with the internal and external resources necessary to desist successfully from further offending'.[25] However, in referring to the GLM, we highlight that no women (or children) have so far been charged with any offence. A core underlying assumption is that humans seek out experiences that are consistent with their personal values and in doing so experience high levels of well-being. The aim of treatment in the GLM is 'the promotion of primary goods or human needs that, once met, enhance psychological well-being'.[26] A basic premise is that offenders, like all humans, hold a set of primary goals. Researchers have argued that if the primary goals of rehabilitation focus on 'friendship, enjoyable work, loving relationships, creative pursuits, sexual satisfaction, positive self-regard, and an intellectually challenging environment' then a reduction in criminogenic needs should follow.[27] In using this approach, participants become invested in the treatment or support process because it explicitly aims to assist them live a fulfilling life in addition to reducing and managing any risks. Hence, we focus on participants' positive attributes, build strengths and use a restorative approach with the support of the immediate families.[28]

Circles of Support and Accountability (CoSA)

At the core of Changing Tides is a Circles of Support and Accountability (CoSA) model, which works to create a web of support for at-risk people.[29] The CoSA model was first developed in Canada for sexual offenders and there are now programmes being developed in New Zealand, Australia, the United States, the UK and European jurisdictions (RMIT University, 2017) using the same CoSA principles for mainstream offenders, such as those involved in drug and alcohol offending.[30] In our framework, it has been re-conceptualized to support case management where we aim to help people[31] who have been exposed to significant trauma or are at risk of engaging in potentially harmful behaviour. The framework recognizes the importance of trauma-informed practices, which are strength-based and grounded on an understanding of, and responsiveness to, the impact of trauma. These practices emphasize physical, psychological and emotional safety for the families, and create opportunities for them to rebuild a sense of control and empowerment once home again.[32]

The CoSA model can be described as a programme of wrap-around care, where an intentional community of trusted relationships is created for a vulnerable person, even if they are exposed to the criminal justice system. It aims to redirect behaviour that is deemed harmful to self or others, while at the same time providing care, support and assistance to influence positive change. Rather than working on individual risks, the model works towards expanding individual qualities in people – hence the GLM and the strength-based approach.[33]

Our framework is primarily geared towards supportive action. However, it can easily be upscaled to also focus on middle (secondary) intervention and tertiary cases, such as when an individual is diverted from the criminal justice system, or if a person progresses through and out of it. The CoSA model also recognizes that in many cases, individual specialist support alone may not address negative behaviours in vulnerable people. Therefore, the teams contained in our framework also aim to work closely with families to provide the necessary care and support to deal with any issues that may arise within any aspect of a family network.

The CoSA model is conceptualized as concentric circles of community, family and specialist support that work closely with each other to provide care and prevent or address any behaviour of concern. The inner circle contains the vulnerable individual and is referred to as the 'Core Member'. A Core Member should demonstrate an understanding of their behaviour and participate on a voluntary basis. They should also be committed to playing an active role in maintaining or developing a positive, non-offending lifestyle. The next circle, the 'community of care', is made up of trusted volunteer family and community members who are identified as important to the Core Member and who can provide positive influence, support and assistance to influence behavioural change. In doing so, a person's strengths are built upon and the new pro-social relationships that are created around them help prevent any negative influences that could harm themselves or others.

The central involvement of families and community members in the planning and implementation of this intervention framework is likely to bring greater benefits for the women and children (and families), as well as improving community safety and well-being. An intervention is also more likely to get a greater level of responsivity or buy-in from the participants if it is conducted with trusted families and community representatives. In this aspect, trust is a crucial component in this framework, which we propose leads to greater responsivity. For example, the team providing the support have established deep levels of trust amongst the families, which is likely to result in the women and children's active participation in activities and support within our framework. This means that their participation will be more likely on a voluntary basis rather than them feeling as though they have to participate because there will be negative repercussions if they do not. Also, by asking family community members to help plan and implement an intervention, it helps develop a sense of ownership where they want the programme to succeed. They are more likely to invest the effort and resources needed to sustain it. Involving the community also makes it easier to obtain the resources and volunteers needed to carry out the programme appropriately and effectively over the longer term.

The community of care could also involve dedicated mentor(s) who focus on providing long-term support to reduce social isolation, monitor and guide their actions (for community safety) and help the Core Member stay committed to the programme. There are several important characteristics of this mentoring relationship that are crucial to this programme. To have a better chance of producing positive results, the mentor must have some degree of empathy and authenticity. Mentors who can identify strengths and positive qualities in the Core Member and who lead by expressing care and concern will have a greater chance of a successful mentoring relationship.[34] Cultural and religious sensitivity is also essential and plays a positive role in the Core Member's perceptions of the mentor's credibility and effectiveness.[35] Lastly, one of the most consistent research findings is the difficulty and importance of maintaining a sufficiently long mentoring relationship with the Core Member. Foreshortened relationships can be extremely problematic – such as relationships lasting less than six months can harm a person, leading to feelings of abandonment and negative outcomes.[36]

The community of care can also play another vital role in introducing other relationships into a circle when professional expertise is required from the next outer circle. This process is facilitated by the transfer of trust from those on the inner circle to those being brought in to provide professional expertise. This circle can include a case manager, psychologists, counsellors, other health professionals and religious scholars and others who can help assess and address any potential problems that could lead to offending or re-offending. If specialist services are not available, the programme would seek to connect with the existing external social service and mental health provider networks. The programme will vary according to the needs of the Core Member. These needs can include criminogenic needs, such as antisocial attitudes, antisocial peers, substance abuse, lack of problem solving and self-control, and other factors leading to criminal behaviour. They can also include health and mental health needs as well as other needs around safe housing, education and employment.[37] Sometimes these needs will revolve around family, where regular follow-up sessions with the participants and families will be crucial. To avoid any potential stigma associated with participating in the programme, it must be highlighted to participants that they are not a 'risk' but are a valued part of their community.

Framework strategy

With the CoSA concept at the core of the framework, the following is a breakdown of the support elements contained within Changing Tides. The key areas of the framework include the following:

Pre-travel education and briefings

At the point of safety and prior to the women and children's travel to Australia, we aim to begin a needs assessment to help with their immediate support on arrival back into Australia. We will also brief them on their safe passage and what to expect on arrival home. This will include the basics about how they will be getting home, their travel documentation, customs and quarantine arrangements, and who will be meeting them on arrival. They will also need to know about the expected processes of psychological assessments or evaluations and health assessments. We aim for the health assessments to be undertaken by family general practitioners recognized within relevant communities. This will be essential so that relevant religious and cultural requirements will be observed and respected.

The reunification with families will not be straightforward, so expectations around accommodation and care arrangements would also need be discussed. However, family engagement will be essential to achieving successful reunification and will focus on fostering the relationships between parent/s, child and immediate relatives. This will require 'emotional preparation' for reunification, which means learning about the emotional side of reunification and coming to terms with what that experience might be like for different family members.

The women will also get an understanding of possible legal proceedings by the Australian Government, the potential media and public interest, and their obligations regarding any requirements placed on them by police and government agencies. Most importantly, they will get reassurance that this framework will support them regardless of any situation that may arise.

Assessments

On arrival, we will conduct individual and family needs assessments, as the women and children and their families (whatever that family structure may look like) will have immediate needs and support, such as health, mental health, childcare, personal hygiene, legal, etc. From this, a holistic plan of care will be developed with the women and families involved in the support. The plan will be dynamic but created specifically for each woman and child. This will be driven by the following short- and long-term objectives:

- They will be safe and secure on return, be proud of their identity and culture, and restore, develop and maintain strong positive community relationships.
- The children will be valued and respected on their return, be supported to learn and develop in their new home environment and be provided opportunities for remediable education prior to returning to formal education.
- The women be supported in their family and community, so that they can learn to be positive, confident and resourceful in re-establishing themselves in the families and community, and that they be given the best opportunities to continue to help their children learn and grow.
- Local communities be provided capacity to support their return, support the relevant families and recognize the importance of the whole community in keeping all the families together to support the reunification.

The plan will help coordinate and centralize all service provision, allowing the women and families a centralized access point for help and services. This access point aims to complement and coordinate services, not duplicate, with the capital of trust already established with the women and children.

Health/mental health assessments and psychological first aid

Also on arrival, a range of individual-based and family-based psychological and health assessments will be conducted in cooperation with immediate family members. We will work on the assumption that the women and children will have experienced many highly stressful and dangerous situations. For the women, this may potentially include emotional, physical or sexual maltreatment while in ISIS-led territory.[38] Appropriately qualified mental health professionals who are experienced in assessing individuals returning from these types of situations will be utilized. From these assessments, relevant health care plans and interventions will be specifically developed and co-managed by the families and support teams.

The assessments will be undertaken simultaneously with psychological first aid.[39] Psychological first aid is widely used in the first hours, days and weeks following someone's experience of a traumatic event or disaster and is based on an understanding that people affected by trauma will experience a range of early reactions (physical, psychological, emotional, behavioural). These reactions may interfere with their ability to cope.

Using a psychological first-aid approach, we will help the women and children with basic principles of support to promote recovery. This will involve helping them to feel safe, connected to others, calm and hopeful, and to access physical, emotional and social support. This is also likely to reduce initial distress, meet current needs, promote flexible coping and encourage adjustment on their return.[40]

Mental health support

It will also be important to address mental health needs. We anticipate several interrelated areas where support may be required to address, for example, post-traumatic stress disorder (PTSD), depression, shame/embarrassment, self-harm, social anxiety, etc. All assistance will be trauma-informed in that we assume varying degrees of trauma have occurred.[41] A trauma-informed system uses that information to design service systems that accommodate the vulnerabilities of trauma survivors and allows services to be delivered in a way that will avoid inadvertent re-traumatization and facilitate participation in treatment.[42]

Several different interventions supporting mental health are included in this framework. We anticipate PTSD will be an example of where intervention support will be required. Common psychological effects of traumatic events include a range of symptoms and behavioural effects. Some of the women may experience a range of mental health conditions, the most common being post-traumatic stress disorder, depression and/or anxiety. The children may also experience similar psychological reactions to trauma as the adult women; however, their clinical presentation will be reflective of their age and development. Presentations may include behavioural issues, sleep concerns, attention difficulties, low self-esteem, friendship difficulties, enuresis and developmental/education concerns, as well as symptoms of anxiety and depression. Parent mental illness affects child well-being and addressing both parent and child mental health will be crucial.[43]

We will focus on strengths, not weaknesses, which is a basic tenet of working with trauma survivors who may see themselves as inherently fragile due to their experiences. Working from a strengths-based perspective is part of a process of relationship and trust building we undertook in setting up this framework. While many 'experts' and government representatives have already made assumptions about the women (and children) being radicalized, our conversations with them will be open-minded and occur within a context of compassion, empathy and humanity. Our primary focus will be on rapport and relationship building, as well as developing the person's own capacity for resilience and healing. This non-authoritarian approach views the women (and children) as the expert in their own life and as a whole person, rather than a potential risk or threat.

Family reunification

Family engagement will be essential to achieving successful reunification and reception. The service will focus on fostering the relationships between parent/s, child and immediate relatives. We expect that some of the women and children may not be ready or willing to talk with service providers or family members about their personal circumstances, but we can nonetheless explain to the families that it is normal and okay for them to experience a wide range of emotions. For example, it will be normal that the women and children have mixed feelings about the transition back to Australia, such as excitement, relief, joy, ambivalence, anxiety, stress, hope, anger and insecurity.

Further, it is expected that the immediate families will primarily be involved in the long-term normalization and integration of the women and children into society. We expect that the immediate family will provide day-to-day support, encourage and assist with schooling, and help with caring for young children whilst the mothers may have to deal with PTSD and other related issues. In addition, in the months and years after arrival, it will be the immediate families that will provide information, support and guidance to assist with the transition and disentanglement from the environment they had been for the previous seven years or more in Syria. Therefore, this is essential in providing the support to the immediate family and resource and supporting them to provide the skills needed.

By establishing trust and confidence with the immediate family members, it is they who will first alert government and non-government services to extra needs, such as psycho-social support, childcare needs or antisocial behaviour.

Child support and protection

We will assist families and extended families to provide children with stable, secure and safe environments that includes care arrangements that meet their social, emotional, cultural, psychological and developmental needs. Using case planning where necessary, we can provide opportunities to identify the strengths, resources and safety concerns of the child's family, extended social network, carers and community and mobilize these in ways that facilitate sustainable reunification for the children. Members of a child's family, including parents, grandparents, relatives, carers and others who are significant in their life, as well as constituents from relevant communities, will be able to offer important insights and experiences to assist in planning for reunification.

A child protection plan will be drawn up for each child, which will set out how the child will be kept safe, how things can be improved for the family and what support is required. We anticipate that some of the women may need help understanding and working through their child's reactions, responding to children's physical and behavioural needs, and dealing with the stress of unforeseen challenges. The following kinds of support and services are closely connected with reunifications and include, but not limited to,

- the provision of information and services to families by outside service providers;
- special educational services for the children where required;
- therapy and intensive family-based services;
- mentoring; and
- coaching and information for families about children's developmental stages and needs.

If at any time any member of the support teams forms a view that a child has experienced or is likely to experience abuse or neglect, the relevant State or Territory child protection authorities will be notified.

Religious support and guidance

In Changing Tides, we acknowledge the importance and significance of religious guidance in support and rehabilitation for the women and children. Research suggests that religiosity and religious participation can increase a person's interpersonal likability, can improve an individual's psychological and physical well-being, and can comfort someone who is facing difficult life circumstances (i.e., imprisonment, family problems, divorce or unemployment). Involvement in any religion may also foster strong social networks and emotional support that constrain criminal behaviour.[44] Religiosity can be associated with a reduction in criminal offending or antisocial behaviours.[45]

In acknowledging the importance of religion in the lives of the women and children, their families and communities, we will provide a range of options for the families to engage with relevant Imams or Sheikhs. Like mentors, it is important that the fit is right; however, decisions around this right religious fit will be up to the families and is something that cannot and should not be decided by anyone external to the families. Our research has shown that getting the wrong religious fit can contribute to negative outcomes and a rejection of the programme or intervention as a whole. In noting this, we understand that religious support is just one element of our framework and there are many other factors that contribute to the success and failure of a programme or intervention.

Governance and support groups

The following groups will be established to support and manage this framework.

Community Advisory Board (CAB)

The CAB will consist of a small number of family members, community representatives, legal and specialist advisors. The Chair of the CAB will act as a key liaison point with government and police agencies. This will be done in consultation with the other board members. The CAB will have several functions, including providing input into the programme agenda, serve as gatekeepers for protection of the women, children, families and communities, formally approve any changes in the framework's direction, and ensure the effective implementation of the interventions.

The CAB will be responsible for calling in interventions based on trigger points and can be escalated according to the process described below in 'case escalation'. Trigger points are many but can include confusion and disorientation; destructive or high-risk behaviour; restless, agitated and disorganized behaviour; significant changes of mood (up or down); suicidal thoughts or acts of self-harm.[46] The responsibility of the CAB actioning on these trigger points will be done in consultation with the Professional Support Group (PSG) and the manager of an external service where required.

Family Support Team (FST)

The FSTs will consist of dedicated and trusted family and community members. It is not a clinical group but will liaise and work closely with the PSG below. Through strength-based approaches, the FSTs will help families adjust to the arrival of the women and children, and for the women and children to settle in their new environment and circumstances. They will offer practical support within a home and help families reach out to external services available to them when required.[47] Initially, they will visit families on a regular basis (adjusted on a case-by-case basis) to support the activities of the case management plan and to assist with any physical and mental health, emotional, developmental and educational needs. Dedicated FSTs will help families (parents, elders, carers, etc.) develop strategies to keep at-risk children out of harm's way in their homes, communities and culture.

In our framework, we also acknowledge that strong bonds have formed between the groups of women and children in the camps. However, on their return to Australia, some women and children will return to families in Melbourne and others to Sydney. Therefore, the FSTs will facilitate communication between the families through the established Australian Family Network to help deal with any anxiety associated with the initial separation of family groups.

Professional Support Group (PSG)

The PSG supporting the families will be multi-faceted, multi-disciplined and includes local, national and international experts. The skills base of the team draws from clinical, forensic, and counselling psychology, youth work, child protection, criminology, sociology and theology. This includes support from psychologists registered with the Psychology Board of Australia and relevant trusted community professionals.[48] Where necessary, the PSG will also coordinate with established services based in relevant state governments.

The PSG will be responsible for coordinating mental health needs assessments and for leading the corresponding interventions. This will include trauma-informed care and counselling, as well as building psychological resilience, emotional well-being and other necessary or specific interventions. The PSG has well-established street credibility and trust and along with respected and relevant members of the Muslim community will help deliver the programme from a 'grassroots perspective'.

Case Support Team (CST)

Situated within the PSG is a system of case management and support found in the CST. A team of dedicated CST members will be developed from within the relevant families and communities and work directly to the PSG. The CST would consist of a team of permanent members, but other experts could be brought in as required. The CST could consist of mentors, councillors and Sheikhs/Imams. Initially, the CST would meet on a weekly basis to see how each case is progressing and to provide direction. The CST will also assist with compiling results that will feed into the evaluation processes and provide progress reports about individual cases.

Figure 11.1 outlines the overall governance structure around case management.

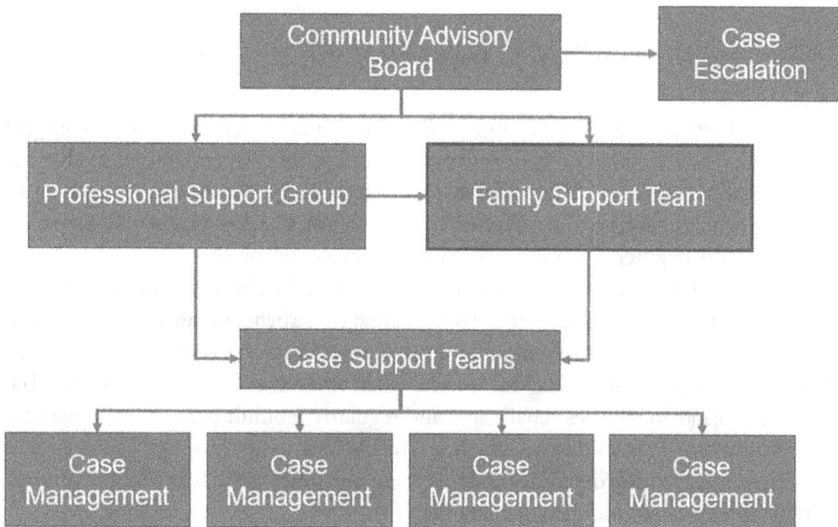

Figure 11.1 Changing tides governance.

Case escalation

In this framework, case escalation can be triggered because of several different possibilities. First and foremost, the safety and well-being of all of the children are the paramount consideration. If at any time any member of the support team forms a view that a child has experienced or is likely to experience abuse or neglect, the relevant State or Territory child protection authorities would be notified. Also, if we ascertain through assessments of the women and children, such as mental health or risk assessments, that any of them have sympathies or support for the Islamic State (or any other terrorist group), we will liaise closely with police to determine a safe and immediate course of action. Similarly, if any member of the support team forms a view that a child or adult requires immediate mental health support or is at risk of harming themselves or someone else, the relevant State or Territory mental health authorities and/or the police will be notified.

However, it is important to note that escalation may not always require intervention by statutory authorities. In many situations, escalation could involve increasing the intensity of support delivered within the existing framework or involve referral to expertise external to the immediate team. Alternatively, an empathic and calm response to a person's distress can assist to de-escalate a situation, as can mobilizing a person's existing supports. All family members, along with the CST and PST, however, will be trained and supported to recognize when a matter needs escalation and to seek relevant external or professional assistance.[49] Regardless of the circumstances, family involvement in the escalation of care will be critical, even if the escalation requires police cooperation or an emergency response. In urgent cases, teams can request a police response should a situation deteriorate quickly to threaten life or property.

Evaluation

Complex interventions like Changing Tides are built up from several complex components, which 'may act both independently and interdependently'.[50] Evaluating complex interventions pose considerable challenges and a substantial investment of time. We will undertake a comprehensive evaluation of Changing Tides based on objectives and key performance indicators co-developed by the teams. The aim of the evaluation will be to demonstrate that the women, the children and families have benefitted in measurable and lasting ways, and that those benefits can be attributable to the framework. While assessment of family outcomes in interventions is an important activity, it is usually problematic due to conceptual and measurement challenges.[51] The CAB will work through these challenges and regularly monitor progress to make sure interventions are on track and on schedule. The PSG will assess how well it has reached the desired intervention outcomes and that these outcomes are in line with the original framework objectives and management plan.

Based on the individual case management strategies and support plans, the PSG will repeat mental health assessments on set intervals. From this, the PSG will be able to determine whether the programmes or interventions have provided measurable benefits to the women and children. For the children, some of the early interventions will include developmental evaluations and assessments, physical therapy, occupational therapy, speech/language therapy, audiology, nutrition services, special education, and psychological and social work services. Individual evaluations of each component will be conducted by the relevant specialists and included in the overall evaluation.

Overall, the evaluation will commence from the start and will be an integral part of the overall framework. The PSG will be running multi-dimensional evaluations (both quantitative and qualitative), utilizing a framework that considers multiple levels:

- Line of Sight Evaluation – evaluating whether the programme is aligned with the Strategic Framework regarding outcomes and capabilities.
- Project Effectiveness Evaluation – evaluating if the framework and associated interventions are meeting the stated goals and objectives (programme logic).
- Outcomes Evaluation – evaluating if the interventions are contributing to projected outcomes.
- Programme Benefit Evaluation – evaluating whether the programme outcomes result in the desired benefits, i.e., disengaging young people from harmful/antisocial behaviours associated with violent extremism. (Note: specific psychological evaluations will be implemented here.)
- Framework Impact – evaluating whether the benefits help realize the framework's original vision of protecting the returnees, the families, and the Australian community as a whole.

Conclusion

There is no doubt that the returning women and children will require a range of different types of support captured in our framework – Changing Tides – to assist in their reintegration back into the Australian community. This will include specific interventions to address a complex array of needs as well as protective mechanisms to ensure their safety on return. In our framework, we recognize the right of families as the fundamental group in society to be leading decision-making around this support and as co-contributors in the development of solutions for their care and ongoing support. Therefore, Changing Tides has been developed in close cooperation with the immediate families so that we are able to address a range of potential immediate and long-term needs. Embedded in this close cooperation is trust, which means that the programme has the full support of the families. With this trust, we are more likely to get the women and children's active participation in any specific interventions when they are required. The element of trust and active participation by families in the design and implementation sets this model apart from other CVE interventions.

We acknowledge that the Australian government may want to implement their own security focused programme for the returnees. There are several existing programmes at the Federal and State levels including the AFP Diversionary Programme, the Victorian Community Integrated Support Programme (CISP) or NSW's Proactive Integrated Support Model (PRISM) run by Corrections NSW. We are fully aware of the potential risks involved in the eventual reintegration, so also embedded in Changing Tides is the need for accountability. In this accountability, we recognize that some situations may require close cooperation and support from law enforcement agencies and government services. Nevertheless, we remain concerned that interventions not specifically designed for this type of situation could potentially add to the stressors or trauma already experienced by the women and children. Therefore, it is important that we do not allow 'responses to be dictated' by assumptions around 'types of offending' rather than addressing individual needs.[52] Finally, as these programmes are CVE-related, we are concerned that they could create the sort of stigmatization and marginalization that may lead to negative outcomes or offending. With our own unique approach outlined in this framework, and with the cooperation of other government and non-government services, we can confidently say the broader Australian community will be safe when the women and children return.

Notes

1   See 'Speed Up Repatriations or Foreign Children Could Be Stuck in North East Syria Camps for Up to 30 Years, Warns Save the Children', *Save the Children International*, 22 May 2022.

2   See https://bringourkidshome.com.au/

3   See https://www.abc.net.au/news/2019-11-16/us-offers-to-rescue-australian-islamic-state-families-in-syria/11710924

4   See https://www.news.com.au/world/middle-east/australian-isis-brides-and-children-wont-come-home-from-syria-due-to-coronavirus/news-story/cc4c6387bdb7abf7ad002add810e5802

5   See https://www.theaustralian.com.au/news/breaking-news/isis-brides-to-remain-in-syrian-prisons-despite-us-government-offer-to-help-repatriate/news-story/b1071ed63eb0b4099ea0cd73ea965adb

6   E. Rosand, B. H. Ellis and S. Weine, 'Minding the Gap: How to Provide More Comprehensive Support to the Children of ISIS', Brookings, 28 January 2020, available at: https://www.brookings.edu/blog/order-from-chaos/2020/01/28/minding-the-gap-how-to-provide-more-comprehensive-support-to-the-children-of-isis/

7   See https://www.savethechildren.org.au/media/media-releases/children-and-their-mothers-trapped-in-al-hol-camp

8   G. Boag-Munroe and M. Evangelou, 'From Hard to Reach to How to Reach: A Systematic Review of the Literature on Hard-to-reach Families', *Research Papers in Education* 27, no. 2 (2012): 209–39. doi: 10.1080/02671522.2010.509515; see also C. Benoit, M. Jansson, A. Millar, and R. Phillips, 'Community-Academic Research on Hard-to-Reach Populations: Benefits and Challenges', *Qualitative Health Research* 15, no. 2 (2005): 263–82. https://doi.org/10.1177/1049732304267752.

9   E. Hopper, E. Bassuk and J. Olivet, 'Shelter from the Storm: Trauma-informed Care in Homelessness Services Settings', *The Open Health Services and Policy Journal* 3 (2010): 80–100.

10 J. T. Edison et al., 'Advancing the Science of Community-level Interventions', *American Journal of Public Health* 101, no. 8 (2011): 1410–19.

11   A. Kundnani, 'Radicalisation: The Journey of a Concept', *Race & Class* 54, no. 2 (2012): 3–25. doi: 10.1177/0306396812454984.

12   Brennan Centre for Justice, 'Why Countering Violent Extremism Programs Are Bad Policy' (2019), available at: https://www.brennancenter.org/our-work/research-reports/why-countering-violent-extremism-programs-are-bad-policy on 26 March 2020.

13   J. Shoultz, M. F. Oneha, L. Magnussen, M. M. Hla, Z. Brees-Saunders, M. D. Cruz, and M. Douglas, 'Finding Solutions to Challenges Faced in Community-based Participatory Research between Academic and Community Organizations', *Journal of Interprofessional Care* 20, no. 2 (2006): 133–44. doi: 10.1080/13561820600577576.

14   J. Carling, M. B. Erdal and R. Ezzati 'Beyond the Insider–Outsider Divide in Migration Research', *Migration Studies* 2, no. 1 (2014): 36–54. doi:10.1093/migration/mnt022

15   Krauss et al., 'Parenting, Community, and Religious Predictors of Positive and Negative Developmental Outcomes among Muslim Adolescents', *Young People & Society* 46, no. 2 (2014): 201–27.

16   See https://www.nctsn.org/what-is-child-trauma/about-child-trauma

17   C. Panter-Brick, M. Grimon and M. Eggerman, 'Caregiver-child Mental Health: A Prospective Study in Conflict and Refugee Settings', *Journal of Child Psychology and Psychiatry* 55, no. 4 (2014): 313–27. doi: 10.1111/jcpp.12167, at p. 314

18   Australian Institute of Family Studies, 'Risk and Protective Factors for Child Abuse and Neglect' (2017), retrieved from https://aifs.gov.au/cfca/publications/risk-and-protective-factors-child-abuse-and-neglect on 16 September 2020.

19   K. Reynolds et al., *Understanding and Strengthening Student Resilience to Radicalisation and Violent Extremism in Schools* (2016) ANU Research School of Psychology (unpublished report).

20   Minkler et al., 'Community-based Participatory Research: Implications for Public Health Funding', *American Journal of Public Health* 93 (2003): 1210–13.

21   Kumpfer, 'Cultural Sensitivity and Adaptation in Family-based Prevention Interventions', *Prevention Science* 3, no. 3 (2002): 241–6. doi:10.1023/A:1019902902119; J. R. Graham, C. Bradshaw and J. L. Trew, 'Addressing Cultural Barriers with Muslim Clients: An Agency Perspective', *Administration in Social Work* 33, no. 4 (2009): 387–406. doi: 10.1080/03643100903172950

22   J. Belsky and M. H. van Ijzendoorn, 'What Works for Whom? Genetic Moderation of Intervention Efficacy', *Development and Psychopathology* 27, no. 1 (2015): 1–6. doi: 10.1017/S0954579414001254.

23   Centre for Innovative Justice, 'Integrating the Indefensible – What Role Should the Community Play?' Issues Paper, RMIT University, 2017, available at: https://cij.org.au/research-projects/integrating-the-indefensible-what-role-should-the-community-play/ on 22 May 2019.

24   Nation et al., 'What Works in Prevention: Principles of Effective Prevention Programs?' *American Psychologist* 58, nos. 6–7 (2003): 449–56. doi: 10.1037/0003-066X.58.6-7.449.

25   G. M. Willis and T. Ward, 'Striving for a Good Life: The Good Lives Model Applied to Released Child Molesters', *Journal of Sexual Aggression* 17, no. 3 (2011): 290–303. doi: 10.1080/13552600.2010.505349, at p. 290.

26   Ibid.

27   Ward and Stewart, 'Criminogenic Needs and Human Needs: A Theoretical Model', *Psychology, Crime & Law* 9 (2003): 125–43. doi: 10.1080/1068316031000116247, at 142.

28   D. A. Andrews, J. Bonta and J. S. Wormith 'The Risk-need-responsivity (RNR) Model: Does Adding the Good Lives Model Contribute to Effective Crime Prevention?' *Criminal Justice and Behavior* 38, no. 7 (2011): 735–55. doi: 10.1177/0093854811406356.

29   S. Bogaerts, M. Höing and B. Vogelvang, 'Circles of Support and Accountability: How and Why They Work for Sex Offenders', *Journal of Forensic Psychology Practice* 13 (2013): 267–95; Centre for Innovative Justice, 2017; Azoulay et al., 'Circles of Support and Accountability (CoSA): A Review of the Development of CoSA and Its International Implementation', *International Review of Psychiatry* (Abingdon, England), 31, no. 2 (2019): 195–205. doi: 10.1080/09540261.2018.1552406.

30   See https://www.thewitnessonline.org/stewardship/circles-of-support-and-accountability-aid-people-struggling-with-addiction/

31   For the purposes of this project, young people are defined as those aged twelve to twenty-five years old. While the age range assigned to 'young people' differs, twelve to twenty-five years of age is commonly used in Australian young people policy to frame young people (J. Bell, A. Vromen and P. Collin, 'Rewriting the Rules for Youth Participation: Inclusion and Diversity in Government and Community Decision Making', 2008).

32   Hopper, Bassuk and Olivet, 'Shelter from the Storm: Trauma-informed Care in Homelessness Services Settings', 80–100.

33   K. J. Fox, 'Civic Commitment: Promoting Desistance through Community Integration', *Punishment and Society* 18, no. 1 (2016): 68–94.

34   Stewart and Openshaw, 'Young People Mentoring: What Is It and What Do We Know?', *Journal of Evidence-based Social Work* 11, no. 4 (2014): 328–36.

35   Suffrin, Todd and Sanchez, 'An Ecological Perspective of Mentor Satisfaction with their Young People Mentoring Relationships', *Journal of Community Psychology* 44, no. 5 (2016): 553–68. doi: 10.1002/jcop.21785.

36   Higley et al., 'Achieving High Quality and Long-lasting Matches in Young People Mentoring Programmes: A Case Study of Results Mentoring', *Child & Family Social Work* 21, no. 2 (2016): 240–8.

37   Latessa and Lowenkamp, 'What Are Criminogenic Needs and Why Are They Important', *For the Record* 4 (2005): 15–16.

38   Alsaba and Kapilashrami, 'Understanding Women's Experience of Violence and the Political Economy of Gender in Conflict: The Case of Syria', *Reproductive Health Matters* 24, no. 47 (2016): 5–17. doi: 10.1016/j.rhm.2016.05.002.

39   Australian Red Cross and the Australian Psychology Society, *Psychological First Aid*, 2013.

40   Ibid.

41   Harris and Fallot, 'Using Trauma Theory to Design Service Systems', *New Directions for Mental Health Services* 89 (2001): 1–103.

42   Harris and Fallot, 'Using Trauma Theory to Design Service Systems'.

43   See https://refugeehealthguide.org.au/psychological-effects-of-torture-trauma/

44   Halama and Lacna, 'Personality Change Following Religious Conversion: Perceptions of Converts and Their Close Acquaintances', *Mental Health, Religion and Culture* 14, no. 8 (2011): 757–68.

45   Johnson, 'Jailhouse Religion, Spiritual Transformation, and Long-term Change. Sagamore Institute', *Justice Quarterly* 17, no. 2 (2016): 377–91.

46   See https://www.betterhealth.vic.gov.au/health/ServicesAndSupport/early-signs-and-intervention-with-mental-illness

47 Save the Children, see https://www.savethechildren.org.au/Our-work/Our-programs/
    Australia/Providing-support-to-families
48 Service professionals can include (but are not limited to) community-based
    psychologists, religious or young people mentors and social workers.
49 See https://www.safetyandquality.gov.au/sites/default/files/2019-06/national-
    consensus-statement-essential-elements-for-recognising-and-responding-to-
    deterioration-in-a-persons-mental-state-july-2017.pdf
50 Campbell et al., 'Designing and Evaluating Complex Interventions to Improve Health
    Care', *Bmj* 334, no. 7591 (2007): 455–9. doi:10.1136/bmj.39108.379965, at 455.
51 Bailey et al., 'Family Outcomes in Early Intervention: A Framework for Program
    Evaluation and Efficacy Research', *Exceptional Children* 64, no. 3 (1998): 313–28.
    doi: 10.1177/001440299806400302.
52 Centre for Innovative Justice, at 5.

Bibliography

Alsaba, K. and Kapilashrami, A. 'Understanding Women's Experience of Violence and
    the Political Economy of Gender in Conflict: The Case of Syria'. *Reproductive Health
    Matters* 24, no. 47 (2016): 5–17. doi: 10.1016/j.rhm.2016.05.002

Andrews, D. A., Bonta, J. and Wormith, J. S. 'The Risk-need-responsivity (RNR)
    Model: Does Adding the Good Lives Model Contribute to Effective Crime
    Prevention?' *Criminal Justice and Behavior* 38, no. 7 (2011): 735–55. doi:
    10.1177/0093854811406356

Australian Institute of Family Studies. 'Risk and Protective Factors for Child Abuse and
    Neglect' (2017). Available at: https://aifs.gov.au/cfca/publications/risk-and-protective-
    factors-child-abuse-and-neglect on 16 September 2020.

Australian Red Cross and the Australian Psychology Society. *Psychological First Aid.* 2013.

Azoulay, N., Winder, B., Murphy, L. and Fedoroff, J. P. 'Circles of Support and
    Accountability (CoSA): A Review of the Development of CoSA and Its International
    Implementation'. *International Review of Psychiatry* (Abingdon, England), 31, no. 2
    (2019): 195–205. doi: 10.1080/09540261.2018.1552406.

Bailey, D. B., McWilliam, R. A., Darkes, L. A., Hebbeler, K., Simeonsson, R. J., Spiker,
    D. and Wagner, M. 'Family Outcomes in Early Intervention: A Framework for Program
    Evaluation and Efficacy Research'. *Exceptional Children* 64, no. 3 (1998): 313–28. doi:
    10.1177/001440299806400302.

Bell, J., Vromen, A. and Collin, P. *Rewriting the Rules for Youth Participation: Inclusion and
    Diversity in Government and Community Decision Making* (2008).

Belsky, J. and van Ijzendoorn, M. H. 'What Works for Whom? Genetic Moderation
    of Intervention Efficacy'. *Development and Psychopathology* 27, no. 1 (2015): 1–6.
    doi: 10.1017/S0954579414001254.

Boag-Munroe, G. and Evangelou, M. 'From Hard to Reach to How to Reach: A Systematic
    Review of the Literature on Hard-to-reach Families'. *Research Papers in Education*
    27, no. 2 (2012): 209–39. doi: 10.1080/02671522.2010.509515.

Bogaerts, S., Höing, M. and Vogelvang, B. 'Circles of Support and Accountability: How
    and Why They Work for Sex Offenders'. *Journal of Forensic Psychology Practice*
    13 (2013): 267–95.

Brennan Centre for Justice. 'Why Countering Violent Extremism Programs Are Bad Policy' (2019). Available at: https://www.brennancenter.org/our-work/research-reports/why-countering-violent-extremism-programs-are-bad-policy on 26 March 2020.

Campbell, N. C., Murray, E., Darbyshire, J., Emery, J., Farmer, A., Griffiths, F. and Kinmonth, A. L. 'Designing and Evaluating Complex Interventions to Improve Health Care'. *Bmj* 334, no. 7591 (2007): 455–9. doi:10.1136/bmj.39108.379965.

Carling, J., Erdal, M. B. and Ezzati, R. 'Beyond the Insider–Outsider Divide in Migration Research'. *Migration Studies* 2, no. 1 (2014): 36–54. doi:10.1093/migration/mnt022.

Centre for Innovative Justice. 'Integrating the Indefensible – What Role Should the Community Play?' Issues Paper, RMIT University, 2017. Available at: https://cij.org.au/research-projects/integrating-the-indefensible-what-role-should-the-community-play/ on 22 May 2019.

Edison, J. T. et al. 'Advancing the Science of Community-level Interventions'. *American Journal of Public Health* 101, no. 8 (2011): 1410–19.

Fox, K. J. 'Civic Commitment: Promoting Desistance through Community Integration'. *Punishment and Society* 18, no. 1 (2016): 68–94.

Halama, P. and Lacna, M. 'Personality Change Following Religious Conversion: Perceptions of Converts and Their Close Acquaintances'. *Mental Health, Religion & Culture* 14, no. 8 (2011): 757–68.

Harris, M. and Fallot, R. D. 'Using Trauma Theory to Design Service Systems'. *New Directions for Mental Health Services* 89 (2001): 1–103.

Higley, E., Walker, S. C., Bishop, A. S. and Fritz, C. 'Achieving High Quality and Long-lasting Matches in Young People Mentoring Programmes: A Case Study of Results Mentoring'. *Child & Family Social Work* 21, no. 2 (2016): 240–8.

Hopper, E., Bassuk, E. and Olivet, J. 'Shelter from the Storm: Trauma-informed Care in Homelessness Services Settings'. *The Open Health Services and Policy Journal.* 3 (2010): 80–100.

Johnson, B. 'Jailhouse Religion, Spiritual Transformation, and Long-term Change. Sagamore Institute'. *Justice Quarterly* 17, no. 2 (2016): 377–91.

Krauss, S. E., Hamzah, A., Ismail, I. A., Suandi, T., Hamzah, S. R., Dahalan, D. and Idris, F. 'Parenting, Community, and Religious Predictors of Positive and Negative Developmental Outcomes among Muslim Adolescents'. *Young People and Society* 46, no. 2 (2014): 201–27.

Kumpfer, K. L., Alvarado, R., Smith, P. and Bellamy, N. 'Cultural Sensitivity and Adaptation in Family-based Prevention Interventions'. *Prevention Science* 3, no. 3 (2002): 241–6. doi:10.1023/A:1019902902119; see also Graham, J. R., Bradshaw, C. and Trew, J. L. 'Addressing Cultural Barriers with Muslim Clients: An Agency Perspective'. *Administration in Social Work* 33, no. 4 (2009): 387–406. doi: 10.1080/03643100903172950.

Kundnani, A. 'Radicalisation: The Journey of a Concept'. *Race & Class* 54, no. 2 (2012): 3–25. doi: 10.1177/0306396812454984.

Latessa, E. J. and Lowenkamp, C. 'What Are Criminogenic Needs and Why Are They Important'. *For the Record* 4 (2005): 15–16.

Minkler, M., Glover Blackwell, A., Thompson, M. and Tamir, H. 'Community-based Participatory Research: Implications for Public Health Funding'. *American Journal of Public Health* 93 (2003): 1210–13.

Nation, M., Crusto, C., Wandersman, A., Kumpfer, K. L., Seybolt, D., Morrissey-Kane, E. and Davino, K. 'What Works in Prevention: Principles of Effective Prevention

Programs?'. *American Psychologist* 58, nos. 6–7 (2003): 449–56. doi: 10.1037/0003-066X.58.6-7.449.

Panter-Brick, C., Grimon, M. and Eggerman, M. 'Caregiver-child Mental Health: A Prospective Study in Conflict and Refugee Settings'. *Journal of Child Psychology and Psychiatry* 55, no. 4 (2014): 313–27. doi: 10.1111/jcpp.12167.

Phillips, R. 'Community-academic Research on Hard-to-Reach Populations: Benefits and Challenges'. *Qualitative Health Research* 15, no. 2 (2005): 263–82. doi: 10.1177/1049732304267752.

Reynolds, K., Jones, C., Klik, K., Saydan, S., Rahman, D. and Chia, K. *Understanding and Strengthening Student Resilience to Radicalisation and Violent Extremism in Schools* (2016) ANU Research School of Psychology (unpublished report).

RMIT University. 'Integrating the Indefensible – What Role Should the Community Play?' Centre for Innovative Justice Issues Paper, December 2017.

Rosand, E., Ellis, B.H. and Weine, S. 'Minding the Gap: How to Provide More Comprehensive Support to the Children of ISIS'. Brookings, 28 January 2020. Available at: https://www.brookings.edu/blog/order-from-chaos/2020/01/28/minding-the-gap-how-to-provide-more-comprehensive-support-to-the-children-of-isis/

Save the Children. Retrieved from 'Speed Up Repatriations or Foreign Children Could Be Stuck in North East Syria Camps for up to 30 Years, Warns Save the Children' | Save the Children International on 22 May 2022.

Shoultz, J., Oneha, M. F., Magnussen, L., Hla, M. M., Brees-Saunders, Z., Cruz, M. D. and Douglas, M. 'Finding Solutions to Challenges Faced in Community-based Participatory Research between Academic and Community Organizations'. *Journal of Interprofessional Care* 20, no. 2 (2006): 133–44. doi: 10.1080/13561820600577576.

Stewart, C. and Openshaw, L. 'Young People Mentoring: What Is It and What Do We Know?'. *Journal of Evidence-based Social Work* 11, no. 4 (2014): 328–36.

Suffrin, R. L., Todd, N. R. and Sanchez, B. 'An Ecological Perspective of Mentor Satisfaction with Their Young People Mentoring Relationships'. *Journal of Community Psychology* 44, no. 5 (2016): 553–68. doi: 10.1002/jcop.21785.

Ward, T. and Stewart, C. 'Criminogenic Needs and Human Needs: A Theoretical Model'. *Psychology, Crime & Law* 9 (2003): 125–43. doi: 10.1080/1068316031000116247.

Willis, G. M. and Ward, T. 'Striving for a Good Life: The Good Lives Model Applied to Released Child Molesters'. *Journal of Sexual Aggression* 17, no. 3 (2011): 290–303. doi: 10.1080/13552600.2010.505349.

Part Six

Cautionary contributions

12

Finding the off-ramps: The challenges of diversion programming in the P/CVE space

Amarnath Amarasingam, David Jones and Bradley Galloway

Introduction

Violent extremism, from Islamist groups to white supremacist organizations, continues to present a pressing public safety issue for governments around the world. While the motivation to address violent extremism generally exists, the target of policy interventions represents a matter without consensus. On the one hand, many government interventions have focused on policing as a strategy to address violent extremism, using tactics such as surveillance of particular group activities to identify, charge and isolate violent extremists. In terrorism studies, borrowing from public health models, this is often referred to as a tertiary level of intervention. More upstream approaches (i.e., preventative approaches) to preventing violent extremism have also been identified by governments as key policy initiatives worth developing.

In this chapter, the authors draw on insights from interviews conducted with former members of hate-motivated or violent extremist groups, human service providers and community leaders to examine more closely the challenges of upstream interventions. More specifically, by asking former extremists to consider the various factors that contributed to them joining violent extremist groups, the authors attempted to identify key 'root causes' that may serve as targets for diversion programming or secondary interventions. These interventions target individuals at risk for radicalization into violence and divert them off this pathway before tertiary strategies become necessary. As will be shown below, this task is not easy and many of these former extremists, after having had time to consider their own pathways into extremism, still struggle to pinpoint anything that could have helped avoid joining altogether.

The challenge identified by the authors across the thirty interviews conducted with former members of the far-right is that myriad risk factors or 'root causes' exist as drivers to join violent extremist groups. While a sense of a lack of belonging or a traumatic childhood did recur as a theme that eventually resulted in an individual joining extremist groups, many interviewees noted that in hindsight, there was little that could have been done to divert them from radicalization. While primary interventions, which target such broad, root causes, could have been effective in diverting some of the individuals interviewed, identifying more specific risk factors for intervention was difficult.

In other words, while many of our interviewees experienced clear vulnerabilities to radicalization, from experiencing poverty to a sense of isolation, there were few, if any, clear, common factors that made them *specifically* likely to join a violent extremist group. Many of these broader risk factors are indeed ones shared by hundreds of thousands, if not millions of people, in a particular country – and the vast majority of these individuals do not join hate movements of any kind. After a brief methodology section, and a literature review, the authors present three case studies of former members of far-right organizations. The case studies are presented in narrative format, largely in their own words, to present the full expanse of their life story. We argue that narratives such as these help researchers and practitioners better understand the difficulty of pinpointing particular moments in an individual's life where some sort of intervention might have been possible. We conclude the chapter by drawing out some commonalities from these case studies.

Methodology

The primary source of data for this chapter came from a series of interviews that were conducted by the authors over the last three years with former members of hate-motivated or violent extremist groups. In total, we conducted thirty interviews. These interviews with formers focused on the nature of their pathways in and out of extremist groups and encouraged them to reflect on different factors that they thought could have either prevented their initial involvement, the primary focus of this chapter, or supported their disengagement. Interviews ranged in length from 15 minutes to 120 minutes and were conducted both in-person and over video conferencing software.

These interviews relied on snowball sampling; respondents were encouraged to identify other individuals who would be interested in speaking to us. The emergence of organizations like Life after Hate, which provide psychosocial and peer-support programming to former extremists, have facilitated the development of networks between formers. These networks can be useful to researchers during the data collection phase and reduce some of the search costs associated with recruiting interviewees from what was previously a relatively inaccessible population. All interviews were then transcribed and thematically coded for analysis. However, because this volume is largely aimed at a practitioner audience, we argue that more long-form case studies of particular individuals will be more useful in teasing out the specific trajectory of an individual's life and showcase the difficulty of primary intervention programming.

Emergence of diversionary programming

Scholars studying preventing/countering violent extremism (P/CVE) have moved towards adopting a 'public health' model for understanding and classifying programming.[1] Within this framework, there are usually three levels of programming identified: primary, secondary and tertiary.[2] Secondary programming tends to deal with individuals already demonstrating some defined risk factors ('symptomatic' or 'pre-clinical')[3] whereas tertiary involved those who are currently or formerly active in an extremist movement (rehabilitation or acute treatment).[4] Of interest in this chapter are the secondary and tertiary levels of programming, sometimes referred to as off-ramping, disengagement or diversion.[5]

Put differently, primary prevention programming aims to build resilience to, and remove or reduce the occurrence of, risk factors thought to be associated with radicalization to violence whereas secondary and tertiary prevention work on an individual level and aim to promote behavioural change and address manifested risk factors. Before addressing the opportunities and challenges associated with diversionary programming, it is helpful to understand its emergence and function.

Secondary and tertiary programming recognizes that although radicalization is a societal issue, it manifests at an individual level and therefore proposes that working with individuals may be a more fruitful approach to prevention than population-level initiatives. This level of intervention, which draws heavily from the methods developed in adjacent areas of human service work, such as gang prevention programming, aims to develop a supportive network in place around the at-risk individual and either prevent their entry into extremism or facilitate their exit. These sorts of interventions with individuals are predicated on three interrelated assumptions. The first is that individuals who become involved in extremism do so because of some underlying unmet need, broadly defined; the second is that an intervention programme can place resources around the individual to help them fulfill this need, which will in turn cause them to cease their involvement. Finally, and what will be the focus of this chapter, is the belief that there are clearly demarcated and identifiable intervention points on a person's journey into violent extremism.

While this individual-level intervention approach was pioneered in states like Denmark and the UK,[6] it is now increasingly common in countries around the world, from Kazakhstan[7] to Canada.[8] Operationally, these programmes tend to rely on a team of human service practitioners, broadly defined, who work with individual clients. The nucleus of most of these teams are youth or social workers and mental health practitioners, often psychologists or psychiatrists. Many programmes also involve additional supports including youth workers, ethnocultural community organizations, religious leaders, mentors or former extremists.

However, as will be discussed below, diversion itself presents several underappreciated challenges. Broadly speaking, these challenges relate to the contingent nature of radicalization and the varied pathways people follow into and out of involvement with violent extremism. While a move away from population-level, or primary prevention, presents a positive evolution, effective diversionary programming remains a complex endeavour.

Diversion in a changing threat environment

An emerging challenge that faces diversionary or secondary programming is the evolving nature of the threat landscape. When early structured P/CVE initiatives began to emerge, many of them were implicitly or explicitly predicated on a belief that their client base would mostly be individuals with some affinity for, or links to, groups like

Al-Qaeda, al-Shabaab or the Islamic State. However, the nature of violent extremism is evolving, and programmes are beginning to see older participants who are more likely to be influenced by violent far right, anti-government beliefs, or more nebulous engagement with any number of conspiracy theories.[9] For example, the number of right-wing extremism-related cases discussed at CHANNEL panels in the UK rose from 189 in 2015/16 to 542 in 2018/19, while Islamist-related[10] cases declined during the same period from 819 to 536.[11]

Similarly, there is also already evidence of an age cohort shift in the CHANNEL data. For example, in the one-year period between April 2018 and March 2019, individuals over the age of thirty accounted for 25 per cent of total referrals to the programme.[12] By comparison, in the period between April 2015 and March 2016, only 18 per cent of referrals were over the age of thirty.[13] The longstanding operating assumption that involvement in violent extremism is primarily or exclusively a 'young person's game' is no longer entirely supported by the data. The trend towards older individuals' late entrance into extremist movements complicates the automatic assumption the education sector or youth-serving agencies should be the default sites of diversionary or intervention programming. While there are perhaps concepts or curricula that could be introduced into schools or youth programmes to build resilience against radicalization to violence over a longer period, there is a pronounced need for more research and policy development targeted towards this older cohort of individuals involved in extremism.

Below we provide three in-depth case studies of one male and two females who were once part of far-right movements in their respective countries. We have anonymized their identities, are not mentioning the countries in which they are based and have redacted other possible identifying information. We argue that a case study approach, one that closely examines an individual's whole life story, provides important insights for practitioners, not only about the entire social ecology that led an individual down a violent path, but also about how difficult it can be to precisely pinpoint when things went wrong.

Case studies

Sarah

Sarah became involved with the white power movement just as she was finishing high school in the mid-2000s. Sarah described her upbringing as at least superficially perfect, saying that she came 'from a loving family. It kind of looks like your typical white picket fence … both parents and then young brother and of course the dog too.'

Upon further reflection, Sarah acknowledged that there were some issues below the surface at home. Her grandfather was an alcoholic and his racism went unchallenged in the family home. Additionally, Sarah realized between the ages of thirteen and fourteen that she was bisexual and did not feel comfortable disclosing this to either of her parents. Sarah also believes, looking back, that she struggled with anxiety and codependence through most of her formative years but never received formal treatment or support.

Things began to take a turn for her towards the end of high school. Her father, who worked in law enforcement, suddenly died. Sarah was especially close with him, and her relationship with her mother began to decline after her father's death. Within a year, Sarah stumbled upon an individual within the movement who later became her recruiter.

Sarah's recounting of her recruitment focused on how the individual went about establishing a connection built on shared interests and trust. Two specific events stood out to Sarah and are important to understanding how she came to be involved. The first being a chance interaction with the recruiter on a Facebook page devoted to metal music, and the second being the way in which the recruiter demonstrated what she perceived at the time as a sense of caring towards her.

I meet my recruiter online and he's sending me all of these national socialist black metal songs. I grew up on metal, so he knew how to twist my interest to fit his own needs. And I'm also a bass player so I could tell that, you know, these guys did have some talent. It's just the lyrics had a really dark undertone to them ... I think the fact that it was so talented – it was really attractive and made the movement look attractive too. We chatted more and more. I for whatever reason felt comfortable telling him about my personal life and then we meet up and stuff, and I got to admit he was pretty obnoxious, but I did find that funny – like, yelling at random people on the street.

So, the way my recruiter really pushed me over the edge. It's a little personal but I'll tell ya anyways. Yeah so, I got touched inappropriately by a guy at my school. At my high school, and the only person that I told about this was my recruiter because I trusted him at the time. So he's sending this guy death threats and stuff online – scared the guy into not even being able to look at me in school. And I'm thinking, wow okay, this guy's awesome. He just protected me. He's intimidating. This is kind of what I want. The way he kind of used this one as a vulnerability of mine. He said, 'well everybody in the movement, they'll take care of you this same way'. And then the coaxing goes further and he's telling me about, 'well what you saw out of this guy is nothing compared to what a coloured person would do to you'. So, yeah, so it was a bunch of fear instilled in me.

Once Sarah joined the movement, she became antagonistic towards both her prior friend group and her mother, and often found herself in protracted ideological debates. This behaviour eventually resulted in her mother kicking her out of the house and onto the streets at age eighteen. Sarah's being made homeless rendered her unable to attend college and narrowed the opportunities she had before her.

This breakdown in her pre-existing relationships also cemented her involvement with the white power movement, which was simultaneously reinforced by the increasingly close friendship with the individual who recruited her. Separating herself from the movement during the initial stages of involvement was then further complicated by the fact that she soon began to date another member of the movement at age eighteen. Sarah's membership in two white power groups – Hammerskins and

Blood & Honour – lasted for a period of roughly four years, during which she moved between both groups somewhat fluidly.

Three factors facilitated Sarah's departure from white supremacist groups. First was her diagnosis and treatment for PTSD. She recalled that through treatment, she came to understand the link between her PTSD and her participation with white supremacist groups: 'For me, everything was tied to stuff that I saw while I was in the white power movement.' Second, Sarah's friend from the movement, who she described as 'the male version of myself', died after being stabbed in a botched home invasion and robbery. Sarah added, 'I saw myself eventually going down the same path as him if I didn't change or leave.' Third, after Sarah moved jobs and began working in construction, she was placed in a crew with mostly Black co-workers. She described how 'they showed me more respect than I'd ever been given in my whole life', and given the risky nature of the job, the need to 'take care of each other' on site.

To leave the movement, Sarah 'fell off the face of the earth. Changed my phone number, took all of [her contacts] off Facebook, made a new profile'. Despite some contacts still being able to find her email and social media accounts, she has blocked any accounts who have sent messages and managed to keep her home address hidden. She continues to work in construction.

Jane

Another of our interviewees, Jane, became involved with Identity Europa, a white nationalist group, in late 2016, officially being accepted into the group at the start of January 2017. Jane noted that to some, her childhood may have appeared idyllic: 'On a good day, I'll tell people I was raised on a farm … every day was beautiful. But the reality of it is … my father was an alcoholic. And I guess I didn't realise how bad it was until one day, I was like, "Yeah my dad only broke the furniture in the basement and beat me with it once – it's not a big deal." And my friend was like, "Once is too much."'

Jane's relationship with her parents was complex. She felt like she spent much of her childhood feeling like the mediator between her parents, who had a tense relationship. 'I was extremely combative with my mother, and I worshipped my father. My dad was never home 'cause he was always drinking.' Her mother, on the other hand, worked three jobs to support the family.

Jane also described a somewhat 'weird dynamic between [her] and [her] brother', as she 'was academically inclined, and I guess I was a cute kid, so I got a lot of attention'. Her younger brother 'was quiet, he was sensitive, and because my parents were so hyper-focused on me being their retirement plan … for my brother they were just kind of like, "If he passes the class, that's good enough. Like, who cares?"' Moreover, as her parents were often out of the house drinking or working, she described how she 'took on the role of provider for him'.

In high school, Jane recalled fitting in pretty well: 'I was able to, you know, mingle with all the groups. I was never part of any group, but I swam, I was on the debate team … I was everything that I chose to be, and I was embraced by every community.' However, she added, 'I personally never felt like I fit anywhere. So I wouldn't say that I was popular, but I wasn't like an outcast.' In her freshman year of high school, however, Jane admitted that she had attempted suicide. She partially attributed this, upon reflection, to her complicated relationship with her parents, as well as a thyroid disorder that disrupted her hormones: 'I just felt things so intensely … I was really upset my first years of high school all the time.' By her second year of high school, she started dating someone and made a close group of friends.

However, her parents decided to move her family to Florida for her last two years of high school. Jane identified this as a very upsetting change for her that affected her behaviour: 'I started smoking weed a lot more, I was doing drugs. I started shoplifting. I was completely defiant to everything … I had no desire to put forth any effort to anything other than being mad at the world.' This move to Florida, as Jane's mother said to her at one point, 'was to save their marriage … my mother point blank said, like, your dad won't know where any of the bars are'. Jane saw this, however, as them running from their problems in their marriage.

This move also strained Jane's relationship further with her mother, with whom she got into a physical altercation after the move to Florida. She described the conflict in her house as 'cyclical'. Both her father and mother would come home 'miserable', and she added she used to think, 'I don't like my mom. And of course, why would anyone like my mom, she's miserable.' Jane 'fucking hated' living in Florida and tried to leave as much as she could. Finally, she came across a job opportunity in South Carolina, where she moved.

A pivotal moment came for Jane when she was twenty-one and had been working in South Carolina for two years. Her father called her while drunk, and Jane recalls how he said on the phone that 'he never loved my mom. They never really wanted to marry. They thought they were supposed to, they never really wanted kids, but that when they had me, he took all the love he should have for a wife and felt it towards me'. Jane's father also asked her to tell her mother that he was having an affair. 'So when my dad called me, I just had this, this moment of like, "I'm finally building this life that I love, I'm dating people, I'm going out, making friends, I'm doing these great things" … and then I just completely spiraled. My dad never sexually abused me, but there was a lot of psychological stuff that went on in there that definitely impacted my relationships with men, my relationships with women, how I saw myself.'

This call was critical for Jane in starting to see her childhood and relationship with her parents in a new light: 'In that very moment, I had realised that, like, my mother and I were never combative, we were competitive … we were in competition with each other.' She added, 'I even knew that growing up, my childhood wasn't normal … but I guess I didn't recognise all the components of it that made it so specifically insular.' Following this call, Jane recalled thinking to herself, 'I'm going to drink about this for a little bit', which, she says, she continued to do for years as her struggle with alcohol escalated.

About three months after the call with her father, Jane met a man with whom she started a relationship and that allowed her to avoid her familial issues. She described how at the time, 'he could do everything … in my head it was just like, "he's the one, he's the stability that I want and I need. And if I want to be anyone, I want to be what he wants"'. When Jane was about twenty-two or twenty-three and early in her relationship with this man, however, she got pregnant, and later, miscarried, which devastated both her and her boyfriend. She began to use more drugs and felt that her boyfriend had emotionally withdrawn from her. About six months following her miscarriage, Jane broke up with her boyfriend, changed her career and got sober, though she remained in periodic contact with her now ex-boyfriend: 'I rebuilt this whole life myself, all with the intention of getting back with him' over about a year or year and a half period.

Finally, in August of 2016, Jane felt 'ready to be with him' again and she and her boyfriend got back together. Almost immediately, she felt that they 'were combative again, he was a little bit more controlling, but in my head, I was like, 'I did all this work and I want to be with you, so I don't care. Like, I will deal with it. I will, you know, just take a couple of cues out of my childhood playbook, and just, you know, do whatever I need to make you okay.' Over the period where Jane had been rebuilding her life, however, her boyfriend had begun frequenting manosphere and white supremacist websites and began powerlifting. Eventually, Jane confronted him over it, and her boyfriend described himself as a fascist. Jane, whose politics were very leftist at the time, broke up with him for about five days. She decided, however, 'I've done all this work to be with him, and I'm going to be with him. So, I guess I'm a fascist too.' This marked a turning point for Jane, where she began to be exposed increasingly to alt-right ideologies.

Jane's boyfriend desired 'a woman who was docile and subservient to him', and she 'wanted to be whatever he wanted [her] to be'. Thus, motivated by a desire to please her boyfriend, Jane applied to join Identity Europa in late 2016. While at first, Jane admitted she had little sincere interest in the group, she eventually became more convinced by the ideology. Though she attempted to leave the group in March, she was convinced to stay by the leadership, who also promoted her to a gatekeeper position in the group, such that she would introduce new members to the group. Throughout her ten-month tenure in Identity Europa, Jane stayed in regular contact with her brother, mother and best friend, who continued to challenge her ideology.

In the second half of her ten months in Identity Europa, Jane began to question their ideology quietly. Following the death of her grandmother in October 2017, Jane realized 'she had nothing to be proud of', and resigned from the group shortly thereafter. At the time, she was living with a prominent member of the alt-right who abused her physically and emotionally, so she slowly planned her escape, which she eventually completed in December of 2017. She joined Life after Hate after her escape, and she plans to attend postsecondary school in the near future.

Tom

Tom, a thirty-four-year-old interviewee from the UK, had helped form the Make Britain Great Again pressure group, which was affiliated with the UK Independence Party (UKIP) and was partially inspired by Donald Trump's slogan. Tom described his childhood growing up in a family of 'hardcore Jehovah's Witnesses' that believe 'school is, sort of, from the devil.' As such, Tom had no formal education as a child, though he was taught to read so that he could read the Bible to his congregation. 'Other than the religion', he described his parents, who had also been born into the same conservative group of Jehovah Witnesses, as 'good parents', referring to some of the conflict Tom experienced later in life as part of his community of Jehovah's Witnesses.

From a young age, Tom had many questions he could not reconcile about his faith, such as 'if God exists, who made God?' However, he was 'told just to, to trust and to wait and "eventually one day you'll understand"'. He also struggled to understand his community's position on education, as from a young age, Tom took a keen interest in computing. Computing, however, 'was viewed as a sort of … they call it worldly, meaning it's the opposite of spiritual … something that could pull you away from God'. Despite this, in his teenage years, Tom managed to build a computer from parts he found in a waste container near his home.

Regarding his adolescence, Tom recalled, 'I never aggressively pushed back through my teenage years … I tried to go along with it, please my parents, this is what I was taught, I really didn't know much about the outside world.' He also began working as a cleaner and started participating in community door-knocking campaigns, similarly 'trying to please [his parents]'. But, into his early twenties, Tom 'found this very difficult because … there's a lot of hypocrisy … you're told, you know, you don't need an education, "just trust in God and Jehovah and He'll provide," and you actually find it's very difficult to pay the bills if you don't have an education, especially as rent's going up and house prices increase'. As such, he had more trouble quashing the questions that had troubled him since his childhood.

Eventually, Tom began to attract attention from the Elders in his religious community as he increasingly began to question their policies in his early twenties, for example, their policy on education which he 'wasn't entirely comfortable with'. He added, 'I wasn't really convinced that the university was worse than the world in general. Like, for a short time, I worked in electronic stores stacking shelves, and those guys were shooting drugs and reading pornography. And I'm told university is dangerous because it has drugs and pornography, but I'm thinking, so does this place I'm working in. So how am I protecting my morality by working in this place instead of a university?' In time, Tom was brought before 'religious courts … a few times … for thinking … for questioning things too much … I was told it was an attitude problem'.

Despite being 'actually fairly passionate about' his faith, 'it just didn't work out'. One event around 2010 in particular catalysed Tom's departure from the group: 'I went over to this [Elder's] house to … help him do something with his … some filing or some paperwork … and his computer history was full of all this pornography, and I noticed, and next thing he was trying to throw me outside of the religion … in case I told anyone. So, that's kind of how I ended up leaving it. Basically, I got chucked out.' After finding this pornography, the community leadership decided that Tom had to leave the community, and that he would be disfellowshipped.[14] At the age of twenty-six, thus, his family shunned him: 'They're literally told to treat you as if you're dead, which they do. So that's my parents, my cousins, uncles, aunts, grandparents, everyone I knew as a child … So, just one day, every single human I knew never spoke to me again.' Tom admitted, 'I don't think it did a lot of good for me psychologically. So that might explain it, I'm not blaming that for what happened later, but I'm thinking that I was in a very bad place.'

Tom found this experience very difficult: 'I was quite lost at first … very bad problems with depression … went to see a therapist who didn't really understand.' His concerns about finances also persisted as his job cleaning was not sufficient to pay his bills. At one point, Tom also became homeless. However, he eventually managed to buy an old computer and began practising coding, before landing an internship role in computer programming about three years following his disfellowshipping. Even for internships afterwards, however, Tom's experience with being disfellowshipped and not having a formal education did not 'really help with job applications ... it was quite difficult, which, um, probably wasn't helping my mental state as well. I had the feeling that the world was against me ... it was really difficult to afford rent anywhere ... to pay the bills sometimes'. These difficulties laid the foundation for Tom's interest in politics, and eventually, his participation with UKIP.

Other experiences Tom had while working started to push him towards politics. For example, he noted, 'when I started doing things like having to take the train to get to work ... you'll pay all this money for this train ticket ... the trains are so crowded, you don't even get a seat and you paid all this money for this ticket, which is a big chunk of your wage. And, um, things like this really started to annoy me. The trains are falling apart'. This in turn, made him feel like 'I had to push back against something'. Similar frustrations with the UK health system also sharpened Tom's interest in politics: 'Health services are meant to be free in this country, but it's actually really poor quality even though you pay for that in your wages. But meanwhile, Google is not paying tax.' Further, Tom described feeling 'very uncomfortable with the world around me ... hearing people talking about things like abortion, which I'd been told was wrong', and generally feeling caught in a 'culture clash' between his childhood experiences and the world outside of his community.

By June of 2016, Tom had joined the Conservative Party in the UK, as he initially felt they cared about 'family values' and addressed some of the economic concerns he had. However, he realized that 'all they're interested in is just free market economics ... you don't really see how it's going to help me or anyone. So, I lost interest in that. And after that, I just switched to the UKIP party.' Shortly thereafter, Tom helped create Make Britain Great Again, the Trump-inspired pressure group affiliated with UKIP.

With UKIP, Tom described feeling 'a sense of camaraderie. They were friendly, go and get a drink at the pub. And I didn't really know anyone outside the religion ... I enjoyed their company initially until the infighting started ... they seemed to understand some of the things I was frustrated with.' Tom claimed that initially, UKIP was more focused on economic issues, such as skyrocketing housing prices, low wages and unfair taxes. Moreover, UKIP appeared to stand for 'traditional family values' vis-à-vis issues such as abortion (which Tom added they actually did not), so he was 'drawn towards that'. He admitted that despite his fraught relationship with his religious upbringing, he still held many of the values of his community and sought those in UKIP. Later, UKIP became more outspoken against terrorism and critical of Islam, which aligned with Tom's views. Tom was 'uncomfortable about the terrorist attacks happening' in the UK, and 'thought a high number [of Muslims] were radical', though he claimed he 'never had a problem with moderate Islam'.

His motivation to create Make Britain Great Again was inspired also by Donald Trump's rhetoric and the American, Republican brand of conservatism. Tom recalled being 'drawn to the idea of Trump, because he seemed like this rebellious person who was questioning the establishment and going to shake things up'. Tom was also 'feeling very uncomfortable with political correctness and [Trump] was questioning that'. Trump's rhetoric about bringing manufacturing jobs back from China to the United States also resonated with Tom, who had seen a similar haemorrhage of mining jobs in Wales, where he spent part of his childhood. Furthermore, he described how the American Republicans 'cultural views are very similar to those I grew up with. I mean, they are, like, very anti-abortion ... I sort of connected at that time with that very much, having recently left that religious environment ... So with MBGA, I was pushing for some sort of cultural conservatism, not racial, just cultural, and that I wanted it to be about traditional family'.

About two years ago, Tom left the party after a highly publicized altercation. Prior to this point, he had also begun experiencing significant conflict with other MGBA and UKIP members, as the leadership had started to welcome Generation Identity, an explicitly white nationalist group, into the youth wing of UKIP. Since leaving UKIP and MGBA, he has started studying at university, and he hopes to use his education to 'atone for what I've done', perhaps even by contributing in some way to a P/CVE initiative.

Diversion in hindsight

As the case studies above demonstrate, the process of radicalization and of becoming involved with violent extremism is marked by contingency and variability. Reflecting on their involvement, many former extremists we have spoken with alluded to the highly individualized and seemingly random process of becoming involved. As no two individuals join a movement in exactly the same way, a generic or 'one-size-fits-all' approach to diversion is unlikely to be effective.

Most of the former extremists we interviewed had a somewhat fatalistic view of their involvement. There were very few formers we spoke with who could readily identify the contours of a programme or piece of curriculum which they thought would have successfully prevented their involvement or promoted their disengagement at an early stage. This was true even for formers now involved in P/CVE work. When asked what could have prevented him from joining the violent far-right, one respondent answered: 'Nothing. I don't think there's anything that could have stopped me. Yeah. I don't think there was anything.' Others expressed similar scepticism:

I don't think so because I was already involved with doing drugs when I was, you know, growing up and I went to prison, there was no stopping in going into prison. I did what I did, and I went to prison. So, I mean regardless, I was getting ... I was bound to join some kind of organization.

Another noted:

I don't think I really, really grasped what it was that I was doing when I became involved with it. So, like, I can't really say for sure if there is one thing or another that could've stopped me from getting involved with it.

Even when individuals we interviewed offered up some suggestions as to what effective programming could look like, several remarked that they did not think it would have worked for them. As one noted:

> *No. No, I had been in politics since I was like 12 or 13. Yeah. And with music and it just, I think it just pulled me in and that, for me personally, no. For other kids, probably but for me, no.*

Jane, introduced above, noted:

> *When you first learn all this stuff and you first start to believe it, it's, I mean, it really does feel like the veil has been lifted. Like, it's just like this weird, miraculous thing where you're just like, 'Oh my God, I have been asleep. I am a sheep, I am, I am a fool to media. Whatever the TV tells me, I do.' And I thought I was above it. I didn't watch TV. I listened to NPR ... I thought I was smart enough for all of it ... Outside of myself being honest with myself about it, I don't think [diversion would have worked].*

Jane did tentatively suggest that more accessible online content about people who had formerly been involved in extremist movements may had been helpful for her later on in her radicalization.

> *I wish I would have looked up [the movement online]. Well, I guess at the time, and that's kind of why I do interviews and why I'm doing media, is because there wasn't anyone who had left the alt-right at that point and said, 'well, this is what it's really like.' You know, all of these, these cute little euphemisms and all the rhetoric that they use, it is all bullshit. It is all violence. So, I think if there was someone like that, that could have helped.*

This echoes other calls by former members of extremist groups, who advocate for informal, interpersonal relationships with other former members as a diversion strategy.

Conclusion

In this chapter, the authors have presented data from interviews with former members of extremist groups, to explore the factors that contributed to their radicalization, as well as diversion tactics that may have been useful. Generally, interviewees identified a whole host of factors that contributed to their radicalization, from dysfunctional family relationships to a poor sense of self. Moreover, the interviewees broadly claimed that diversion strategies would have been largely ineffective for them once they had started on the pathway to radicalization. In summary, these results suggest that primary and tertiary interventions remain more promising for preventing and responding to violent extremist groups, rather than interventions at the secondary level – interventions targeted at individuals who have already begun to radicalize and who are 'at-risk', but who have not yet engaged in criminality. As the authors argue, the data here points towards the challenge of secondary interventions.

However, two elements of this studies' methodology limit the conclusions made here. First, the sample of interviewees, by virtue of being former members, biases the data towards individuals who were *not* diverted from radicalization, rather than individuals who may have been successfully diverted. As such, the conclusion that diversionary programming is of limited utility is nuanced by the population sampled who may have been, for various reasons, less likely to be convinced by diversion tactics. Second, given the retrospective nature of the interviews, participants may have been biased towards claiming that there were no interventions that would have been effective in diverting them from the path to radicalization. Still, with these limitations in mind, three key takeaways emerged for human service providers interested in contributing to diversionary interventions.

First, human service providers should understand the broad and varied root causes that may drive individuals to join extremist violence and seek to design diversionary programming in a way that can be flexible and adaptive to individual clients' needs as opposed to presupposing what services or supports individuals may need. While practitioners may read the above accounts and see commonalities between these individuals and clients in other fields they may have interacted with, discounting the uniqueness of the ideological and political grievances these individuals hold may impede effective programme design. While a lack of sense of self and belonging or complicated family relationships emerged frequently as themes that contributed to joining extremist groups, they clearly are not specific to individuals who join extremist groups. In other words, most people who experience similar difficulties *do not* often turn to extremist organizations.

Second, while diversionary programming is important, upstream or primary interventions on the part of human service providers can and should be considered as a part of a comprehensive terrorism prevention strategy. For example, programming that offers community support or counselling for family-related conflicts may have been effective in diverting some of the interviewees away from the radicalization pathway before they started onto it.

Third, human service providers should appreciate the difficulty in intervening once the radicalization process had begun and prepare for what can be an intensive intervention. Many interviewees noted strong scepticism that diversion programming would have helped them to avoid joining an extremist group. Moreover, family members and close friends were often ineffective in diverting individuals from radicalization once they had started. As such, it should be no surprise that human service providers may also have a difficult time encouraging diversion, given the determination of some individuals to join such groups, and the difficulties that those who were close to them experienced in encouraging diversion. Broadening the remit of a diversion programme to include providing support to family members of individuals radicalizing is crucial.

Diversion represents a promising new approach to P/CVE by partially circumventing the specificity issue and by offering support to individuals before they engage in criminality or violence. However, diversion should not be understood as a panacea and, in some ways, working with clients in the secondary space may be more challenging than working with those in the tertiary space. Practitioners designing diversionary programming must think through how to provide tailored, often intensive, interventions to clients and their families to raise the probability of success.

Notes

1   Shandon Harris-Hogan, Kate Barrelle and Andrew Zammit, 'What Is Countering Violent Extremism? Exploring CVE Policy and Practice in Australia', *Behavioral Sciences of Terrorism and Political Aggression* 8, no. 1 (2016): 6–24; Stevan Weine, et al., 'Addressing Violent Extremism as Public Health Policy and Practice', *Behavioral Sciences of Terrorism and Political Aggression* 9, no. 3 (2017): 208–21, https://doi.org/10.1080/19434472.2016.1198413.

2   Some models include 'primordial prevention', which operates at the level below primary, again as a population-level intervention. The distinction between primordial prevention and primary prevention in the context of CVE however is unclear.

3   *Countering Violent Extremism through Public Health: Proceedings of a Workshop* (Washington, DC: The National Academies Press, 2017), 63–8, https://doi.org/10.17226/24638.

4   *Countering Violent Extremism through Public Health: Proceedings of a Workshop*, 63–8.

5   Eric Rosand, 'Taking the Off-ramp: A Path to Preventing Terrorism', *War on the Rocks*, 2016, https://warontherocks.com/2016/07/taking-the-off-ramp-a-path-to-preventing-terrorism/

6   Rosand, 'Taking the Off-Ramp'.

7   Stevan M. Weine, 'Rehabilitating the Islamic State's Women and Children Returnees in Kazakhstan', *JustSecurity*, 2019, https://www.justsecurity.org/67694/rehabilitating-the-islamic-states-women-and-children-returnees-in-kazakhstan/

8   Public Safety Canada, 'Intervention Programs in Canada', 2019, https://www.publicsafety.gc.ca/cnt/bt/cc/ntrvntn-en.aspx

9   Amarnath Amarasingam and Marc-Andre Argentino, 'The QAnon Conspiracy Theory: A Security Threat in the Making?' *CTC Sentinel* 13, no. 7 (2020), https://ctc.westpoint.edu/the-qanon-conspiracy-theory-a-security-threat-in-the-making/; Organization for the Prevention of Violence, 'Evolve Program: The First Two Years' (Edmonton, Alberta, 2021), https://preventviolence.ca/publication/evolve-program-the-first-two-years/

10 'Islamist' reflects the Home Office's terminology.

11 Home Office, 'Individuals Referred to and Supported through the Prevent Programme, April 2018 to March 2019', 2019, Annex A.D.03, https://www.gov.uk/government/statistics/individuals-referred-to-and-supported-through-the-prevent-programme-april-2018-to-march-2019; Home Office, 'Individuals Referred to and Supported through the Prevent Programme, April 2015 to March 2016', 2017, Annex A.D.03, https://www.gov.uk/government/statistics/individuals-referred-to-and-supported-through-the-prevent-programme-april-2015-to-march-2016

12 Home Office, 'Individuals Referred to and Supported through the Prevent Programme, April 2018 to March 2019', Annex A.D.01.

13   Home Office, 'Individuals Referred to and Supported through the Prevent
      Programme, April 2015 to March 2016', Annex A.D.01.
14   *Disfellowshipping* is a process unique to Jehovah's Witnesses, but can be understood
      as similar to excommunication.

Bibliography

Amarasingam, Amarnath and Argentino, Marc-Andre. 'The QAnon Conspiracy Theory:
    A Security Threat in the Making?" *CTC Sentinel* 13, no. 7 (2020). Available at: https://
    ctc.westpoint.edu/the-qanon-conspiracy-theory-a-security-threat-in-the-making/.
Countering Violent Extremism through Public Health: Proceedings of a Workshop.
    Washington, DC: The National Academies Press, 2017. https://doi.org/10.17226/24638.
Harris-Hogan, Shandon, Barrelle, Kate and Zammit, Andrew. 'What Is Countering
    Violent Extremism? Exploring CVE Policy and Practice in Australia'. *Behavioral
    Sciences of Terrorism and Political Aggression* 8, no. 1 (2016): 6–24.
Home Office. 'Individuals Referred to and Supported through the Prevent Programme,
    April 2015 to March 2016', 2017. Available at: https://www.gov.uk/government/
    statistics/individuals-referred-to-and-supported-through-the-prevent-programme-
    april-2015-to-march-2016.
Home Office. 'Individuals Referred to and Supported through the Prevent Programme,
    April 2018 to March 2019'. 2019. Available at: https://www.gov.uk/government/
    statistics/individuals-referred-to-and-supported-through-the-prevent-programme-
    april-2018-to-march-2019.
Organization for the Prevention of Violence. 'Evolve Program: The First Two Years'.
    Edmonton, Alberta, 2021. Available at: https://preventviolence.ca/publication/evolve-
    program-the-first-two-years/.
Public Safety Canada. 'Intervention Programs in Canada', 2019. Available at: https://www.
    publicsafety.gc.ca/cnt/bt/cc/ntrvntn-en.aspx.
Rosand, Eric. 'Taking the Off-Ramp: A Path to Preventing Terrorism'. *War on the Rocks*,
    2016. Available at: https://warontherocks.com/2016/07/taking-the-off-ramp-a-path-to-
    preventing-terrorism/.
Weine, Stevan, Eisenman, David P., Kinsler, Janni, Glik, Deborah C., and Polutnik, Chloe.
    'Addressing Violent Extremism as Public Health Policy and Practice'. *Behavioral
    Sciences of Terrorism and Political Aggression* 9, no. 3 (2017): 208–21. Available at:
    https://doi.org/10.1080/19434472.2016.1198413.
Weine, Stevan M. 'Rehabilitating the Islamic State's Women and Children Returnees
    in Kazakhstan'. *JustSecurity*, 2019. Available at: https://www.justsecurity.org/67694/
    rehabilitating-the-islamic-states-women-and-children-returnees-in-kazakhstan/.

13

School-based prevention of radicalization and extremism involving former extremists: Insights gained from practice and research in Germany

Maria Walsh and Antje Gansewig

Introduction

Like a host of other countries, Germany has been confronted with extremist movements. Besides counterterrorism, preventive and interventive measures offered by the state and civil society have been employed to counteract efforts to undermine democracy. Since the early 2000s, former extremists have played a role in these efforts. This chapter is primarily concerned with 'off-ramp' interventions involving former extremists in Germany.[1]

Background: Political extremism and preventing violent extremism in Germany

For several years, political extremism in Germany has manifested as five main types, with varying degrees of intensity.[2] These are right- and left-wing extremism, Islamist extremism, the so-called Reich Citizen ('*Reichsbürger*') and Sovereign Citizen ('*Selbstverwalter*') movements, and extremist groups of foreigners. Each type manifests in several different ways, with various objectives.[3] Right- and left-wing extremism as well as Islamist extremism are united by the overriding goal of the partial or complete elimination of the democratic state and society. While right-wing extremists, with their particularly nationalistic, anti-Semitic, racist and xenophobic worldview, strive for an ethnically and racially defined 'national community',[4] left-wing extremists aim for a 'communist system or rather a "domination-free" anarchist society'.[5] Islamist extremism, with its various forms, is a religion-based type of political extremism that with its rejection of secularism pursues the subjugation of the entire political and social life to religion-based norms.[6] The Reich Citizen and Sovereign Citizen movements categorically reject the German constitutional state. While Reich Citizens deny the legitimacy of the Federal Republic of Germany or its existence, Sovereign Citizens are convinced that they can effectively secede from the Federal Republic and declare their land a sovereign state territory.[7] Foreign-linked extremist groups – communities that have a strong connection to foreign countries without being associated with Islamist extremist ideologies, and where right-wing and left-wing extremist ideological elements as well as separatist aspirations can be found (e.g., the Kurdistan Workers' Party, the Ülkücü movement) – want to achieve a change in their home countries, sometimes through violent activities there. They support their home organizations through propaganda and by supplying money, material and newly recruited fighters from Germany.[8]

Following the xenophobic riots in the years after German reunification,[9] the first state programmes and measures to prevent right-wing extremism were launched in 1992. Since 2001, these initiatives have also taken place in the field of democracy promotion.[10] Measures to promote democracy are 'offers, structures, and procedures that strengthen democratic thinking and action, promote a democratic political culture based on the value-based constitution, and stimulate corresponding educational processes and forms of engagement'.[11] Notwithstanding the fact that the main focus is on the prevention of right-wing extremism, since 2010 there have similarly been prevention initiatives against the anti-democratic forms of left-wing extremism and Islamist extremism. Since 2015, initiatives against other extremist movements, such as Kurdish and Turkish ultranationalism, have also been undertaken.[12]

In addition to the work of the intelligence services, the police and the judicial system, the prevention of radicalization and extremism has established itself as an integral part of German security architecture.[13] The federal government defines the prevention of extremism as 'measures that prevent and counteract the rejection of the values of the Basic Law and the democratic constitutional state and, in this context, also serve the security of citizens'.[14] The prevention of political extremism in Germany is understood as a task for society as a whole, in which joint action by state and civil society/non-governmental organizations at the federal, state and local levels is indispensable.[15] Consequently, there are numerous state and civil society structures and services focusing on primary, secondary and tertiary prevention at both the federal and state level, as well as at the local and regional levels.[16, 17] In Germany, civil society and non-governmental organizations have a significant role in the prevention of extremism. Most projects carried out by civil society actors are (partially) financed by the state. According to a survey by the German Federal Criminal Police Office on extremism prevention initiatives, for example, at the end of 2018, 60 per cent of the 1,642 initiatives surveyed were implemented at the municipal and state levels by civil society organizations.[18]

The most recent inventory of extremism prevention within Germany concentrated on measures and projects that (1) addressed the phenomenon of right-wing extremism and Islamist extremism; (2) were classified as needing secondary or tertiary prevention;[19] (3) worked directly with persons at risk of radicalization, radicalized persons eager to exit an extremist community, or former extremists; and (4) were either state-run (e.g., disengagement and deradicalization programmes of the Office for the Protection of the Constitution) or supported by public funds.[20] The fourth criterion assumed that basic transparency would accompany these activities, which, however, turned out to be unfounded due to the low willingness of practitioners in the field to participate in the survey.[21] At the beginning of 2018, the inventory identified ninety-six projects and measures that were engaged in secondary or tertiary prevention addressing right-wing extremism and Islamist extremism. This revealed an approximately equal distribution of projects in the areas of right-wing extremism (44.5 per cent) and Islamist extremism (42.7 per cent). The remaining projects pursued a cross-phenomenon approach, meaning that they addressed both right-wing extremism and Islamist extremism.

Quality assurance and evaluation

There is a general research gap in the prevention of (violent) extremism because most measures to prevent and counter violent extremism (P/CVE) have not been evaluated empirically.[22] This also applies to Germany, where there appears to be a considerable need for optimization regarding the scientific monitoring and review of P/CVE measures.[23] The findings of a study conducted by the Federal Criminal Police Office reflect this gap. Of the 721 prevention projects carried out in 2014 and 2015 (mostly nationwide projects; 47 per cent state and 53 per cent civic), only 59 per cent provided information on whether an evaluation had already been carried out or was still being planned. Apart from the state initiatives in the context of the federal programme of the Federal Ministry for Family Affairs, Senior Citizens, Women and Youth (*Bundesministerium für Familie, Senioren, Frauen und Jugend*, BMFSFJ), which is accompanied by a programme evaluation and whose results are available to the public, only a few of the evaluation concepts and results could be investigated. Therefore, the authors concluded: 'This makes a concrete assessment of existing projects and learning from each other enormously difficult or even impossible'.[24] In addition, Meier's study points to deficits in the field of P/CVE: On the one hand, the field proved to be opaque (e.g., regarding case numbers, concepts and methods) and – despite being financed by public funds or located with public agencies – practitioners were reluctant to participate in empirical research. On the other hand, deficits were revealed in the establishment of and compliance with quality standards. For example, the evaluation of the programme of the BMFSFJ, which has been carried out for years, refers to possible chains of impact using the logical model as an evaluation instrument. However, this approach does not allow any conclusions to be made about the actual impact of prevention efforts.[25]

Although the federal government acknowledged the need for evaluation research years ago[26] and scientific monitoring of prevention and intervention measures has been increasingly recognized as a field of activity in recent years, the situation is far from satisfactory. This is even more surprising as the accompanying research on projects and initiatives serves the purpose of quality control and is the only way to investigate what the effects are and what can be achieved with certain P/CVE interventions. In Germany, an adequate nationwide evaluation culture around P/CVE has yet to be established. This has a clear requirement for external processes and impact evaluations, followed by the publication of results.[27] However, realistic expectations should be attached to it. In particular, impact studies of measures targeting extremism are subject to special challenges and require suitable funding and time.[28] As Meier rightly points out, it is not a question of initiatives committed to the idea of P/CVE in their objectives, but ensuring that these objectives are verifiably achieved.[29] In this context, ethical considerations should also be taken into account: often, P/CVE interventions take place in an obligatory or coercive context – for example, compulsory school events, prison programmes or probation orders. From an ethical point of view, this is justifiable under certain conditions if the respective intervention has been proven to cause no harm.[30]

Former extremists in P/CVE

Former extremists (especially former right-wing extremists and Islamist extremists) have been in the public eye in Germany as well as in other countries[31] for several years. They write autobiographies, appear on talk shows on television or run their own channels on social media, and are involved in P/CVE. Apart from Reich Citizens and Sovereign Citizens, former adherents of all extremist movements in Germany are active in P/CVE, with former right-wing extremists being represented for the longest period and the most frequently.[32] While there are former extremists who individually conduct their own P/CVE offerings unconnected with any institutional affiliation or official initiative, the vast majority of them are institutionally linked to deradicalization and disengagement programmes. These initiatives are organized in Germany by both the state and civil society. In addition to their work in CVE (including within prison walls), formers are particularly involved in school-based and extracurricular PVE with children and juveniles.[33] Such arrangements are known to at least three state institutions; two of them are affiliated with State Offices for the Protection of the Constitution and one with a district police department in cooperation with one city administration.[34] The best-known and oldest provider is the civil society initiative 'EXIT-Germany'.[35] The public relations and educational work of and with former right-wing extremists is controversial in both civil society and state deradicalization and disengagement programmes. One of the main criticisms is that this type of work can entail an increased security risk for the former extremists and that it would make it difficult for them to build a new life.[36]

Most prevention interventions in schools with former extremists in Germany focus on a primary preventive target group;[37] they are mainly carried out by male former right-wing extremists in all school types and usually as one-off events from seventh grade onwards (where the age of the students is approximately thirteen years).[38] The duration, costs, use of media reporting, and the methods and content – regardless of biographical individuality – of the individual interventions are diverse. Furthermore, such information is rarely publicly available.[39] This lack of transparency is reflected in the fact that, usually, no detail about the former extremists, project concepts, target groups, impact assumptions and what was tried during the interventions is publicly accessible. The same is true for information on cost aspects, quality assurance, evaluations and how these interventions impacted the students. This lack of transparency extends to the absence of any published evaluations, notwithstanding the fact that evaluations or their results are being used to advertise certain projects.[40]

Research findings on the impact of school PVE involving former extremists

To date, no scientific study of the activities of former extremists in school PVE has concluded, based on reliable data, that this involvement has lasting extremism- or crime-preventing effects on school students. Few meaningful surveys of students' assessments of these interventions are available. Therefore, the impact of these preventive interventions – of either a primary or a secondary preventive orientation – on school students remains unclear.[41] Given this gap, between 2017 and 2019, the authors conducted a research project on school-based PVE involving former extremists in Germany at the German National Centre for Crime Prevention.[42] Various questions were approached through multiple methods and from different perspectives. Besides conducting a survey of the status quo of relevant activities by means of semi-structured interviews,[43] we carried out a nationwide postal survey of relevant state actors and a media analysis.[44] Finally, we undertook an impact and process evaluation of school-based PVE intervention of a former right-wing extremist.

The investigated primary prevention intervention is oriented in particular to the biography of the former and concerns, for instance, the topics of right-wing extremism and crime in general. It comprised four school hours and had the goal of preventing right-wing extremism, violence and crime. In conducting the intervention, the former extremist used a schedule he had drafted himself. Methodologically, the intervention is primarily focused on the former's monologue; at some points, the students were motivated to participate actively through, for example, asking direct questions of the former extremist as well as role-playing. According to the former right-wing extremist, he had been living in several violence-prone subcultures for twenty years. Today, he is in his forties and admits to having been involved in a variety of right-wing extremist contexts for over ten years where, among other things, he sold associated music and led an active group. After that, he became the leader of an outlaw motorcycle club and turned to organized crime.[45] As reasons for distancing himself from right-wing extremism and crime, he mentions, *inter alia*, psychological and physical impairments and quarrels within the respective subcultures. He states that he voluntarily underwent psychotherapy while in prison; in this he found the support he needed to reflect on his previous life, leading him to disengage and deradicalize. After his release from prison, he started conducting P/CVE initiatives not linked to any institutional affiliation in the summer of 2016.[46]

The evaluation study took place in fifty ninth-grade classes (average age of students: fifteen years) at public community schools in a randomized control group design.[47] Data were collected in writing in both the experimental and control group before the intervention (t_0: EG: $n = 297$; CG: $n = 247$) and, on average, five and a half months after it was carried out (t_1: EG: $n = 300$; CG: $n = 264$). Moreover, the experimental group received a questionnaire after the intervention ($n = 490$) as well as further questions about the intervention and the referee at time t_1 ($n = 448$). In addition, we carried out systematic participatory observations of seven interventions.[48] The results of the impact study did not indicate any influence of the PVE intervention investigated on right-wing extremist attitudes, violence and delinquency. Furthermore, no significant differences were found between the participants and the control group regarding an increase in knowledge of or non-school preoccupation with the topic of right-wing extremism.[49] The findings of the student surveys and participating observations delineate a differentiated picture of student perspectives and specifics: for example, most of the 490 young people rated the former extremist (90 per cent) and the intervention (81 per cent) as 'very good' and 'good'. Female students tended to give more positive assessments. The format of the event and the former extremist were well received by most of the students.[50] When asked what they liked about the intervention (*n* = 464), 65.5 per cent of the answers referred to former-specific components (authenticity, appearance and presentation style). Content-related aspects and learning effects played marginal roles, at 10 per cent and 5 per cent, respectively; 16 per cent of all respondents and a quarter of the girls felt uncomfortable at one point during the workshop. This discomfort was mostly triggered by content related to violence.[51] Both positive and critical aspects were identified in the participating observations: for example, the former extremist's performance (e.g., using language to which the youth could relate directly) was seen as being specifically adapted to the target group with the aim of reducing distance. However, the occasional detailed depictions of violence and the use of crude language (including swearing and insensitive terms) by the speaker conflicted with his position as a role model.[52]

Nevertheless, the content analyses of the students' answers and the impact study identified no fascination with a right-wing and/or criminal lifestyle, nor were there any indications in students, e.g., with a migrant biography of possible traumatization from discussions of right-wing violence or re-traumatization in those previously affected by right-wing violence.[53] It should be noted that, in contrast to common practice, participation was voluntary and based on the consent of parents or guardians, which might have led to a pre-selection of the participating students. Consequently – in addition to assuming that positive effects would occur and while being aware that no effects might occur – the possibility of negative effects must be taken into account.[54]

Challenges of involving former extremists in school PVE

Biography-based interventions – that is, interventions largely based on biographical narratives – in school education are not only common in the prevention of extremism but can also be found, for example, in the teaching of history or the prevention of violence and addiction.[55] The assumption often seems to prevail that a topic could be taught particularly well by people who have personal experience of it. In this context, authenticity and insider knowledge are often cited as unique selling points. According to a staff member of a civil society deradicalization and disengagement programme who accompanies former right-wing extremists to school-based PVEs, for example, involving former extremists in PVE is the best way to illustrate the dangers and associated personal consequences of right-wing extremism 'through lively narratives based on facts and experiences'.[56] This view implies that inevitably positive effects will occur through encounters and personal narration, though this ignores the characteristics and challenges of biographical work. These consist, for instance, of the individual biographical character and the subjectivity of the narratives, which are influenced by processing, the current perspective and the (anticipated) reactions of the audience. Moreover, autobiographical reporting is always personally motivated, guided by interests, and influenced by one's own self-image. An inherent challenge of personal encounters is the inhibition of critical questioning of what is heard.[57]

As stated in the European Commission's Radicalisation Awareness Network (RAN) standards on the use of former right-wing extremists, motives based on attention or self-promotion might counteract the actual goals of prevention activities.[58] Regarding former extremists active in prevention work, a review of motives would accordingly be appropriate. Drawing on the research results of Maruna on former offenders, it could be assumed that making amends often plays a role in the decision to become involved in prevention.[59] However, it cannot be ruled out that other motives could play a part, depending on the personality of the individual, for example. Indications of this are to be found in individual statements by former extremists (e.g., 'Working in prevention is helpful for me, too. [...]. The appreciation and the applause, an awesome feeling.'[60]) and correspondingly appear in the media analysis conducted by the authors (representation as a former leader, advertising aspects, etc.[61]). Therefore, the motives and the personalities of the former extremists should be considered when selecting them for P/CVE. Moreover, it should be noted that not every former extremist may be suitable for every target group.[62]

As Koehler notes, there has been a development over the last few years of establishing 'professional former extremists' who have made their past the basis of their professional existence and status. Inherent in this is the insoluble dilemma that working in the field of prevention requires appropriate vocational training; however, such training increases the probability that formers will turn their past into a career.[63] The results of the media analysis additionally pointed towards professional formers.[64] Through the publication of autobiographies, the operation of channels on social media and TV appearances, some former extremists in Germany have become public figures who are frequently described as 'extremism or terrorism experts' and who are in some cases regarded as celebrities.[65] This promotion of former extremists may run counter to the actual prevention goal; after all, the message conveyed here is that membership in an extremist community or a criminal milieu could make one rich and famous after one has left it.

With regard to the involvement of former extremists in school PVE, the danger of a (further) fascination of the students through personal encounters and narrations from the time in the community has been noted.[66] For example, an employee of a civil society deradicalization and disengagement programme, which has been conducting workshops in schools with former right-wing extremists for years, states that they refrained from conducting them in schools where students with affinities have been identified or specific incidents have occurred. The reasons for this are, on the one hand, that 'talking sense, despite the best of intentions, is not effective with young people'. On the other hand, there was 'the danger that young people with affinities would develop even more fascination for the community and its ideology'.[67] A similar situation was reported years ago from the civil society initiative 'Exit-Sweden':

> For many years Exit was recognisable to mainly students in schools because of numerous lectures about what it is like to be a former Nazi and the road to transformation. But by this time Exit started to question this work for many reasons. It can serve as a small flame that dies out after we leave the school. It might not change anything, says [a staff member of the disengagement programme]. It has been suggested that lectures in schools with former criminals, Nazis and drug addicts sometimes can be counter-productive: some listeners get to be more fascinated than discouraged, in spite of good intentions to show the negative sides.[68]

Such fascination could lead to the intervention having a counter-productive effect. Besides, there are the considerations of partly critical content being conveyed, such as detailed depictions of violence and use of inappropriate language.[69] The possibility that students might be enthusiastic about the former extremist himself, even beyond the encounter at school, is illustrated by the results of the evaluation study conducted by the authors as well: the former extremist was particularly mentioned in the answers to the question of what the students liked most about the intervention.[70] In addition, five and a half months after the intervention, on average, half of the students interviewed ($n = 231$) stated that they had started following the former extremist on social media. Eight per cent of the respondents contacted him via social media.[71]

Off-ramp interventions

Most of the school-based interventions involving former extremists in Germany can be classified as primary prevention: that is, aimed at all students in a class or grade. Some interventions, however, are directed at people who are at risk of radicalization or take place because of issues observed at a school and are thus classified as off-ramp interventions. Let us now examine two model projects from the field of off-ramp interventions in more detail. These projects were considered because relevant information on them is publicly available. Both model projects are official secondary prevention interventions carried out for students. The projects mainly intend to prevent radicalization using biographical narrations of former extremists. One of them targets right-wing extremism and the other left-wing extremism. Both are located in the area of the federal programme of the BMFSFJ whose target group consists of children and young people 'who are in the process of becoming radicalized or who develop characteristics of attitudes hostile to democracy, who are members or sympathizers of correspondingly radicalized cliques, groups, or communities, or who display violent behaviour'.[72]

Model project for the prevention of right-wing extremism

The model project 'Borderline Experiences' ('*Grenzerfahrungen*') for the prevention of radicalization was carried out by an independent organization for youth, social and educational work. It was funded between 2017 and December 2019 by the BMFSFJ. The project was executed by one trained social worker and one former right-wing extremist who is now 'after over twenty years within the community' working 'with young people as a deradicalization and anti-violence trainer'.[73] It was conducted 'in schools of all types from Grade Eight onwards' (age approximately fourteen years); it intended to educate students on the subject of extremism, teach them democratic values and inform them 'about content, methods and dangers of the right-wing extremist community'.[74]

This model project was investigated in the context of the programme evaluation of the federal ministry. Overall, the project was classified as 'knowledge transfer to raise awareness' by the evaluators.[75] In addition, it was concluded that a further 'involvement of young people regarding their own contents and interests, and the gathering of their own experiences, cannot be achieved. A (guided) reflection on the knowledge and thus a further transfer into the world of the young people take place only very partially and is (mainly) left to themselves at the end' of the project.[76] Moreover, the evaluation results show the project's 'universal approach': the former extremist and the social worker themselves consider 'all young people to be potentially at risk (…) of slipping into extremist structures'.[77] Accordingly, the project focuses on primary prevention, despite its official secondary prevention orientation.[78] Therefore, the practical application stands in contrast both to the funding guidelines of the programme and to the target group specified in the project description.[79] However, further information on the biographical background of the former extremist involved, the theoretical background of the concept, quality standards, mechanics, and the process within the intervention, or the project's results, is not publicly available. Even though the final brochure on the project concludes that 'in particular the biographically authentic background of the former extremist and the pedagogical support of the employee on site proved to be an effective method of prevention work',[80] neither the evaluation nor any other source available from those who were responsible or the funders provide a justification for or proof of this statement.

Model project for the prevention of left-wing extremism

One of the few model projects in the field of left-wing extremism prevention in Germany is meant to address 'young people at risk'; it aims to educate them through various seminars about left-wing extremism and violence. The project 'Left-wing militancy in history and the present. Educating young people at risk about left-wing extremism and violence' (*'Linke Militanz in Geschichte und Gegenwart. Aufklärung gefährdeter Jugendlicher über Linksextremismus und Gewalt'*) – which is affiliated with a memorial located on the site of the main remand centre of the Ministry of State Security of the former German Democratic Republic – primarily addresses young people between sixteen and twenty-seven years of age. Since 2011, the BFMSFJ has funded the seminars.[81] A former left-wing extremist was involved in the module 'Left-wing extremism today – Contemporary witnesses' report' (*'Linksextremismus in Deutschland – Zeitzeugen berichten'*) between 2017 and December 2019. The module's description included the statement: 'Nothing is as exciting as meeting contemporary witnesses. Victims, police officers, and former extremists narrate their personal experiences with the left-wing extremist milieu'.[82] Regarding the former extremist, the engagement and disengagement processes, his associated feelings, and his current view of his past engagement and of the left-wing community in general have been dealt with, but his criminal actions have not been addressed.[83]

The authors interviewed the staff of this project for the research project on former extremists in prevention work.[84] According to the information provided by those carrying out the project, the model project uses a 'peer group approach', which is intended to promote independent examination of the topic, dialogue and discussion, while at the same time raising awareness. Staff refer to it as a 'knowledge project' with the primary goal of imparting knowledge, especially for school classes.[85] Furthermore, flyers advertising the project state it is 'for students and other interested parties'.[86] Apparently, the model project, which is explicitly publicly funded within the framework of secondary prevention and is intended to address young people at risk, addresses regular school classes. It does not seem to reach the intended target group of the project. An additional point of concern is that no information is publicly available on the former extremist involved nor the theoretical background of the concept, mechanics and process in the intervention, or how well the project worked. Even though the module was advertised with the statement that the encounter with the so-called contemporary witnesses and their stories 'makes an abstract topic come alive, the examination of which is particularly sustainable',[87] no justification or proof of this by the responsible or funding parties can be found. This does not only apply to the module but to the project as a whole. Even though Hildebrand and Prause reveal numbers of participants and refer to feedback surveys and evaluations, they do not address any results. Instead, they make assumptions and claims regarding the impact of their project, such as: 'It can be assumed that for some young people – although it is difficult to measure – it was possible to promote "an exit prior to an entry" into the left-wing extremist community, and to lessen radicalization processes'.[88]

Reaching the target group

The definition of the actual target group is crucial. As the two examples show, projects are labelled by those responsible as secondary prevention without adequate conceptual adaptation and despite addressing regular school classes. One could assume that this labelling is related to funding practice. Some results of the aforementioned research project conducted by the authors indicate an undifferentiated application of primary preventive interventions as secondary prevention.[89] In this respect, the first question that arises is how exactly persons at risk of radicalization, or who already have some affinities, are to be identified and classified.[90] In this case, the problem of differentiation leads to a shift of what is actually a secondary prevention objective into the area of primary prevention. Such shifting appears to play a role in comparable interventions in other countries as well.[91] Fischer et al., for example, describe such shifts as problematic, since the target groups are indirectly accused of unlawful behaviour; this stigmatization potential could result in self-fulfilling prophecies.[92]

Similarly, the German survey by Meier on secondary and tertiary prevention in the area of right-wing extremism and Islamist extremism points to challenges for practice in this area.[93] This survey analyzed project concepts and questioned practitioners both in writing and in interviews. This revealed clear ambiguities regarding the question of how exactly the identification and classification of the targeted persons should be carried out; subjective impressions and 'gut feelings' were cited instead of objectively defined criteria.[94] This subjective approach played a particularly important role in the field of preventing Islamist extremism – a rather new prevention field in Germany. The study revealed that the number of cases declared by projects in the field of Islamist extremism was significantly higher than that of projects targeting right-wing extremism (18.5 vs. 5.5 cases, on average). However, as the interviews showed, these high case numbers were not the result of persons with actual tendencies towards radicalization; rather, they resulted from consultations with persons who turned out not to be at risk of radicalization. The number of persons who were to be classified as actually being radicalized or at risk of radicalization was significantly lower. According to the author, this raised doubts about the validity of the case numbers reported in the written survey.[95]

Recommendations and basic principles

In view of the numerous challenges associated with the integration of former extremists in school PVE and its application in Germany, we have developed recommendations based on the state of the art of biography-based school interventions and our empirical research.[96] These refer to practical principles and recommendations for action that should be considered when planning and implementing such interventions:

If you are considering a PVE intervention from or with a former extremist at your school, it may be helpful to consider, *inter alia*, the following questions in advance:

- Who is the target group?
- What would you like to achieve with the intervention?
- What are the organizational connections, qualifications of the former extremist and the (pedagogical) design of the proposed intervention? Does the provider ensure appropriate quality standards? Do the former and the programme appear legitimate and reputable?
- Is there scientific evidence available regarding the intervention?
- How much funding could or should be allocated?

If you have chosen to run a biography-based PVE, it may be helpful to note, *inter alia*, the following aspects:

- Framework conditions: e.g., voluntary participation and consent of parent/legal guardian, educational preparation and follow-up, small groups, from the age of fifteeen upwards, presence of school staff, breaks;
- Content: e.g., focus on the process of turning towards extremism, as well as disengagement and deradicalization; emphasize the sequential nature of these processes; include the victims' perspective; refrain from detailed narratives on criminal/violent behaviour;

- Methods: e.g., involve the students, refrain from displaying propaganda material and playing extremist music; and
- Former-specific aspects: e.g., credibility of disengagement and deradicalization, ensure that behaviour and language are suitable for students.[97]

However, these recommendations do not constitute a guarantee for implementation in line with the prevention objectives. As a reminder, to date, no scientific study of the activities of former extremists in school PVE has concluded, based on reliable data, that this involvement has lasting effects on students for the prevention of extremism or crime.[98] On the contrary, the international state of research makes it clear that primary prevention in schools must be designed for the longer term to achieve positive effects.[99] This is manifested in primary studies of biographical interventions for the prevention of extremism: both the evaluation of a Basque and a Northern Irish project point to positive effects of prevention measures that are embedded in the curriculum.[100] However, as the findings of the research project by the authors illustrate, the involvement of former extremists in PVE in German schools is usually not embedded in the curriculum but takes place mostly as a one-off event that spans all classes – such a lecture does not represent an adequate prevention project. Considering these points and the international state of research, such implementation should be reconsidered. A basic condition for such PVE to make a sustainable contribution to the intended effects would be its embedding in a school-based prevention concept in addition to an educational concept underlying the intervention, suitable preparation and follow-up by educational staff.[101]

Hence, due to the various former extremists' personalities and biographies, as well as different ways of implementation (in terms of content and form), each of these interventions would have to be accompanied by adequate scientific research. What applies in particular to the use of formers at school should similarly play a common role when involving former extremists in P/CVE: 'In general, it seems advisable to apply this form of school-based prevention work with care. Thus, it should be considered carefully, if and, where necessary, with whom and in what way it is to be carried out at the school.'[102]

Conclusions

The preceding investigation provides some insight into the situation regarding German radicalization and extremism prevention, focusing on the engagement of former extremists in PVE. Generally, their involvement in PVE to dissuade people from taking a comparable path in life might be positive. However, this commitment is subject to special conditions and challenges, especially when addressing children and juveniles; therefore, a positive impact by former extremists should by no means be assumed per se. This needs to be examined empirically in each individual case. Overall, it is apparent that improvements are needed, particularly as regards professionalization and transparency in the field, as well as quality assurance and an adequate culture of evaluation. Thus, the present situation carries, for instance, the risk of misinvesting public funding.[103] To answer the question 'What works for whom under what circumstances?',[104] well-founded evaluation research is key. However, considering scientific findings and transferring them into practice is important as well.[105] In this context, there is a similar need for improvement. Nevertheless, it hardly seems possible to implement these requirements for improvement without major rethinking – including on the political level. The German federal government's increased attention to research needs regarding the prevention of extremism in general, using 'statistical surveys, quality and impact research and the necessary scientific monitoring and evaluation of all projects and measures',[106] promises positive developments.

The two off-ramp interventions described above present difficulties with the differentiation of the target group, which also appeared clearly in the authors' large-scale research project on former extremists in school-based PVE. Although these interventions usually pursue a primary prevention orientation by addressing a universal target group, they are apparently, as the given examples show, in some cases considered as a form of secondary prevention. In other words, there is a lack of differentiation between focusing on protecting people from developing a given problem and focusing on halting the progress of a given problem.[107] For the implementation, which does not show any conceptual adaptation of the intervention for secondary prevention goals and does not differ from the primary prevention application (e.g., content, methods, and target group), this illustrates that it is merely a matter of labelling.[108] Such net-widening effects, *id est* the extension to people who do not belong to the addressed target group,[109] in principle, among other things, harbour a potential for stigmatization.[110] In general, several challenges were addressed that arise from involving former extremists in P/CVE, ranging from factors that could be eliminated by appropriate conceptual and content-related adjustments to seemingly insoluble conflicts, and hence the need is clear for reliable, wide-ranging and interdisciplinary research. Overall, research findings on the prevention of extremism, violence and crime in schools indicate that projects to promote social skills, the introduction of binding rules of conduct and school development work tend to be superior to purely knowledge-based information events of an educational and sensitizing nature.[111]

Notes

1   This chapter was written in May 2020 and the last content update was in April 2021.
2   In this chapter, political extremism is defined as the most significant anti-democratic tendency. All extremist forms have in common the rejection, elimination or restriction of the democratic constitutional state and advocate, propagate or even practise violence as a means to achieve their respective goals. In addition, the theoretical approach assumes that political extremisms are characterized by common dimensions (including fanaticism, absolutism, friend–foe stereotypes), each of which can take on a specific ideological orientation (A. Gansewig, 'Prävention von politischem Extremismus in Deutschland. Eine Betrachtung zur Bedarfs- und Angebotslage', in *Evidenzorientierte Kriminalprävention in Deutschland. Ein Leitfaden für Politik und Praxis*, M. Walsh, B. Pniewski, M. Kober and A. Armborst, eds., 465 et seq (Wiesbaden: Springer, 2018)).

3   Germany, Bundesministerium des Innern, für Bau und Heimat (Federal Ministry of the Interior, Building and Community), *Verfassungsschutzbericht 2019* (Berlin: Bundesministerium des Innern, für Bau und Heimat, 2020).

4   Bundesministerium des Innern, für Bau und Heimat (Federal Ministry of the Interior, Building and Community), *Verfassungsschutzbericht 2019*, 46.

5   Ibid., 112; as translated by the authors.

6   Bundesministerium des Innern, für Bau und Heimat (Federal Ministry of the Interior, Building and Community), *Verfassungsschutzbericht 2019*, 172.

7   Ibid., 102.

8   Ibid., 232.

9   After the end of the Second World War (from 1949 to 1990), Germany was divided into two states: The Federal Republic of Germany in the west and the German Democratic Republic in the east.

10   Germany, Die Bundesregierung (The Federal Government), *Strategie der Bundesregierung zur Extremismusprävention und Demokratieförderung* (Berlin: Die Bundesregierung, 2016), 7.

11   Ibid., 11; as translated by the authors.

12   Gansewig, 'Prävention von politischem Extremismus in Deutschland. Eine Betrachtung zur Bedarfs- und Angebotslage', 476 et seq.

13   According to Horgan, radicalization is 'the social and psychological process of incrementally experienced commitment, to extremist political or religious ideology'. See J. G. Horgan, *Walking Away from Terrorism: Accounts of Disengagement from Radical and Extremist Movements* (New York: Routledge, 2009), 152.

14   Die Bundesregierung, *Strategie der Bundesregierung zur Extremismusprävention und Demokratieförderung*, 11; as translated by the authors.

15   The Federal Republic of Germany is a federation with sixteen states. The exercise of administrative power is divided between the federal government and the states by the constitution.

16   'Primary prevention focuses on protecting people from developing a given problem. (…) Secondary prevention focuses on halting progress of a given problem (…). Tertiary prevention encompasses the remediation of a problem among those who concretely manifest a given problem.' See M. J. Williams, J. G. Horgan and W. P. Evans, *Evaluation of a Multi-faceted, U.S. Community-based, Muslim-led CVE Program* (Washington, DC: National Institute of Justice, 2016), 10–11.

17   Gansewig, 'Prävention von politischem Extremismus in Deutschland. Eine Betrachtung zur Bedarfs- und Angebotslage', 476 et seq.

18   S. Lützinger, F. Gruber and A. Hedayat, 'Extremismuspräventionslandschaft. Eine Bestandsaufnahme präventiver Angebote in Deutschland sowie ausgewählter Präventionsstrategien aus dem europäischen Ausland', in *Handbuch Extremismusprävention – Gesamtgesellschaftlich. Phänomenübergreifend*, B. Ben Slama and U. Kemmesies, eds. (Wiesbaden: Bundeskriminalamt, 2020), 602.

19   See Endnote 16.

20   In accordance with Horgan, disengagement refers to the behavioural level, whereas deradicalization describes changes regarding attitudes. See Horgan, *Walking Away from Terrorism*, 151 et seq.

21   B.-D. Meier, 'Analyse selektiver und indizierter Extremismusprävention', in *'Sag, wie hast du's mit der Kriminologie?' – Die Kriminologie im Gespräch mit ihren*

Nachbardisziplinen, C. Grafl, M. Stempkowski, K. Beclin and I. Haider, eds. (Mönchengladbach: Forum Verlag Godesberg, 2020).

22 cf. Williams, Horgan and Evans, *Evaluation of a Multi-faceted, U.S. Community-based, Muslim-led CVE Program.*

23 Gansewig, 'Prävention von politischem Extremismus in Deutschland. Eine Betrachtung zur Bedarfs- und Angebotslage', 476 et seq.

24 F. Gruber and S. Lützinger, *Extremismusprävention in Deutschland – Erhebung und Darstellung der Präventionslandschaft. Modulabschlussbericht* (Wiesbaden: Bundeskriminalamt, 2017), 33; as translated by the authors.

25 B.-D. Meier, 'Ausstiegsbegleitung und Deradikalisierung in Deutschland: Eher C64 als PlayStation 4?', in *Auf neuen Wegen. Kriminologie, Kriminalpolitik und Polizeiwissenschaft aus interdisziplinärer Perspektive. Festschrift für Thomas Feltes zum 70. Geburtstag,* A. Ruch and T. Singelnstein, eds. (Berlin: Duncker & Humblot, 2021).

26 Die Bundesregierung, *Strategie der Bundesregierung zur Extremismusprävention und Demokratieförderung,* 31.

27 Gansewig, 'Prävention von politischem Extremismus in Deutschland. Eine Betrachtung zur Bedarfs- und Angebotslage', 476 et seq.

28 For example, T. Widmer, 'Wirkungsevaluation zu Maßnahmen der Demokratieförderung', in *Evaluation von Programmen und Projekten für eine demokratische Kultur,* R. Strobl, O. Lobermeier and W. Heitmeyer, eds. (Wiesbaden: Springer VS, 2012), 57 et seq.

29 Meier, 'Ausstiegsbegleitung und Deradikalisierung in Deutschland: Eher C64 als PlayStation 4?'

30 M. Walsh, 'Evidenzorientierung in der deutschen Kriminalprävention und -politik. Entwicklung und Überlegungen zum Stand der Dinge', *Neue Kriminalpolitik* 32, no. 1 (2020): 24–34.

31 M. Tapley and G. Clubb, 'The Role of Formers in Countering Violent Extremism', *The International Centre for Counter-Terrorism – The Hague* 10 (2019); See also D. Koehler, 'Involvement of Formers it Countering Violent Extremism: A Critical Perspective on Commonly Held Assumptions', in *Frühere Extremisten in der schulischen Präventionsarbeit: Perspektiven aus Wissenschaft und Praxis,* M. Walsh and A. Gansewig, eds. (Bonn: Nationales Zentrum für Kriminalprävention, 2020), 15–22.

32 A. Gansewig and M. Walsh, *Biografiebasierte Maßnahmen in der schulischen Präventions- und Bildungsarbeit. Eine empirische Betrachtung des Einsatzes von Aussteigern aus extremistischen Szenen unter besonderer Berücksichtigung ehemaliger Rechtsextremer* (Baden-Baden: Nomos, 2020).

33 Ibid.

34 Ibid.

35 From 2001 on, EXIT-Germany has been offering events with various former right-wing extremists for schools. Information about, e.g., project concepts, selection criteria of the respective former extremists, and costs is not publicly available. Furthermore, there are no meaningful evaluations and differentiated considerations of students' views (with state from 23 April 2021).

36 Gansewig and Walsh, *Biografiebasierte Maßnahmen in der schulischen Präventions- und Bildungsarbeit. Eine empirische Betrachtung des Einsatzes von Aussteigern aus extremistischen Szenen unter besonderer Berücksichtigung ehemaliger Rechtsextremer,* 100 et seq.

37 See Endnote 16.

38 This presented, *inter alia*, a media analysis of the authors regarding school-based PVE involving former extremists in Germany. For further information, see Endnote 44.

39 Gansewig and Walsh, *Biografiebasierte Maßnahmen in der schulischen Präventions- und Bildungsarbeit. Eine empirische Betrachtung des Einsatzes von Aussteigern aus extremistischen Szenen unter besonderer Berücksichtigung ehemaliger Rechtsextremer*, 100 et seq.

40 Ibid., 418; see also A. Gansewig and M. Walsh, '"That Is Simply One Thing That Goes with It": Former Extremists in School Settings and Empirical Evidence', *Educational Review* (2022).

41 A. Gansewig and M. Walsh, 'Aussteiger aus extremistischen Szenen in der Schule. Ein Plädoyer für eine Fokusverschiebung auf die Schülerperspektive und deren differenzierte Betrachtung', in *Frühere Extremisten in der schulischen Präventionsarbeit. Perspektiven aus Wissenschaft und Praxis*, M. Walsh and A. Gansewig, eds. (Bonn: Nationales Zentrum für Kriminalprävention, 2020), 23–35; see also Gansewig and Walsh, *Biografiebasierte Maßnahmen in der schulischen Präventions- und Bildungsarbeit. Eine empirische Betrachtung des Einsatzes von Aussteigern aus extremistischen Szenen unter besonderer Berücksichtigung ehemaliger Rechtsextremer* and R. Scrivens, S. Windisch and P. Simi, 'Former Extremists in Radicalization and Counter-radicalization Research', *Sociology of Crime, Law and Deviance* 25 (2020): 209–24.

42 The overall results of the research project are published in Gansewig and Walsh, *Biografiebasierte Maßnahmen in der schulischen Präventions- und Bildungsarbeit. Eine empirische Betrachtung des Einsatzes von Aussteigern aus extremistischen Szenen unter besonderer Berücksichtigung ehemaliger Rechtsextremer*.

43 See M. Walsh and A. Gansewig, 'Long-term Experience Means Professionalization – Or Does It? An In-depth Look on the Involvement of Former Extremists in German Prevention and Education', *Journal for Deradicalization* 27 (2021): 108–45.

44 The media analysis was based on newspaper articles and notifications on 465 events in the period from January 2001 to April 2019, and 424 of the 465 lectures included solely former right-wing extremists. Of the thirty-two former extremists clearly identified in this time period, twenty-seven were former right-wing extremists, one was formerly active in the far-left autonomous community and two each formerly belonged to the Islamist community or other extremist movements (Turkish and Kurdish extremist groups). See Gansewig and Walsh, *Biografiebasierte Maßnahmen in der schulischen Präventions- und Bildungsarbeit. Eine empirische Betrachtung des Einsatzes von Aussteigern aus extremistischen Szenen unter besonderer Berücksichtigung ehemaliger Rechtsextremer*, 186 et seq. and A. Gansewig and M. Walsh, 'Preventing Violent Extremism with Former Extremists in Schools: A Media Analysis of the Situation in Germany', *Terrorism and Political Violence* (2021).

45 A motorcycle club is an association of several people with a strict hierarchical structure with close personal ties between the club members, little willingness to cooperate with the police, and strict, self-created rules and statutes. Rocker crime includes all crimes committed by individual or several members of a rocker club, which, in terms of motivation for behaviour, are directly related to membership in the club and solidarity with it. Rocker crime is defined by the motivation for the crimes committed, which is directly related to the motorcycle club. In Germany, investigations are being increasingly conducted against biker clubs, because it has been established that outlaw motorcycle clubs also collaborate with other organized

crime groups (violent, drug, weapons crime, etc.). As translated by the authors from Bundeskriminalamt (BKA), 'Rockerkriminalität' (2021), available online: https://www.bka.de/DE/UnsereAufgaben/Deliktsbereiche/Rockerkriminalitaet/rockerkriminalitaet_node.html (accessed 24 April 2021).

46 For further information about the former extremist and the intervention investigated, see M. Walsh and A. Gansewig, 'A Former Right-wing Extremist in School-based Prevention Work: Research Findings from Germany', *Journal for Deradicalization* 21 (2019/20): 4; Gansewig and Walsh, *Biografiebasierte Maßnahmen in der schulischen Präventions- und Bildungsarbeit. Eine empirische Betrachtung des Einsatzes von Aussteigern aus extremistischen Szenen unter besonderer Berücksichtigung ehemaliger Rechtsextremer.*

47 Walsh and Gansewig, 'A Former Right-wing Extremist in School-based Prevention Work: Research Findings from Germany', 1–42.

48 Furthermore, the teaching staff participating in the twenty-five interventions and the respective school contact persons were interviewed in writing. See Gansewig and Walsh, *Biografiebasierte Maßnahmen in der schulischen Präventions- und Bildungsarbeit. Eine empirische Betrachtung des Einsatzes von Aussteigern aus extremistischen Szenen unter besonderer Berücksichtigung ehemaliger Rechtsextremer*, 266 et seq.

49 Ibid.

50 Ibid.

51 Ibid.

52 Walsh and Gansewig, 'A Former Right-wing Extremist in School-based Prevention Work: Research Findings from Germany', 1–42.

53 Gansewig and Walsh, *Biografiebasierte Maßnahmen in der schulischen Präventions- und Bildungsarbeit. Eine empirische Betrachtung des Einsatzes von Aussteigern aus extremistischen Szenen unter besonderer Berücksichtigung ehemaliger Rechtsextremer*, 363 et seq.

54 cf. A. Petrosino, C. Turpin-Petrosino and J. Finckenauer, 'Well-meaning Programs Can Have Harmful Effects! Lessons from Experiments from Programs Such as Scared Straight', *Crime & Delinquency* 46, no. 3 (2000): 354–79; see also European Society for Prevention Research (EUSPR), *Position of the European Society for Prevention Research on Ineffective and Potentially Harmful Approaches in Substance Use Prevention* (Palma: EUSPR, 2019) and Gansewig and Walsh, '"That Is Simply One Thing That Goes with It": Former Extremists in School Settings and Empirical Evidence'.

55 Gansewig and Walsh, *Biografiebasierte Maßnahmen in der schulischen Präventions- und Bildungsarbeit. Eine empirische Betrachtung des Einsatzes von Aussteigern aus extremistischen Szenen unter besonderer Berücksichtigung ehemaliger Rechtsextremer*, 64 et seq.

56 I. van den Berg, '*Und dann wollte ich raus*'. *Extreme politische Szenen verlassen: am Beispiel Sachsens* (Leipzig: Edition Leipzig, 2017), 61 et seq.; as translated by the authors.

57 Gansewig and Walsh, *Biografiebasierte Maßnahmen in der schulischen Präventions- und Bildungsarbeit. Eine empirische Betrachtung des Einsatzes von Aussteigern aus extremistischen Szenen unter besonderer Berücksichtigung ehemaliger Rechtsextremer*, 407 et seq.

58 Radicalisation Awareness Network (RAN) (eds.), *Dos and Don'ts of Involving Formers in PVE/CVE Work. Ex Ante Paper Working with Formers in Exit Work and Online* (Brussels: European Commission, 2017).

59   S. Maruna, *Making Good. How Ex-convicts Reform and Rebuild Their Lives* (Washington, DC: American Psychological Association, 2001).

60   van den Berg, '*Und dann wollte ich raus'. Extreme politische Szenen verlassen: am Beispiel Sachsens*, 50; translated by the authors.

61   Gansewig and Walsh, *Biografiebasierte Maßnahmen in der schulischen Präventions- und Bildungsarbeit. Eine empirische Betrachtung des Einsatzes von Aussteigern aus extremistischen Szenen unter besonderer Berücksichtigung ehemaliger Rechtsextremer*, 208 et seq.; see also Gansewig and Walsh, 'Preventing Violent Extremism with Former Extremists in Schools: A Media Analysis of the Situation in Germany'.

62   Gansewig and Walsh, *Biografiebasierte Maßnahmen in der schulischen Präventions- und Bildungsarbeit. Eine empirische Betrachtung des Einsatzes von Aussteigern aus extremistischen Szenen unter besonderer Berücksichtigung ehemaliger Rechtsextremer*.

63   Koehler, 'Involvement of Formers in Countering Violent Extremism: A Critical Perspective on Commonly Held Assumptions'.

64   Gansewig and Walsh, *Biografiebasierte Maßnahmen in der schulischen Präventions- und Bildungsarbeit. Eine empirische Betrachtung des Einsatzes von Aussteigern aus extremistischen Szenen unter besonderer Berücksichtigung ehemaliger Rechtsextremer*, 203 et seq.

65   Gansewig and Walsh, 'Aussteiger aus extremistischen Szenen in der Schule. Ein Plädoyer für eine Fokusverschiebung auf die Schülerperspektive und deren differenzierte Betrachtung'; see also Gansewig and Walsh, *Biografiebasierte Maßnahmen in der schulischen Präventions- und Bildungsarbeit. Eine empirische Betrachtung des Einsatzes von Aussteigern aus extremistischen Szenen unter besonderer Berücksichtigung ehemaliger Rechtsextremer*.

66   Gansewig and Walsh, *Biografiebasierte Maßnahmen in der schulischen Präventions- und Bildungsarbeit. Eine empirische Betrachtung des Einsatzes von Aussteigern aus extremistischen Szenen unter besonderer Berücksichtigung ehemaliger Rechtsextremer*.

67   F. Lange, 'Zwischen den Stühlen. Erfahrungen und Qualitätsstandards in der Bildungsarbeit mit Ausgestiegenen von NinA NRW', in *Frühere Extremisten in der schulischen Präventionsarbeit. Perspektiven aus Wissenschaft und Praxis*, M. Walsh and A. Gansewig, eds. (Bonn: Nationales Zentrum für Kriminalprävention, 2020), 62; as translated by the authors.

68   A.-L. Lodenius, *To Leave a Destructive Life Full of Hate. The Story of Exit in Sweden* (Stockholm: Exit Fryshuset, 2010), 13.

69   Gansewig and Walsh, 'Preventing Violent Extremism with Former Extremists in Schools: A Media Analysis of the Situation in Germany'.

70   Walsh and Gansewig, 'A Former Right-wing Extremist in School-based Prevention Work: Research Findings from Germany'.

71   Gansewig and Walsh, *Biografiebasierte Maßnahmen in der schulischen Präventions- und Bildungsarbeit. Eine empirische Betrachtung des Einsatzes von Aussteigern aus extremistischen Szenen unter besonderer Berücksichtigung ehemaliger Rechtsextremer*, 343 et seq.

72   Germany, Bundesministerium für Familie, Senioren, Frauen und Jugend (Federal Ministry for Family Affairs, Senior Citizens, Women and Youth), *Abschlussbericht des Bundesprogramms 'Initiative Demokratie Stärken'* (Berlin: Bundesministerium für Familie, Senioren, Frauen und Jugend, 2014), 6; as translated by the authors.

73   As translated by the authors from Internationaler Bund, '*#grenzerfahrung. Rückblick Ausblick Methoden*' (2019), available online: https://grenzerfahrungen.ib.de/

fileadmin/user_upload/storage_ib_redaktion/IB_Grenzerfahrungen/Start_seite/
Abschlussbroschüre_Grenzerfahrungen_PDF.pdf (accessed 20 July 2020), 17.

74 Ibid., as translated by the authors from Internationaler Bund, 'Projektstandorte',
available online: https://grenzerfahrungen.ib.de/projektstandorte (accessed
24 April 2021).

75 C. Figlestahler, F. Greuel, D. Grunow, J. Langner, K. Schau, M. Schott, D. Zierold
and M. Zschach, *Vierter Bericht: Modellprojekte E. Programmevaluation
'Demokratie leben!'. Wissenschaftliche Begleitung der Modellprojekte zur
Radikalisierungsprävention. Zwischenbericht 2018* (Halle/Saale: Deutsches
Jugendinstitut, 2019), 60; as translated by the authors.

76 Ibid., 61; as translated by the authors.

77 Ibid., as translated by the authors.

78 For definitions of primary and secondary prevention, see Endnote 16.

79 Gansewig and Walsh, 'Aussteiger aus extremistischen Szenen in der Schule. Ein
Plädoyer für eine Fokusverschiebung auf die Schülerperspektive und deren
differenzierte Betrachtung'.

80 As translated by the authors from Internationaler Bund, '*#grenzerfahrung. Rückblick
Ausblick Methoden*' (2019), 17.

81 G. Hildebrand and A. Prause, '"Linke Militanz in Geschichte und Gegenwart". Ein
Präventionsprojekt der Gedenkstätte Berlin-Hohenschönhausen', in *Linke Militanz.
Pädagogische Arbeit in Theorie und Praxis*, A.-K. Meinhardt and B. Redlich, eds.
(Bonn: Bundeszentrale für politische Bildung, 2021), 170–80.

82 Gedenkstätte Berlin-Hohenschönhausen, *Alles Geschichte? Linksextremismus
in Deutschland heute. Seminare und Workshops der Gedenkstätte Berlin-
Hohenschönhausen* (Berlin: Gedenkstätte Berlin-Hohenschönhausen, n.d.); as
translated by the authors.

83 Walsh and Gansewig, 'Long-term Experience Means Professionalization – Or
Does It? An In-depth Look on the Involvement of Former Extremists in German
Prevention and Education'.

84 Gansewig and Walsh, *Biografiebasierte Maßnahmen in der schulischen Präventions-
und Bildungsarbeit. Eine empirische Betrachtung des Einsatzes von Aussteigern aus
extremistischen Szenen unter besonderer Berücksichtigung ehemaliger Rechtsextremer*,
126 et seq.

85 Ibid., 136 et seq.

86 Gedenkstätte Berlin-Hohenschönhausen, *Alles Geschichte? Linksextremismus
in Deutschland heute. Seminare und Workshops der Gedenkstätte Berlin-
Hohenschönhausen*; as translated by the authors.

87 Ibid., as translated by the authors.

88 Hildebrand and Prause, '"Linke Militanz in Geschichte und Gegenwart". Ein
Präventionsprojekt der Gedenkstätte Berlin-Hohenschönhausen', 179; as translated
by the authors.

89 Gansewig and Walsh, *Biografiebasierte Maßnahmen in der schulischen Präventions-
und Bildungsarbeit. Eine empirische Betrachtung des Einsatzes von Aussteigern aus
extremistischen Szenen unter besonderer Berücksichtigung ehemaliger Rechtsextremer*.

90 cf. Meier, 'Ausstiegsbegleitung und Deradikalisierung in Deutschland: Eher C64 als
PlayStation 4?'

91 For example, see D. Parker and L. Lindekilde, 'Preventing Extremism with
Extremists: A Double-edged Sword? An Analysis of the Impact of Using Former
Extremists in Danish Schools', *Education Sciences* 10 (2020): 111.

92   T. Fischer, B. Holthusen, A. Schmoll and D. Willems, 'Prävention von Delinquenz im Kindes- und Jugendalter – Ein komplexer Gegenstand für Evaluation', in *Evidenzorientierte Kriminalprävention in Deutschland. Ein Leitfaden für Politik und Praxis*, M. Walsh, B. Pniewski, M. Kober and A. Armborst, eds. (Wiesbaden: Springer, 2018), 333–48.

93   Meier, 'Analyse selektiver und indizierter Extremismusprävention'; see also Meier, 'Ausstiegsbegleitung und Deradikalisierung in Deutschland: Eher C64 als PlayStation 4?'

94   Meier, 'Ausstiegsbegleitung und Deradikalisierung in Deutschland: Eher C64 als PlayStation 4?'

95   Ibid.

96   M. Walsh and A. Gansewig, *Former Right-wing Extremists in School-based Prevention Work. Recommendations for Educators* (Bonn: Nationales Zentrum für Kriminalprävention, 2019).

97   Ibid., 8 et seq.

98   Gansewig and Walsh, *Biografiebasierte Maßnahmen in der schulischen Präventions- und Bildungsarbeit. Eine empirische Betrachtung des Einsatzes von Aussteigern aus extremistischen Szenen unter besonderer Berücksichtigung ehemaliger Rechtsextremer.*

99   D. P. Farrington, M. M. Ttofi and F. Lösel, 'Developmental and Social Prevention', in *Springer Series on Evidence-based Crime Policy. What Works in Crime Prevention and Rehabilitation: Lessons from Systematic Reviews*, D. Weisburd, D. P. Farrington and C. Gill, eds. (New York: Springer, 2016), 15–75.

100 M. Garaigordobil, 'Evaluation of a Program to Prevent Political Violence in the Basque Conflict: Effects on the Capacity of Empathy, Anger Management and the Definition of Peace', *Gaceta Sanitaria* 26, no. 3 (2012): 211–16; see also L. Emerson, K. Orr and P. Connolly, *Evaluation of the Effectiveness of the 'Prison to Peace: Learning from the Experience of Political Ex-prisoners' Education Programme* (Belfast: Centre for Effective Education, Queen's University Belfast, 2014).

101 Walsh and Gansewig, *Former Right-wing Extremists in School-based Prevention Work. Recommendations for Educators.*

102 Ibid., 4.

103 Meier, 'Ausstiegsbegleitung und Deradikalisierung in Deutschland: Eher C64 als PlayStation 4?'

104 A. Cherney, 'Beyond Technicism: Broadening the "What Works" Paradigm in Crime Prevention', *Crime Prevention and Community Safety*, no. 3 (2002): 49–59.

105 Gansewig, 'Prävention von politischem Extremismus in Deutschland. Eine Betrachtung zur Bedarfs- und Angebotslage'.

106 Die Bundesregierung (The Federal Government), *Strategie der Bundesregierung zur Extremismusprävention und Demokratieförderung*, 31; as translated by the authors.

107 cf. Williams, Horgan and Evans, *Evaluation of a Multi-faceted, U.S. Community-based, Muslim-led CVE Program*, 10 et seq.

108 cf. Gansewig and Walsh, *Biografiebasierte Maßnahmen in der schulischen Präventions- und Bildungsarbeit. Eine empirische Betrachtung des Einsatzes von Aussteigern aus extremistischen Szenen unter besonderer Berücksichtigung ehemaliger Rechtsextremer.*

109 M. Ezell, 'Juvenile Arbitration: Net Widening and Other Unintended Consequences', *Journal of Research in Crime and Delinquency*, no. 4 (1989): 358–77.

110 cf. L. Holdaway and R. Simpson, *Improving the Impact of Preventing Violent Extremism Programming. A Toolkit for Design, Monitoring and Evaluation* (Oslo: United Nations Development Programme, Oslo Governance Centre, 2018), 23 et seq.

111 cf. A. Beelmann, *Grundlagen einer entwicklungsorientierten Prävention des Rechtsextremismus. Gutachten im Rahmen des Wissenschafts-Praxis-Dialogs zwischen dem Landespräventionsrat Niedersachsen und der Friedrich-Schiller-Universität Jena* (Jena: Friedrich-Schiller-Universität Jena, 2017); see also Gansewig and Walsh, *Biografiebasierte Maßnahmen in der schulischen Präventions- und Bildungsarbeit. Eine empirische Betrachtung des Einsatzes von Aussteigern aus extremistischen Szenen unter besonderer Berücksichtigung ehemaliger Rechtsextremer.*

Bibliography

Beelmann, A. *Grundlagen einer entwicklungsorientierten Prävention des Rechtsextremismus. Gutachten im Rahmen des Wissenschafts-Praxis-Dialogs zwischen dem Landespräventionsrat Niedersachsen und der Friedrich-Schiller-Universität Jena.* Jena: Friedrich-Schiller-Universität Jena, 2017, 5–75.

Bundesministerium des Innern, für Bau und Heimat (Federal Ministry of the Interior, Building and Community). *Verfassungsschutzbericht 2019.* Berlin: Bundesministerium des Innern, für Bau und Heimat, 2020, 22–281.

Bundesministerium für Familie, Senioren, Frauen und Jugend (Federal Ministry for Family Affairs, Senior Citizens, Women and Youth). *Abschlussbericht des Bundesprogramms "Initiative Demokratie Stärken".* Berlin: Bundesministerium für Familie, Senioren, Frauen und Jugend, Referat Öffentlichkeitsarbeit, 2014, 3–57.

Cherney, A. 'Beyond Technicism: Broadening the "What Works" Paradigm in Crime Prevention'. *Crime Prevention and Community Safety*, no. 3 (2002): 49–59.

Die Bundesregierung (The Federal Government). *Strategie der Bundesregierung zur Extremismusprävention und Demokratieförderung.* Germany: Die Bundesregierung, 2016, 7–61.

Emerson, L., Orr, K. and Connolly, P. *Evaluation of the Effectiveness of the 'Prison to Peace: Learning from the Experience of Political Ex-prisoners' Education Programme.* Belfast: Centre for Effective Education, Queen's University Belfast, 2014, 1–161.

European Society for Prevention Research (EUSPR), *Position of the European Society for Prevention Research on Ineffective and Potentially Harmful Approaches in Substance Use Prevention.* Palma, Spain: EUSPR, 2019, 1–9.

Ezell, M. 'Juvenile Arbitration: Net Widening and Other Unintended Consequences'. *Journal of Research in Crime and Delinquency* 1, no. 4 (1989): 358–77.

Farrington, D. P., Ttofi, M. M. and Lösel, F. A. 'Developmental and Social Prevention'. In *Springer Series on Evidence-based Crime Policy. What Works in Crime Prevention and Rehabilitation: Lessons from Systematic Reviews*, D. Weisburd, D. P. Farrington and C. Gill, eds., 15–75. New York: Springer, 2016.

Figlestahler, C., Greuel, F., Grunow, D., Langner, J., Schau, K., Schott, M., Zierold, D. and Zschach, M. *Vierter Bericht: Modellprojekte E. Programmevaluation 'Demokratie leben!' Wissenschaftliche Begleitung der Modellprojekte zur Radikalisierungsprävention. Zwischenbericht 2018.* Halle/Saale: Deutsches Jugendinstitut, 2019, 1–161.

Fischer, T. A., Holthusen, B., Schmoll, A. and Willems, D. 'Prävention von Delinquenz im Kindes- und Jugendalter – Ein komplexer Gegenstand für Evaluation'. In *Evidenzorientierte Kriminalprävention in Deutschland. Ein Leitfaden für Politik und Praxis*, M. Walsh, B. Pniewski, M. Kober and A. Armborst, eds., 333–48. Wiesbaden: Springer, 2018.

Gansewig, A. 'Prävention von politischem Extremismus in Deutschland. Eine Betrachtung zur Bedarfs- und Angebotslage'. In *Evidenzorientierte Kriminalprävention in Deutschland. Ein Leitfaden für Politik und Praxis*, M. Walsh, B. Pniewski, M. Kober and A. Armborst, eds., 465–88. Wiesbaden: Springer, 2018.

Gansewig, A. and Walsh, M. 'Aussteiger aus extremistischen Szenen in der Schule. Ein Plädoyer für eine Fokusverschiebung auf die Schülerperspektive und deren differenzierte Betrachtung'. In *Frühere Extremisten in der schulischen Präventionsarbeit: Perspektiven aus Wissenschaft und Praxis*, M. Walsh and A. Gansewig, eds., 23–35. Bonn: Nationales Zentrum für Kriminalprävention, 2020.

Gansewig, A. and Walsh, M. *Biografiebasierte Maßnahmen in der schulischen Präventions- und Bildungsarbeit. Eine empirische Betrachtung des Einsatzes von Aussteigern aus extremistischen Szenen unter besonderer Berücksichtigung ehemaliger Rechtsextremer.* Baden-Baden: Nomos, 2020.

Gansewig, A. and Walsh, M. 'Preventing Violent Extremism with Former Extremists in Schools: A Media Analysis of the Situation in Germany'. *Terrorism and Political Violence* (2021): 1–18.

Gansewig, A. and Walsh, M. '"That Is Simply One Thing That Goes with It": Former Extremists in School Settings and Empirical Evidence', *Educational Review* (2022): 1–22.

Garaigordobil, M. 'Evaluation of a Program to Prevent Political Violence in the Basque Conflict: Effects on the Capacity of Empathy, Anger Management and the Definition of Peace'. *Gaceta Sanitaria* 26, no. 3 (2012): 211–16.

Gedenkstätte Berlin-Hohenschönhausen. *Alles Geschichte? Linksextremismus in Deutschland heute. Seminare und Workshops der Gedenkstätte Berlin-Hohenschönhausen.* Berlin: Gedenkstätte Berlin-Hohenschönhausen, n.d., 1–2.

Gruber, F. and Lützinger, S. *Extremismusprävention in Deutschland – Erhebung und Darstellung der Präventionslandschaft. Modulabschlussbericht.* Wiesbaden: Bundeskriminalamt, 2017.

Hildebrand, G. and Prause, A. '"Linke Militanz in Geschichte und Gegenwart." Ein Präventionsprojekt der Gedenkstätte Berlin-Hohenschönhausen'. In *Linke Militanz. Pädagogische Arbeit in Theorie und Praxis*, A.-K. Meinhardt and B. Redlich, eds., 170–80. Bonn: Bundeszentrale für politische Bildung, 2021.

Holdaway, L. and Simpson, R. *Improving the Impact of Preventing Violent Extremism Programming. A Toolkit for Design, Monitoring and Evaluation.* Oslo: United Nations Development Programme, Oslo Governance Centre, 2018.

Horgan, J. G. *Walking away from Terrorism: Accounts of Disengagement from Radical and Extremist Movements.* New York: Routledge, 2009.

Koehler, D. 'Involvement of Formers in Countering Violent Extremism: A Critical Perspective on Commonly Held Assumptions'. In *Frühere Extremisten in der schulischen Präventionsarbeit: Perspektiven aus Wissenschaft und Praxis*, M. Walsh and A. Gansewig, eds., 15–22. Bonn: Nationales Zentrum für Kriminalprävention, 2020.

Lange, F. 'Zwischen den Stühlen. Erfahrungen und Qualitätsstandards in der Bildungsarbeit mit Ausgestiegenen von NinA NRW'. In *Frühere Extremisten in der schulischen Präventionsarbeit. Perspektiven aus Wissenschaft und Praxis*, M. Walsh and A. Gansewig, eds., 61–7. Bonn: Nationales Zentrum für Kriminalprävention, 2020.

Lodenius, A.-L. *To Leave a Destructive Life Full of Hate. The Story of Exit in Sweden.* Stockholm: Exit Fryshuset, 2010.

Lützinger, S., Gruber F. and Hedayat, A. 'Extremismuspräventionslandschaft. Eine Bestandsaufnahme präventiver Angebote in Deutschland sowie ausgewählter

Präventionsstrategien aus dem europäischen Ausland'. In *Handbuch Extremismusprävention – Gesamtgesellschaftlich. Phänomenübergreifend*, B. Ben Slama and U. Kemmesies, eds., 597–626. Wiesbaden: Bundeskriminalamt, 2020.

Maruna, S. *Making Good. How Ex-convicts Reform and Rebuild Their Lives*. Washington, DC: American Psychological Association, 2001.

Meier, B.-D. 'Analyse selektiver und indizierter Extremismusprävention'. In '*Sag, wie hast du's mit der Kriminologie?' – Die Kriminologie im Gespräch mit ihren Nachbardisziplinen*, C. Grafl, M. Stempkowski, K. Beclin and I. Haider, eds., 405–21. Mönchengladbach: Forum Verlag Godesberg, 2020.

Meier, B.-D. 'Ausstiegsbegleitung und Deradikalisierung in Deutschland: Eher C64 als PlayStation 4?' In *Auf neuen Wegen. Kriminologie, Kriminalpolitik und Polizeiwissenschaft aus interdisziplinärer Perspektive. Festschrift für Thomas Feltes zum 70. Geburtstag*, A. Ruch and T. Singelnstein, eds., 187–97. Berlin: Duncker & Humblot, 2021.

Parker, D. and Lindekilde, L. 'Preventing Extremism with Extremists: A Double-edged Sword? An Analysis of the Impact of Using Former Extremists in Danish Schools'. *Education Sciences* 10 (2020): 1–19.

Petrosino, A., Turpin-Petrosino, C. and Finckenauer, J. 'Well-meaning Programs Can Have Harmful Effects! Lessons from Experiments from Programs Such as Scared Straight'. *Crime & Delinquency* 46, no. 3 (2000): 354–79.

Radicalisation Awareness Network (RAN) (eds.). *Dos and Don'ts of Involving Formers in PVE/CVE Work. Ex ante Paper Working with Formers in Exit Work and Online*. Brussels: European Commission, 2017, 1–8.

Scrivens, R., Windisch S. and Simi, P. 'Former Extremists in Radicalization and Counter-radicalization Research'. *Sociology of Crime, Law and Deviance* 25 (2020): 209–24.

Tapley, M. and Clubb, G. 'The Role of Formers in Countering Violent Extremism'. *The International Centre for Counter-terrorism – The Hague* 10 (2019): 1–20.

van den Berg, I. '*Und dann wollte ich raus*'. *Extreme politische Szenen verlassen: am Beispiel Sachsens*. Leipzig: Edition Leipzig, 2017.

Walsh, M. 'Evidenzorientierung in der deutschen Kriminalprävention und -politik. Entwicklung und Überlegungen zum Stand der Dinge'. *Neue Kriminalpolitik* 32, no. 1 (2020): 24–34.

Walsh, M. and Gansewig, A. *Former Right-wing Extremists in School-based Prevention Work. Recommendations for Educators*. Bonn: Nationales Zentrum für Kriminalprävention, 2019.

Walsh, M. and Gansewig, A. 'A Former Right-wing Extremist in School-based Prevention Work: Research Findings from Germany'. *Journal for Deradicalization* 21 (2019/20): 1–42.

Walsh, M. and Gansewig, A. 'Long-term Experience Means Professionalization – Or Does It? An In-depth Look on the Involvement of Former Extremists in German Prevention and Education'. *Journal for Deradicalization* 27 (2021): 108–45.

Widmer, T. 'Wirkungsevaluation zu Maßnahmen der Demokratieförderung'. In *Evaluation von Programmen und Projekten für eine demokratische Kultur*, R. Strobl, O. Lobermeier and W. Heitmeyer, eds., 41–68. Wiesbaden: Springer VS, 2012.

Williams, M. J., Horgan, J. G. and Evans, W. P. *Evaluation of a Multi-faceted, U.S. Community-based, Muslim-led CVE Program*. Washington, DC: National Institute of Justice, 2016.

Index